# Kitty O'Shea

## An Irish Affair

### Jane Jordan

SUTTON PUBLISHING

*To my father and mother,*
*John and Mary Tucker*

First published in the United Kingdom in 2005 by
Sutton Publishing Limited · Phoenix Mill
Thrupp · Stroud · Gloucestershire · GL5 2BU

British Library Cataloguing in Publication Data
A catalogue record for this book is available from the British Library.

ISBN 0-7509-3342-9

Typeset in 11/13.5pt Sabon.
Typesetting and origination by
Sutton Publishing Limited.
Printed and bound in England by
J.H. Haynes & Co. Ltd, Sparkford.

# Contents

# Acknowledgements

I could not have written this book without the support of my husband, Tim Jordan, who has been indefatigable in his willingness to read countless drafts. I don't have the words to express my gratitude to him. I am also greatly indebted to Cathy Wells-Cole, who suggested amendments to late drafts and who helped me to foreground Katharine's story. Cathy has been a great friend to this book.

I also owe particular thanks to the following: Ciara McDonnell, Assistant Keeper in the Department of Manuscripts, National Library of Ireland, who gave me every assistance in tracking down Katharine's letter of August 1886, a complete version of which exists only as a lawyer's shorthand copy; Susan Henry at Kingston University, who worked on this copy and produced a transcript for me to work from; Ruth Clayton, who told me about the correspondence in the Gladstone Papers regarding Gladstone's knowledge of Katharine's affair with Parnell; Steven Davies, County Archivist at the Flintshire Record Office; Martin Killeen, Special Collections Reference Librarian at the University of Birmingham; staff at the British Library; and Niamh O'Sullivan, archivist at Kilmainham Gaol Museum, for her generous help and for the material she has shared with me. Just when I thought Katharine's story was finished, the Parnell relics at Kilmainham opened up another story about Katharine and Parnell's daughters and grandson.

I would also like to thank my agent Simon Trewin for his belief in this project, and at Sutton, Jaqueline Mitchell for her advice and guidance, Hilary Walford, Jane Entrican and Alison Duncan for their involvement in the production of the book. At Kingston University, I thank my students, my colleague Meg Jensen, and in particular David Rogers and Avril Horner for their warm support.

The author and the publisher would like to thank the following for permission to reproduce illustrations: plates 8, 16, 17, 18 and 23 by courtesy of the British Library; plates 6 and 19 by courtesy of Getty Images; plates 7, 9, 10, 13 and 14 by courtesy of the Mary Evans Picture Library; plate 15 by courtesy of Topham Picturepoint. Plates 1, 2, 3, 4 and 11 are reproduced from Katharine's biography of Parrnell, *Charles Stewart Parnell: His Love Story and Political Life*. Plate 5 is the author's own.

# List of Illustrations

The grass shall cease to grow,
The river's stream to run,
The stars shall ponder in their course.
No more shall shine the sun;
The moon shall never wane or grow,
The tide shall cease to ebb and flow,
    Ere I shall cease to love you.

           (Poem written by Parnell
             for Katharine O'Shea)


No man has a right to fix the boundary to the march of a nation.
No man has a right to say to his country, 'Thus far shalt thou go
And no further.'

                  (Charles Stewart Parnell)

# Introduction

Kitty O'Shea was not Irish. In fact, she never set foot in Ireland. Nor was that her real name. Katharine O'Shea, known familiarly as Kate or Katie, was the English wife of an Irish MP, who from 1880 to 1890 had a love affair with the leader of the Irish Parliamentary Party, Charles Stewart Parnell. She was called Kitty only after the notorious divorce case of November 1890. It was meant derisively.

For the Irish, Kitty O'Shea remains a deeply distrusted figure, and understandably so. She was seen to be the cause of a disastrous political scandal. The divorce came at a time when Parnell had entered into negotiations with the Liberals on a second Home Rule bill: its revelations were fatal to Parnell's political career and also, it seemed at the time, to hopes for the restoration of an Irish Parliament.

In 1914, Katharine published a record of her life with Parnell, *Charles Stewart Parnell: His Love Story and Political Life*. Her reprinting of a great many letters she received from him served only to revive Irish feeling against her. In one letter in particular, written when Parnell was imprisoned in Dublin's Kilmainham Gaol (at a time when Katharine was carrying their first child), he offered to resign from Parliament and give up his political cause in order to live with her. This stunned his old political colleagues. In their view, the Irish leader had 'proposed to forsake his comrades in the most critical hour', and retire from Ireland's political struggle 'at a *woman's whim*'.[1]

For the British, too, in the early twentieth century at least, Katharine remained a problematic figure. On Parnell's behalf, she had enjoyed a privileged access to Gladstone, corresponding with the Prime Minister over a period of years and meeting him for private interviews at Downing Street. The publication of her book in 1914 exposed this close political relationship, which was not consistent with the prevailing view of the Liberal leader, and right up until the late 1930s Gladstone's sons sought to defend their father's moral reputation by strenuously denying the extent of his contact with Mrs O'Shea, in particular her contention that their father had known that she was Parnell's mistress when he first met her.[2]

Katharine's political role as Parnell's chosen intermediary with the British Government was particularly distasteful to Irish Nationalist opinion, and there has been a widespread attempt on the part of Irish historians and biographers of Parnell to deny the significance of her testimony. When Katharine did break her silence, her book was treated with reserve, if not distrust. While her reprinting of so much of Parnell's intimate correspondence has been regarded as the book's 'great contribution' to Irish history,[3] there is a prevailing uneasiness about the Parnell that is revealed, a Parnell in thrall, as it were, to Katharine O'Shea. Prominent Nationalists such as T.P. O'Connor and Tim Healy, neither of whom met Katharine, saw her as a dominant figure who sapped Parnell's strength. She was regarded as a Delilah. There is also a rather prurient dislike of her surprisingly frank telling of her story, involving as it does the history of an unhappy marriage and of a love affair which was both a grand passion and an oddly domesticated 'marriage', made vastly more problematic by its political implications. What emerges is not exactly a struggle between his personal and public life, but a love for Katharine so vitally necessary to him that he was prepared to confront, endure, at times recklessly ignore, all manner of political consequences.

There are also lesser objections to Katharine's book. It has been noted that her dating of documents or events is not always reliable,[4] whereas, in fact, such errors are on the whole insignificant and easily corrected. Reservations about the tone of some of the letters are less easy to dismiss. For F.S.L. Lyons, whose monumental biography of Parnell was published in 1977, 'Parnell's fumbling endearments are pathetic to the point of embarrassment'.[5] This has to be conceded, but of course these are utterly private letters of Parnell's, and Katharine does at least appear to present them to us in unedited form.

It was Henry Harrison's conviction that a considerable portion of Katharine's book was in fact ghost-written, or clumsily edited (without her knowledge, he implies), by her son Gerard: 'One seems to detect composite authorship and patchwork, as well as writing definitely not done by Mrs Parnell.'[6] Harrison was a young Parnellite MP who had interviewed Katharine during the months immediately after Parnell's death in October 1891. He claimed that she had told him a story which is obscured in her book, and that she made it much more clear to him that her husband had known about the affair from its inception, and had indeed encouraged the intimacy for his own political and financial advantage. There is at crucial points an ambivalence in Katharine's book about this central question, whereas, according to what she is said to have told Harrison, theirs was an open secret, known to O'Shea, to Parnell's colleagues, to Cabinet Ministers and high-ranking civil servants: 'Nobody wanted publicity. Nobody wanted the conventions so openly disregarded.'[7] Regrettably, at the time of their interviews in 1891–2 Harrison took no notes, and he frankly admits that, after a gap of forty years (his own study of the affair was not published until 1931), he was unable to reproduce Katharine's authentic voice, even though she had at the time expressed herself 'with a good deal of vigour and some occasional picturesqueness of phrase'.[8]

Aside from her much mistrusted memoirs, there is precious little surviving documentary evidence which captures that authentic voice. The fifty or so letters that Katharine wrote to Gladstone on Parnell's behalf remain the largest single primary source for writers on the subject, yet they have been largely ignored, even by biographers of Katharine.[9] Some of her correspondence with O'Shea (and also O'Shea's correspondence with Parnell) was produced in the divorce court and reprinted verbatim in *The Times*'s account of the trial, and a few other letters, which were not in the event submitted as evidence, exist as lawyers' copies. Katharine's book reproduces many more letters from Parnell and from her husband, the latter often differing from the recorded testimonies given by O'Shea to the divorce court and, earlier, to a Special Commission, in 1888. His statements regarding his political and fraternal relationship with Parnell frequently contradict each other, and prove that he was prepared to lie on oath in order to safeguard his own reputation. O'Shea's version of the truth is always a slippery one.

There also remain significant gaps in the narrative. Katharine led an isolated life at Eltham, then a village in south-east London. She was rarely seen in society and appears to have had no close female friends besides her sisters, and certainly no female confidante. The only contemporary commentators on the case (several of Parnell's colleagues published their memoirs or wrote early biographies of Parnell[10]) were necessarily people who had never even met Katharine, or who had no close knowledge of her. Clare and Katie, the two surviving daughters, are not mentioned in their mother's book, and their existence was only briefly alluded to during the divorce trial. It is therefore impossible to determine how Parnell fitted into the family, and how he was regarded by O'Shea's young children and by his own.[11] Katharine describes a particular day at Eltham when Parnell had cut his finger and asked her children to bring him cobwebs to wrap around the wound in order to 'stop the poison', something he had learned from his housekeeper in Ireland: 'My children, with delighted interest, produced cobwebs (and spiders) from the cellar.'[12] It is an anecdote suggestive of Parnell's ease and familiarity within the family, yet it is the only one of its kind in the whole of Katharine's book.

For biographers, the scarcity of documentary evidence and the disputed accuracy of Katharine's recollections 'point up the complications we face in reconstructing the truth in this controversial love affair'.[13] From his own rigorous analysis of the discrepancies between the various sources, Henry

Harrison made the confident claim that his own study of the affair could indisputably 'establish its claim to be *the truth*',[14] yet we will never know exactly how Captain O'Shea reconciled himself to his wife's love affair with Parnell, or the fact that she bore him three children, or exactly when he discovered that she had been unfaithful to him. What needs to be borne in mind is that this was not simply an adulterous love affair, which, if revealed, would bring them social disgrace. Clearly, this was something that they could have borne. They knew, though, that exposure would be politically disastrous to Parnell and his cause, as indeed it proved.

This book offers only a partial truth. It is necessarily a story of three people, not simply a biography of Katharine O'Shea, but it does attempt to resuscitate her voice, which is, as Roy Foster has remarked, wonderfully 'original'.[15] It is a surprisingly modern voice, one which conveys the frustrations of a woman living in the late nineteenth century, who, having found true love outside her marriage, was bound by a unjust 'law that tied husband and wife together and forced Mr Parnell to play the part of clandestine intriguer'.[16]

# CHAPTER 1

## Katharine O'Shea

On the morning of Saturday 15 November 1890, a surging crowd was struggling to gain admittance to Divorce Court No. 1 at the Royal Courts of Justice on the Strand. At 10.30 a.m. the divorce hearing of O'Shea v. O'Shea and Parnell (Steele Intervening) was scheduled to begin. It was one of the scandals of the age. The suit was brought by William Henry O'Shea, a retired Captain of the 18th Hussars and former Irish MP (1880–1886), whose wife Katharine stood accused of committing adultery with the leader of the Irish Parliamentary Party, Mr Charles Stewart Parnell. An impeccably dressed O'Shea, 'looking rather pale', yet 'quite unembarrassed', entered the courtroom shortly before half-past, bringing with him his 20-year-old son Gerard, who had been subpoenaed to give evidence against his mother. Yet neither Parnell nor Katharine O'Shea appeared. Parnell was not even represented, and, once the jury were sworn in, Katharine's counsel Frank Lockwood announced to the court that he would take no part in the proceedings: 'This is news to me,' remarked Justice Butt. Since the case was undefended, counsel for the petitioner, Sir Edward Clarke, proposed to alter his evidence accordingly, but first, he said, it was necessary for him to draw the attention of the jury to the 'remarkable' counter-charges entered by the respondent at different periods since the suit was first filed on 24 December 1889. In answer to her husband's simple charge of adultery, Katharine accused her husband of being an accessory to the love affair, from 1880 to the spring of 1886, 'by inducing, directing and requiring the respondent to form the acquaintance of the co-respondent, and to see him alone in the interest and for the advantage of the petitioner'. This was, said Clarke, not only an admission of her adultery, but a gross insult to a man already 'gravely injured'. Katharine made further counter-charges of infidelity against her husband, including the 'cruel' accusation that he had committed adultery with her own sister, Anna.[1]

While there was no longer any necessity for Clarke to call upon Katharine's own children as witnesses, there was ample evidence of their adultery. This was supplied by a number of maids ('Mrs O'Shea told me if anybody asked if he had been there I was to say no'[2]), grooms and stable-hands, cab-drivers, seaside landladies and estate agents, who all came forward to testify to the use of aliases and disguises, houses taken under false names, drawing-room doors locked in the middle of the afternoon, shared bedrooms, and an escape from a first-floor balcony. This in itself would have acted as a reminder to well-to-do Victorian people of how many pairs of eyes were upon them as they went about their daily lives. Besides the testimonies of servants and employees, hundreds of confidential letters between husband and wife were laid before the court, which appeared to reveal a ruthless and systematic deception practised upon Captain O'Shea for the past ten years. From 1880 to 1890, Katharine and Parnell had behaved with apparent disregard for moral law and social convention. The *Daily Chronicle* spoke for many when it asked how it was that Parnell should wreck not only his career but his country's chances of Home Rule, 'merely for the gratification of a guilty passion'.[3] A similar question can be asked of Katharine: how was it that this woman, after thirteen years of marriage, could enter into an adulterous relationship with her husband's parliamentary leader, fully aware of the social ignominy she would endure if the affair were discovered, and risking the loss of the custody of her three young children?

It was not a decision to be taken lightly by any woman in the late nineteenth century, and certainly Katharine understood the serious implications of her love for Parnell. She knew what it was to live without love. The fact is that her marriage to O'Shea was knowingly misrepresented to the divorce court when Sir Edward Clarke described the O'Sheas' marriage from 1867 to 1880 as being one of 'unbroken domestic happiness'.[4] Since O'Shea and his witnesses were not cross-examined, this statement passed unchallenged. It is true that two jurors were uneasy about the question of neglect and, with the permission of the judge, asked O'Shea why, after he became an MP in 1880, he lived apart from the family home in Eltham, south-east London, which was only an hour's drive away from Parliament. Even the judge admitted that there was evidence of neglect, yet he chose to use his discretionary powers 'not [to] allow any such defence to avail the defendants in this case'.[5]

The truth was that Katharine had suffered deplorable neglect from her husband since the earliest years of their marriage. No more children were born after 1874, and from that time on O'Shea had contributed nothing towards the upkeep of his family.[6] By 1880 he had become a virtual 'stranger'. Katharine suspected that O'Shea was guilty of countless infidelities, and regarded any attempt on his part to renew former intimacies with 'repugnance': 'She did not believe in its reality on his side.'[7] She also felt extremely uncomfortable about the way in which O'Shea would commandeer her attractions to charm business associates and potential investors: 'He was always in need of money, always "wanting" money, always hatching plans to make money, to get money and promoting schemes that required the co-operation of monied people. "He used to press me into the service", she said, "he was not particular".' This was how Katharine came to seek the company of the Irish leader after the General Election of April 1880. This, too, was '"part of the system of my trying to help Captain O'Shea in his career"'.[8]

This was not part of the world in which Katharine O'Shea, née Wood, had been brought up, at Rivenhall Place in Essex. She was a woman of impeccable social connections. All her near male relatives were in the Army or Navy,[9] the Church, or involved in Liberal politics. Her brother, Field Marshal Sir Evelyn Wood (at the time of the divorce, Major-General Wood, KCB), was a veteran of the Crimean War, the Indian Mutiny (during which he won a VC), the Zulu War, and the relief of Khartoum. Her father, Sir John Page Wood, was vicar of St Peter's Cornhill and of the parish of Cressing in Essex, where his thirteenth child Katharine was born on 30 January 1845. Her uncle William Page Wood, later Baron Hatherley,[10] became Liberal MP for Oxford in 1847 and Gladstone's Lord Chancellor in 1868, the year after Katharine's marriage to O'Shea. Emma, her older sister, was married to Sir Thomas Barrett Lennard, whose country seat was Belhus Park, also in Essex.[11]

Yet the Woods' social position came from business; they had only recently 'arrived'. It is a remarkable story. Katharine's grandfather, Matthew Wood, laboured as a child in his father's serge-making business in Tiverton and at the age of 14 was apprenticed to a cousin, a chemist at Exeter. At some point he moved to London and by the age of 27 had set up his own business, eventually becoming an extensive hop merchant. At 39 he was an alderman of the City of London, and two years later he was elected sheriff of London and Middlesex. He was twice Lord Mayor of London (1815/16, re-elected 1816/17) and, 'a consistent radical and a strenuous supporter of all the whig ministeries',[12] represented the City of London as a Liberal MP from 1817 to 1843. When the young Queen Victoria ascended the throne in 1837, his was the first title she created.

In a single generation Matthew Wood rose from child labourer to a hereditary title through his own ambition and through the economic opportunity made possible in the early nineteenth century: his dates, 1768–1843, correspond neatly with those of the Industrial Revolution. The baronetcy was, no doubt, an acknowledgment of his services to Victoria's father, the Duke of Kent, whose estates he had administered while the Duke was abroad on military and diplomatic service (there survives a copy of a letter of Sir Evelyn Wood's which refers to the Queen in the early 1880s expressing her gratitude for his family's kindness to her father[13]), but also perhaps for services to her late aunt, Queen Caroline, the estranged wife of George IV. They had lived apart since 1796, Caroline for many years on the Continent, but on the death of George III in 1820 she refused to renounce her claim to the title of Queen.[14] She was supported in this wish by the Whigs, among them Katharine's grandfather, who travelled to Burgundy to meet the Princess and accompany her back to England. Remarkably, the Wood family were involved in two of the greatest scandals of the nineteenth century, one towards its beginning, the other at its end.

Matthew Wood sat in Queen Caroline's landau when she entered London on 6 June 1820, and for some time she was a guest at his house. His son William (not yet 19) was employed as her translator, and Katharine's father John (ordained one year earlier) as her chaplain and private secretary. Katharine's mother, who had married John Page Wood in February 1820, became a lady of the bedchamber to the Queen.

As a sign of her gratitude they were each given a ring bearing a personal inscription and a lock of her hair. The coronation ceremony, from which Caroline was forcibly excluded, took place the following year, in July 1821. She was to die a few weeks later, at the age of 53, John Page Wood 'performing the last offices for her', and 'attending her body to its final resting-place in Brunswick'.[15] (At the time of her death she had been knitting a baby's sock for the Woods' first child, born that year.) For a brief period, Katharine's father now became chaplain to the King's younger brother, Augustus Frederick, the Duke of Sussex. The family had come a long way.

Besides Katharine's grandfather Sir Matthew and uncle William, Lord Hatherley, her great-uncle Benjamin Wood, a wealthy brewer who was married to her mother's sister, was Liberal MP for Southwark from 1840 to 1845; her father's younger brother Western Wood served briefly as Liberal MP for the City of London, from 1861 until his death two years later, and her brother Charles stood (unsuccessfully) as the Liberal candidate for Essex East in 1880. Her own father she called 'a thorough-going Whig [who] became a great influence in the county during election times'. One of Katharine's proudest memories of her father was of driving him to a canvassing, her dress decorated loudly with the Liberal colours, and hearing the crowd respond to his speeches with 'cheers for "Sir John's man"'.[16] As Katharine would later confide to the Liberal Prime Minister William Ewart Gladstone, 'Our admiration of you has always been almost akin to a religion in my family.'[17]

Katharine's happiest moments as a child were those quiet evenings spent in the company of her father when her brothers were away from home, and her mother and Anna were absorbed in their books or their sketches. (Anna had returned home to Rivenhall in 1858, after being married for a matter of weeks to a Captain Charles Steel.[18]) She would preside over her father's tea and toast while he read *The Times* by the fire, or put down his paper to listen to his daughter's childish compositions featuring 'blood-stained bandits'.[19] They 'took long walks and hunted for wild flowers together'.[20] Years later she would sit in attendance on Parnell in just the same way, and take such walks with him.

As Katharine herself said, 'had it not been for my father I should have been a very lonely child'.[21] She was the youngest child by five years. In fact, twenty-four years separated the births of the Woods' first child, John Page Wood, who died at the age of 3, and Katharine, born in 1845. As many as four other children died in infancy, and her sister Clarissa at the age of 17 when Katharine was just 2 years old. Of her remaining six siblings, her eldest sister Maria married a Colonel Chambers that same year, 1847, the couple immediately departing for India, while Frank, her senior by fourteen years, had a commission in the Army and was also away from home. Katharine 'really knew only four at all well':[22] Emma, who married when Katharine was 8, Charles (b. 1836), who farmed locally and lived at Wakes Colne Hall, Evelyn (b. 1838) and Anna (b. 1840).

As the youngest child, Katharine was patronised by her mother and Anna, who 'laughingly offered to buy my "plot" in order to "write it up" into a novel', and teased by her brothers.[23] She says that she was treated as the fool of the family. Evelyn's general advice to her was to 'look lovely and keep your mouth shut!' in the company of house-guests, and when the young John Morley, then a rising journalist and seven years her senior, was invited to Rivenhall and parcelled off onto Katharine during the day, one of her sisters told her, 'You, dear Katie, don't matter, as no one expects you to know anything!'[24] Yet this was a defining moment for Katharine, then 'so young in knowledge', as she puts it, and 'so excessively and shyly conscious of his superiority'. Since Morley was apparently well aware of her alarm, he did not talk down to her, but happily chatted away about the things that mattered to her – 'horses and dogs, books and their authors . . . my father, soldiers, and "going to London"' – so that 'I had in this little episode lost all awe of cleverness as such'.[25] As a Liberal politician, of course, Morley became closely involved with the Irish Question – he was Chief Secretary for Ireland in 1886 – and would have further dealings with Katharine and Parnell.[26]

O'Shea was first introduced to Katharine when she was 15. He thought to patronise her in the same way as her brothers, but 'nettled' by the condescension of a stranger, she bamboozled the young Captain with literary talk and reduced him to 'a bewildered and shocked silence'. He was not used to young women like Katharine, but he quickly grew to appreciate her freedom of manner, and even composed a little poem which praised her 'witsome speech'.[27]

O'Shea's origins were perhaps more obscure, although he was of the Irish Catholic landowning gentry, and had titled relatives in Spain, who had gone there as Catholic émigrés in the seventeenth century. Like Katharine's uncle, Lord Hatherley, O'Shea's father (the name was pronounced 'O'Shee') had also worked his way up in the law, but as a Dublin solicitor. Katharine glosses over the source of her father-in-law's wealth, stating that he had 'a perfect genius for pulling together estates that appeared to be hopelessly bankrupt', and that 'business flowed in to him'.[28] The truth was possibly less reputable. According to T.P. O'Connor, O'Shea 'belonged to a class which is well known in Ireland': the sons of men who exploited landlords bankrupted in the Famine by buying up estates at knockdown prices.[29] Significantly, O'Shea, his mother and sister turned their backs on the native country to which they owed their fortune. Catharine Quinlan O'Shea, a Countess of the Holy Roman Empire, settled permanently in Paris with her daughter, Mary. By the time Katharine met her sister-in-law, Mary O'Shea spoke English with an '(unaffected) French accent'.[30] O'Shea's French was also perfect, and his 'cosmopolitan education had given him an ease of manner and self-assurance'.[31] His father had moulded him to be an English gentleman, sending him first to the Catholic seminary outside Birmingham, Oscott College, and then (for the sum of £5,000) buying him a commission in the 18th Hussars. Katharine was quick to observe the contrast between father and son: the one speaking in a charming 'brogue that was music to the ear', the other in 'clear, clipped English'.[32] Yet while he might have lost his Irish accent, O'Shea would try too hard to speak and write like an English gentleman, and bewildered his recipients with airy circumlocutions. His hand-writing, too, gave him away, 'the large rounded copper-plate' being 'copy-book perfection without one touch of character'.[33]

There was a good deal of veneer with O'Shea. When in 1880 he became a Nationalist MP, T.P. O'Connor observed that the newcomer 'stood out from all his colleagues as . . . a real dandy, though a tasteful one . . . He gave me at once the impression of a man who had "lived", and had just come direct from the enjoyments of a club at St James's.'[34] His taste for fine things dated from the time of his army commission in 1858, when his father apparently instructed him, 'First become a smart officer; secondly, do what the other men do and send the bill in to me!'[35] He did just that, running up long-standing debts of £15,000. So while he came from a rising middle-class background, O'Shea spent money like an officer with a private income, and this was a habit that never left him. Years later he made something of a boast to Joseph Chamberlain about his 'extravagant personal outlay'.[36] When Katharine first saw him he was dressed in a style as meticulous as it was ostentatious, with conspicuous jewellery. She recalled 'a brown velvet coat, cut rather fully, seal-skin waistcoat, black-and-white check trousers, and an enormous carbuncle and diamond pin in his curiously folded scarf'. Yet, the youthful and vivacious officer pleased her eye. His dress was showy, but 'perfectly correct then for a young officer in the 18th Hussars'.[37]

This first introduction came when her brother Frank (in the 17th Foot) recommended O'Shea to ride one of the racehorses belonging to their sister Emma's husband, Sir Thomas Barrett Lennard, at the Brentwood Steeplechase. O'Shea's was 'a sporting regiment' and he had quickly gained a reputation for his skilled horsemanship, with 'a perfect seat and hands'.[38] The Barrett Lennards welcomed him. No doubt they had something in common. They too owned land in Ireland, with an estate in Clones, County Monaghan, which had been in the family since the sixteenth century. Yet although O'Shea's prowess as a horseman won their admiration, and his political leanings were in calculated sympathy with the Woods and Barrett Lennards, O'Shea's absorption into this family was not entire. For one thing, his Catholicism stood out in this firmly Anglican clan (O'Shea never did compromise his faith, and he maintained close contacts with the Catholic hierarchy in Ireland). O'Shea's Irishness, initially, at least, was the butt of jokes among Katharine's brothers and sisters, as it was among his regiment. Was it to make fun of O'Shea that the Woods chose him to impersonate Queen Elizabeth I in an amateur production of *Betsey Baker*, in flaming false hair and full skirts? If so, the embarrassment was doubled by the efforts of his fellow officers who were heard singing *sotto voce* 'O She is a jolly good fellow' as he made his appearance on stage. Katharine describes how 'a shout of laughter went up as Willie, who was then (and always) sensitive as to foolish puns upon his name, glowered at them', and as the whole house picked up the tune, 'with a look of withering scorn, picked up his skirts and stalked off "left" with as much dignity as he could muster'.[39] It was a joke that took some time to die. Before dinner one evening at the Barrett Lennards', Sir Thomas asked Katharine's sister, 'Who is Katie to go in with, milady?', to which Emma replied, 'Oh, *she* shall go in with O'Shea.'[40]

Katharine and O'Shea met again when she was 17, and were perhaps better able to get to know each other than other courting couples because of the theatricals started up by Emma and Sir Thomas at Belhus Park. Although the company was very much amateur, people with the Barrett Lennards' money and social standing could afford to hire the services of well-known professional actors and actresses, who would come down to Belhus in order to coach the players. In the spring of 1862, the actor Robert Keeley was advising them on a play called *Plot & Passion*. In 1861, Keeley recommended to them the comic actor John Clarke to advise the company on a burlesque of *Romeo and Juliet*, while Keeley's wife, Mrs Mary Ann Keeley, a famous comedic actress in her own right, gave assistance with the songs.[41] Lady Wood herself painted the drop curtain and all the scenery. As their ambition grew, Belhus theatricals took their productions to the largest towns in the county, Chelmsford and Colchester, and even performed in London. Yet while the performances terrified Katharine, who like Anna, was often chosen for the lead, the main attraction of the theatricals was of course in the rehearsals, during which an intimacy between Captain O'Shea and Katharine was not only possible but inevitable; he took to presenting Katharine with elaborate bouquets after her performances.

Yet for all this marked attention, O'Shea's courtship of Katharine was fitful. That first summer at Belhus Park, they were permitted to ramble the grounds unchaperoned, but Katharine says that 'she was content to drift along' with O'Shea, 'thinking not at all of the future'.[42] Nevertheless, she had a vague sense of 'belonging to Willie', and he to her, as he once demonstrated by kissing her 'full on the lips' in front of another officer who was attracted to her.[43] Then, back with his regiment, O'Shea was nearly killed when he was thrown from his horse and lay unconscious for weeks, apparently: 'for six unhappy weeks', says Katharine, 'I did little else than watch for news of him.' When he was safe to be moved, the Barrett Lennards had him transferred to Belhus, and Katharine and Anna were permitted to meet O'Shea in London and accompany him back to Essex. During the journey, 'he slipped a ring from his finger on to mine and pressed my hand under cover of the rugs'. At Belhus, he monopolised her, and catching her alone on the sofa after dinner, 'slipped a gold and turquoise locket on a long gold and blue enamel chain round my neck'. She was 'very happy to know how much Willie cared for me'.[44]

Once he had fully recovered, Lady Wood made efforts to bring the courtship to a swift conclusion, taking Katharine with her on a visit to Brighton, where O'Shea now was, even hiring her daughter a horse so that she could go for long rides on the Downs with him. Yet nothing happened. O'Shea's father Henry had earlier come over from Ireland to help look after his son, and would certainly have discussed with him the suitability of Katharine as a wife. It may have been that Henry O'Shea advised his son against the marriage on the grounds that Katharine's father was unable to provide much by way of a marriage settlement. Katharine herself seems to have taken fright at the situation, unnerved by the overtly sexual nature of his attraction to her ('I wished him away when he looked fondly at me'). After an accidental meeting at a dance, O'Shea said that he would call on her the following day, but when he arrived at the house he was met by Lady Wood, who wished to interview him. Katharine says, 'I fancy my mother understood me better than anyone.' Perhaps, too, Lady Wood was mindful here of her daughter Anna's violent reaction to her own early marriage. O'Shea was dismissed, and passed Katharine on the stairs as he made his way out. He gave her a curt goodbye, but 'I only remember a feeling of relief'.[45]

Within a few months, he would be called back. The Woods spent Christmas 1865 at Belhus, where Katharine's father began noticeably to decline. In the New Year he became increasingly feeble and feverish, and, six months short of his seventieth birthday, John Page Wood died on 21 February 1866. During the last fortnight, Katharine barely left his side for a moment, and even slept on a sofa at the foot of his bed. Her uncle Hatherley came at the last and said the Lord's Prayer over her father, Katharine's hand in his, but when it was over Katharine fell across the bed in a dead faint and had to be carried out of the room. Oddly, her mother's response was to telegraph O'Shea to come and comfort her daughter. He could stay only briefly, because he was now involved in his uncle's banking business in Spain, but he did a very tender thing: he brought with him a King Charles spaniel for Katharine. It was a desolate time for her. She was deeply affected by the loss of her father: 'I felt that I could not bear the sadness and longing for him.' She had, too, to face the reality of her mother's financial situation, who was 'left almost penniless'.[46] John Page Wood left something under £6,000 to his wife, yet this seems to have been swallowed up by the estate, for it was necessary for Lady Wood's sister, Anna Maria, the rich widow of Benjamin Wood, to settle a yearly income on her, 'thus saving her from all future anxiety'.[47] Lady Wood's ambivalent attitude towards O'Shea, and her unexpected encouragement of his suit after her husband's death, may well be explained by an anxiety to see her youngest daughter married and off her hands. Katharine and O'Shea were married 'very quietly' from the Barrett Lennards' house in Brighton, on 24 January 1867, six days before her twenty-second birthday, the wedding taking place at the parish church of St Nicholas.

Why, then, did O'Shea marry her? His own father had died in 1865, which maybe left him with an independent income, but Katharine Wood was not an heiress. Besides a gift of £5,000 which her aunt, Mrs Wood, made to all her nephews and nieces when they married, Katharine's marriage settlement was a meagre £120 a year.[48] But marriage to Katharine provided him with a secure entrée into a privileged social milieu. Her father and brother-in-law were baronets, her uncle was at the head of the legal profession and at the centre of political power. There was, also, the likelihood that Katharine would inherit something from her childless Aunt Wood, or indeed from Lord Hatherley, who, though married, also had no children. Both generously bailed out Katharine and her husband in the early years of the marriage, and O'Shea saw that Katharine kept up her connection with her influential uncle. Whereas O'Shea would generally excuse himself from the churchy dinners at George Street, he always expected Katharine to go and 'insisted upon *his* wife being perfectly gowned on these occasions'.[49] On his death in 1881, Baron Hatherley's estate was valued at £105,247. Katharine was left £1,150, pointedly 'for her separate use absolutely independent of any husband',[50] that is, outside the O'Sheas' marriage settlement. O'Shea had been disappointed, too, with the Hatherleys' wedding gift to Katharine, a delicate bracelet worked in gold and turquoise: '*this* will do for the dog', he announced, and snapped it round the neck of the spaniel, Prince.[51] Anna's gift of a carbuncle locket with a diamond centre was more to his taste. His own present to Katharine was a gold-mounted dressing-bag, while her sister Emma provided Katharine's trousseau.

O'Shea had previously sold his commission in the Army and bought a partnership in his uncle's bank, but a year spent in Madrid ended in some business disagreement with his uncle, and they returned to England, where O'Shea took over a stud farm at Bennington Park in Hertfordshire. He had a good understanding of horses, but in taking on Bennington, he was clearly over-reaching himself. The society of gentlemen was the attraction for O'Shea, naturally, but he was quite unable to keep his clients up to settling their accounts. He was running a large business, employing twenty 'lads' and looking after many brood-mares,[52] but had no wish to appear to need to press his clients to settle up. Heavy expenses were entailed, and not just in the stables. There was far too much lavish entertaining: O'Shea was often away at the races and would bring his sporting friends back with him ('most of the sporting world of that day were welcome visitors to Bennington'[53]). In addition, since O'Shea liked to 'keep up with the county', there were 'long, heavy' dinners to be got through, which led to 'such an absolutely painful boredom' in Katharine that she would sometimes hide the invitations. She admits that they were a handsome pair, 'and people liked to have us about': horse-talk always went down well, and besides, O'Shea had a natural wit. Katharine's response to her boredom was to develop a reputation for being 'delightfully unusual'. She would place a dull-witted conventional county lady next to a fast young man 'with a fund of racy anecdote', or, contravening the rules of etiquette, would not depart after dinner to take tea with the ladies, but stay to play chess with a male partner. She also encouraged flirting between the prim girls who accompanied their parents and the ineligible sporting type of young man they often had about the place, and on one occasion, having come in from the horses late, with no time for her maid to dress her hair, Katharine came down to dinner 'with my then abundant hair hanging loosely to below my waist, twisted through with a wide blue ribbon'.[54]

O'Shea was as shocked by Katharine's behaviour as his guests, but she boldly assured the party that it was the latest fashion from Paris. Yet though she despised Bennington society, it would have occasion to exclaim, as O'Shea began to absent himself, forgetting to come home for their own dinner parties or those to which they had been invited, that the O'Sheas' marriage was 'very odd'.

The Bennington experience was soon to come to an end. In an attempt to get rid of their ever worsening debts, O'Shea took to gambling heavily, and the losses only made worse their financial situation. The bank foreclosed on him within a year, and O'Shea was declared a bankrupt. Emma's husband, Sir Thomas, relieved them of the mares for £500, which enabled them to pay off their employees and servants.

Katharine was now expecting their first child, and Aunt Wood stepped in to pay for a house in Brighton; indeed, she managed to secure 6 Lewes Crescent, near the sea front, and next door to the Barrett Lennards' Brighton home. Here Katharine was left with just three servants in attendance: her old nurse, Lucy Goldsmith, her French maid, Caroline, and the groom, Selby. Gerard Henry William O'Shea was born on 4 April 1870. The birth affected Katharine badly and her mother stayed in the house to nurse her, yet there is no suggestion that O'Shea stayed, too. On the birth certificate, registered by O'Shea one week later, Gerard is simply identified as a male child. It seems inconceivable that Katharine and O'Shea had not yet agreed upon a name for their first child, although it may be that, in O'Shea's absence, they had not discussed the matter fully.

After O'Shea's solicitor had boldly applied on his behalf to Lord Hatherley in case there was a vacant post at the Treasury suitable for Katharine's husband, a generous cheque was delivered to the Brighton house, again significantly in Katharine's name alone: Baron Hatherley sent his best wishes to the young couple but regretted that he could do nothing for Captain O'Shea. Thereafter, O'Shea remained up in London. He 'often was away for days',[55] pursuing various business ventures in the city, yet their finances showed no improvement. Katharine moved into a rather more modest rented house on Marine Parade, and then, still dependent upon her aunt's generosity, into a cottage at Patcham, on the outskirts of Brighton.

Patcham was a beautiful village against the Downs, and Katharine enjoyed walking and riding (she was able to have her old pony there). She also had before her the stalwart example of Caroline and Selby, who put up with the new situation and refused to leave their mistress. Selby, who had had 'more than twenty underlings to do his bidding' at Bennington, went down from '£200 a year for doing practically nothing' to ten shillings a week, while Caroline, 'whose hardest task had been to dress my hair and wash my little dog, now with the utmost cheerfulness took to cooking, scrubbing, cleaning, and being literally a maid-of-all-work'.[56] Yet although Katharine had, as she says, 'the consolation of my beautiful babe', O'Shea would only make 'flying' visits, and in her loneliness Katharine would drive daily to her sister's in Brighton. When a cousin of O'Shea's, a Mrs Vaughan, came on a visit, irritation was added to loneliness as her guest was 'perpetually wondering what Willie was doing that kept him so much away'.[57] Finally, Katharine would tolerate his neglect no longer and 'told him that I must join him in London if he meant to be there so much'.

O'Shea agreed, but the home he brought her to was a poky house on the Harrow Road with a recurring view of funeral processions to the Kensal Green Cemetery. Thereafter, their financial situation improved dramatically, although Katharine gives little information about the sort of business her husband was involved in – investment schemes, no doubt, for she noted acerbically that he 'always drew up a prospectus excellently; on reading it one could hardly help believing – as he invariably did – that here at last was the golden opportunity of speculators'.[58] Their debts paid, they now took a house in Beaufort Gardens, off the Brompton Road, O'Shea typically insisting upon Parisian wallpaper of silver and blue, which 'showed up the extreme ugliness of our furniture to great disadvantage'.[59] A butler was hired, with a staff of maids to run the household, and Caroline's privileged position of lady's-maid was restored. Katharine was again pregnant, but 'Willie insisted upon my making many new acquaintances', acquaintances who would do him good professionally, one assumes. She was called upon to keep up her connections with her uncle, now Lord Chancellor, 'and we were a good deal at his house, both at "functions" and privately', although Lord Hatherley was a very pious man and O'Shea found the company of so many churchmen tedious. Most often Katharine would be sent alone. Here, too, she had to endure the pity of her relatives, who would say to her, 'Dear Katie, alone again! poor dear girl, where *does* he go?'[60]

'We soon found ourselves in a social swirl of visits, visitors and entertainments. I had always disliked society, as such, and this appeared to me to be almost as bad as the Bennington dinner-party days.'[61] Katharine was expected to reflect O'Shea's glorious self-image. When she found that the fashionable French style of wearing the hair in loops of braid did not suit her, he 'insisted' that she buy false hair to increase the number of braids, and 'was always worrying me to dress in the latest fashion'.[62] This becomes a familiar refrain in her account of the early years of her marriage to O'Shea. Katharine's complaint may be interpreted as a discreet protest against her husband's taste for ostentation, and her own wish for a less public, more intimate marital relationship, one that was not always on display. Finally, she refused the services of the French hairdresser, and, striking a characteristically modern tone, did so 'in defence of my own personality'.[63]

Katharine's relationship with O'Shea was one of extremes: she either suffered neglect (after a ball or party he would frequently drop her off at Beaufort Gardens in order to 'finish up the night' with his new-found friends), or was asked to perform the role of contented wife in the company of people she did not know, 'a life I found so wearisome'.[64] The 'personality' valued by O'Shea was Katharine's ability to charm, her cultured conversation, the assurance of her social background. He was a stranger to her inner self, an inner self which suffered still more in Katharine's growing aversion to her husband's faith. Two daughters were born to her while she was living in Chelsea: Mary Norah Kathleen (known as Norah), on 10 January 1873, and Anna Maria del Carmen (known as Carmen) nineteen months later, on 4 August 1874, the relative nearness of the births no doubt a consequence of O'Shea's occupying the same house as Katharine for a continuous period. Their names, like their brother's, reflect O'Shea's background: one typically Irish, the other typically Spanish, although Aunt Anna Maria Wood is also kept in view. The girls, of course, were baptised in the Catholic Church.

Katharine describes how, in her loneliness, she would seek respite from tense domestic scenes with O'Shea ('Willie and I were beginning to jar upon one another a good deal now') by taking solitary walks through the London parks. She was within easy reach of Kensington Gardens, Hyde Park and Green Park, and on her return from Kensington Gardens would often stop at the Brompton Oratory where, despite its being a Catholic church, she would sit for a few minutes' rest before heading back to Beaufort Gardens. She describes these quiet moments as 'a comfort to me when suffering from the fret and worry of my domestic life'.[65] Shortly after Norah's baptism at the Oratory, perhaps at O'Shea's suggestion, a priest called on Katharine with the intention of giving her instruction. She undertook to read all the books that she was given and clearly tried with great patience to understand the Catholic faith, but she had what she calls two stumbling-blocks: the fact that her husband was a type of 'careless Catholic', while her mother- and sister-in-law were the embodiment of 'such a fierce bigotry and deadly dullness of outlook, such an immense piety and so small a charity', that, she says, her 'whole being revolted', and she not only turned away abruptly from Catholicism but from 'all forms and creeds'. The crisis for Katharine was the occasion of her daughter Carmen's baptism in 1874, when she refused even to enter the church and 'stood waiting in the porch': 'I felt that my children were taken from me, and that I was very lonely.'[66]

As with Gerard's birth, Katharine took a long time to recover her health that autumn and winter. Despite what was now once more a worsening financial situation, or perhaps for the sake of appearances, O'Shea, not satisfied with the diagnosis of their local doctor, insisted that he consult with two leading physicians of the day: Sir William Gull, who had attended the Prince of Wales in 1871, and would later become Queen Victoria's physician, and Sir William Jenner, Royal Physician in the early 1860s. Katharine was recommended a recuperative stay on the Isle of Wight and prescribed a course of sleeping draughts. Aunt Wood 'played fairy godmother once more, and sent Willie a cheque', which enabled the whole family to take rooms at a hotel in Niton over Christmas, but finding this expensive, O'Shea moved Katharine, the children and nurses, into rented lodgings at Ventnor, 'and, finding the place decidedly dull, returned to London'.[67] He never came back.

While a local doctor got her off the sleeping draughts and onto beef tea, Katharine found that her new setting played on her nerves more than anything. She was surrounded by fellow patients, many consumptive, who seemed a warning of what she might become. She determined to get away, and, without informing O'Shea, got one of her Barrett Lennard nephews to escort her and her young family back to the mainland and to St Leonards, where O'Shea did eventually come to them.

As Katharine grew stronger, O'Shea encouraged her to call on her aunt, to thank her for her generosity. As with the earlier visits to Lord Hatherley, this was a very calculated attention to Katharine's childless aunt, who had lived in seclusion since her husband's death in 1845. She had only once been on a train and never left Eltham Lodge except for a daily airing in her carriage about the neighbourhood. Yet, although in her late seventies, and enjoying relatively little society, Aunt Wood was astute enough to recognise the difficulties in the O'Shea marriage and to sense that her niece was 'much alone'.[68] She may also have been told details of what her niece had undergone by her sister, Lady Wood, who had not only witnessed O'Shea's careless attitude to his wife and young family, but would have heard further stories from Emma in Brighton.

Katharine's mother is the missing figure in this drama. Katharine greatly admired her beauty, and tells us that she was a fine painter and musician and became a successful novelist (as did her sister Anna[69]), but after mentioning that her mother looked after her in Brighton after the birth of Gerard, Katharine never again alludes to her, not even to record her death, which took place on 13 December 1879. It may be that the distance she felt from her mother as a child persisted – she comments upon her mother being 'so entirely wrapped up in Evelyn' and of her being 'devoted' to Katharine's sister Emma[70] – and that Katharine's relationship with her elderly aunt was a substitute for the friendship she never quite had with her own mother.

Whatever the source of her information, the solution proposed by Anna Maria Wood was serious and immediate. After taking legal advice, Aunt Wood (or Aunt Ben as she was also known) proposed to Katharine that, in exchange for her undertaking the duties of a companion, she would buy her a house in the neighbourhood of her own home in Eltham, 'and arranged to settle a regular income on me and to educate my children'.[71] She was undoubtedly very fond of Katharine, the youngest of her sister's children, but her proposal was made not just for her own benefit and to meet Katharine's domestic necessities, but for the sake of her niece's reputation: 'She considered that this arrangement would be more "seemly" for me, as Willie was obliged to be away from home so much.'[72] The house she found, a large recently built detached Victorian villa, Wonersh Lodge, backed onto North Park, in which Eltham Lodge,[73] a grand house built in the Restoration period, was situated; a gate was made in the fence, allowing Katharine to cross the grounds to her aunt's home daily on foot without having to drive by road. It was, says Katharine, a 'comfortable' house, not of course the style of house she had lived in as a child, but the sort of villa to suit a prosperous middle-class family. Her aunt's house, however, was indeed the kind that Katharine was accustomed to, and 'after the restraint of town life', the freedom her children enjoyed in North Park made a considerable difference. Katharine could now afford nurses for the girls and a governess for Gerard until he was old enough to attend school at Blackheath. Mrs Wood also furnished the whole house, which numbered a formal dining-room and drawing-room, besides two sitting-rooms, one of which opened into the garden and the other into a conservatory. There were also 'excellent stables'.[74]

Katharine's life was now of value to another person. She makes a point of saying that her aunt was 'someone who wanted me always'.[75] Her life, too, now had routine and structure: 'I was generally with my aunt from the first thing in the morning, returning to my children at lunchtime, and in the afternoon I got home for dinner, should Willie happen to return.'[76] There was little likelihood of that in the early days at Wonersh Lodge. O'Shea was at this time launching his Spanish sulphur mining company, which kept him largely in London, soliciting investments. He was then appointed manager and left for Spain. He would not return for another eighteen months. He depended upon Katharine to communicate his wishes to the board in London: 'I had to pay frequent visits to London when samples of the sulphur were sent home for testing purposes . . . and to place the constant demands for new machinery in as ingratiating a way as possible before various members of the "board".'[77] Katharine seems to have understood that O'Shea was calculating that her natural charm would work its way with the board. He would send her long reports ('in hot language') that she was to pass on to the company directors. His reliance upon her had developed naturally throughout their early marriage, as his absences from home required her to become more and more independent, responsible and resourceful. Starved of intellectual stimulus, Katharine evidently took an interest in her husband's business and enjoyed this role as his representative at board meetings and company dinners. After various setbacks in the extraction process, however, the Spanish sulphur proved too expensive to extract and the company folded, which seems to have been an outcome typical of O'Shea's business ventures.

One intriguing question remains: did Katharine have an affair with Christopher Weguelin, an old friend of the days of the Belhus theatricals, and one with an interest in the company, while her husband was out of the country for eighteen months (when presumably O'Shea felt under no pressure to be sexually abstemious)? Certainly Katharine attracted a number of admirers in her early years of marriage. Tim Healy claimed that there was a letter which was evidence of an affair with Weguelin, but all we have to go on is Katharine's passing reference that she made a number of visits to see him.[78]

On O'Shea's return to England in 1878 he came back to Wonersh Lodge for a time: 'We were pleased to see one another again, but once more the wearing friction caused by our totally dissimilar temperaments began to make us feel that close companionship was impossible.' The decision they came to, to live separately, O'Shea taking rooms in London, was apparently an amicable, mutual agreement, one greatly smoothed, no doubt, by the fact that O'Shea's 'separate establishment in London' was also paid for by Katharine's aunt.[79] O'Shea was to come down to Eltham at the weekends, when he would sometimes call at the Lodge to read French to Aunt Wood,[80] yet although he could generally be depended upon to arrive on Sunday mornings to take the children to Mass at nearby Chislehurst, 'the regularity of his weekend visits became very much broken'.[81] His informal separation from Katharine suited O'Shea in so many ways, but he was equally as sensitive as Katharine's aunt that appearances should be maintained. Occasional dinner parties were held at Eltham, but more often Katharine would be asked to come up to London in order to help host a dinner at the London hotel always used by her parents, Thomas's Hotel, Berkeley Square: 'here I used to help Willie with his parties, and to suffer the boredom incidental to this form of entertainment. He never seemed to have anyone at all amusing.' O'Shea was insistent that 'if only for the sake of our children I ought not to "drop out of everything"',[82] yet even then he often forgot his wife's existence. Katharine records her anger and mortification at having submitted to her husband's nagging demand that she attend a particular ball given by a countess she had never heard of, only to be stood up. She came up to Thomas's Hotel the afternoon of the ball, was ready and dressed at half an hour to midnight with her carriage at the door. At one o'clock she went to bed, O'Shea finally turning up the next morning having forgotten all about the ball. It was not just her husband's slighting her that caused Katharine so much aggravation, but the fact that her humiliation was clear to both manageress and head waiter, who had known 'Miss Katie' since she was a child, and fussed over her rather too familiarly when O'Shea did not appear.

When, in early 1880, O'Shea was encouraged by his Irish friends, Sir George and Lady O'Donnell, to stand for an Irish constituency at the forthcoming General Election, Katharine 'wrote back strongly encouraging him to stand, for I knew it would give him occupation he liked and keep us apart – and therefore good friends'.[83] This was one field in which Katharine's Liberal connections might be useful to O'Shea. Although his only chance of a safe seat at the 1880 General Election was as an Irish Nationalist, O'Shea was wholly a landowning Liberal, who sat on the Liberal benches and voted consistently with the Liberal Government. He was duly returned for County Clare. His campaign partner was the O'Gorman Mahon, and Katharine, or rather her aunt, was expected to cover their joint election expenses of £2,000. As Katharine later told Henry Harrison, 'Captain O'Shea was always coming to me to get money from her for him – and he got quite a lot.'[84] Over supper with Katharine at Greenwich, Mahon gave O'Shea his cue: 'Now, Willie, 'twill slip easier into her ear from you!'[85]

The Irish Parliamentary Party had returned sixty MPs, and had now to elect a new party chairman. For the past year, since the death of Isaac Butt in May 1879, the moderate William Shaw had served as chairman, but the O'Gorman Mahon now proposed a contender, the 35-year-old Charles Stewart Parnell. O'Shea voted for him, even though he feared, as he telegraphed Katharine, 'that Mr Parnell might be too "advanced"'.[86] Parnell's victory was narrow: twenty-three MPs voted for him, eighteen for Shaw. Among Parnell's supporters were the core of the future party: Tim Healy, T.P. O'Connor, Justin McCarthy, John Barry, Thomas Sexton, T.D. Sullivan, and Joseph Biggar, who was also a member of the supreme council of the extremist Irish Republican Brotherhood. O'Shea, whose attempts to fashion himself as an English gentleman had been a matter of such care, became a member of the Irish Parliamentary Party at the very moment it became, under Parnell's leadership, a revolutionary movement.

As with O'Shea, an English schooling and four years at Magdalene College, Cambridge, had rid Parnell of any trace of an Irish accent. Rusticated from Cambridge in 1869 for drunken rowdiness (it seems that he could have returned to the university but refused to apologise for his behaviour[87]), he returned to his home at Avondale, in County Wicklow, to all appearances perfectly suited to the life of a country gentleman: 'His pleasures were as uncomplicated as those of any country squire.'[88] Not a scholar, nor by any means a literary man, Parnell's interests were practical and scientific: besides riding and hunting, he developed industries on his land – sawmills, quarries, and mines for copper, iron, and gold.[89] Like Katharine's, his was also a political family. His own father showed little interest in politics, but Parnell's family had been MPs in either the Irish Parliament (before the Act of Union, 1800) or at Westminster for much of the past two centuries, Sir John Parnell, his great-grandfather, becoming Chancellor of the Irish Exchequer and admired among Nationalists for his opposition to the Act of Union.[90] Parnell's sisters, Fanny and Anna Parnell, were also active in Nationalist politics, but from a more extreme position than their brother's. They formed the Ladies' Land League, Fanny in America, Anna in Ireland, a radical movement which created difficulties for Parnell and which, therefore, he acted to suppress.[91]

The Parnell family's Irish patriotism featured strongly in Parnell's own electioneering campaigns: 'the family mystique was necessarily evoked.'[92] After failing to win a seat at the 1874 General Election, he was elected MP for Meath the following year, but spent the next couple of years in more or less political anonymity. He first came to public notice in 1876, when he caused a stir in the Commons by interrupting the Irish Chief Secretary to state his opinion that the Manchester policeman who had been accidentally shot during a botched attempt to rescue two Fenian prisoners from a prison van in 1867 had not been 'murdered'.[93] In 1877, in direct opposition to the wishes of the then party chairman, Isaac Butt, Parnell, together with Joseph Biggar, threw himself into a new concentrated phase of 'Obstruction', in which the business of the Commons was held up by time-wasting speeches from members of the Opposition.

By now, 'Parnell was the effective leader of the Irish in England and Scotland'.[94] He was able to wrest power from Isaac Butt because Butt offered the party no effective leadership. Butt's position was essentially defeatist. He felt that the British Government could never be brought to reform the land question, and he had founded the Home Rule League in 1873 with no real expectation that an Irish Parliament could be achieved in his lifetime. Parnell, on the contrary, believed that the British Government could, and would, deliver both land reform and Home Rule, if only sufficient political pressure was applied. Butt's conduct in Parliament was 'a model of courtesy and moderation'. He 'hoped by moderation and friendliness to remove English prejudice', whereas Parnell vowed to the Irish people that he would 'help you to punish the English'.[95] When at one meeting a voice from the crowd told him that it would take 'an earthquake to settle the land question', he replied, 'Then we must have an earthquake.'[96] Faced with extremist organisations like the Irish Republican Brotherhood, and the American Clan-na-Gael (which had severed links with the Irish Parliamentary Party believing that the House of Commons was 'a school for Anglicising Irishmen'[97]), he had to convince them that legislative reform could be achieved if it had their support. Katharine puts it well when she says that it was Parnell's mission 'to unite all the warring elements of the Nationalist movements into one force to be hurled against England'.[98]

Parnell took over from Butt as the head of the Home Rule Confederation of Great Britain in 1877, and in 1879 became the first elected President of the newly formed Irish National Land League, the main force behind which was Michael Davitt, also a member of the supreme council of the IRB, currently on ticket-of-leave, having served half of a fourteen-year prison sentence for gathering arms. The Land League was pledged to support legislative reform of the land question (their ultimate aim being peasant ownership), and to defend 'those who may be threatened with eviction for refusing to pay unjust rents'.[99] The situation in Ireland was at that time so grave, after bad harvests in 1878 and 1879, that the West of Ireland was threatened 'with the worst economic disaster since the Great Famine'.[100]

The new land movement was crucial for Parnell on two counts. He maintained the belief that the two questions of Land and Home Rule were inextricably linked: once the practice of rack-renting was abolished, and the source of tension removed between landlord and tenant, conditions would be conducive to a united call for Home Rule. The land-owning class would no longer look to England for protection of their interests, but would regard themselves as Irish, with a responsibility to return an Irish Parliament.[101] The Land League itself, however, was an organisation which attracted many extremists,[102] and this new movement symbolised what was known as the 'New Departure' – what amounted to an offer of support to Parnell's parliamentary campaign from the revolutionary force of political extremists.

In December 1879, Parnell left for America in the company of Davitt on a fund-raising tour on behalf of the newly founded Land League. He returned home for the General Election in April 1880, at which he was elected MP for Cork City.[103] The election as party chairman followed on 17 May. As leader of the Irish Parliamentary Party, and with a mandate from the League and the country, he made a phenomenal impact on the House of Commons. Sir Charles Dilke later accounted for Parnell's success in an interview with R. Barry O'Brien, saying that, 'He hated England, English ways, English modes of thought. He would have nothing to do with us. He acted like a foreigner. We could not get at him as at any other man in English public life. He was not one of us in any sense. Dealing with him was like dealing with a foreign Power.'[104]

If Parnell was an enigma to the political establishment, the course he now took in his private and political life was extraordinary. This was a man who had never married ('he was not a sociable or a marrying man,' noted William O'Brien[105]), and who seems to have had only one previous experience of love (in 1871, at the age of 25, he was jilted by his American fiancée, a Miss Woods[106]). At the age of 35, he fell in love, at first sight, with a woman married to one of his own MPs, jeopardising not only his own career but the Irish Nationalist movement, of which he had only recently become the leader. She was an English woman, moreover,[107] and of a privileged social background, a woman who knew nothing of the plight of the poor in Ireland, indeed, whose husband and brother-in-law could both be described as absentee Irish landlords. Katharine, too, was risking a great deal – her three children, her reputation and social standing – for the sake of a man who was a 'Revolutionist',[108] identified with Fenians and defying a Liberal Government of the kind her family had served for the past two generations.

There is no shortage of reasons why she did so. Clearly he found her irresistibly sexually attractive, and she him. What is more, he took her seriously. From the first he encouraged her to attend Irish debates from the Ladies' Gallery in the House of Commons, and what began as her help with his correspondence developed into a role as political confidante and wholly trusted go-between in Parnell's dealings with the Prime Minister. He needed her help, and needed her to attend on him daily, and nurse him when he was in poor health, as he often was. He simply could not bear to be separated from her. When he was away from her, in Ireland, or France, he would write to Katharine, and need to hear back from her, daily. They were also of the same social class and shared the same Protestant background, yet neither was a practising member of the Established Church, and neither felt bound by its moral strictures: 'Parnell contravened certain social laws, not regarding them as binding him in any way,' writes Katharine, and 'I joined him in this contravention since his love made all else of no account to me'.[109] Above all, he loved her. She recalls his meeting her at Charing Cross Station, at a time when she was deeply troubled about whether to enter into a relationship with him. She had been away to the Downs above Brighton, to think about her life, 'narrow, narrow, narrow, and so deadly dull'. On the train to Eltham he whispered to her, 'I love you, I love you. Oh my dear, how I love you.'[110] They did not expect to be forgiven by the upholders of conventional morality, nor did they resent 'the consequences that were inevitable and always foreseen'.[111]

# CHAPTER 2

## *Parnell*

Katharine's husband was now an MP and, no doubt to help establish him in the London political world, the O'Sheas held a number of dinner parties at Thomas's Hotel. O'Shea's parliamentary leader, Parnell, was always invited, always accepted, yet never appeared. Their guests teased Katharine over his empty chair and told her 'how he ignored the invitations of the most important political hostesses in London, and of his dislike of all social intercourse'. Some one 'laughingly defied me to fill' the empty chair,[1] and, piqued by his aloofness, Katharine determined that he would be present at the next dinner they gave. So, on a bright summer's day at the beginning of July 1880, Katharine picked up her sister, Anna Steele, at St James's Street, drove to the House of Commons, 'and sent in a card asking Mr Parnell to come out and speak to us in Palace Yard'. It all seems to have been rather playfully done. Yet the man who came out to meet her carriage was not a man to be taken so lightly. Very handsome, she thought him, with an 'aristocratic face':

> He came out, a tall, gaunt figure, thin and deadly pale. He looked straight at me smiling, and his curiously burning eyes looked into mine with a wonderful intentness that threw into my brain the sudden thought: 'This man is wonderful – and different.'

Parnell apologised for not having read his mail for days (his rooms were scattered with unanswered letters – as Justin McCarthy put it, he had 'never been trained to the habits of a man of business'[2]), and promised to come to dinner with the O'Sheas, if the invitation still stood, once he had returned from Paris where he was to attend his sister Theodosia's wedding the following week. Then, as Katharine leant forward in the carriage to say goodbye a rose fastened in her bodice dropped onto her skirts: 'He picked it up and, touching it lightly with his lips, placed it in his button-hole. This rose I found long years afterwards, done up in an envelope, with my name and the date, among his most private papers.'[3] It is an account much discredited by Parnell biographers. F.S.L. Lyons regards it as 'no doubt romanticised', and prefers to believe that for Parnell the dinner invitation was 'a tiresome obligation he could no longer avoid'.[4] This is a view not supported by the flirtatiousness of Parnell's letters written shortly after he met Katharine. Presumably, she renewed her invitation, asking Parnell when he would be free. He replied:

> London,
> July 17, 1880
>
> My dear Mrs O'Shea,
> We have all been in such a 'disturbed' condition lately that I have been quite unable to wander further from here than a radius of about one hundred [paces]. And this notwithstanding the powerful attractions which have been tending to seduce me from my duty towards my country in the direction of Thomas's Hotel.[5]

This is the first letter that Katharine received from Parnell. It was an extraordinary letter to write to the wife of one of his own MPs, a woman to whom he had been only formally introduced.

Parnell was then busy drafting amendments to the Liberal Government's Compensation for Disturbance Bill, which offered protection against eviction to Irish tenants unable to pay their rent because of bad harvests: this measure would empower them to appeal to the Land Court for compensation if they could prove that they were willing to negotiate a fair rent on the property, but that the landlord had refused their terms. In practice, it would have had the effect of suspending evictions in Ireland. Parnell had some success in widening the terms of the bill, which comfortably passed its second reading on 5 July, the Irish party voting with the Government. The third reading was due in three weeks' time.

Towards the end of July, allowing Parnell to name a suitable date, the O'Sheas arranged a 'quiet dinner' at Thomas's Hotel, inviting only Anna, her fellow novelist and Irish MP Justin McCarthy, Katharine's nephew Sir Matthew Wood,[6] and a couple of other guests. Despite Katharine being 'really anxious that he should have an agreeable evening', she seems to have lost her tongue at table, overshadowed by her sister's brilliant talk which 'kept him interested and amused'. Parnell may have been nervous, too, since he addressed most of his conversation to Anna. After dinner, the party took a box at the Gaiety Theatre in the Strand, famous for its burlesques, and here, away from the formality of the dinner table, Parnell and Katharine 'seemed to fall naturally into our places in the dark corner of the box' behind the others.[7] Here in the darkness he immediately began to address her personally, and intimately.

Katharine's memory of this, their first private conversation, is vivid. He had begun to speak to her about his recent American tour when, 'turning more to me, he paused; and, as the light from the stage caught his eyes, they seemed like sudden flames. I leaned a little towards him . . . and his eyes smiled into mine.'[8] What made him hesitate was his impulse to tell Katharine about his broken engagement to a young woman in America. This story has also been doubted by biographers, quick to point out that Parnell's former fiancée had been married to a Boston lawyer for ten years.[9] Yet, we might consider that Parnell was taking the first opportunity he had to talk confidentially to Katharine to let her know that he had no emotional ties to any other woman. Surprisingly, this was before he knew the precise details of the O'Sheas' matrimonial situation. The long-established informal separation between husband and wife is unlikely to have been party gossip, since O'Shea, an MP of three months' standing, was relatively unknown to them, and to all appearances husband and wife put on a united show.

A courtship began and persisted through the repercussions of the Lords' rejection of the Compensation for Disturbance Bill on 3 August. The defeat was crushing – 282 to 51 – and was 'the signal for extreme agitation in Ireland'. R. Barry O'Brien notes that 'There were riots at evictions; tenants who had ventured to take the place of the evicted occupiers were assaulted, their property damaged, their ricks burned, [and] their cattle maimed,' and a Fenian arms robbery was carried out on a ship in Cork harbour.[10] The defeat in the Lords also drove Parnell to take more aggressive action. On 6 August he called a meeting of MPs who resolved upon an immediate policy of obstruction in the House, and then 'to place themselves at the disposal of the country' once the session was over.[11] On 24 August they forced an all-night sitting on the constabulary estimates for Ireland. 'We must compel the people to listen to us,' Parnell told Justin McCarthy, 'and the only way to do it is by insisting that if our claims are not heard no other business shall be done'.[12]

Parnell pressed Katharine to attend the Irish debates, and whenever she was able to get away from North Park for an afternoon she would take a place in the Ladies' Gallery. She says that she did not let Parnell know when to expect her, but he always found out that she was there and would come up for a few words. If the Wednesday sittings did not require his presence, he would ask Katharine to take a drive with him along the river. According to Katharine, one of the things they discussed was the question of her husband's chances of being re-elected for County Clare 'in case another election is sprung on us'. O'Shea's concern was that in the likely event of the O'Gorman Mahon's retirement or death his own position in Clare would be vulnerable without Parnell's support: 'Both Willie and I were very anxious to secure Mr Parnell's promise about this.'[13] Yet she and Parnell also found time to walk out along the Mortlake meadows, and 'sit there through the summer afternoon, watching the gay traffic on the river . . . till the growing shadows warned us that it was time to drive back to London'.[14]

Katharine's published account of Parnell's leisured, almost casual, courtship during the late summer months of 1880 perhaps conceals more urgent, passionate assignations. Tim Healy was alert to his leader's showing signs of distraction at this time, and he was disturbed that Parnell was prepared to leave the work of parliamentary obstruction to his deputies. He began to ask himself why, having promised Healy to keep the House sitting for days over a particular question, his leader was in such a hurry to leave the Commons as he had been, two or three times that week. 'There must be a lady in the case,' he concluded.[15] There was certainly an exhilaration about him which could be seen in his delightful behaviour as best man at the London wedding of his election agent M.J. Horgan. 'Dressed magnificently and looking so handsome,'[16] he carried off the nervous groom to a nearby hotel, where he ordered a bottle of champagne. Unexpectedly, he stayed to the wedding luncheon and, as Horgan later told R. Barry O'Brien, 'entered quite into the spirit of the whole business', not leaving until after the bride and groom.[17]

At about this time, O'Shea was away holding meetings in his County Clare constituency, and in his absence Katharine and Parnell saw more and more of each other. She was invited to a lunch party on Wednesday 1 September at her sister Anna's London house in fashionable St James's Street, off Piccadilly. The only other guests were Justin McCarthy and Parnell. The parliamentary session was drawing to a close and Parnell talked of his longing to leave England for the partridge-shooting at Avondale. Katharine held back from the conversation while her sister and McCarthy 'chaffed' Parnell for caring so little for their society, but his studied reply was for Katharine: 'I have the partridges there, and here I cannot always have your society.'[18]

After lunch, she had to break up the party in order to get back to her aunt, and Parnell offered to accompany her to Charing Cross Station. They just missed the Eltham train, and, hailing a cab, Parnell persuaded Katharine that 'it would be much pleasanter to drive down on such a beautiful afternoon'. The hour-long drive, during which they could talk intimately in safe seclusion, must indeed have been pleasant, and there seems little doubt that once they reached Eltham, Parnell anticipated an invitation into the house, which made Katharine nervous. She seems to have felt that he was rushing her. It was no doubt one thing to go on romantic drives along the Thames and to parry Parnell's flirtatious speeches, but quite another to invite him into her home while her husband was in Ireland – a home occupied by her three children and Katharine's old nurse, 85-year-old Lucy Goldsmith. Katharine reminded him that she had to call on her aunt, and Parnell 'reluctantly returned to London',[19] but not before he made her promise to have dinner with him at Thomas's Hotel the following Wednesday. With O'Shea safely out of the country, he seems to have assumed that she was at liberty to see him alone.

Here again, he was moving much faster than Katharine. It is an episode which bears little relation to the myth of Katharine as a calculated seductress, an older, sexually dominant woman, who, according to William O'Brien, 'hunted him down'.[20] Even their mutual friend, Justin McCarthy, later observed that 'he was a very young man when it began . . . she was considerably older than he'.[21] In fact, she was older by a year and a half.

Parnell had arranged to meet Katharine's afternoon train as it came into Cannon Street Station. He then ushered her into the Station Hotel, where he had taken some rooms. He had clearly done so with the intention of seducing her. Looking in at the dining-room door Parnell saw a group of his own MPs, or so he claimed to Katharine, 'and said it would be more comfortable for us in his private sitting-room'.[22] Whether she knew what was in his mind or not, Katharine said that she thought he had rooms in Keppel Street, and Parnell, apparently abashed, was obliged to pretend that he had recently taken rooms at the hotel. She did agree to have tea with him in his private rooms, but seems to have been unnerved by the prospect of sharing a hotel bedroom with him. He talked politics to her until she was at her ease, 'and then lapsed into one of those long silences of his that I was already beginning to know were dangerous in the complete sympathy they evoked between us'. Rather than engage with this dangerous sympathy, Katharine reminded him of their dinner engagement at Thomas's: 'he rose without a word and followed me downstairs.'[23]

After dinner, Parnell took the morning mail to Dublin and later in the day she received a further indication of his feelings towards her: 'I don't feel quite so content at the prospect of ten days' absence from London amongst the hills and valleys of Wicklow as I should have done some three months since. The cause is mysterious, but perhaps you will help me to find it, or her, on my return.'[24] Two days later, about to go into the Wicklow hills for the shooting, where he would be 'removed from post offices and such like consolations for broken-hearted politicians', he wrote again: 'I am still in the land of the living, notwithstanding the real difficulty of either living or being, which every moment becomes more evident, in the absence of a certain kind and fair face.'[25]

While Parnell recovered his strength at Avondale, the Land League had organised a series of weekly meetings up and down the country. On 19 September, Parnell, sharing a public platform with eight local priests, made his now famous speech at Ennis, County Clare, in which he stirringly set forth a system of defeating the eviction process through passive resistance:

'Slowly, calmly, deliberately, without a quiver of passion, a note of rhetoric, or an exclamation of anger, but in a tone that penetrated his audience like the touch of cold steel, he proclaimed war against all who should resist the mandates of the League.'[26] The English Parliament had failed the Irish people, he told them. The character of the Land Bill promised next session would be decided by action taken by the people this winter. 'Now,' he asked the assembled masses, 'what are you to do to a tenant who bids for a farm from which his neighbour has been evicted?'. Here, there were excited shouts of 'Kill him!', 'Shoot him!', but Parnell, with his hands behind his back, stood calmly, waiting for absolute silence until he resumed:

> When a man takes a farm from which another has been evicted, you must show him on the roadside when you meet him, you must show him in the streets of the town – (A voice: 'Shun him!') – you must show him at the shop counter, you must show him in the fair and in the market-place, and even in the house of worship, by leaving him severely alone, by putting him into a sort of moral Coventry, by isolating him from his kind as if he was a leper of old.[27]

The effects were immediate and staggering. On 22 September, three days after Parnell's Ennis speech, eviction notices were due to be served on the tenants of Lord Erne's estates in Connaught, where Lord Erne's agent, Captain Boycott, had previously rejected the tenants' proposal of a reduced 'just rent'. The tenants responded by refusing to harvest their crops. They successfully persuaded all domestic servants and farm labourers to leave, while local shop-keepers and tradesmen were enjoined to have no dealings at all with Captain Boycott, a process which quickly became known as 'boycotting'. The agent was forced to apply to Dublin Castle for assistance in bringing in Lord Erne's crops. Fifty Ulster Orangemen, who volunteered for the job, arrived under military escort with two cannons, and the crops were harvested without any resistance. But no evictions took place on the estate. Indeed, in many areas of the country, as noted by Conor Cruise O'Brien, 'The landlords, through the general fear whether of outrage or of boycotting, had temporarily lost their power.'[28]

At the height of the land campaign in Ireland, Parnell was tempted to travel to London on the off-chance of seeing Katharine, however briefly. Returning to Dublin from Ennis, he wrote a note to Katharine to say that he had found two of her letters waiting for him at Morrison's Hotel: 'you may write me even nicer ones with perfect confidence,' she was assured.[29] They had already planned to meet in London in a week's time, yet on 22 September, only a fortnight after their dinner at Thomas's Hotel, Parnell announced that he was setting off for London that very night. He could not bear the separation from Katharine: 'I cannot keep myself away from you any longer . . . Please wire me to 16 Keppel Street, Russell Square, if I may hope to see you to-morrow and where, after 4 p.m. Yours always, C.S.P.'[30]

He set off never thinking that Katharine might be unable to see him. In her book, Katharine states that she was sitting at Lucy Goldsmith's death-bed, although in this she is not quite accurate. The elderly woman had had a severe stroke at Wonersh Lodge on 17 September which left her paralysed down one side, partially blind and unable to form words. She was reduced to running her fingers over Katharine's rings, 'that she might know that I was with her'. She died five days later, on 21 September, the day before Parnell's letter. It is not entirely clear why Katharine was unable to meet Parnell in London two days after the death of a domestic servant, however well loved, although it is likely that O'Shea had come down to Eltham to assist Katharine in making preparations for the funeral. (He would accompany the coffin back to Cressing, where Lucy was to be buried near Katharine's parents.) Katharine telegraphed Keppel Street to explain to Parnell that she could not possibly meet him in London on his arrival, but that, if at all possible, she would try to be at London Bridge Station at 12.15 the next day. For some reason she did not keep the appointment. Writing to her that evening from Euston Station, waiting for the night train, Parnell blamed 'the telegraph people' for adding to the confusion, but nothing could disguise his exasperation at not seeing her, 'especially as I must return to Ireland to-night – I came on purpose for you, and had no other business . . . Your very disappointed C.S.P.'[31]

The next morning, realising how full of complaint his letter must have sounded, he wrote again, contritely. He begged Katharine to continue writing to him, and let her know of his movements. He was committed to speak at further meetings at New Ross and Cork, the latter on 3 October, but proposed as soon as they were over to 'renew my attempt to gain a glimpse of you'. He hoped to hear that she would be able to meet him in London on the following Tuesday. In answer to her concern that he should make such a journey to see her just briefly, he wrote, 'Of course, I am going on purpose to see you', thus establishing what must have been an exhausting pattern of sudden dashes to see her and dutiful returns to the campaign in Ireland. If she needed any further proof of the strength of his feeling for her, Parnell assured her that, 'somehow or other something from you seems a necessary part of my daily existence, and if I have to go a day or two without even a telegram it seems dreadful'.[32] On this occasion, his crossing delayed by bad weather, Parnell finally met Katharine in London on the evening of Wednesday 6 October.

Despite his persistent pressure upon Katharine to consummate their relationship, she had, throughout the month of September, managed to defer doing so. She would later tell Henry Harrison that when she had first met Parnell she believed herself to be a free woman, and that 'sex love' between herself and her husband 'was long since dead'.[33] Her last child had been born six years earlier, in 1874, and on O'Shea's return from Spain in 1878 the financial terms of their informal separation had been agreed. Yet it can have been no easy matter for Katharine to respond to Parnell's sexual advances. Now in her thirty-fifth year, long separated from a philandering husband, Katharine's emotional life was claimed by her three children, aged 6, 7 and 10, and by the responsibility she felt for her elderly aunt. Nonetheless, bound to the routine of life at Eltham, Katharine admits that she was newly conscious of 'sudden gusts of unrest and revolt against these leisured, peaceful days'.[34]

It was at this time that, 'restless and unhappy', Katharine took herself off to Brighton early one morning in order to prepare herself to take the step: 'I . . . wished to be alone.'[35] Not wanting to run into her sister or any of the family at Brighton Station, Katharine got off the train at the previous station and ordered a cab to take her to the edge of the Downs. She walked a good way, and despite feeling tired and hungry, resisted the temptation to walk down into Brighton to her sister's house: 'I did not want to see anybody who loved me and could bias my mind.' Nor did she want to answer questions about O'Shea, whom she saw 'rarely enough'.[36]

It is one of the episodes in her life which Katharine represents in what may be a rather novelistic manner. Yet, what can be said of the experience she relates is that, at the very least, her choices and their implications are set out before her. She decides not to go to the comfort of her sister's home and begins 'deliberately to climb up the hill onto the Downs again', asking, 'Why should I be supposed to have no other interests than Willie and my children?'[37] Sheltering from the gathering mist and 'drifting rain', she sees her brother-in-law returning home on foot across the Downs from Lewes and keeps herself hidden from him. And then a young horsewoman stops to ask her the way. Katharine recognises her as the grown-up daughter of a woman she had met when she was living in Brighton in the early years of her marriage. The mother had been at the centre of a notorious scandal, and had warned Katharine never to gamble for love, 'but if you do, be sure that the stake is the only thing in the world to you'.[38] Once the girl on horseback had turned away, Katharine involuntarily cried out to her friend, since dead, 'I am afraid; I tell you, I am afraid'. Now, walking back down to the station, Katharine reflected: 'I thought more quietly how the daughter . . . had grown to happy womanhood in spite of all.'[39]

It was on this occasion that Parnell met her at Charing Cross and went with her on the train back to Eltham. They were careful not to acknowledge each other in public: 'As our eyes met he turned and walked by my side.' The train was crowded, and they sat opposite one another, still not having exchanged a word. Katharine was so nervous that she could not even look at him. Seeing that she was damp and cold, Parnell leant over and put his coat round her, and then moved into the seat next to her: 'and, leaning over me to fold the coat more closely round my knees,' he whispered his declaration of love. Katharine's decision had been made: 'I slipped my hand into his, and knew I was not afraid.'[40]

This was clearly a development not expected by O'Shea, who, at some time in the autumn of 1880, had invited Parnell to stay for a few days at Wonersh Lodge. According to what Katharine later told Henry Harrison, her husband 'wished her – to use Mrs Parnell's own phrase – to "establish an influence" over Parnell . . . and, to this end, "he rather threw me at (Parnell's) head", or, at any rate, "into unchaperoned companionship"'.[41] Lyons believes that Parnell's first openly acknowledged stay at Eltham dates from the second week of October. We cannot be certain of the precise dates of the visit because Katharine reprints no formal acknowledgement of an invitation, as she does elsewhere, yet if it took place at some point in October, they had been seeing each other for three months or so and he was already in love with Katharine, if not her lover.

Katharine's home at Eltham was one which she shared with her three children and her female domestics, who included the children's governess, the parlour-maid Mary Francis and the cook Ellen Delany from Tipperary, whom she had recently hired. It was a home to which Katharine had at first been reluctant to bring Parnell on account of its being 'shabby'.[42] She took on a new maid at this time, Jane Lennister, who, at the divorce trial, ten years later, recalled that she first saw Mr Parnell 'very soon after' she was employed at Wonersh Lodge.[43] The very fact that Katharine hired a new cook and maid in the autumn of 1880 also accords with the efforts she describes to make the house attractive to their eminent guest, such as her buying in hothouse flowers and potted palms to dress up the drawing-room.

The O'Sheas had invited Parnell to be their guest ostensibly because of his poor state of health, owing to the strain of the campaign in the south-west of Ireland and the many open-air mass meetings. He was put into the spare bedroom nearest the stairs and during the day rested in the drawing-room, watched over by Katharine. He was suffering from a sore throat and exhaustion, and 'looked so terribly ill when – as he often did now – he fell asleep from sheer weakness on the sofa before the fire'.[44] During this time, Katharine 'nursed him assiduously, making him take nourishment at regular intervals, seeing that these day-sleeps of his were not disturbed, and forcing him to take fresh air in long drives through the country around us'.[45] On this, and subsequent more covert visits to Eltham, Parnell would sit up late at night, and 'speaking in that low, broken monotone, that with him always betokened intense feeling strongly held in check', confide in Katharine the terrible reality of the mass evictions carried out in Ireland that autumn: of the sick and elderly, of women and children, 'all thrust from the little squalid cabins which were all they had for home, thrust out on the roadside to perish, or to live as they could'.[46] Such reports made Katharine's 'heart sick', and she 'never wondered at the implacable hatred of England that can never really die out of the Irish heart'.[47] Yet despite being the wife of an Irish landlord, at this stage she became aware that she knew very little of the situation of the poor in Ireland: 'I in my English ignorance used to say: "Why did they not go into the workhouse or to neighbours?" and Parnell would look wonderingly at me.' Workhouses were 'few and far between', while neighbours 'were in the same trouble'.[48]

Speculation continues about what attracted Parnell to Katharine O'Shea. Lyons perhaps overplays his conclusion that it was her 'quality of maternal solicitude which attracted [Parnell] from the outset'. His restrained account of how 'acquaintance ripened into friendship' is not borne out by the documentary evidence supplied by Katharine, although his later assessment of their relationship is perhaps more astute: 'though passion lay at the root of his infatuation with her, tender domesticity was much more the key-note of their love-affair.'[49] Tender domesticity was something Parnell lacked. At the time they met, he was living in what T.P. O'Connor referred to as 'miserable lodgings' at Keppel Street, where he worked during the day and then, 'from four till four the next morning', he was at the House of Commons: he 'had no time left for women'.[50] Another of Parnell's colleagues sympathised with his leader's 'craving for womanly companionship in an immeasurably lonely life'.[51]

Keppel Street was a short passageway connecting Gower Street and Malet Street where once-grand old houses were subdivided into flats and rented, largely to law and medical students. It was certainly very different from Captain O'Shea's distinguished lodgings in Charles Street (where Conservative Party hostess Lady Dorothy Nevill lived at No. 45), yet Parnell had a near neighbour in Justin McCarthy, whose family resided in Gower Street, and at whose dinner parties Parnell was introduced to notable political figures. Frank Hugh O'Donnell, whose speculations about the Parnell–O'Shea triangle are generally wild and fanciful, may be close to the truth when he says of Parnell's friendship with Justin McCarthy that 'the London-refined man of letters and fine appreciation' was the one colleague 'with whom Parnell, a man of breeding, ever found himself at home'.[52] He became one of the family at the McCarthys', dropping in on his friend on odd afternoons, before the evening sittings began, 'a great favourite'[53] with the little children, earnestly talking cricket with the boys, or asking McCarthy's elder daughter about her art studies at the Slade School and telling her about his sister Fanny's painting.

Wonersh Lodge, with its domestic clutter, must have had its comforts. Within weeks Parnell regarded it as 'home', declaring himself 'quite homesick' when away from Eltham.[54] While he returned frequently to his family home at Avondale, he went chiefly for the shooting or to oversee the development of mines and works on the estate. His mother had returned to her native America, and Avondale, as a result of Parnell's generosity, was effectively the home of his sister Emily and her financially insolvent, increasingly alcoholic husband, Arthur Dickinson. At this time, a reporter from the *World* described the house as having 'a rather barren and neglectful look'. Anything but a homely home. 'One could fancy that the coverings had just been drawn off the furniture at the expiration of a Chancery suit.'[55]

It is possible, too, that McCarthy's influence can be detected in Parnell's being drawn towards another man's wife for intellectual companionship. McCarthy famously enjoyed a long, platonic friendship with his literary collaborator, Mrs Campbell Praed. He wrote her letters full of detailed political analysis, and encouraged her to attend Commons' debates from the Ladies' Gallery, where he would join her: 'He was one of the few men who believe in the trustworthiness of women as confidantes and even counsellors.' As McCarthy himself said of his attitude towards women:

You know I don't go in . . . for making dolls and pets of women . . . No. I like a woman to be a man's companion, to be his comrade: to be able to comfort him and soothe him when he needs soothing – and the strongest man does need a woman's soothing and does get strength from her in his turn, even as he gives her strength.[56]

He could as well be describing Parnell's relationship with Katharine O'Shea. Parnell himself told Katharine, 'I sometimes think that is why you came to me, for I was very ill then and you kept the life in me and the will to go on . . . you have stood to me for comfort and strength and my very life.'[57] At first his nurse, Katharine would in time become his political confidante, his trusted secretary and messenger. Frank Harris, one of the few commentators on the divorce case to have actually met Katharine, judged her, 'evidently a lively, clever woman and excellent company'.[58] Frank Hugh O'Donnell, who claimed to have met her in the early 1880s, was 'struck by her clever conversation', although he became rather worn-down by 'her persistent questioning. She wanted to know everything about everything.' Unused to the company of women who took such an earnest interest in politics he concluded that her 'intellectuality was slightly aggressive'.[59] Parnell, though, was comfortable in the company of women. His father had died when he was young, and he had grown up in a household made up of his mother, two brothers and six sisters. Also, through the political activity of his sisters Fanny and Anna, he was familiar with the idea of independent-minded women.

Katharine was also, of course, an unusual woman for her time in terms of her independence from her husband, and it is important to establish exactly what Katharine and O'Shea understood by the terms of their 'agreed arrangement [which] secured her personal freedom' at the time that Katharine began her love-affair with Parnell. 'Captain O'Shea was in the position of a stranger', she explained to Henry Harrison. 'That is, his visits were regarded as dependent upon definite invitation.'[60] Their informal separation is nowhere more clearly demonstrated than in the census return for 1881. O'Shea is registered as lodging at 16 and 17 Charles Street, Westminster, while Katharine is listed as the 'Head' of the household of Wonersh Lodge. Explicitly, Katharine claimed that she had secured her 'personal freedom' from her husband's insisting upon his conjugal rights: 'she wished to be free from any distasteful remains of it.' Thus when she became Parnell's lover, Katharine told Harrison, 'we believed ourselves to be fully justified . . . and we never repented it . . . Mr Parnell, so long as he knew me, never regarded me as Captain O'Shea's wife at all', a statement entirely consistent with what she says in her book: 'To Parnell's heart and conscience I was no more the wife of Captain O'Shea when he (Parnell) first met me than I was after Captain O'Shea divorced me, ten years later.'[61]

Katharine was also the perfect mistress. She talks of her husband's anxiety lest she 'drop out of everything', and claims that he 'worried' her into accepting social invitations,[62] but in reality the O'Sheas' separation meant that Katharine was isolated at Eltham, where Parnell could call discreetly without fear of discovery and without fear that Katharine's reputation would be compromised.

Katharine's maid Jane Lennister would state that O'Shea was present at Eltham for the duration of Parnell's first stay (according to O'Shea's recollection, Parnell was there for only 'two or three days'[63]), yet it has been suggested that it was during their brief time together in early October that Katharine's relationship with Parnell became intimate. Evidence for this is the 17 October letter from Dublin which Parnell sent not to Eltham but to the Charing Cross Post Office, in which he addressed Katharine for the first time as 'My own love': 'You cannot imagine how much you have occupied my thoughts all day and how very greatly the prospect of seeing you again very soon comforts me.'[64] T.P. O'Connor, who was his guest at Avondale at the time, records that Parnell was so sensitive about his thinning hair ('He would often speak of the subject'[65]) that he shaved his head in the hope that it would make his hair grow thicker! From Avondale, Parnell posted Katharine sprigs of heather and vowed that she was 'the one dear object whose presence has ever been a great happiness to me'.[66]

The affair resumed a fortnight later, when Parnell, again in the spare room as a guest, would have been able to pass undiscovered into Katharine's bedroom through a connecting dressing-room door. He had wanted desperately to see her again before the end of the month, but he was already committed to giving speeches in Ireland on the last two Sundays of October, and nothing is heard from him until he addresses a formal letter to 'Mrs O'Shea' on 4 November, thanking her 'for all your kindness, which made my stay at Eltham so happy and pleasant'. Since he spoke at Tipperary on Sunday 31 October, this second visit to Eltham has the appearance of being brief. That it also took place in O'Shea's absence is clear. Parnell writes that he will be in London the following week, when he trusts 'to be more fortunate in seeing Captain O'Shea'.[67] The deception practised upon O'Shea went further than that, however, for Katharine states that the letters she reproduces from 4 to 6 November, which are all sent from Dublin, were actually written at Eltham and sent over to Dublin to be posted back from there.

When Parnell did return to Ireland it was with a set of keys for Wonersh Lodge in his pocket. Within a week he was trying to set up another meeting in London, writing to Katharine, 'It is quite impossible for me to tell you just how very much you have changed my life, what a small interest I take in what is going on about me, and how I detest everything which has happened during the last few days to keep me away from you'. He wanted no more of her 'artificial letters': 'I want as much of your own self as you can transfer into written words, or else none at all.' Katharine was further notified that she and her husband would both receive telegrams from Parnell, presumably describing his movements in the forthcoming weeks, 'which are by no means strictly accurate'.[68]

Significantly, it can thus be established that Parnell was at Eltham on his second, clandestine, visit when he got news of the announcement made on 2 November that the Government intended to prosecute the leaders of the Land League for thwarting the rule of law in Ireland. While there was little belief that these trials would lead to successful prosecutions, it was a way for the Government to make clear the state of lawlessness in Ireland and a necessary step towards the introduction of coercive legislation in order to prevent 'something like a general massacre of all landlords and agents not under police protection'.[69] Throughout the autumn, Lord Cowper, Lord-Lieutenant of Ireland, had forwarded to the Cabinet desperate accounts of the situation. He believed that 'there never has been such a state of panic on one side and lawlessness and ill-will on the other'.[70] In the words of

R. Barry O'Brien, the Land League had become 'in truth, nothing more nor less than a provisional Irish Government', so that 'the question really was, whether Lord Cowper or Parnell should rule Ireland'.[71]

Besides Parnell, four other MPs were named in the 2 November announcement: John Dillon (who had threatened the Commons with 'bloodshed and massacre', and called publicly for farmers to be coerced into joining the League[72]), Joseph Biggar, T.D. Sullivan and Thomas Sexton, together with nine League organisers. Parnell seems not to have taken the prosecutions seriously. According to Katharine, he considered them to be farcical, 'an impotent effort of the Government to intimidate him'.[73] He knew that no Irish jury would convict him.

At the end of November, Parnell left Ireland to make a third and more prolonged visit to Eltham. Writing a formal letter of thanks a fortnight later, he spoke of having been away from Ireland for a substantial 'interval', and regretted having had to leave Eltham 'so suddenly' after such a 'pleasant and charming' stay. It seems likely that this visit, too, was made in O'Shea's at least partial absence. Parnell writes of Katharine having gone with him up to London, perhaps accompanying him as far as London Bridge or Victoria, and of his getting to Euston 'with just ten minutes to spare' to catch the night-train to Dublin. It is a sentence which conveys a good deal: the lovers' reluctance to part, Parnell's putting off his departure until the last minute, and Katharine's willingness to risk her reputation by travelling publicly in his company late at night. Parnell's postscript suggests as much, noting that he has been 'exceedingly anxious all day at not receiving your promised telegram to hear how you got home'.[74]

For the first two weeks of December Parnell was in Dublin, or at Avondale, awaiting the commencement of the Land League trial, news of which fills his letters to Katharine. On 4 December he wrote, 'it turns out that we need not necessarily attend the trial unless absolutely directed to do so by the Court', and he was confident that the members of the special jury panel, a list of whose names he had received the night before, were unlikely to form a unanimous verdict.[75] He hoped to 'run down' to Eltham on Monday 13 December (O'Shea was then in Paris), but had to put off this visit in order, first, to see the jury sworn in 'before giving final instructions',[76] and then to support Tim Healy at the latter's trial at the Cork Assizes, where he was charged with having, on 18 October, made an incendiary speech at Bantry on the south-east coast. Healy had condemned the eviction of a local farmer, McGrath, who had subsequently died of exposure, after seeking shelter with his family under an upturned boat on the seashore. The jury found Healy not guilty, and Parnell retained Healy's defence attorney, Peter O'Brien, for the state trials which would begin on 28 December.

Katharine reprints no letters from Parnell until late December, but it does appear that they were together at Christmas. Katharine's own reference to Parnell's having 'tipped my servants generously'[77] at Christmas 1880 is perhaps the strongest indication of his having been a familiar guest at Wonersh Lodge throughout the autumn and winter. Another clue is provided in a letter Parnell wrote to Katharine on Christmas Eve 1881, in which she was urged to put behind her all memory of 'our squabble of last Xmas Day'.[78] There is further documentary evidence to suggest that Parnell stayed at Eltham over Christmas, even though O'Shea does not appear to have left for Madrid, on yet another business trip, until 27 December, and that on Boxing Day, Katharine accompanied her lover to London, where he caught the Irish Mail. The next day, safe in the knowledge that O'Shea had left for Spain, Parnell was free to write to his 'dearest Wifie'. It is his closing words which give an indication as to what their Christmas 'squabble' had been about: 'I was immensely relieved by your letter this morning. You must take great care of yourself for my sake and your and my future.'[79] Writing two days' later, the reason for his solicitude now becomes more clear.

> My dearest Love,
>
> . . . I fear I was very foolish to allow you to come with me the day of my departure; I felt sure it would do much harm, and until your first letter arrived I was in a continual panic lest some dreadful disaster had happened.
>
> That my poor love should have suffered so much makes my heart very sore, and she must take great care of herself for the sake of *our* future.[80]

Such concern seems to suggest that, in late December 1880, having been Parnell's mistress for less than three months, Katharine believed herself to be carrying her lover's child. The phrases quoted from Parnell's letters are identical to those he uses when Katharine is pregnant with their daughter Claude in 1881. It would then follow that the Christmas Day 'squabble' is likely to have concerned how the pregnancy was to affect both their relationship and Katharine's marriage to O'Shea. Of course, we do not know precisely what Parnell was alluding to. There is certainly no surviving reference to a miscarriage, and Parnell's letters to Katharine sent from Paris in late February 1881 make no specific allusion to her state of health, whether with child or not. The few letters she reprints from that spring refer only to Katharine's by now familiar unhappiness at being parted from her lover for long stretches of time. It would appear that Katharine was simply mistaken about this pregnancy. Her first child by Parnell would be conceived in mid-May the following year.

One final piece of evidence that Parnell was at Eltham this Christmas is perhaps provided in the delightful anecdote Katharine tells about her servants' adoration of him. When he first began to visit Wonersh Lodge, the new cook, Ellen Delany, was so excited to learn that she was to cook for the Irish leader that Katharine had to ask Parnell to introduce himself so that Ellen could 'settle to her cooking': on being shown in to the drawing-room Ellen dropped to her knees 'and kissed his hands, much to his horror'. By Christmas, emotions below stairs had calmed somewhat, but Ellen now paraded the Irish leader's portrait in 'an enormous gold locket' about her bosom, and consequently Mary the parlour-maid (both were single women in their late twenties) appeared with another of the same design, 'and wore it with an air of defiance, when bringing in tea, on New Year's Day'. Such displays were not expected of serving maids, but also threatened to make trouble between O'Shea and Parnell, who now took it upon himself gently to explain to Mary that her mistress allowed him to come down there for a rest, and if people knew he was there, he would be 'worried to death with politics and people calling'. Mary promised to keep her locket inside her gown in future, 'and Ellen came running in to promise too'.[81]

It is an attractive story because of what it tells us of the day-to-day atmosphere at Wonersh Lodge, one thoroughly domestic, in which Parnell and Katharine appear utterly at their ease in front of the servants. Yet, as so often, there is a problem with the dating of the episode. The anecdote may date instead from Christmas Day, or from a separate occasion entirely, because at the New Year Parnell was in Dublin, where he had gone for the Land League hearing. From there he wrote on New Year's Eve: 'I felt very much tempted to run over and spend the New Year and Sunday with you, but feared you might not be alone.'[82]

# CHAPTER 3

## *Discovery*

The Land League hearings opened in Dublin on 28 December, with Parnell and his fellow accused escorted to the court by twenty-four MPs and a great crowd of demonstrators. The trials had gone ahead despite the Irish Chief Secretary Forster's awareness that they would result in increased political support for Parnell and the Land League, and that they would end in acquittal. By 23 January the jury had disagreed and Forster had been proved right on both counts. As Katharine later wrote, 'My lover was the leader of a nation in revolt.'[1] Meanwhile, Parnell had returned to Eltham on 5 January 1881. Katharine recalls that they spent some days together and that she took Parnell to Eltham Lodge to call on Aunt Wood who was, she says, 'much charmed with him. His quiet manners and soft, clear voice pleased her greatly, as also did his personal appearance,' and she spoke to him of having met the 'Liberator', Daniel O'Connell, at the House of Commons some forty years earlier. She much preferred Parnell's soft tones to O'Connell's, whose 'enunciation was startling to me', she told him.[2] There can be no doubt, of course, that Aunt Wood was not made aware of the true nature of Katharine's relationship with Parnell.

Parnell had returned to England for the opening of Parliament on 7 January. Throughout the following months, for all his quiet manners and soft voice, in the Commons he was to be at his most obstreperous. As expected, the Queen's Speech announced two new pieces of legislation designed to tackle the increasingly lawless situation in Ireland: firstly a bill to maintain law and order, and then a Land Bill to ensure fair rents for tenant farmers. The Queen spoke of the 'alarming character' of agrarian violence in Ireland, which had 'multiplied far beyond the experience of recent years' so that a 'system of terror has . . . been established in various parts of the country'.[3] In order to protect life and property the Government were to be given special powers to suspend the ordinary law in 'proclaimed' districts. On 24 January – on the eve of the collapse of the state trials in Dublin – Forster introduced the long-threatened Protection of Person and Property (Ireland) Bill. This was what became known as the Coercion Bill, which would enable the Lord-Lieutenant 'to arrest any person whom he reasonably suspected of treasonable practices or agrarian offences, and to keep such persons in prison for any period up to September 30, 1882'.[4] All Land League leaders were vulnerable to arrest.

Nationalist MPs had already taken up their seats on the Opposition benches under a resolution passed by Parnell at the party meeting in Dublin on 27 December. When Parnell's efforts failed to have the Land Bill made law and given a chance to work before the imposition of coercive measures (the vote on his amendment went 435 to 57), the Irish party vowed to prevent the passage of the first stage of the Coercion Bill and to disrupt all business of the House: 'obstruction, not argument, was the weapon on which the Irish leader relied.'[5] This return to obstructive tactics was very effective. In the words of T.P. O'Connor, 'The great Imperial Parliament [was] held up for week after week by twenty young men.'[6] On 25 January the House was forced to sit for twenty-two hours; on 31 January, for forty-one hours. Parnell personally threw himself into the work, and Katharine writes of her 'pride in him as I watched from the Ladies' Gallery'.[7] During the debate on the first reading, which would last six nights, R. Barry O'Brien stood by his side while Parnell searched through parliamentary records in the House of Commons Library looking for reports of earlier struggles over coercion: 'He plunged into the books, marking with a blue pencil the passages that specially interested him . . . "By Jove!", he would repeat, "this is very good."'[8] He maintained a constant barrage of interruptions to parliamentary proceedings and kept his men up to the mark.

At a time of such intense political effort, Parnell also found time for secret meetings with Katharine. During the all-night sittings he would take a few hours' rest at the Westminster Palace Hotel and then 'drove quickly to one of our meeting places to tell me of his plans before I went down to Eltham'.[9] From the grille of the Ladies' Gallery she would watch for a particular touch of his handkerchief by which Parnell signalled for her to wait for him at a London railway terminus or hotel: 'So very many hours I waited for him at various stations!', Katharine would recall, yet she 'always returned at night to see that my children were all right'.[10] Waterloo Junction, as it was then known, proved the most convenient, if uncomfortable, meeting place since it stayed open into the early hours of the morning. At other stations, Katharine might be moved along 'from one waiting-room to another as the lights were put out' and would be forced 'to take to a steady tramp up and down the station platform', until her 'husband' would at last arrive and take her away in a hansom cab: 'I think the officials must have known who Parnell was, as I always had a free pass (from him) for all these lines, but they never intruded, and . . . received and kept his telegrams for me . . . with perfect tact.' The porters were good to her, too, often keeping waiting room fires alight after they had had to turn off the gas-lighting, saying 'it will be fairly cheerful like with the firelight ma'am'.[11]

Katharine and Parnell may have been taking great risks by meeting in such public places, but they could not always rely upon O'Shea to keep away from Eltham. Katharine noted that in January of this year he 'came down to Eltham suddenly, very angry indeed with me',[12] but not, as she must have feared, because he had discovered her relationship with Parnell. Quite the reverse. O'Shea had spotted detectives keeping watch on his lodgings at Charles Street and began to suspect that they had been hired by Katharine to produce evidence of her husband's infidelities. 'As I had never had an idea of doing anything of the sort I was extremely annoyed, and a violent quarrel was the result.' (In fact, it was a fellow lodger who was being watched, whose wife would divorce him.) Katharine says little more about this episode, and it is not immediately apparent why she should have been 'extremely annoyed' by it. One would have expected her to feel immense relief.

The notorious 41-hour sitting over the Coercion Bill was brought to an abrupt end on 2 February by the Speaker, who demanded a vote on the first reading, and the next day Gladstone put forward a motion to expedite 'urgent' public business which effectively defeated Obstructionism. That same evening, Thursday 3 February, the re-arrest of Michael Davitt, one of the leaders of the Land League, was announced to the House by Sir William Harcourt. During the furore which followed, John Dillon was 'named' by the Speaker, suspended, and then forcibly removed from the chamber. Parnell, in a 'semi-revolutionary gesture',[13] followed Dillon, as did every one of the thirty-six Irish MPs sitting on the Opposition Benches. Parnell and a number of his inner circle then decided to meet in Paris the following Sunday, at the Hotel Brighton, Rue de Rivoli (it was in Paris that the Fenian Pat Egan was holding the League funds), in order to frame a manifesto protesting against the Coercion Bill. This was an extremely delicate matter for Parnell, since on 17 January he had declared that the first arrest under the Coercion Act was to be the signal for a strike against rent across Ireland. Davitt had now been re-arrested, and while the bill had not yet become law, Parnell had to persuade the League, his party, and, most crucially, American support, that the way forward was through 'parliamentary action'.[14]

The significance of the Land League meeting in Paris in February has, however, been overshadowed by the suggestion that, before Parnell's arrival there, the secret of his relationship with Katharine had been discovered by his closest colleagues. Tim Healy is the sole witness to record the episode of the 'opened letter'. He describes how Sunday 6 January came and went without any sign of Parnell. A whole week passed, and still there was no word from him. Parnell appears by this time to have given up his lodgings at Keppel Street for rooms at the Westminster Palace Hotel, but where he was the rest of the time became a matter of guesswork for Healy, then acting as Parnell's secretary: 'Inquisitive pressmen from London came to Paris to try to penetrate the mystery. Our uneasiness became extreme.'[15] Late on Saturday 12 January, Healy was pressed by his colleagues to give up any correspondence which might throw light on their leader's whereabouts. The only letters he had about him which might in any way prove useful, apparently, were those 'in a woman's hand' which had accumulated over a fortnight or so before the departure for Paris, and which Healy had brought with him from England. Despite his scruples, and after a vote was taken, Healy allowed Dillon and Egan to open one letter. The contents have never been revealed, but it was decided that Healy and Biggar should depart immediately for an address in London, and, if Parnell could not be traced there, to employ detectives known to them to find him. However, as they drove round to the Gare du Nord to catch the 7 a.m. train, Parnell's cab passed them in the street. Arriving at the hotel, he took to his bed for the rest of the day, and though courteous to Healy, said not a word to his colleagues about what had detained him.

It was Tim Healy's later belief, certainly, that Parnell's mysterious delay in reaching Paris was due to the fact that 'he had then taken up with Mrs O'Shea'.[16] However, the reason for Parnell's staying at Eltham may have been rather different from the one implied by Healy. Although Parnell's attitude to the state trials had been dismissive, the atmosphere surrounding the Coercion Bill made him much more cautious. Katharine states that 'on one occasion in 1880' (she appears to mean the winter of 1880–1), Parnell had come to her as usual after a late sitting, but told her that he needed to 'disappear', and that she 'must hide him for a few weeks'.[17] He had information 'that his arrest for "sedition" was being urged upon the Government', and he had been advised to go abroad for a short while. Katharine says that she managed to hide him in 'a little boudoir dressing-room' leading from her bedroom, which was large enough for a sofa, and brought food up to him at night, and that for a fortnight no one knew that he was in the house.[18] It has been found difficult to establish exactly when in the winter of 1880 this particular visit to Eltham could have taken place, but the episode concludes with Parnell's departure for Paris, where he had arranged to go on business connected with the Land League. Wary of imminent arrest, Parnell travelled to Paris by a 'roundabout route' via Harwich, accompanied by Katharine as far as the port. In the train, she bundled him up in rugs against the intense cold, and 'a lady and gentleman in the carriage remarked to me – thinking he slept – that my husband looked terribly ill'. A 'little smile of content' flitted over her 'husband's' face.[19] When in Paris, Parnell bought a wide, hollow bracelet made of gold for Katharine, not wholly for sentimental reasons: it was in order to secrete 'two papers that he did not wish left even here [at Eltham], and, fearing arrest, could not carry on him'.[20]

The episode of the opened letter takes up four pages of Healy's memoirs, but he consistently denied that the letter was from Katharine. Indeed, he offers instead an unlikely story of a Manchester barmaid and her child, discovered by a 'friend' of Biggar's in a garret-room in Holloway, with 'a likeness of Parnell (cut from the Dublin *Weekly News*) . . . pinned to her counterpane'.[21] Neither Healy nor Biggar ever met this woman, whose real name has never been confirmed.[22] Michael Davitt, at the time in prison after his re-arrest, was convinced that the letter opened in Paris was Katharine's and called it a 'painful discovery', since none of Parnell's closest associates had any suspicion of 'the liaison in which he was found entangled'.[23] This was certainly Katharine's own belief, although she, of course, would have been told as much by Parnell.[24] Healy, though, goes out of his way to make it clear that Katharine's name 'was unknown to us at the time', and another of Parnell's closest colleagues, T.P. O'Connor, also states, 'with confidence', that for several years 'there was not among members of the Irish Party a breath, perhaps not even a suspicion, of the real state of affairs'.[25] Whatever the truth of the opened letter, it is a fact that it was Healy and Biggar who, years later at the Galway by-election in 1886, would be the two Irish MPs most vociferous in their denunciation of Parnell's relationship with the wife of O'Shea.

Certainly it is difficult to see why Healy should have been so disturbed by the letter if it were not so scandalous as to involve an affair between Parnell and the wife of one of his MPs. 'The breaking open of the letter so upset me', explains Healy, that the day after their return to London, 'I told Parnell . . . in the Tea-room of the House of Commons I could no longer continue as his secretary'.[26] The fact that Parnell knew that a letter of Katharine's had been tampered with, and that Healy must be in possession of his secret, may well explain the subsequent deterioration in their relationship. Yet for five years more Healy kept the secret, and in his memoirs he repeatedly defends the actions of his colleagues, saying, perhaps ambiguously, that 'None sought knowledge of any intrigue'. He goes on to commend them for never having 'revealed or made use of the incident' after the divorce trial, when they 'confined themselves to the publicly known facts of the O'Shea case'.[27]

The whole story is a puzzle, and may reflect an unwillingness in Parnell's colleagues to be seen to have been complicit in his affair with Katharine. After all, they could not afford to lose him as their leader. Yet, while the story of the barmaid seems melodramatic and improbable, it is equally improbable that a whole packet of Katharine's letters could have accumulated without Parnell knowing of it. They had become practised at sending each other private letters, used secret enclosures, innocuous postmarks, wrote in code and adopted pseudonyms. They also kept a tally of where and when each letter was sent so that if any went astray they could protect themselves. Katharine did address letters and coded telegrams directly to Parnell's Paris hotel and to another safe address he gave her. When, on Sunday 27 February, after returning to Paris for further meetings, Parnell found no communication waiting for him 'at the usual address', he feared that 'something may have gone wrong' and forwarded Katharine yet another address which would enable her to 'write me freely in my own name' (Thomas Adams and Co., Limited, 33 Rue d'Hauteville, Paris).[28] He had received five letters from her since his arrival in Paris, and this was his third to her. The following Tuesday more of her letters arrived: 'My dearest love, – Today I have received your four letters, the earliest of which was written on Saturday. You do not seem to have written to me on Friday.'[29] His added instruction to Katharine, 'Best not post your letters at Eltham',[30] is a typical caution on Parnell's part. There is in these letters a heightened anxiety that Katharine's correspondence might be intercepted, but this did not stop them writing to each other, even for a short period.

Parnell was still in Paris when the Coercion Bill became law on 2 March. In the coming months he would be under constant fear of arrest, and had already got word from Dublin that there was 'some plot on foot against us'. He wired Katharine that his sudden return to Paris was 'influenced by information of reliable kind that my arrest was intended . . . and that bail would be refused'.[31] He felt that he had been watched in Paris, and on his brief return to London between the two Paris trips, he challenged a detective who attempted to trail him when he left the Commons at three o'clock in the morning. On 18 February he asked the House by whose authority he was being watched: the British Embassy or the Home Office?[32] Yet, even though hundreds of Land Leaguers were imprisoned in Dublin's Kilmainham Gaol throughout the spring and summer of 1881, the Government held off arresting the leader himself, despite the worsening situation in Ireland, which, it was feared, 'might actually be the beginning of a small civil war'.[33]

On 7 April, one month after the passing of the Coercion Act, Gladstone introduced the Land Bill. This offered the 'three Fs' – fixity of tenure, fair rents, and free sale – and effectively stripped the landlords of their autonomous power to set rents. Its concessions to the Land League, 'one of the most lawless movements which had ever convulsed any country', made it 'revolutionary'.[34] Understandably, many within the Irish party determined to back the bill, yet there were those, Dillon among them, who suspected that the concessions offered by the bill were designed specifically to 'kill the Land League' by pacifying tenant farmers.[35] Others feared that a positive measure dealing with the land question might in the long run detract attention from the most important political question for Ireland, that of Home Rule. Parnell had therefore to respond to the bill very cautiously. He kept quiet during the Easter recess, and then, just before the second reading was due on 19 May, safe in the knowledge that the bill would pass comfortably with or without the Irish vote, he demanded that the whole party vote against it.

The bill now went to committee, where it would stay from 26 May to 27 July, although there is evidence that Parnell himself left much of this somewhat tedious work of opposing and recommending amendments to his deputies. Tim Healy complained that Parnell 'seldom attended', even when appealed to, and that 'his mind was far away'.[36] At around this time, T.P. O'Connor went down to the telegraph office at the Westminster Palace Hotel and found Parnell in the act of writing a telegram. The sight of a colleague apparently disturbed him: 'I observed that Parnell was not in his usual composed temper. He tried to write; finding the pencil somewhat blunt, he threw it from him with an angry gesture and an angry face.'[37] Not until years later did O'Connor wonder whether Parnell had been trying to arrange a meeting with Katharine O'Shea.

Parnell and Katharine were about to arrange their boldest assignation yet. At some point in the late spring of 1881, Katharine was able to get away to Brighton for as long as a month while her aunt had an old friend to stay with her at Eltham. When Katharine's maid, Jane Lennister, was examined at the divorce trial she recalled returning to Wonersh Lodge from Brighton 'about the end of April or the beginning of May 1881'.[38] We can be more precise about the time that Katharine and the children were at Brighton because months later Parnell talked of returning there, 'to listen to the waves breaking as we used those mornings of spring last May'.[39] Evidently, he regarded their time at Brighton as a sort of honeymoon. Katharine presented him with a gold signet ring which he wore on the little finger of his left hand, and it is almost certain that their first child was conceived there. Nine months later, on 15 February 1882, Claude Sophie was born at Eltham.

Katharine describes how she had gone down to Brighton before the children to take rooms for them all. At Brighton Station she was approached by a tall man who was a stranger to her for a moment, until he said quietly, 'Don't you recognise me?' Knowing that she was going to Brighton that day, Parnell left his colleagues at the Commons and boarded the train at Clapham Junction. On the train, he had cut off his beard with his pocket scissors in order to disguise himself. Then, wrapping a white muffler around his neck and jaw, he checked into Katharine's hotel as 'Mr Stewart', telling the manageress that he was suffering from toothache. When Katharine told him that she 'could not bear his appearance', he found a barber's and cleaned himself up, re-emerging at the hotel to announce his relief that his 'tooth' was out.[40] The lengths to which Parnell went to alter his appearance, spontaneous and clumsy though they were, demonstrate how nervous he was of discovery, yet also the risks he was prepared to take in order to spend a night, or nights, with Katharine, undisturbed by her children, her servants, or her husband.

On their return from the holiday in Brighton, Parnell seems to have risked staying at Eltham for longer periods: 'he certainly was there a great deal', Jane Lennister testified, and 'remain[ed] there when Captain O'Shea was away'.[41] Her description of Parnell's domestically regular habits, his generally getting back to Wonersh Lodge at 1.30 in the morning, then sleeping until the afternoon when he would have a 'breakfast' and sit around in the drawing-room until it was time to return to the House, is confirmed by Katharine. 'As a rule' he would get a cab down to Eltham in order to avoid being recognised on the local train ('He used to say that it was such a relief to get right away from the House when a sitting was over', and he enjoyed the 8-mile drive through country lanes[42]), and would enter the house through the conservatory at the back where Katharine would be waiting in her sitting-room: 'I would have supper ready for him before the fire, with his smoking-jacket and slippers ready to put on. He seldom spoke after his first greeting. He would take off his frock-coat and his boots, and, when I slipped on the others for him, he would eat his supper quite silently . . . I never worried him with talk. Supper finished, he would light a cigar and sit down in his own arm-chair.' Only then would he tell her of the night's debate: 'Once he began to talk he confided all his thoughts to me unreservedly.'[43] Then, during the afternoons before he went back to the Commons, they would work together on his official correspondence. This peaceful domesticity lasted just two months.

It was shattered when, on the evening of Tuesday 13 July, O'Shea came down to Eltham unannounced. We know little of Parnell's relations with Captain O'Shea during the first part of 1881, although it would appear that Katharine's husband was far busier in ensuring the safe passage of the Land Bill than Parnell was himself. On 9 June, having already proved himself an unwavering supporter of the Government (voting, against Parnell's instruction, for the second reading of the bill, and then again for its third reading), O'Shea conceived of an amendment to the Land Bill, mentioned it to Parnell and apparently got his approval. Instead of putting his proposal through the Parliamentary Committee, O'Shea spoke directly to the Prime Minister the next afternoon, and by the evening had produced a 'Confidential Memorandum' for Gladstone to put before the Cabinet. As early as September 1880, O'Shea had introduced himself to Gladstone, sending congratulations from his constituents on the Prime Minister's recovery from pneumonia, reminding him 'that my wife is neice [*sic*] of a member of your former Cabinet, Lord Hatherley'![44] O'Shea now proposed a measure which would ensure the success of the Land Bill by offering financial compensation (no less than two and a half million pounds) to Irish landlords, some of whom the Land Court 'would reduce to beggary', he suggested.[45] His intervention was motivated not by a regard for impoverished tenant farmers (none more so than in O'Shea's constituency of County Clare) but a wish to protect his own, landowning, class. The Exchequer had no intention of setting aside such a fund and nothing ever came of his proposal. However, what is of interest about the two letters O'Shea wrote to Gladstone is the way in which O'Shea presents himself as the moderating influence upon the Irish leader, his confidential guide and adviser.[46] It is as if he were supremely confident of the terms of their relationship. Unknown to O'Shea at the time he wrote this letter, his wife was pregnant with Parnell's child.

O'Shea's sudden arrival at Wonersh Lodge on 13 July 1881 resulted in his discovery of Parnell's portmanteau in the upstairs room connected to Katharine's by a small dressing-room. The very fact that Katharine had not hidden away Parnell's clothes suggests that her husband's visits to the house were infrequent. According to the evidence Sir Edward Clarke put before the jury at the divorce trial, the Captain 'was furiously angry, and after a scene with his wife left the house that night and walked to London in the early hours of the morning, proceeding to St James's Street, near Buckingham Palace, where Mrs Steele, his wife's sister, lived'.[47] Katharine herself says as much, although she gives a rather different interpretation of the angry 'scene' between the estranged husband and wife: 'Willie and I were quarrelling because he, my lawful husband, had come down without the invitation that was now (for some years) understood as due to the courtesy of friends, and because he had become vaguely suspicious.'[48] Before leaving the house that night, he packed the portmanteau off to Charing Cross Station and told Katharine that he would challenge Parnell to a duel and would shoot him. The challenge was issued the next day:

Salisbury Club
13th July 1881

Sir, – Will you be so kind as to be in Lille, or in any other town in the north of France which may suit your convenience, on Saturday next, the 16th inst.? Please to let me know by 1 p.m. today where to expect you on that date, so that I may be able to inform you of the sign of the inn at which I shall be staying. I await your answer in order to lose no time in arranging with a friend to accompany me.

I am, your obedient servant,
W.H. O'Shea[49]

His choice of 'friend' was his campaign partner, the O'Gorman Mahon, appropriately a man who 'had fought, in his day, more duels than he could remember'.[50]

While O'Shea's letter made its way to the Westminster Palace Hotel, Anna Steele went to the hotel in person. She called on Parnell at his rooms that morning where, according to Sir Edward Clarke, he 'assured her that there were no grounds for the jealous suspicions which Captain O'Shea had formed. He also promised her that in future he would not see Mrs O'Shea or give any cause for the suspicions that had been excited.'[51] Parnell, it seems, was caught on the back foot and all he felt able to do was to attempt a convincing denial of any impropriety. Unable to discuss the matter with Katharine, he appears to have sent a similarly phrased denial to O'Shea, and left open the question of a duel. O'Shea's response was to accuse Parnell of failing to reply, as a gentleman, to his challenge or to make preparations for the journey to northern France: 'Your luggage is at Charing Cross Station,' O'Shea declared![52]

The following day, Katharine received a guarded letter from Parnell telling her that her husband had written him 'a very insulting letter, and I shall be obliged to send a friend to him if I do not have a satisfactory reply'.[53] Apparently, as soon as O'Shea comprehended that Parnell did indeed intend to fight him, Katharine told Harrison, 'he worked upon my fears for Mr Parnell to get him out of it . . . – of course I hated the idea of a duel'.[54] O'Shea's sister-in-law also acted to avert a public scandal by advising him to withdraw his threat, and she eventually persuaded him to return to Eltham, where she promised to accompany him, to sort things out with Katharine. There was another 'stormy scene', apparently, 'in the course of which Captain O'Shea said he would no longer live with his wife' (which was a nonsense since he had not been 'living' with his wife for a number of years past). But the divorce court was told that Katharine 'implored' her husband to 'dismiss the suspicions, the truth of which she emphatically denied'.[55]

A duel, of course, would have been disastrous for Parnell, and perhaps for all parties involved, however it turned out. The whole matter is complicated by the accusation made by Katharine during the divorce proceedings, that O'Shea and her sister Anna were adulterous lovers and had committed adultery on the very night of the row over the portmanteau. When later asked about this accusation by Henry Harrison, Katharine exclaimed, 'Oh, yes . . . Anna and he had constantly been hunting in couples for many years.'[56] There appears to have been a degree of complacency all round, but on this occasion it was seriously disturbed.

It has been suggested by Joyce Marlow that the fraught atmosphere at Eltham was caused by Katharine's confession to her husband that she was carrying Parnell's child.[57] Yet this supposition does not square with O'Shea's behaviour at the time – either his reaction to his discovery of the portmanteau, or his subsequent attentiveness towards Katharine as her pregnancy advanced. The most likely explanation for the July quarrel is that O'Shea, 'vaguely suspicious', as Katharine put it, that Parnell had secretly been visiting Wonersh Lodge, called unannounced late one evening to try to catch them out. Parnell was not there, but the evidence that he had been was enough to make O'Shea, now in a fit of jealousy, force himself upon Katharine, either then or around that time, in order to assert his mastery of his wife and, indeed, their marital home. He continued to claim his conjugal rights as the year went on, and he could continue to believe that Claude Sophie was conceived in July, rather than May, 1881.

The question of how Katharine and Parnell planned to deal with her pregnancy is a crucial one. For if we accept that their first child Claude Sophie was conceived in mid-May 1881, Katharine would have known for certain that she was pregnant by June, or early July, at the very latest. She may even have waited unduly to make certain, since her belief that she was pregnant as early as December 1880 was an awkward mistake. The question is whether Katharine resumed sexual relations with her husband on or before 13 July in order to convince O'Shea that the baby was his.

The mere possibility of such an explanation has resulted in violent reactions from twentieth-century historians and biographers: Harrison calls it 'a vile picture' and simply cannot believe that Katharine would have compromised her relationship with Parnell; Jules Abels is convinced that Katharine took this decision alone (he even dramatises an imaginary conversation in which Katharine makes her confession to Parnell); while Lyons is relieved that the 'unpleasant hypothesis' that she was, in 1881 at least, having sexual relations with both men, 'remains only a theory'.[58]

Captain O'Shea told the divorce court that, largely owing to Anna Steele's intervention at Eltham on the afternoon of 14 July, and 'having accepted the assurances' of both sisters, 'I became reconciled to my wife'. His barrister went further, saying that O'Shea eventually 'listened to [Katharine] and agreed that their relations should be resumed as before'.[59] Husband and wife, of course, interpreted this last phrase very differently. The divorce court heard that normal marital relations were restored: 'the affectionate relations which had always existed between Captain O'Shea and his wife were resumed.'[60] Katharine, on the contrary, regarded this whole episode as cementing the terms of her relationship with Parnell: 'From the date of this bitter quarrel Parnell and I were one, without further scruple, without fear, and without remorse.'[61]

When interviewed by Henry Harrison in the months immediately following Parnell's death, Katharine would claim that her sister's intervention on 14 July was prompted by the desire, not to save the marriage by assuring O'Shea of the innocence of Parnell's friendship with Katharine, but to save the appearance of a marriage by arranging things with O'Shea so that Katharine's independence was safeguarded at Eltham, where she could continue to receive Parnell. Harrison recalls Katharine telling him that 'between us we managed to settle it': 'We were on a perfectly clear basis from that onwards. My freedom was to be respected; appearances were to be preserved; scandal and all cause for scandal were to be avoided.' Nothing had been said directly, 'but Anna and Captain O'Shea and I all understood'.[62]

Katharine convinced Harrison that from the moment O'Shea accepted 'the tacit agreement negotiated by Mrs Steele', he 'consciously and deliberately shut his eyes to what was going on'.[63] Yet this new arrangement between husband and wife is flatly contradicted by the few short, scrupulously formal, letters Parnell sent her from London in the latter part of July, which suggest not only that O'Shea resumed his visits to Eltham, but also – stung by jealousy of his wife's attraction to Parnell – resumed sexual relations with Katharine. On 20 July, for example, we have Parnell writing to 'My dear Mrs O'Shea, – Just a line to say that I am very well and wondering when I shall see you again', a letter which supposes that Mr O'Shea is resident at Eltham.[64] Two days later, he writes again, and significantly makes reference to the still fractious mood of Katharine's husband:

House of Commons
Thursday night, July 22, 1881

My dear Mrs O'Shea, – I have received both your very kind letters quite safely, and am looking forward to seeing you somewhere or somehow tomorrow.

I am very much troubled at everything you have to undergo, and trust that it will not last long. – Yours always,

Chas. S. Parnell

I am quite well. Thank you very much for enclosure.[65]

On the evening of Sunday 25 July, from his rooms at the Westminster Palace Hotel, Parnell wrote that he had been 'very lonely all today and yesterday. Have not seen anyone that I know.'[66] Together, these letters tell us how serious the July row with O'Shea was. While Sir Edward Clarke neatly tied up the episode, stating that once Captain O'Shea had been won over by his wife's assurances, the 'incident was then terminated',[67] Katharine's independent situation at Eltham was clearly under threat. More than that, she was now two months' pregnant with her lover's child, a lover who, despite her version of events, appears to have been staying cautiously clear of her house.

In the immediate aftermath of the July argument, Katharine was left in a very vulnerable position at Eltham, while political events kept Parnell in Ireland. For while the majority of the party had voted for the Land Bill, which passed its third reading on 29 July, extremist opinion in America was hostile to the Act and continued to demand a no-rent strike in Ireland. Parnell's problem was that, while he was convinced that the Nationalist cause was best served through the parliamentary process, Irish-Americans, on whose funds their movement depended, needed reassurance that it was a truly revolutionary movement. According to R. Barry O'Brien, 'It was Parnell who got the Land Act . . . though he refused to make himself responsible for it, and even appeared hostile to it. He played a deep game.'[68] Consistent with this, in a calculated manoeuvre, Parnell 'deliberately picked a quarrel with the Speaker, by repeatedly demanding a day for the discussion of arrests in Ireland under the coercion act'.[69] This had the result that he intended: he was 'named', suspended for the remainder of the session, and departed the next day for Ireland where his presence was urgently needed to unite moderates and extremists behind the Land Bill, which would become law on 22 August. The compromise offered by Parnell was to try the legislation by observing a number of 'test cases' selected by the Land League. Only if these proved successful were tenant-farmers to be encouraged to go wholesale to the Land Court. Parnell's policy of stalling agitation in Ireland by watching 'test cases' was accepted by the Land League convention held in Dublin between 15 and 17 September.

The policy of observing test cases did not mean that Parnell was quiescent. Throughout the remainder of September and early October 1881, and perhaps partly with the Irish-Americans in mind, Parnell made uncompromising public attacks not only on the Act itself but on the Liberal Government responsible for it. Forster was so angered at this apparent call to boycott the Act that he recommended to Gladstone the mass arrest and imprisonment of all 'the central leaders who conduct the boycott', the priority being Parnell himself: 'Unless we can strike down the boycotting weapon, Parnell will beat us.'[70] For now, Gladstone chose merely to denounce Parnell's behaviour at a speech he gave in Leeds on 7 October. Parnell responded in kind two days later, at Wexford, where, in 'a speech of calculated insolence' and invoking 'the men of '98' and other past uprisings, he talked of Gladstone supporting the plunder of the landlords 'by his bayonets and his buckshot'. The assembled crowds were told that the Land Act was but 'a fraction of that to which you are entitled', and Parnell announced that it was time for the Irish people 'to regain their lost land and their legislative independence'.[71] Quite simply, he dared the

Government to call for his arrest. Tim Healy, who describes how he and Parnell composed this speech in the train down to Wexford, records how the people were 'stirred to their entrails', and that when Parnell was presented with the Freedom of the Borough the next day a procession followed his carriage through the narrow streets, bombarding them with roses: 'Women flew handkerchiefs from the windows; crowds cheered from the footpaths; men went wild with fervour.'[72]

In all this time, it seems that Parnell was only able to get across to England a couple of times to see Katharine briefly, although they continued to write or wire each other every day. On 10 September he posted her from Morrison's Hotel a formal note (to which O'Shea would have been unable to take exception), requesting that she forward an enclosure for him. Of course the enclosure was a private letter, a letter to 'My own Wifie', telling Katharine that a telegram from Eltham had just been put into his hand, and expressing his relief 'to know that your trouble has not returned since I left',[73] another reference, perhaps, to O'Shea's unwanted sexual attentions.

In early October, O'Shea was in Dublin, where Parnell went out of his way to seek his company. Parnell's persistence in tracking him down demonstrates how important it was for him to smooth things over after the events of mid-July. Back in August Parnell had written to Katharine, 'I had a very satisfactory conversation yesterday, and things look much straighter.'[74] In October, he described to her how he had waited for *three* hours for O'Shea at the Shelbourne Hotel on the off chance of arranging an appointment. O'Shea finally walked in just after Parnell returned at 11 p.m. that night. His invitation to Parnell to dinner at the Shelbourne the following evening caused one discerning juror at the divorce trial to put a question to the Captain: 'How do you account for your conduct in, after having challenged Mr Parnell to a duel, inviting him again to dinner?'[75] O'Shea, no doubt feeling the strain of undergoing cross-examination for the first time during the trial, denied the Dublin dinner, confusing it with an earlier dinner at Eltham, and thus offered no satisfactory account of his relationship with Parnell immediately *after* the events of July 1881.

The suggestion that O'Shea was still very much on his guard is borne out by Parnell's cautious message to Katharine after seeing her husband at his hotel. Of the Captain's movements, Parnell had this to report: 'He *says* that he leaves tomorrow (Friday) evening, and stops to shoot on Saturday in Wales, and goes on Tuesday to Paris to see the Papal Nuncio, who he says has requested him to come.'[76] Parnell, though, suspected that he was bluffing, and warned Katharine that he would not send her any more letters directly to Eltham. He hoped to get to London early in the week, but asked her whether they should meet in London or at Eltham. The next day, Saturday 8 October, he was more definite, telling her that after speaking at

Wexford on Sunday he would be free to leave, and planned to meet her in London on the Tuesday or Wednesday.

Katharine's side of the correspondence has not survived, but it seems plain that she felt abandoned: subject to moody visitations from her estranged husband, and five months' pregnant with her lover's child, a lover whose possible arrest was a great anxiety to her, and who, in between political business, found time to visit Avondale (Katharine reprints a letter dated Tuesday 4 October, which is solely concerned with the mines on his land; he doesn't think to ask how she is). She needed to be reassured of Parnell's love for her: 'My dearest little Wifie, – Your husband has been very good since he left you, and is longing to see you again. He has kept his eyes, thought, and love all for you, and my sweetest love may be assured that he always will,' he wrote on 8 October, and gave the further encouragement that the Dublin convention and subsequent public meetings had all gone so well that he hoped he would only have to make 'an occasional appearance in Ireland during the rest of the autumn and winter'.[77] But when the day came that they had hoped to meet in London, Tuesday 11 October, Parnell was still in Ireland, about to depart for a public meeting in Naas, Kildare, to the west of Dublin. He hoped to journey to London on the Friday, 'but I cannot be sure of this'.[78] Besides the constant fear of arrest, there was a meeting of the Executive scheduled for Saturday 15 October which he really ought to stay for: 'However, Wifie knows I will do the best I can, and she will get a wire from me on Friday . . . telling her what I have done. If I arrive London Friday night shall go to same hotel and shall wait for my darling. Will she mind asking for my number?'

There was to be no reunion in a London hotel room. Parnell's immediate arrest 'on suspicion of treasonable practices'[79] had been authorised at a meeting of the Cabinet, and Forster himself set off to Dublin with the warrant, arriving in the early hours of 13 October. Parnell was arrested soon after he awoke that morning at Morrison's Hotel. The arrests of three other MPs, Sexton, Dillon and O'Kelly, two League secretaries, Thomas Brennan and Andrew Kettle, and William O'Brien, the editor of Parnell's paper, *United Ireland*, followed shortly. On the evening of Parnell's arrest, Gladstone announced the news to the Guildhall, London, where the Prime Minister was presented with the freedom of the city: 'The great meeting rose *en masse*, frantic with excitement and joy, and rounds of applause rang again and again throughout the hall, until the speaker himself was astonished, and perhaps startled, at the savage enthusiasm which this announcement called forth.'[80] With Parnell safely in prison, 'The British Empire breathed once more' was R. Barry O'Brien's sardonic comment. Katharine would not see Parnell for another six months.

# CHAPTER 4

## *Kilmainham Gaol*

For some time now, Katharine had taken care of Parnell's correspondence and had thus known that her lover's arrest was imminent. Indeed she claims to have had prior knowledge of Forster's crossing to Ireland to authorise it. She 'could not bear the thought of his arrest'. She had by now 'so much of his business in hand . . . I felt almost unable to cope'. Earlier that week she telegraphed to ask whether he could meet her at Holyhead, but Parnell replied in code to the effect that his arrest must come soon and that he 'would be careful when in Kilmainham so that his imprisonment should be of short duration'. She took comfort from 'his confident spirit and loving messages'.[1]

On 13 October, the day of his arrest, Katharine was woken early at Eltham by a tremendous storm and, before the house was up, dressed and walked out into her aunt's park, where 'the fierce wind blowing through my hair braced me'. The violence of the wind was such that a great branch was torn from the very tree she leant against. In 'the havoc of the storm', 'crimson and russet leaves were swirled across the park' and 'old trees bowed beneath the gale' until 'the whole of one side of the avenue fell, ripping and tearing till I thought every tree in the place was coming down'.[2] Elsewhere, telegraph poles came down across England and Ireland, and in the Irish Channel vessels were run ashore or wrecked. Tim Healy says that the people believed 'the elements protested against the arrest of Parnell'.[3]

O'Shea had written telling her to expect him for dinner that evening, and having spent the day with her aunt as usual, Katharine returned to Wonersh Lodge to arrange for the evening papers to be sent over from Blackheath. O'Shea was there before her, and she knew of the arrest as soon as she saw his face. Since she was prepared for it, 'I did not flinch, but replied languidly that I had thought Parnell "couldn't keep out of gaol much longer, didn't you?"'.[4] The pleasure O'Shea clearly took in Parnell's imprisonment shocked Katharine's maids, 'ardent Parnellites', and Katharine, overwrought, responded with what was a 'laugh of jangled nerves and misery'. It satisfied her husband, however, and, in what became a recognisable pattern of behaviour, observing her 'closely', he set out to make wounding criticisms of Parnell. Over dinner he enlarged upon the 'wickedness and folly' of Parnell's policy and boasted that the Irish question would be settled if left 'in his [own] hands and those who thought with him'. Calm again, Katharine smilingly reminded O'Shea that she was now 'as ardent a Parnellite as Parnell himself': she had already worked so hard for 'the cause' that her politics were far more 'reactionary' (by which she clearly means reactive to the injustices of the Irish question) than when she had first met Parnell.[5] Ultimately, she was able to turn the conversation away from Parnell to general questions about the treatment he might expect in Kilmainham: 'Willie, as are so many men, was never so happy as when giving information',[6] she commented acutely.

That morning, Parnell had been wakened at Morrison's Hotel with the news that two detectives were waiting below. His first thought was for Katharine, and he kept the men out of his room while writing her 'a few hasty words of comfort and hope, for I knew the shock would be very terrible to my sweet love. I feared that I could not post it, but they stopped the cab just before reaching the prison and allowed me to drop the letter into a pillar box'.[7] In this letter Katharine was told to be 'a brave little woman' and a 'brave, dear little wifie'.[8] From Kilmainham the next day, Parnell wrote that he had been tortured by the fear that 'the shock may have hurt you or our child'.[9] He heard nothing from Katharine until the morning of 17 October, his fourth day at Kilmainham. Some time between 14 and 17 October, in desperation (because she had often said that the news of his arrest would kill her), Parnell sent a telegram to Anna Steele, to find out how Katharine was, but since Anna was then away from home, the telegram was returned, undelivered.

Of his arrest itself and his imprisonment, Parnell took a pragmatic view. As he explained to Katharine, 'Politically it is a fortunate thing for me that I have been arrested, as the movement is breaking fast, and all will be quiet in a few months, when I shall be released'.[10] The Land League's response to Parnell's arrest was to issue a 'No Rent Manifesto', 'calling upon the tenants to pay no agrarian rents, under any circumstances, until the Government had restored the constitutional rights of the people'.[11] Its only effect was to outlaw the Land League itself. On 17 October the manifesto was published in *United Ireland*. Within three days the League was suppressed.

In prison, Parnell was inconvenienced for a while by the posting of new sentries outside his door and window each night ('we are all in disgrace on account of the manifesto'), but otherwise he felt that the Government 'have let us off very easily'.[12] In the first letter he was able to get out of Kilmainham, he told Katharine that he was comfortably settled in 'a beautiful room facing the sun – the best in the prison'.[13] This may have been partly to reassure Katharine, but it was evidently no more than the truth. A friend who had visited him there exclaimed to R. Barry O'Brien, 'what a room! . . . The table strewn with everything, newspapers, books, magazines, light literature, Blue Books, illustrated periodicals, fruit, addresses from public bodies, presents of every description, all lying in one indiscriminate heap before him.'[14] Indeed, all these years later it does seem to be a surprisingly commodious room, certainly in comparison with the narrow, cramped cells nearby. Parnell was, in fact, 'exceedingly comfortable and not in the slightest degree dull'.[15] After a week's confinement he declared that he had quite forgotten he was in prison. He had possession of a good-sized, perfectly dry room fitted with a coal fire and gas lighting, and his colleagues were all close by. He was allowed to read the morning newspaper in bed, even to have his breakfast in bed, and could get up or retire at whatever hour he liked. Forster's arrangements were 'unquestionably humane': young William O'Brien was permitted to make regular visits to see his mother at the Sisters of Charity hospice, and Parnell himself 'was virtually under no prison rules except a bar against his walking out of Kilmainham. No indignity beyond detention was offered to him.'[16] Political prisoners were allowed to play ball – something Parnell hadn't done for twenty years – and he clearly enjoyed the physical exercise, boasting, 'I expect to be so fresh when I get out that even Wifie won't be able to hold me, although her bonds are very strong and pleasant.'[17] In January they got a new exercise yard and were even permitted to practise with an air-gun! Unlike Katharine's, his time passed lightly: 'I admire supremely my life of ease, laziness, absence of care and responsibility here.'[18] Another prisoner was assigned to look after Parnell, and did so as assiduously as Katharine's parlour-maid, Mary:

He makes me a soda and lemon in the morning, and then gives me my breakfast. At dinner he takes care that I get all the nicest bits and concocts the most perfect black coffee in a 'Kaffee Kanne' out of berries, which he roasts and grinds each day. Finally, in the evening, just before we are separated for the night, he brews me a steaming tumbler of hot whisky. He has marked all my clothes for me also, and sees that the washerwoman does not rob me. Don't you begin to feel jealous?[19]

It has been suggested that Katharine made 'heavy weather of a pregnancy which had come upon her after a long interval'.[20] In fact, none of her pregnancies could be described as easy, but this time, certainly, Parnell's arrest hit her hard. It must have been a desperate situation for her: she found the prolonged separation unbearable. She describes her day-to-day life from Parnell's arrest onwards as 'a curiously subconscious existence', following the normal pattern of her life, 'but feeling that all that was of life in me had gone with my lover to prison, and only came back to me in the letters that were my only mark of time'.[21] For the sake of their unborn child Parnell urged Katharine that 'it will be wicked of you to grieve, as I can never have any other wife but you, and if anything happens to you I must die childless'.[22] While the initial shock did not cause her to miscarry, she was unwell at the end of October, and unable to get word to Parnell because O'Shea was with her at Eltham. He became concerned for her health and wanted to visit the house more often than she would allow. As Katharine puts it, O'Shea thought the birth of the baby 'would seal our reconciliation, whereas I knew it would cement the cold hatred I felt towards him'.[23]

The fact that O'Shea insisted upon his conjugal rights for the duration of Parnell's confinement in Kilmainham, almost up to the time of the birth, is suggested fairly strongly in the letters reprinted by Katharine. In November and December, Parnell expresses his disgust that Katharine was having to submit to the 'intolerable annoyance' of O'Shea's presence at Eltham: 'It is frightful that you should be exposed to such daily torture.'[24] That the 'intolerable annoyance' was specifically sexual can be inferred from the comments made by Parnell whenever O'Shea left Eltham. Katharine will be free 'to get some sleep for her husband's sake and for our child's sake, who must be suffering much also'.[25] More explicit is the reference made by Parnell on 7 January: 'It is perfectly dreadful that Wifie should be so *worried at night*. I had hoped that the doctor's orders would have prevented that.'[26] When, a few days later, he heard that O'Shea had left Eltham, Parnell wrote, in similar vein: 'I do trust you have been now relieved for a time by his departure, and that you are getting a little sleep. It is enough to have killed you several times over, my own Queenie.'[27] One of the surprising things which the Kilmainham letters reveal about the relationship between Katharine and Parnell is the extraordinary frankness with which they appear able to discuss this continuing intimacy between the legal husband and wife. She seems to have made no attempt to hide unpalatable details from her lover, while on his part, Parnell expresses not his own jealousy, as one would expect, but only solicitude for Katharine.

It was an intolerable situation for Katharine, and the question of when her lover would be released from prison became the pressing issue. When first arrested, Parnell encouraged her to believe that he would be out by the New Year: 'I am told the Government don't exactly know what to do with us now they have got us.'[28] A month later he thought he might even be home for Christmas. But there seemed no sense of urgency on his side. In the meantime he kept up Katharine's hopes of visiting him at the prison. Of course, as her pregnancy advanced, this became less and less likely, but the planning continued, for her sake as much as for his. In fact, in her first private letter to him at Kilmainham (her first two letters were formal enquiries from 'Mrs O'Shea'), Katharine seems to have expected to be able to visit him somehow. She was gently dissuaded. There were half a dozen men in rooms adjacent to Parnell's who knew about everybody who visited him: 'Besides, you would not be permitted to see me except in the presence of two warders, and it might only make you more unhappy.'[29] In his next letter, Parnell did consider that if she was strong enough, she might, at some point, come over to visit him. At present, though, owing to the issuing of the No Rent Manifesto, he was denied all visitors. On 1 November, she was told that Forster had refused to allow him any visitors 'except in the cage', a humiliation which Parnell refused to submit to.[30] Yet a day later, he was able to send Katharine a private message which suggested that he would indeed get her over to Dublin 'as soon as I hear that W[illie] is firmly fixed'.[31] The plan put forward was for Katharine to impersonate a cousin of Parnell's or a married sister. Yet Parnell does not appear to have gone about this with anything like the same energy that he put into ensuring that he and Katharine were able to write to each other freely during his imprisonment.

One of the things that got Katharine through the pregnancy, perhaps *the* thing, was that Parnell could send and receive private letters while in prison. His safest time for writing to her was when they had all been locked up for the night, and 'everything is quiet and I am alone'.[32] He wrote formal letters to 'Mrs O'Shea' at Eltham, but employed several subterfuges in order to send much more intimate letters to 'My Darling Wifie' or 'My own Queenie'. He spent the evenings reading and then wrote letters until twelve or one o'clock, looking fondly at Katharine's portrait: 'with your sweet face before me I can give my thoughts up entirely to my Queen, and talk to you almost as well as if you were in my arms. It seems to me a long, long time since our hasty goodbye.'[33] Parnell writes tenderly and lovingly, 'Promise your husband that you will . . . look as beautiful when we meet again as the last time I pressed your sweet lips';[34] 'With a thousand kisses to my own Wifie, and hoping soon to lay my head in its old place'.[35] By mid-November he had begun to send his 'Best love to our child', and on 1 December Katharine wrote to him about the baby's vigorous kicking: 'Am rejoiced to learn that Wifie hopes our child will be strong,' was his reply.[36]

Parnell was quick to devise a means of corresponding secretly with Katharine the very day after his arrival at Kilmainham. She was sent an envelope in which she was instructed to place her own letters within an inner envelope marked with her initials: 'Oh, darling, write or wire me as soon as you get this that you are well . . . You may wire me here. I have your beautiful face with me here; it is such a comfort. I kiss it every morning.'[37] Later, he asked that she put her 'proper initials' on the inner envelope, 'thus, K.P.'.[38] Separately, Katharine and O'Shea had written Parnell formal letters 'which reached me safely after having been duly perused by the Governor' – hence the need for extreme caution. 'Mrs O'Shea' received a formal reply, letting her know that Morrison's had forwarded her last letter to him there, and giving her the following instruction: 'If you have not done so already, please inquire in London about the messages you were expecting, and about any others that may arrive in future, and let me know in your next whether you have received them.'[39]

It is clear from this letter that, even before Parnell was arrested, he and Katharine had established a safe system for exchanging correspondence through a London address, 34 Woburn Place, Russell Square.[40] Katharine explains that she would pick up letters in London under the anonymous enough pseudonym of 'Mrs Carpenter'.[41] Yet this was not enough for Parnell, and perhaps the increasingly convoluted system he organised for corresponding with Katharine would have been a welcome diversion during her months of solitude and anxiety at Eltham. As well as continuing to send the occasional formal letter from Eltham, she was advised at the end of November that, 'the Woolwich or Charlton post offices will do very well'.[42] Later, Katharine would also send letters through Parnell's land agent, William Kerr, at Casino, Rathdrum. Believing that the outside envelope of one of her letters had been tampered with – one of the envelopes he had sent her for the purpose – he suggested that it would be safer for her to 'direct the next envelopes in a feigned hand . . . Gum your inside envelopes well'.[43]

During the first week of December, Parnell somehow got hold of a more effective, and far more intriguing, method of communication: invisible ink. After a few days of experimenting in his cell, he sent Katharine a 'prescription' for the two concoctions: 'No. 1 is for writing. No. 2 is for bringing it out.' She was advised to test out the strength of each and refine them accordingly, and that 'The secret writing should be with a clean quill pen, and should be written lightly . . . Use unglazed rough paper.'[44] Despite its being a fiddly business (Katharine was repeatedly chided for pressing the pen too heavily, for using too much ink and the wrong kind of paper), the fact that she could send and receive intimate letters at Eltham saved her, as her pregnancy advanced, from much arduous journeying to London. She was told to 'brush any letters I write you to E. with No. 2 solution', since he would try to direct most of his letters to her at home.[45] Yet this did not always work. On 17 January Parnell warned her that there was 'a very sharp-eyed man over the letters' (a warder refused him permission to send one particular letter, and he had to burn another), and at the end of the month he explained that he had decided to direct her letters again to London, 'lest there should be any mistake, especially as my paper is not very suitable'.[46] It is alarming to think that within a fortnight before the birth of her baby Katharine was continuing to travel to London through the cold January fog to pick up word from her lover. Parnell was certainly concerned about this. He did not like her going to London so often, and asked if there was an address nearer home that might be used.

As well as fatiguing herself with such journeys, Katharine was anxious about Parnell's health. She had the *Freeman's Journal* delivered at Eltham, which, for political purposes, carried exaggerated accounts of his poor health. Reports of his spells in the infirmary and scare stories about prison fare were put out by the prisoners themselves in order to ensure that their stay was as comfortable as possible. In fact the infirmary, where each patient had his own room, was more comfortable than being in a cell. The prisoners had 'longer hours of association, from 8 a.m. to 8 p.m., instead of being locked up at 6 and obliged to eat by yourself'. Parnell also invented 'little maladies for myself from day to day in order to give Dr Kenny an excuse for keeping me in . . . The latest discovery is heart affection.'[47] This does appear to have been a real concern of Dr Kenny, but aside from getting an obligatory dose of diarrhoea, the 'mal du prison', which Kenny saw off with mustard and chlorodyne, as well as the odd cold and passing 'indisposition', Parnell constantly sought to assure Katharine that he was not concealing the truth from her, and that he 'never felt so well in his life'.[48] 'You must not mind the reports about my health', she was told, 'I have a first-rate appetite'.[49]

Parnell explained that the political prisoners were to announce that they had 'gone on Government food' in order to prompt a public subscription fund, as they wanted to use the American funds for political purposes.[50] It was estimated that the Ladies' Land League,* led by his sister Anna, were spending £400 a week to provide food for the many Land League members who had been imprisoned. On 3 November the 'Prisoners' Sustentation Fund' was launched through the *Freeman's Journal* and raised an astonishing £20,000. Parnell himself had little intention of going on 'P.F.' (Prison Fare), 'but Wifie must not tell anybody'.[51] In any case, all those in the infirmary were on a special diet and could have anything Dr Kenny ordered for them, even game. They were permitted one meal a day from outside if they had the money, but besides that Parnell and Dillon lunched daily on smuggled chops and they always had some cold ham on hand,

---

* The Government had not named the Ladies' Land League when they ordered the suspension of the Land League in October 1881.

besides dinners provided from the Governor's private kitchen. 'The "one meal a day" is only a pretence,' he told her. In fact, he was getting 'Chops or grilled turkey or eggs and bacon for breakfast, soup and chops for luncheon, and joint and vegetables, etc., for dinner, and sometimes oysters'.[52]

Of Katharine's side of the correspondence all we know is what we can divine from brief references to her letters in Parnell's own. In her book, throughout the period covering Parnell's confinement in Kilmainham, Katharine fills two chapters with nearly sixty of her lover's letters, yet she reprints none of hers, and comments very little on her state of mind at this time. The impression given is that she was entirely alone and unable to confide in anyone except Parnell himself. At no point does she mention so much as a letter or a visit from any of her brothers or sisters.[53] By the time she was writing the book, however, she had long fallen out with them and perhaps for this reason or in order to safeguard their privacy she deliberately avoided mention of them. To have acknowledged their support, if indeed there was any, might have raised the question of their knowledge and complicity. Anna, certainly, would have realised that Katharine must already have been pregnant at the very time her husband accused her of an illicit relationship with Parnell and threatened the latter to a duel.

In fact, Katharine's letters appear to have kept to a familiar theme: her 'loneliness and weariness', and also rather more extreme states of mind. They were letters which left her lover 'very nervous'.[54] As Christmas approached, with still no word on the possible release of the prisoners, she grew desperate. On 14 December Parnell received a letter accusing him of 'surely killing' her and their child. Remarkably, Parnell made his now notorious proposition: 'Rather than that my beautiful Wifie should run any risk I will resign my seat, leave politics, and go away somewhere with my own Queenie, as soon as she wishes.'[55] He asked her to let him know if it was safe for her if he was to remain in prison. This should be seen as a measure of the strength of his feeling for Katharine, but when Tim Healy read Katharine's book he called this document, and its revelation that Parnell was prepared for her sake to 'desert his colleagues and the Irish Cause' at the height of the struggle, 'the strangest State Paper in Irish History'. He was tempted to disbelieve it, except that Katharine printed a facsimile of the letter in Parnell's hand.[56] Likewise, his colleagues were incredulous to read Parnell's stated relief that the days of making platform speeches were behind him, saying, with reference to the Land League, 'I cannot describe to you the disgust I always felt with those meetings, knowing as I did how hollow and wanting in solidity everything connected with the movement was.'[57]

How serious was Parnell's intention to resign is highly questionable. In his postscript to the 14 December letter he advised Katharine that the prisoners would probably all be let out at the opening of Parliament (7 February 1882). He wrote that her letter 'frightened me more than I can tell you', and once more assured her that, 'Nothing in the world is worth the risk of any harm or injury to you. How could I ever live without my Katie? – and if you are in danger, my darling, I will come to you at once.'[58] Katharine perhaps knew better than to force him to choose between his political career and herself, another man's wife, yet carrying Parnell's child of seven months. She did ask whether some sort of compromise with the Government might not be possible, but he explained that he 'could not well make any arrangement or enter into any undertaking . . . unless I retired altogether'.[59] The subject was not mentioned again until early April. All that Katharine had wanted was to know that he continued to love her and intended to return to her, and her alone, on his release. 'I do not receive any letters from ladies I know,' he protested. 'Am glad to say that none of my "young women" have written.'[60] This appears to have been in response to jealous enquiries from Katharine, but Parnell did not at all have a reputation as a womaniser. His letters from Kilmainham are consistently expressive of his love and concern for Katharine. At Christmas, she asked for a token of that love, a lock of hair, perhaps, for she received a letter dated Christmas Eve, in which Parnell wrote, 'I send my own love what she has asked me for, and trust that it will make her forget our squabble of last Xmas Day, as I had long forgotten it. My darling, you are and always will be everything to me, and every day you become more and more, if possible, more than everything to me.'[61] At New Year, more confident than ever that their release was imminent, he assured her, 'My own Queenie, – Yes, I will go to you, my love, immediately I am released.'[62]

By mid-February this had turned into hopes that they would be released by the middle of March, since it would then be known how tenants had responded to the Land Act, and they would be able to decide whether it was worth their while remaining in prison any longer. There had been the possibility that the tenants would find the assurances provided by the Act and the rents set by the Land Court acceptable, but, according to Lyons, the winter of 1881–2 was 'one of the most violent in living memory' and, prior to this, the effect of the Land League had been to contain rather than to instigate 'agrarian anarchy'.[63] There is evidence to suggest that by this time Parnell had begun to conceive of a deal by which he could persuade the Government to extend the terms of the Land Act to those farmers presently excluded from it (that is, lease-holders, and also the very poorest tenants who, because of bad harvests, owed a whole year's rent or more with no prospect of paying), or even to introduce a separate piece of legislation relating exclusively to the question of arrears, in return for an end to the agitation in the country, thus making a renewal of the Coercion Act unnecessary. Some time in February or March he surprised William O'Brien by asking if he did not think they had 'got about enough of this thing', and in April said, 'with one of his brightest smiles', 'Don't pitch into me too hard, O'Brien, if . . . I sign conditions and go out.'[64]

Katharine gave birth to a baby girl on 15 February 1882. A careful reading of the letters Parnell sent her as the birth approached proves beyond doubt that the child was Parnell's, but suggests also that O'Shea had grounds to believe that it was his. Indeed, Katharine was under great strain because of the deception she had to practise towards her husband (in her book, she states that 'he had no suspicion of the truth'[65]). He appears, as has been noted, to have insisted upon his conjugal rights from 13 July onwards and therefore would have expected his child to be born some time in late March or even early April 1882. In the passage from Katharine's book quoted above, she does say that O'Shea 'thought February would seal our reconciliation', but this later commentary is belied by the evidence of the letters which reveal that only Katharine and Parnell knew that the baby would be delivered as early as February. This is the sequence of events which can be inferred from three letters Parnell sent Katharine as the correct time of the birth approached. On 30 December 1881, Parnell was clearly anxious that the baby might be born before she had doctors to attend her, and that she should 'at all events *tell one of them the right time*, so that he may be on hand, otherwise you may not have one at all. It will never do to run this risk.'[66] After the New Year he renewed his plea to Katharine that she 'must be sure to have at least one doctor in February. It will never do to let it trust to chance,'[67] advice which becomes more transparent when he wrote again, even more urgently, on 7 January, 'You must tell the doctor, and never mind about ———.'[68]

On 14 February, a day before she went into labour, Katharine managed to write Parnell two notes, which were presumably posted by her maid, Mary. These may have expressed fears that she might die in childbirth: whatever it was she managed to scribble down made Parnell 'burst into tears'. He told her that he 'could not hold up his head or think of anything until my darling's note arrived that everything was right', and was unable to describe to her 'how hopeless and utterly miserable I felt'.[69] The baby, a daughter bearing 'the brown eyes of her father', was safely delivered at Wonersh Lodge on 15 February. Parnell didn't get word for two days: 'I cannot describe to you what a relief your little note was that everything was quite right . . . My own, you must be very good and quiet until you are quite strong again, and do not be in a hurry to get up.'[70] There was little chance of that. Katharine says that 'the joy of possessing Parnell's child carried me through my trouble',[71] but she was in fact very ill (she had actually lost weight before the birth), and didn't leave her bed for over a month. For three weeks she was unable to write again to Parnell, leading him to address 'Mrs O'Shea' on 5 March, 'It is so long since I have heard from you that I sometimes wonder whether you have quite forgotten me.'[72] That prompted a rush of letters, and the response, 'You are very good to your husband in writing so often and so lovingly to your King, even when you must have been suffering terribly.'[73] Their intimate correspondence was resumed, and Parnell received a lock of his daughter's hair, which he put in his locket next to a lock of Katharine's: 'there is a splendid golden tint in it which is quite exceptional,' he declared.[74]

On 16 March, Katharine received a beautifully tender letter in which Parnell put aside her disappointment – whether for Parnell or for herself we do not know – that their first child was not a boy: 'I shall love her very much better than if it had been a son; indeed, my darling, I love her very much already, and feel very much like a father.'[75] He had been 'training up' the chairman of the Prisons Board to allow him to be visited privately by his married sisters. His sister Emily had been to see him that day, a visit consistent with Parnell's intention at some point of passing off Katharine as another married sister. The letter closes by trying to persuade Katharine, who was so weak that she was still confined to her room, to give the nursing of their child over to a wet nurse: 'The idea of nursing our little daughter was too preposterous. Do, my own darling, think of yourself and take great, great care of your husband's own little Wifie.' He wanted Katharine 'to be an even younger little Wifie than when I gave her that last kiss'.[76] There is, it must be said, a rather selfish preoccupation with the restoration of Katharine's sexual attractiveness to him in this and later letters.

Knowing how weak she was, Parnell sent bulletins of his own good health, writing on 23 March, 'I have not been weighed yet, but shall try today and send my own darling the true weight. It must be considerably more than 12-5.'[77] Indeed, the question of his weight had become obsessive just at the moment that Katharine must have been preoccupied with the arrival of their daughter. He comments on his weight in at least seven letters at around this time. On 27 March, for instance, while declaring himself 'very anxious about our little daughter', his only item of news from Kilmainham was his weight: 'Was weighed yesterday – 12 st. 7 lb. Have certainly gained five or six pounds since I have been here.'[78] It is as if there is a sense of rivalry involved. On 29 March, he says that he does not want Katharine to nurse the baby because 'She is much too good and beautiful for anything of the kind.'[79]

Katharine did submit to his wish about the wet nurse, but the baby, too, was in delicate health, and it may have been a question of whether

Katharine could feed her adequately. Of course, the whole question of the nursing of the baby needs to be seen in the context of what would have been customary practice among upper-class women of the time. Parnell's attitudes, too, need to be related to their time. What can be said for him is that in the 16 March letter he discouraged Katharine from nursing, in part at least, because of concern for her health, only to regret, in the 29 March letter, that she 'must have been exhausted by all that hunting about for nurses'.[80]

Some five weeks after the birth of baby Claude, Anna Steele wrote independently to Parnell with a bulletin of her sister's health. Parnell was unsure how to respond and pressed Katharine for advice: 'Mrs S. has written me that she has "seen you recently", and that you "have not left your room", assuming that I know all about it. What am I to say to her?'[81] Katharine did not reply to this question for almost a week. She had taken the delivery hard, and had fresh worries that week concerning the baby's health (causing Parnell to write, 'Is it dangerous?'[82]). Finally, on 29 March, Parnell received his instructions and wrote back to assure Katharine: 'Shall write Mrs —— as you suggest, and say am sorry to hear you had not yet left your room, and that I had seen the event in the *Times* and hoped you would soon be quite well again.'[83] Parnell's request for guidance, and Katharine's advice of a guarded response to her sister's enquiry, are interesting for the light they shed on the so-called 'understanding' of July 1881 in which Anna's mediatory role was so significant. Parnell's discretion in dealing with Katharine's sister casts doubt upon the claim made to Harrison that Anna knew of the affair, and had indeed orchestrated an arrangement whereby her brother-in-law would turn a blind eye to it. One further crucial point is established in the letter referred to above. For Parnell continues, 'If my own can make an arrangement now for him [O'Shea] to keep away, I think she ought to do so. It will be too intolerable having him about always.' The next day, he repeats that she had best make 'some arrangement' with O'Shea.[84] In other words, Parnell demanded, now that he and Katharine had a child together, that 'an arrangement' with Captain O'Shea *should* be made, specifically *not* a 'new', secondary, arrangement, relating to an agreement concluded in July 1881.

Although it was clear to Parnell that the present situation could not continue once their child was born and he was released from prison, it is not at all clear how he envisaged their future life together. He does say, 'When I see Wifie again or am released, I can consider the situation,'[85] but the question remains: how was Katharine to arrange a complete separation from her husband when he had been led to believe that the new baby was his? When Katharine had first become pregnant, she and Parnell had, so she says, 'agreed that it would be safe to have the child christened as a

Catholic'.[86] That is to say that they had agreed to have the child baptised and registered as an O'Shea in order to pass the child off as O'Shea's. This was a curious decision in view of Parnell's insistence on addressing Katharine as his 'Wifie', and his wanting her to sign her initials as 'K.P.'. He seems not even to have considered that he should have any part in naming his child. A month and a day after the birth of his daughter, he thought to ask Katharine, 'What do you intend to call her?'[87] This enquiry came two days late. O'Shea had officially registered the birth of 'Claude O'Shea' on 14 March. It is surely very odd that Katharine had not informed Parnell of the choice of name. Odder still is the tentative suggestion made by Parnell a fortnight later, on 30 March, that 'Sophie' might 'make a nice second name'. It was the name of the sister who most resembled him, but, he added, 'possibly it might make suspicions'.[88] Possibly, although Parnell's sister Sophia or 'Sophy' had died in 1877.

Little Claude, wrote Katharine, 'rarely cried, but lay watching me with eyes thoughtful and searching beyond the possibility of her little life'.[89] She was a big baby, and apparently healthy (Katharine reported her to be 'strong and good-tempered'), but she began to have problems in her fifth week and grew more and more delicate. 'Give my best love and ever so many kisses to our little daughter,' wrote Parnell: 'I am very much troubled about her health, and hope it will not make her permanently delicate.'[90] But Katharine has described how, 'Slowly she faded from me . . . and my pain was the greater in that I feared her father would never see her now.'[91] The doctors told her that the child was dying and that there was nothing they could do for her. O'Shea asked his local Catholic priest Father Hart to conduct the baptism at the house, since by then Claude could not be moved, and Katharine made an altar of flowers in her drawing-room. And then came an act of fate. The 20-year-old son of Parnell's sister Delia died in Paris of typhoid fever. Parnell immediately applied to Forster for permission to attend the funeral and at 11.30 p.m. on Sunday 9 April word came through that he had been granted parole. The next morning he was on the mail train to London, and from there to Eltham.

# CHAPTER 5

## The Kilmainham Treaty

The Government's ready agreement to Parnell's request for parole in order to attend his nephew's funeral in Paris was a clear sign that they were in a mood to release the political prisoners before long. They would do so through the agency of O'Shea. In the coming weeks, O'Shea, as Parnell's self-appointed spokesman, came to the fore, and Katharine's emerging role as her lover's political confidante and secretary, for a time at least, was put to one side. So too is Katharine's side of the story. Her brief reunion with Parnell after their six-month separation, and the agony of watching their baby daughter slowly dying just when Parnell seemed about to be freed, goes largely unrecorded, save for the discreet references Katharine makes in her book to these intensely private scenes. Just two weeks earlier, as we have seen, Parnell and Katharine were anticipating an agreement with O'Shea whereby the two lovers would be able to live at Eltham undisturbed. The fact that her husband was now helping to negotiate what became known as the 'Kilmainham treaty', which involved not only Parnell's release from prison but a new phase of cooperation with the British Government, meant that the continuing ordeal of their domestic arrangements had to be borne a little while longer.

Parnell left Kilmainham at six o'clock on the morning of Monday 10 April and crossed over to England. Waiting for his connection at Chester Station, he was recognised by a reporter for *The Times*, but refused to be drawn into political discussion: 'He was travelling as hastily as possible to Paris via London' was all that he would say.[1] By the evening a vast crowd had assembled at Euston Station to meet the Irish Mail, where some of his MPs had got a carriage ready to drive Parnell straight to Charing Cross. Instead, Parnell was headed off at Willesden Junction by Justin McCarthy, Frank Hugh O'Donnell and Frank Byrne, who took him off to McCarthy's house, now in Jermyn Street. This much was known to the Government, but O'Shea, whom Parnell saw in London the following day, wrote to Gladstone with further details of the visit. He could assure the Prime Minister that at Jermyn Street Parnell conversed with his colleagues 'with great reticence', and left 'as early as possible'. Then, having missed the Paris Mail, Parnell decided to stay with O'Shea, 'as he was anxious to speak with me'.[2]

What emerges is that from Jermyn Street Parnell went straight to Katharine and arrived at Wonersh Lodge in the early hours of Tuesday morning. Not until Tuesday evening did he call on O'Shea, now living at 1 Albert Mansions, Victoria Street. From there he caught the night-train to Paris. Katharine says that she had known for some days that she would have the 'unspeakable comfort' that her lover would 'perhaps see his child while she lived'. At dawn on the morning of 11 April, 'when the air was fragrant with the sweet freshness of the spring flowers and the very breath of life was in the wind, Parnell came to me and I put his dying child into his arms'.[3] Claude Sophie would live for another ten days.

From Paris, Parnell managed to send private as well as formal letters to Katharine. Delia was 'very much cut up' by her son's death, he told her, but 'my coming has picked her up very much'.[4] Parnell was staying at the Grand Hotel even though his sister's house had been disinfected of typhoid fever, and he assured Katharine that he would take precautions, including a Turkish bath every day. He remained there a week, his departure delayed by a slight cold.

While Parnell was away, O'Shea made an extraordinary proposal to the Prime Minister, offering to mediate on Parnell's behalf, and warning Gladstone that, 'you must cease to ignore an important Irishman'. A whole paragraph of this letter is taken up with O'Shea's credentials. For all their differences in political matters, it was apparently to O'Shea that Parnell turned for counsel: 'He considers, I believe, that I am not without insight into Irish affairs.' He claimed that Parnell had even, eighteen months earlier, tried to persuade him to become the leader of the Irish party (a fact 'known only to two or three besides ourselves'[5]). Why O'Shea should make such an absurd claim is difficult to comprehend, given the strongly divergent opinion and the powerful personalities within the party.

Whether or not Gladstone credited O'Shea's self-advertisement, he seems to have accepted unquestioningly what he said about his moderating influence over Parnell: 'no apology can be required either for the length or for the freedom of your letter', wrote Gladstone in reply. Nothing, he said, would 'prevent the Government from treading whatever path may most safely and shortly lead to the pacification of Ireland'.[6] As R. Barry O'Brien remarked, the incidence of murders and crimes involving firearms had grown alarmingly: the increasingly lawless country was 'drifting out of [Parnell's] hands', and his release from Kilmainham was 'a matter of paramount importance' for both Parnell and Gladstone.[7] Each was asking himself how to bring about a *modus vivendi* with the other. O'Shea, given warm encouragement by Gladstone (and with the apparent agreement of Parnell), stepped forward at precisely the right moment.

Parnell had told O'Shea to expect him at the end of the week, yet he told Katharine that he would be with her as early as Tuesday 18 April. He was able to spend Wednesday and Thursday alone with Katharine and their dying child. Only then did he telegraph O'Shea, to say that he was at Eltham and asking him to come down in order to continue their political discussions. O'Shea was later to admit that he knew Parnell had returned from Paris earlier than expected, but gave contradictory evidence as to whether or not Parnell was staying at Eltham at the time.[8] Of course, beside the fact that Parnell may have deceived O'Shea for a few days as to his whereabouts, there is also the question of why the terms of Parnell's parole were apparently so relaxed as to allow him to spend several days in London before returning to Dublin on the evening of Monday 24 April. In his telegram to Forster requesting permission to attend his nephew's funeral, Parnell had stated, 'Will undertake not to take part in any political matters during absence.'[9] Yet, after the overtures to the Government made by O'Shea, Joseph Chamberlain (who, as President of the Board of Trade, had no specific responsibility for these matters but who had been approached by O'Shea as a radical voice in the Cabinet) had suggested to Gladstone the political benefits of extending the parole. Parnell's prolonged stay in England was given official sanction: 'he was away from prison', recalled Sir Charles Dilke, 'at Mr Gladstone's wish, unnecessarily long, and staying in London with Captain and Mrs O'Shea'.[10] At the time, Gladstone's secretary noted approvingly in his diary that 'Parnell seems to be scrupulously anxious not to contravene in the smallest way the conditions of his parole. Among the few friends he saw while passing through was O'Shea [who] makes himself out to be Parnell's special confidant.'[11] Of Parnell's private visits to Katharine, either side of his week in Paris, the Government apparently knew nothing.

O'Shea did not go down to Eltham until the evening of Friday 21 April, where, after dinner, he and Parnell withdrew to the drawing-room to discuss in detail the terms of the proposal Parnell intended to offer the Government in order to lift Ireland out of the present state of crisis. Katharine was invited to stay – 'Willie wanted me to join them' – but she deliberately excused herself from discussion of the treaty, saying that 'I would not leave my baby'.[12] She herself says that, although she had not previously 'ventured to influence Parnell in any way politically', during the two or three days she had alone with him that week, she 'threw the whole strength of my influence on the side of the treaty of conciliation', urging 'the greater good for Ireland' that was likely to come from his making immediate peace: it was 'my great fear for him', she believed, which made him sign the Kilmainham treaty.[13] Frank Hugh O'Donnell goes so far as to say that it was Katharine alone who 'negotiated the Kilmainham treaty between the prisoner and the Premier', an idea which has persisted.[14] The notion that Katharine had any material influence upon the actual terms of the treaty while nursing her dying 9-week-old baby is surely doubtful. So too is the idea that her husband really made a significant contribution to them. Tim Healy would later express his disgust at the fact that the Kilmainham treaty was arranged at Eltham,[15] yet it is likely that the terms of the document Parnell and O'Shea discussed that night had already been determined upon by Parnell while he was in Kilmainham, and that the invitation to O'Shea to collaborate on the treaty served to prolong Parnell's presence at Eltham. No doubt he did ask O'Shea for his thoughts on this and that point. O'Shea's conviction that he exerted a great influence upon Parnell must have had some origin.

'When daylight came', Katharine wrote, 'and they went to lie down for a few hours' rest before Parnell left for Ireland, my little one died as my lover stole in to kiss us both and say good-bye'.[16] It is a touching account in its spareness of detail. Yet it falters on two points: Claude Sophie did not die in the daylight hours of 22 April (her death was certified by the local doctor as taking place on 21 April), and Parnell did not catch the early morning boat-train to Ireland but stayed on at Wonersh Lodge. He left London on the Sunday evening, arriving back at Kilmainham on Monday 24 April. It may be that in recalling her distress at this period Katharine misremembered certain details. As one commentator has observed, this was a 'piercing hour for a man and a woman who had to mask what they felt except when alone with each other'.[17] Quite possibly, too, the pathos of her account enabled her to gloss over the difficulties of her relationship with the two men.

Presumably, first thing on the morning of Saturday 22 April, O'Shea summoned Dr Rickett to the house to confirm the cause of death, which was obstructive jaundice. He wired *The Times* to put in an announcement of the death of Claude O'Shea in Monday's edition of the paper, and may also have called on Father Hart to arrange a date for the funeral. Yet during the ensuing week he was too taken up with political events to register the death of the baby daughter he believed to be his own. It was left to the hired nurse to do so.

At the Cabinet meeting held on the Saturday, Chamberlain was given 'full leave to enter into negotiations with Parnell through O'Shea'. These negotiations were to be 'disavowed if he failed'.[18] Chamberlain invited O'Shea to his house at Prince's Gate that evening and heard that Parnell was then at Eltham. O'Shea had left his guest and his grieving wife alone together (he referred at the time to the 'wretched state of the house'[19]), and on the Sunday morning he sent a message to Eltham asking Parnell to meet him at Albert Mansions before five o'clock that afternoon, so as to discuss Chamberlain's view of his proposals. However, having given O'Shea every belief in his own significance, Parnell then cut him, deliberately avoiding him before departing for Dublin. Instead, he kept an appointment with Justin McCarthy, discussed with him the precise terms of the 'treaty' he proposed to put before the Government, and then, ignoring O'Shea's request, he appears to have taken a cab back to Eltham to make his farewells to Katharine before leaving for Euston. He clearly had a political preference for working through McCarthy as well as the strongest personal reasons, at such a time, for keeping away from O'Shea, who hung on at Victoria Street until eight o'clock, beside himself to have missed Parnell.[20]

Thus, O'Shea was not, as he believed, the sole negotiator. No doubt it was the sheer awkwardness of the situation as well as, perhaps, a feeling that he could not wholly trust O'Shea that led Parnell also to confide in McCarthy. To Davitt, O'Shea was 'more of an emissary of the Government than a Home-Rule member', although both men, 'who were in no sense extreme', would have been acceptable to the Government as intermediaries.[21] Parnell, no doubt, would rather have negotiated through McCarthy, a man unambiguously associated with the Nationalist cause, even though the Government had so relaxed the terms of his parole in order specifically that he have 'ample opportunity'[22] to confer with O'Shea. It was the unresolved nature of his relationship with Katharine at this time that forced him to accommodate her husband's self-interested manoeuvring.

On 25 April, back in Kilmainham, Parnell sent Justin McCarthy 'a letter embodying our conversation' which McCarthy was authorised to show to Chamberlain: 'Do not let it out of your hands,' he was warned.[23] In this letter, Parnell expressed his concern that the Government should act on the question of rent arrears for tenant farmers and provide measures for the greater protection of lease-holders. In return – the precise terms of the bargain could not be more explicit – the Irish party would withdraw the No Rent Manifesto, and 'put a stop to the outrages which are unhappily so prevalent', to ensure that the Government was in a position to 'allow the Coercion Act to lapse'.[24] This was the substance of the 'Kilmainham treaty'. Chamberlain responded eagerly to McCarthy's message: 'I only wish it could be published, for the knowledge that the question still under discussion will be treated *in this conciliatory spirit* would have a great effect on public opinion.'[25]

Yet O'Shea was not to be denied his part in these proceedings. From London on Monday 24 April, he wrote two letters to Parnell, one in code, the first explaining that the reason he had wished '*most particularly*'[26] to see Parnell on Sunday was to request from him a letter of recommendation (for Chamberlain to put before the next Cabinet meeting), saying that he was pleased to have been able to discuss the matter fully with O'Shea, 'and that I have your confidence'. Unaware that Parnell had now determined to communicate with Chamberlain through McCarthy, O'Shea announced, 'I shall today ask for an unopened correspondence between us for a week.'[27]

The Cabinet met on Tuesday 25 April, the day of Claude Sophie's funeral: 'My dear Sir', O'Shea reminded Chamberlain, 'My child is to be buried at Chislehurst this afternoon and I do not intend to return to town unless you want to see me. In this case telegraph to Eltham.'[28] At Eltham, Katharine received words of consolation from Parnell: 'I have been thinking all day of how desolate and lonely my Queenie must be in her sorrow. It is too terrible to think that on this the saddest day of all others – and, let us hope, the saddest that we *both* shall ever see again – my Wifie should have nobody with her.'[29]

The phrase used here by Parnell, that Katharine had 'nobody with her', no doubt alludes primarily to his own absence from their baby daughter's funeral. But it is significant that he makes no reference to Katharine's sisters supporting her at this most difficult time. One would have expected Anna, at least, who after all lived in London, to have called at Eltham to see Katharine's baby and then to have stayed with her sister after Claude's death, yet Katharine makes no mention of her. The only letter of condolence she prints is that from her sister-in-law, Mary O'Shea, who wrote from Paris on 21 May to express her own and her mother's sympathies and good wishes for Katharine's recovery. In passing, Mary mentions that they had heard from Lady O'Donnell, a great friend of O'Shea's, who described to them her own recent visit to Eltham: 'She loved your dear little Claude, and shares your grief at losing her.'[30] Katharine's motive for reprinting Mary O'Shea's long letter was to prove that her husband's family were thoroughly convinced of the baby's paternity. The apparent lack of sympathy from her own family suggests that her brothers and sisters may have had reservations about Katharine's unexpectedly giving birth to a child eight years after the birth of Carmen and Katharine's effective separation from her husband.

At all events, Parnell was confident, this time with good grounds, that he would soon be released, and that they would not be apart for much longer. Katharine herself was fully aware that, in his negotiations with the Government, Parnell's intended intermediary was Justin McCarthy, and not her husband. Parnell sent her O'Shea's coded letter of the previous day, which stated his intention of visiting Parnell at Kilmainham, asking, 'What do you think I had best say?': 'I told my friend in Jermyn Street [i.e. McCarthy] what steps to take, so that the matter referred to in enclosed will probably go on all right without, or with, the further participation of the writer.'[31] Yet O'Shea persisted. On 28 April he applied to Forster for permission to visit Parnell in prison, in spite of the fact that Parnell had advised him particularly *not* to come. Parnell eventually replied to O'Shea on 27 April, his chief advice being 'to wait and see what proposals are made, as any appearance of anxiety on your part might be injurious'. Very specifically, O'Shea was warned, 'If you come to Ireland, I think you had best not see me.'[32]

It is possible that Parnell's letter was unduly delayed, but one suspects that, by the time it reached Albert Mansions, O'Shea had already got Forster's permission to visit Kilmainham, and pretended not to have received it. Harrison argues very persuasively that it was at Chamberlain's prodding that O'Shea's visit went ahead, because Chamberlain would have wanted to put before the Cabinet a treaty secured by his own messenger, O'Shea, rather than by McCarthy, who was Parnell's.[33] Yet O'Shea would have needed little prodding. He arrived in Dublin on the morning of Saturday 29 April, and was with Parnell from eleven o'clock until five in the afternoon.

As soon as O'Shea left Kilmainham, Parnell sat down to write to Katharine. After letting her know that that day he had received 'two letters from my own lovie', he explained that he had been completely taken aback by O'Shea's visit: 'He came over to see me, so I thought it best to give him a letter, as he would have been dreadfully mortified if he had had nothing to show.'[34] In order to obscure the fact that the Cabinet had sent O'Shea to Dublin 'to get the letter . . . from him',[35] which would have been an embarrassment had it got out (and did indeed prove so), Parnell backdated the letter he gave O'Shea to the previous day, 28 April 1882, and addressed him as if continuing discussions the two had already had at Wonersh Lodge: 'I was very sorry that you had left Albert Mansions before I reached London from Eltham . . .'.[36]

O'Shea remained unaware of the letter authorising McCarthy to negotiate with Chamberlain. One point alone distinguished the Kilmainham treaty as described in these two letters:[37] O'Shea's contained an unequivocal assurance from Parnell that he would in future cooperate fully with the Government. It would be this final paragraph which would prove so contentious, to Liberals and Irish Nationalists alike.

The letter O'Shea brought back from Kilmainham proposed this wholly new relationship between the two parties, but for O'Shea the wider political considerations were subordinate to his own importance in negotiating Parnell's freedom, despite the fact that Parnell had given him very specific instructions: 'Never mind the suspects [i.e. himself and his fellow detainees] . . . Try and get the question of arrears satisfactorily adjusted . . . The great object to be obtained is to stay evictions by an Arrears Bill.'[38] Forever after he would speak of his having secured the release of the Irish leader and the other Nationalist prisoners as if that were Parnell's sole objective. He felt that Parnell should regard Chamberlain as his 'benefactor'![39]

Chamberlain's view of O'Shea's part in these proceedings was merely as a messenger: 'He took no initiative. He simply took what I said to Parnell, and brought back what Parnell said to me.'[40] O'Shea saw things rather differently and, perhaps carried away by his sense of his own importance, he then side-stepped Chamberlain and, first thing on the morning of Sunday 30 April, made straight for Forster, the Chief Secretary for Ireland, at his house in Eccleston Square. This was a rather strange move to make. Forster was known to be hostile to the Irish party and was not at all a political ally of Chamberlain. By eleven o'clock that morning he had dictated to his wife a comprehensive summary of his interview with O'Shea which he sent directly to Gladstone, enclosing, in Parnell's hand, proposals for the Kilmainham treaty. Forster admitted his bewilderment at O'Shea's way of doing business. When he suggested disappointment that certain of Parnell's assurances to the Government were not worded more explicitly, O'Shea twice volunteered to 'supplement' phrases used by Parnell. Further, and more damagingly, when Forster appeared sceptical of Parnell's particular undertaking that, in return for specific legislative measures, he would exert himself to stop 'outrages and intimidation of all kinds', O'Shea took it upon himself to spell out exactly what the Irish leader had in mind: '"what is obtained is" – and here he used *the* most remarkable words – "that the conspiracy which has been used to get up boycotting and outrages, will now be used to put them down"'.[41]

Gladstone interpreted Parnell's letter very differently, viewing the whole as sagacious and carefully worded. As for the concluding paragraph, in which Parnell hoped 'to co-operate cordially for the future with the Liberal Party in forwarding Liberal principles',[42] Gladstone regarded this an 'an *hors d'oeuvre* which we had no right to expect', and added: 'I cannot help feeling indebted to O'Shea.'[43] As Michael Davitt observed, Gladstone's reaction 'sealed and sanctioned the Kilmainham treaty'.[44] The next day, 1 May, Gladstone called a Cabinet meeting at which expiration of the Coercion Act and the immediate release of Parnell, O'Kelly and Dillon were discussed. The day after, Gladstone instructed Lord Cowper to authorise the release of the prisoners, to which the Lord-Lieutenant answered with his resignation. Forster soon followed suit.

Thus, on the evening of Tuesday 2 May, exactly one week after the funeral of Claude Sophie, Parnell was released from Kilmainham Gaol. Whether or not Parnell himself understood that the release of the prisoners would so quickly follow O'Shea's delivery to Forster of the Kilmainham proposals, Katharine, ironically, was given up-to-the-minute information by her husband. On the Monday O'Shea wrote his wife a long letter telling her to expect Gladstone's announcement of the release of Parnell, O'Kelly and Dillon at 9 p.m. on Tuesday 2 May, and warning her that Forster ('a duffer', in O'Shea's estimation) would be required to answer questions about the nature of the negotiations that had taken place with the prisoners. O'Shea had had two meetings with Chamberlain that day and had been told 'that if a row occurred and an explanation was called for we were agreed that no negotiations had taken place between us, but only conversations'.[45]

It is impossible to deduce the state of the O'Shea marriage from this letter. O'Shea continues to use their familiar nicknames, 'Dick' and 'Boysie', and he lets Katharine know that he intends to stay in town that night in case Chamberlain needs to say anything more to him: 'I will try to run down to Eltham if possible in the afternoon, unless I hear you are taking the Chicks anywhere.' The letter gives every appearance of theirs being a relaxed intimacy, with Katharine both mother of his 'Chicks' and her husband's political confidante. Yet when Parnell arrived back in England, he was able to go straight to Katharine at Eltham, and slept there for four consecutive nights, apparently without any fear of disturbance.

After resting briefly at Avondale, Parnell arrived in London in time to hear Forster's resignation speech in the House on the night of Thursday 4 May. Indeed, just as Forster was referring to the imprisonment of the 'member for the city of Cork', Parnell walked in to tremendous applause.[46]

O'Shea, of course, regarded this as *his* hour of triumph and had continued to bombard the Prime Minister with confidences. On 3 May ('astonished at my audacity, but having insight into so many details of Irish affairs, political and personal'[47]), he had advised Gladstone to appoint Chamberlain as Forster's replacement, but had to change tack smartly the next day when Gladstone informed him of his choice of Sir Frederick Cavendish as the new Chief Secretary. O'Shea's sense of his own importance to the process was quite unshakeable: 'I am anxious, and I think with a fair view to usefulness, to make the better acquaintance of Lord Frederick Cavendish' was his reply![48]

On the night of his reappearance in the House, before he took a cab down to Eltham, Parnell went back with O'Shea to Albert Mansions, where he asked him to bear a further message to the Government, requesting that extremists like Patrick Sheridan and Patrick Egan be permitted to return to Ireland without the threat of arrest, in order that he could '*actively employ them in the restoration of obedience to the law*'.[49] Parnell presumably thought that this was a job he could entrust to O'Shea, who, however, not only made a great deal more of the situation than was necessary, but, as in his dealings with Forster, continued to implicate Parnell in the coordination of extremist activity in Ireland. The next day, at a private interview with the Prime Minister, he left no doubt in Gladstone's mind that Parnell 'had used lawlessness for his [own] ends': 'nothing can be clearer' was Gladstone's assessment of the interview to Cowper's successor, Lord Spencer.[50] O'Shea seems to have been acting in such a way, perhaps mischievously, but also to perpetuate his own key role as the friend of the Government who would ensure that Parnell honoured the precise terms of the Kilmainham treaty.

Meanwhile, O'Shea had remained in London, and Katharine and Parnell were able to adjust themselves to the resumption of their relationship in the privacy of Eltham. Apart from the few brief days in April, they had been separated under the most trying circumstances for more than six months. Any peaceful respite that they enjoyed was short-lived. On Saturday 6 May Parnell left her briefly in order to take the train down to Weymouth to accompany Michael Davitt back to London. Davitt, whose release from Portland Prison was announced on 2 May, had been confined for the past fifteen months, and Parnell needed to explain a great deal to him: 'Mr Parnell was in a most optimistic mood,' assuring Davitt that they were 'on the eve of something like Home Rule', but he put off proper discussions until the next day.[51] On the train back to London, Parnell light-heartedly suggested that if he ever became Prime Minister of Ireland he would appoint Davitt 'Director of Irish Prisons'.[52] Yet, according to Davitt, he did not say a word about the Kilmainham treaty and the fact that he had committed the Irish party to collaboration with the Liberals.[53]

A 'throng' of friends met them at Waterloo Station, and from there they drove straight to the Westminster Palace Hotel, '"the Home-Rule Parliament of the immediate future" being toasted and drank to in the true spirit of Celtic buoyancy'.[54] After a couple of hours the party broke up, Parnell promising to return in the morning for private political discussion with Davitt. Scarcely had Davitt sat down when a journalist ran into the room and held out a telegram announcing that, in Dublin that evening, Sir Frederick Cavendish and his Under-Secretary Mr Burke had been assassinated with knives.

On the evening of Saturday 6 May, the new Chief Secretary for Ireland, Lord Frederick Cavendish, was strolling through Dublin's Phoenix Park in the company of his Under-Secretary, Thomas Burke, when they were set upon by a group of four or five darkly dressed young men. To a Lieutenant of the Royal Dragoons, out exercising his dogs a few hundred yards away, it appeared to be a bit of drunken horseplay: 'I thought they were larking about,' he would tell reporters. He could see that two men had fallen to the ground while the others jumped into a cab that had been standing by: 'I was watching the men on the ground, and wondering why they did not get up.' To the coroner, speaking at the inquest two days later, 'the attackers could scarcely be called human beings, but demons'.[55] Cavendish and Burke were attacked with surgical knives between 9 and 12 inches in length: Burke suffered two deep wounds in his neck, one reaching towards his spine, and several more across his chest and shoulder-blade, one of these fatally piercing his right lung, from which 'there was a copious haemorrhage into the mouth'. Cavendish had been cut across his arm with such force that the bone was fractured, and other bones were penetrated in wounds to his neck, shoulders, chest and back; death was caused by a deep wound to the armpit – he had presumably raised his arm to ward off his attackers. By the time onlookers had rushed to the scene, both men were dead. Their assailants were members of the Invincibles, a secret society who, in the words of Parnell, speaking in the Commons on Monday 8 May, 'had devised that crime and carried it out as the deadliest blow in their power against his hopes and the new course which the Government had resolved upon'.[56]

The next morning, knowing nothing as yet of the appalling event of the previous evening, Katharine drove with Parnell to Blackheath Station on his way to meet Davitt and Dillon at the Westminster Palace Hotel. As they said goodbye, Katharine asked him to get her the *Sunday Observer* while she stayed in the carriage. From where she sat, she could see Parnell through the door of the station pick up a paper, half turn to smile at her, and then glance at the front page. He was looking for reports of Davitt's release:

> He had now come to the top of the steps and, as he suddenly stopped, I noticed a curious rigidity about his arms – raised in holding the newspaper open. He stood so absolutely still that I was suddenly frightened, horridly, sickeningly afraid – of I knew not what, and, leaning forward, called out, 'King, what is it?' Then he came down the steps to me and, pointing to the headline, said, 'Look!' And I read, 'Murder of Lord Frederick Cavendish and Mr Burke'.[57]

As she got out of the cab, Katharine heard the London train coming into Blackheath, and ushered him back into the station, urging him, 'Quick, you must catch this train. See Davitt and the others . . . you *must* meet them all at once.' Parnell turned away from her saying that he would resign, 'and I answered him as I ran beside him to the platform, "No, you are not a coward."'[58]

Once the train had left, no doubt aware that it would be impolitic to try to contact Parnell herself, she wired a telegram to O'Shea to bring Parnell to dinner at Eltham if at all possible, 'and spent one of the most terrible days of my life considering the effect this awful crime would probably have upon my lover's career'.[59] Her isolation at Eltham must have been terrible. The father of her dead child had been restored to her for just three nights, and Katharine would have been afraid that he was about to be arrested a second time under the existing Coercion Act. Rather than be prevented from seeing him at all, she was arranging for Parnell to spend one more night at Eltham, even if it had to be as the guest of her husband.

At the Westminster Palace Hotel, Davitt recorded how Parnell 'flung himself into a chair in my room and declared he would leave public life. "How can I," he said, "carry on an agitation if I am stabbed in the back in this way?" He was wild. Talk of the calm and callous Parnell. There was not much calmness or callousness about him that morning.'[60] By the time Davitt had begun to draft a manifesto condemning the murders, Healy, Biggar, John Barry and Arthur O'Connor all came rushing into the room, and 'in silence we waited until it was revised by Parnell'.[61] When they had all signed the statement, Barry suggested to Davitt that he come back to the lodgings he shared with Healy, 'lest reprisals might be attempted'.[62]

At some point in the morning Parnell sought out O'Shea at Albert Mansions and gave him the responsibility of delivering an offer of resignation to Gladstone's secretary, Sir Edward Hamilton. He appears to have dictated the note there and then. No doubt Parnell entrusted O'Shea with this message because he was now an established intermediary amenable to the Government. The letter, in O'Shea's hand, which begins abruptly without preliminaries, states simply and clearly Parnell's position: 'I am authorised by Mr Parnell to state that if Mr Gladstone considers it necessary for the maintenance of his (Mr Gladstone's) position and for carrying out his views, that Mr Parnell should resign his seat, Mr Parnell is prepared to do so immediately.'[63] It was Gladstone's recollection that he received Parnell's message through O'Shea at Downing Street, 'while I was at lunch':

> I was much troubled by it. He wrote evidently under strong emotions. He did not ask me whether I would advise him to retire from public life or not. That was not how he put it. He asked me rather what effect I thought the murder would have on English public opinion in relation to his leadership of the Irish party . . . I thought his conduct in the whole matter very praiseworthy.

Gladstone, 'deeply sensible of the honourable motives by which it has been prompted', refused the offer.[64]

That Sunday, the Prime Minister received two further communications from O'Shea. The first was to inform Gladstone of the manifesto drawn up by Davitt that morning ('in somewhat highflown language', as O'Shea put it), and signed by Parnell. O'Shea was in fact less concerned with the official response of the Nationalist Party than to remind Gladstone of his personal efforts, as an 'Irish Liberal'. Continuing to represent himself as Parnell's chief adviser, he stated that 'at his request' Parnell was to wire the mayors of Dublin, Cork, Limerick and Waterford, calling on them to summon special meetings of their corporations to condemn the murders. His letter concludes with a rather presumptuous expression of sympathy: 'Do not consider my tender of sympathy a mere form,' he wrote to Gladstone. 'I feel the blow *as if it were a family misfortune.*'[65] Not content with this, O'Shea addressed yet another note to Downing Street to inform the Prime Minister that, 'Since writing, an unlimited order has been telegraphed to print and post the Manifesto all over Ireland.'[66] It hardly seems likely that Parnell would have wanted him to bother Gladstone with these details. O'Shea's concern was rather to give an impression of his own centrality to the decisions being made.

Writing to Gladstone was not O'Shea's only independent move of the day. That afternoon he received a message asking him to call on the Home Secretary, Lord Harcourt, whose object was enquire whether either Parnell or O'Shea wished to be given police protection. O'Shea appears to have responded eagerly, requesting protection for Parnell at his lodgings, and for himself at 1 Albert Mansions and at Wonersh Lodge ('I was promised that I should be looked after'[67]). Harcourt was delighted to hear that Parnell was 'now suffering some of the tortures he had inflicted on others', and he allowed the story to be leaked to the press.[68]

It is fairly certain that Parnell would never have authorised O'Shea to make such a request. Katharine's own view was that the Government were intent on forcing police protection on Parnell, in order to 'weaken the trust of the Irish in him', which was of course a matter of great concern to Parnell. It would also enable them to keep him under observation, and to ascertain 'the extent of his influence over the Invincibles'.[69] Katharine herself was extremely anxious for her lover's safety in the coming months, and was tempted to ask for such protection for him, but knew that he 'would have died rather than ask for himself'.[70] The way Parnell did respond to the many threatening letters he received at this time (although some of them were held back from him by Katharine) was to carry a revolver, and to insist that Katharine also carry one when they drove back to Eltham late at night.[71] We also have the testimony of Justin McCarthy, whose clear recollection of Sunday 7 May 1882 is that, despite Parnell's having received sympathetic warnings from both Chamberlain and Dilke to take a cab in order to avoid being seen in London, he 'said rather sharply that he would do nothing of the kind . . . he intended to walk in the open streets like anyone else'.[72]

The most intriguing point about this whole episode is O'Shea's request for a police presence at Eltham, which has been taken to indicate both that he was in effect condoning Parnell's continued presence there as his wife's lover, and the opposite: that if he knew he was a cuckold he wouldn't have advertised the fact.[73] The most likely explanation is that he had again got carried away with his own political significance. On the day after the Phoenix Park murders, he was closer to real political power than he had been, even in helping to secure the Kilmainham treaty. He was at the heart of things: employed to carry Parnell's letter of resignation to Downing Street; communicating independently with Gladstone, and in doing so, representing himself as influencing the movements of his political leader; appearing, too, to be influential in discussions with the people who mattered, particularly in his easy access to Joseph Chamberlain, who could be expected to replace Cavendish. In asking for police protection for himself and for Parnell, he was emphasising to the Government that it was under *his* influence that Parnell would continue to cooperate. O'Shea had more cause to ask for police protection at 1 Albert Mansions, fully aware that he might be vulnerable for his part in negotiating a deal which was regarded by party members like Healy, let alone extremist groups like the Invincibles, as 'surrender'.[74]

After making his request for police protection, O'Shea met up again with Parnell and together they made their way to Eltham. Katharine found them 'both very gloomy and depressed'.[75] Parnell was obliged to greet her as if this was the first occasion on which he had seen her since his release, and she, apparently, to refer to him as 'Mr Parnell'. He sat at the dinner table, 'gazing stonily before him, only glancing across at Willie with the stormy flare in his eyes when the latter – who was really sorry for Parnell, as well as shocked at the murders – said something that jarred upon him'.[76] Judging from her account of the evening, Parnell stayed silent while O'Shea, excited by the day's events, became garrulous, telling his wife all that he had seen and heard, including Parnell's continued threats to retire from public life.[77] He urged her to persuade him not to do so, saying that Parnell 'must show that it simply does not touch him politically in any way'. Katharine agreed that it would be 'throwing the whole country over'.[78]

It was a highly charged evening, as Katharine describes in detail. As the parlour-maid Mary came in with coffee, an engraving of the newly elected House of Commons of 1880, hanging on the wall behind Parnell, 'fell to the floor with a crash that, in the state of nervous tension we were all in, brought us to our feet in alarm':

> Willie's chair overturned as he jumped up; but Parnell's was steady, held in a grip that showed his knuckles white as he held it slightly raised off the floor, while he stood, half turned, staring at the picture as it lay among the splintered glass.
> Willie laughed, and coming to help the parlourmaid to pick up the picture, exclaimed: 'There goes Home Rule, Parnell!'

For the superstitious Parnell, 'It was an omen, I think, darling, but for whom? Willie or me?'[79]

At a quarter past four on the afternoon of Monday 8 May, Gladstone rose before the assembled House and promised a new measure on the question of arrears, thus honouring the terms of the Kilmainham treaty. However, he also announced, 'We intend to ask the House on Thursday to permit us to introduce a measure relating to the repression of crime in Ireland.'[80] Parnell then rose to express his sympathies for the deaths of Lord Frederick Cavendish and Thomas Burke. According to Tim Healy, 'something like a groan arose from a small section, but the vast body of the House angrily suppressed it and listened to him with respect'.[81] After further speeches, the House adjourned at 4.40 p.m. 'We have got to begin all over again,' Parnell remarked to William O'Brien.[82]

Yet there was more bad news to follow. The following morning, in the same edition of *The Times* which reported his own carefully phrased condemnation of the murders and the full ghastly details of the coroner's inquest in Dublin, there appeared a letter to the editor from his sister, Anna Parnell, in which she made a forthright defence of acts of terrorism. She informed *The Times* that on Friday 5 May, the day Lord Spencer was sworn in as the new Lord-Lieutenant of Ireland, a group of children were shot down in Ballina 'like mad dogs'. 'Mr Forster butchered men and women,' she remarked; 'for Lord Spencer has been reserved the distinction of butchering children'.[83] There was no parallel in history for the 'outrages on humanity' she had witnessed in Ireland. In Clare, she reported, evicted families were 'living in lanes and ditches'; in Limerick, as many as 600 people were 'liable to death by cold, hardship, and exposure, it being illegal to help them'. (Weeks earlier, Special Magistrate Major Clifford Lloyd had outlawed the erection of temporary housing for evicted tenants by the Ladies' Land League.)[84] Anna concluded that the English should not be 'surprised that the assassin's arm is not idle'.[85]

Parnell saw Anna's letter for what it was: an 'infamous' attempt to thwart 'her brother's endeavours' to come to an understanding with the British Government.[86] Later that day, Parnell spoke to O'Shea of his disgust with his sister's letter, which prompted yet a further O'Shea communication to Downing Street: 'He would prefer giving in, but he feels that it is his duty to destroy the power of mischief . . . of Miss A. Parnell. He is most indignant at what he himself terms her atrocious letter.'[87]

When the House reconvened on 11 May, Sir William Harcourt introduced the new Crimes Bill – in fact, reintroducing Coercion under another name – which sanctioned trials without jury and gave the Executive powers 'to summon witnesses and to carry on inquiries in secret'.[88] The Irish party mounted vociferous opposition to the bill, and O'Shea privately apologised to Gladstone for Tim Healy's 'outrageous speech', in which he spoke of Parnell making 'compacts or compromises' behind his party's back.[89] Having apologised on Parnell's behalf for the conduct of Anna Parnell and Tim Healy, O'Shea obtruded once more with a letter informing the Prime Minister that, 'My object now is to induce Mr Parnell to retire from interference [with the bill] for the present.' A day later, he could offer assurances that the bill was 'safe from Obstruction', and further, that he had got Parnell 'to listen to my suggestions as to some rational amendments which I believe the government would be inclined to consider'.[90]

O'Shea's privileged position as the recognised intermediary between Parnell and the Government was about to suffer a blow. Notice had been given that on Monday 15 May, Charles Lewis MP intended to put a question to the Government 'as to documentary evidence connected with the release of Mr Parnell'.[91] That weekend, Parnell and O'Shea had both been at Eltham in order to discuss what their response would be. Katharine says that at dinner her husband revealed that Gladstone had asked him to read 'a certain letter' to the House, but Parnell felt that it would be better that he himself read out the letter containing the Kilmainham treaty.[92] It would appear that between them they decided to make available to Parliament a version of the treaty in which the final paragraph was suppressed. This was the paragraph in which Parnell had promised to 'co-operate cordially for the future with the Liberal Party in forwarding Liberal principles'. Whether or not Gladstone sanctioned the doctoring of the treaty we do not know.

Before he set off for the Commons on the Monday, O'Shea wrote a hasty note to Charles Lewis, begging him not to put his question, but to no effect. That evening, Lewis proceeded to ask whether documentary evidence was now available 'of the intentions of the recently-imprisoned members of the House with reference to their conduct, if released',[93] and in response Parnell read out O'Shea's copy of the treaty. The description of what follows is Healy's:

> Near by sat Forster, the dismissed Chief Secretary, his furrowed brow and gleaming eyes portending trouble. As Parnell ended Forster, towering to his feet, shrieked, 'That's not the letter!' . . . The House of Commons has known some dramatic moments, but in my thirty-eight years there I never felt such emotion as at that interruption. Parnell paled [and] stammered that it was possible a paragraph had been omitted.[94]

Forster now thrust the original letter towards O'Shea who, 'after some hesitation . . . read it through, paragraph by paragraph'.[95]

No section of the House was more shocked than the Irish party at hearing the exact terms of the treaty, and in particular the final paragraph:

'We felt that the Chief had lowered the flag', wrote Healy, 'and had tried to deceive alike his countrymen and the British'.[96] The blunder meant that Parnell and Gladstone were forced to deny that there existed any 'treaty' between their two parties. Parnell said only that the document produced was a private letter from himself to O'Shea which the Captain had been permitted to show to one other person. It was O'Shea who had decided to show it to Forster, although he did not blame him for doing so. Gladstone, on his part, felt compelled a second time to state: 'I did say, and I repeat now, that there was not the slightest understanding of any kind. (Hear, hear.) The hon. gentleman the member for the City of Cork asked nothing from us, and on our side we asked nothing from him.'[97]

Then, getting on for one o'clock in the morning, O'Shea rose from the Government benches to have his say. He 'was loth to intrude upon the House at that hour, but he felt that he would be doing a grave injustice to the hon. member for Cork unless he made an explanation'.[98] Healy, who was seated next to Parnell, records that he 'muttered to me as he began, "This d—— fellow will make a mess of it as usual!"'[99] O'Shea proceeded to give a personal history of his role as intermediary, of his dealings with Gladstone and Chamberlain, and of the 'many conversations' he claimed to have had with Forster. Regarding the suppression of the final paragraph of the Kilmainham agreement, it was his explanation that the precise phrasing was not liked by Forster, and so, he had taken it upon himself to expunge the passage, 'in order that no member of the Cabinet should suppose that there was any bid for a release' on the part of Parnell.[100] He took all blame upon himself alone, and hoped that the House 'would acquit the hon. member for Cork of any idea of bargaining for his liberty'.[101] Enjoying his own performance, O'Shea then had the audacity to reprimand Forster for wasting the time of the House, saying that he, personally, had 'often been baited very cruelly' by the former Chief Secretary, 'But now the bear was loose. (Cheers and laughter.)'[102]

Forster's reply was devastating as he proceeded to read aloud from the transcription of his interview with O'Shea at his house on 30 April, during which the Captain had linked Parnell to 'the *conspiracy* which has been used to get up boycotting and outrages . . . (Opposition cheers.)'. O'Shea protested that he had said no such thing, but the damage was done. Forster expressed his disgust with the treaty, as he insisted upon calling it, saying that he had come away from the interview with O'Shea regretting that he had had anything to do with the negotiation and wanting 'nothing more to do with it (Cheers from the Opposition.)'.[103]

Clearly O'Shea had blundered in giving the letter containing the treaty to Forster rather than Chamberlain, and in making confidential assurances to Forster which linked Parnell to acts of terrorism. It must be conceded, too, that it was a serious misjudgement by Parnell to make the written promise of collaboration with the Liberals. Such revelations showed that both he and the Government had concealed, from their supporters and enemies alike, the fact that there was a treaty, or an understanding of some kind.

Rather than being crushed by his own blunders, O'Shea actually seems to have grown in political confidence during the weeks and months immediately after the release of the prisoners from Kilmainham, as he established publicly his responsibility for securing the treaty. Yet these very public indiscretions had contributed to an 'unpleasant atmosphere of petty intrigue – almost of deception',[104] and O'Shea, who was at the centre of these embarrassments, and who since the end of April had managed to evade any attempts Parnell had made to exclude him from negotiations with the Government, was now supplanted by his wife.

# CHAPTER 6

## Gladstone

Within days of the Commons debacle over the Kilmainham treaty, Parnell acted swiftly, dropping O'Shea in favour of Katharine. Less than a month after baby Claude's funeral, Katharine was acting for him in negotiations with the British Government. Without O'Shea realising it, his close political relationship with Parnell, sealed by the Kilmainham treaty, effectively ended the moment his wife wrote her first letter to Gladstone. It was certainly an odd situation in which O'Shea, one of Parnell's MPs and someone Parnell would have to deal with almost daily in the Commons, had lost his wife to Parnell, and to that wife any political significance he had had.

On 23 May, Gladstone received a letter from *Mrs* O'Shea, begging him to let Parnell 'have a few minutes *private* conversation with you'. While she was unwilling to go into particulars in writing, she hoped to be able to explain the matter to Gladstone, 'if you would kindly manage to see me for a few minutes after the morning sitting today'. She wrote to him (on North Park notepaper) from Thomas's Hotel, Berkeley Square, the hotel where she and Parnell had first dined alone in September 1880, saying that she would wait there for a message 'all the evening', before returning to Eltham that night. Politely begging Gladstone's forgiveness for troubling him at such a difficult time, on one matter she is firm: 'I am writing in perfect confidence that you will not mention the subject of this letter to *anyone*. I have not, and shall not, even to Captain O'Shea.'[1] Not only did Katharine make it clear that she thought and acted independently of her husband, but also that she could receive letters and private visitors at her chosen London address, Thomas's Hotel, independent of her husband's apartments at Albert Mansions.

Gladstone knew of Katharine only as the wife of Captain O'Shea, a man whom he thought highly of, despite the misgivings of Cabinet Ministers and his Private Secretary, Sir Edward Hamilton. He was a man who had so recently demonstrated his loyalty not only to Parnell personally, but to the Irish–Liberal Alliance. The wife was now writing to him privately on Parnell's behalf, yet *not* in tandem with her husband, indeed, specifically *not* with her husband's knowledge, let alone consent. Here was a puzzle for the Prime Minister. By what right could Parnell ask Mrs O'Shea to act independently of the wishes of her husband, and for what reasons?

T.P. O'Connor declared himself convinced that, until O'Shea began his suit for divorce, Gladstone had 'no idea of the real state of things between Parnell and Mrs O'Shea. He was not the type of man either to look for or to suspect illicit sexual relations.'[2] Sir Edward Hamilton says much the same, noting in his diary on 20 June 1882, with reference to the rumour that Mrs O'Shea was Parnell's mistress, that the Prime Minister 'does not take the view of the "man of the world" in such matters'.[3] That may be, but Gladstone could hardly have been ignorant of the rumour, since another of his private secretaries and members of the Cabinet aired it in his presence.

His most junior secretary at this time was George Leveson Gower (also nephew to the Foreign Secretary, Lord Granville), a young man of 24. Leveson Gower never saw any of Katharine's letters, but he was required to produce copies of Gladstone's replies and became increasingly nervous about the situation: 'even if they – P. & K. – had been quite innocent,' he reasoned, 'it did not seem to me a very dignified way for the P.M. to conduct such negotiations'. He determined to give Gladstone 'a light hint' at his next opportunity.[4] When he did so, he received a sharp reprimand from the Premier: 'Mr G. wheeled round, and with that rather fierce look', demanded to know what proof he had, asking whether it was possible that 'a man in Mr P.'s position . . . would be so far forgetful of his duties – not to speak of morality and the danger of such actions – as to enter into a disloyal & criminal intrigue with the wife of one of his own colleagues?'[5] J.L. Hammond, an early biographer of Gladstone, is confident that 'Gladstone certainly disbelieved the story then, and he continued to disbelieve it'.[6] But Leveson Gower put it rather more strongly, telling Gladstone's son Henry that his father 'chose to disbelieve – or at any rate to disregard' the rumours.[7] Leveson Gower's story, which was later published in a study of the Queen's private secretaries, Paul Emden's *Behind the Throne* (1934), caused significant embarrassment to Gladstone's sons, guardians of his reputation, since, if true, it fixed their father's knowledge of Parnell's relations with Mrs O'Shea as early as 1882.[8] Herbert Gladstone had denied in a court of law that rumours of the affair existed in 1882.[9] It was Sir George Murray who alerted Henry Gladstone to Emden's book, saying that he found it 'incredible that your father – even if he had only heard of *suspicions* – would have been corresponding with Parnell's mistress'. Throughout August and September 1934, Murray and Gladstone tried to bully Leveson Gower into withdrawing his story, but he held to it.[10]

It was not just a junior private secretary who spoke to the Prime Minister about Mrs O'Shea. According to Sir Charles Dilke's diary of 1882, the Home Secretary, Lord Harcourt, had spoken of the affair in Cabinet on 17 May, six days before Katharine wrote Gladstone her first letter:

At this Cabinet Harcourt made himself specially disagreeable. He told the Cabinet that the Kilmainham Treaty would not be popular when the public discovered that it had been negotiated by Captain O'Shea 'the husband of Parnell's mistress'.[11]

Even if we acknowledge the problems with this source (Dilke's diary was written up in 1890; in 1882 he was not in the Cabinet and there is no record of a Cabinet meeting that day), on Wednesday 24 May, the day after the first exchange of letters, the Foreign Secretary Lord Granville personally informed Gladstone that Mrs O'Shea was 'said to be [Parnell's] mistress'.[12] Knowing this, Gladstone agreed to meet her. Moreover, when interviewed in 1897 by R. Barry O'Brien, Gladstone deliberately misrepresented the circumstances of his first meeting with Katharine, stating that she had initiated the meeting thus: 'Well, she told me that she was a niece of Lord Hatherley, and I called to see her.'[13] Yet it was O'Shea who had told the Prime Minister of his wife's family connection back in September 1880 in order to gain access to him.[14] Katharine wrote to Gladstone not as Hatherley's niece, nor as O'Shea's wife, but as Mr Parnell's exclusive confidante.

From Downing Street, Gladstone wrote Katharine a gracious yet firm denial: 'I thank you for your very frank letter, and I will be equally frank in reply, nor will I be less secret than you ask of me – no one being aware of your letter but myself.' It was his concern, in the present situation, that if word got out of any such interview between himself and Parnell it might 'impair any means of action' and even cause 'serious mischief'.[15] Parnell and Katharine let a day go by and then renewed their request. Katharine professed herself 'inexpressibly sorry' that Gladstone had determined against a private meeting with Parnell, but was now writing to beg that he would see *her*: 'I am sure, with your usual kindness, that you will forgive me if I have over rated the importance of what I wish to tell you.'[16] On Friday 26 May, Katharine appears once again to have waited for a message at Thomas's Hotel, only to find waiting for her on her return to Eltham in the early evening a telegram from Downing Street which stated that Gladstone would be out of London. Katharine wired back her 'great regret' and hoped to 'be more fortunate on his return'.[17]

Less than a week later, 'rather surprisingly', Gladstone agreed to meet her: 'Much more surprisingly, he went to her favourite rendezvous.'[18] On Thursday 1 June, on the dot of three o'clock in the afternoon, Katharine had her first interview with the Prime Minister at Thomas's Hotel. She found him 'extremely agreeable and courteous' and possessing a remarkable 'charm of manner', such that with 'perfect courtesy' Gladstone let it be understood that 'he knew before the end of our interview, and allowed me to know that he knew, what I desired that he should know – that my personal interest in

Parnell was my only interest in Irish politics'.[19] The way she expresses this may be somewhat coy, but the implication that from the first Gladstone was fully aware of the nature of her relationship with Parnell is important. The chief reason for the meeting was for Katharine to put to Gladstone various amendments suggested by Parnell to the Prevention of Crimes Bill, a responsibility which would formerly have been her husband's, yet whatever else they talked of that afternoon, one certainty was established, that since Gladstone 'agreed that it would be of considerable convenience to the Government to be in private and amicable communication with Mr Parnell', Katharine's role as intermediary was 'confidently accepted': 'we parted satisfied, I think, on both sides with the afternoon's compact.'[20] Further than that, he sent her away 'feeling that I was at least . . . worthy of the place I held'.[21] Gladstone's gracious manner towards Katharine at that first interview encouraged her to sign her subsequent letters to Downing Street as *Katie O'Shea*, and he was to assure her that, 'Any paper transmitted to me by you will have my early & best attention.'[22]

The fact that Gladstone agreed to meet Katharine a few times is not in dispute. What is contested is the number of such meetings, since Katharine herself gives the impression that she met the Prime Minister several times: 'After this first interview with Mr Gladstone', she writes, 'I had frequently to see him at Downing Street – taking him drafts, clauses, and various proposed amendments [of bills]'.[23] Little evidence of this personal contact survives. Following on from the research of Herbert Gladstone and J.L. Hammond, who both maintained that there were just three meetings, more recent commentators have also denied Katharine's claims, raising the question of whether she enlarged upon the two subsequent visits to Downing Street which are on record, or whether there were other, undocumented meetings.[24] Judging from her surviving correspondence with Gladstone, Katharine clearly expected the contact to be regular. Just over a fortnight after the first meeting, Katharine was entrusted with a 'written proposal' from Parnell which she offered to forward to the Prime Minister in the hope that he would see her for a few minutes the next day at Thomas's Hotel: 'Then perhaps you will allow me the pleasure of receiving a verbal reply from you.'[25] On this occasion, Gladstone was to be away for the weekend.

The extent of Katharine's role as intermediary, and, more specifically the question of just how many times she saw Gladstone personally, has been clouded by his published statements on the question. In the immediate aftermath of the divorce trial, Gladstone told Sir Edward Hamilton that he had met 'Mrs O'Shea twice at Thomas's Hotel in 1882', yet he claimed to have 'no clear recollection of the woman herself or of his conversation'. He further reassured Hamilton that 'It was R[ichard] Grosvenor who was generally made the go-between in those days when communication with

Mrs O'Shea was really necessary.'[26] According to J.L. Hammond's research there were just three interviews: one, the first, at Thomas's Hotel on 1 June 1882, the other two at Downing Street, on 29 August and 14 September. Of the first, Hamilton recorded his alarm that Mrs O'Shea 'has actually inveigled Mr G. into seeing her . . . It would have been far better for Mr G. to decline point blank to see her or communicate with her'. His reason had little to do with her identity as the wife of O'Shea, of whom Hamilton was deeply suspicious, but because 'She seems to be on very intimate terms with Parnell; some say his mistress.'[27] It is interesting, though, that Hamilton appears to have learned of the first meeting three weeks *after* the event (the diary entry just quoted is dated Tuesday 20 June). He may only have become aware of the 1 June interview because Katharine, in the meantime, had written twice to Downing Street requesting a further meeting at Thomas's Hotel. It is also the case that less than a fortnight after having met Katharine for the third time on 14 September, Gladstone assured Lord Spencer, whom he kept closely informed about Katharine's written and verbal communications, that, 'Some time ago I signified to Mrs O'Shea that we had better not meet again'. He continued, airily, 'Her letters I cannot control but do not encourage.'[28]

Gladstone's denial to R. Barry O'Brien that he wrote any *letters* of consequence to Mrs O'Shea suggests that he may have had more interviews with her than his personal secretary was aware of ('all my communications with her were oral'[29]). O'Brien, though, did not pursue this matter and failed to ask when and where these interviews took place. Certainly, when Gladstone told O'Brien that he had only ever received one letter from Parnell, the offer to resign which O'Shea had brought to him the morning after the Phoenix Park murders, he was being disingenuous. Since 1882, Katharine O'Shea had written Gladstone many letters which conveyed the sentiments of the Irish leader, often directly quoted, and which often contained enclosures in Parnell's own hand. It is certainly the case that in the spring of 1885, a period when Katharine was in constant communication with Downing Street, O'Shea twice makes casual reference to her visits to the Prime Minister, as if this was a fairly common occurrence (Katharine subsequently reprinted these two letters in her biography of Parnell).[30]

In fact, besides the few letters of Katharine's which were produced as evidence in the divorce trial, and the shorthand version of a single, unpublished, letter which she wrote to her husband in August 1886,[31] her correspondence with Gladstone is the largest and most significant surviving body of documents in Katharine's hand. Certainly the letters are important for the light they throw upon Parnell's direction of policy, but they are also revealing of Katharine's character and the nature of her political influence upon Parnell, which is another contested issue. In 1914, Katharine stated that she was 'never a "political lady"', and denied specifically the allegations made by some of her late husband's colleagues, 'that I "inspired" certain measures of his, and biased him in various ways politically'. Parnell, she said, was 'self-reliant' and 'the master of his own mind'.[32] It may be that she felt the need to make such statements: an abridged version of her book was about to be serialised in the *Daily Sketch* during May 1914, and although the serialisation did include such political elements as her dealings with Gladstone, it was advertised with strong emphasis on the romance. She may also have sought to distance herself from the militant campaigning of the suffragettes, whose leader, Emmeline Pankhurst, had been arrested six times in the past year. Katharine is perfectly candid in her account of how 'Parnell would sometimes write the rough draft of what he wished to say in the form of a letter',[33] a statement seized upon by Lyons, who reduces Katharine's role to that of simply taking down letters dictated by Parnell: 'his practice seems to have been to dictate to her what she was to say'; 'it is virtually certain that he dictated . . . to her'.[34] However, a comparison of the preparatory notes given her by Parnell, which Katharine reprints in her book, and the letters preserved in the Gladstone Papers suggests a degree of independence. In fact, Lyons does suggest that Katharine sometimes went beyond Parnell's instructions, but feels the need to belittle this by citing as an instance that she 'duly embroidered' information Parnell had given her with reference to Dillon and Davitt.[35] She often preferred to phrase statements in her own words, or would add information that she felt Gladstone should have. And she did not always write self-deprecatingly. When lightly rebuffed for requesting another interview immediately after their first appointment at Thomas's Hotel, Katharine had the spirit to write to the Prime Minister, 'I beg you will not "boycott" me altogether.'[36]

The period of Katharine's first meeting with Gladstone at Thomas's Hotel on 1 June was one of intense involvement in Parnell's political concerns. It is also about this time that her second daughter by Parnell was conceived. She was to be born at Wonersh Lodge on 4 March 1883. If the pregnancy went to full term, and there is no evidence to suggest otherwise, conception must date from the beginning of June 1882. Parnell was out of the country at the end of the first week of June, in Dublin with Dillon, where they were 'to receive the freedom of the city and attend the Irish National Exhibition of Industries',[37] but he must certainly have been with Katharine to discuss how she should phrase her initial correspondence with Downing Street, dated 23 May. Katharine then sent letters to Gladstone fairly regularly in the latter half of June through to early July (seven letters in all, in the space of less than a month). Indeed, on Monday 10 July

Katharine disclosed to Gladstone that Parnell had been with her the whole weekend, and the following day she wrote that she had had still 'further conversation with Mr Parnell'.[38] Such references seem to suggest that, since his release from Kilmainham, Parnell had been able to live with Katharine at Eltham for much of the time without interference from her husband.

Katharine's political role brought new purpose to her life. She continued, of course, to visit her aunt daily. This was a pleasant duty, but Aunt Wood, widowed in 1845, the year of Katharine's birth, 'was so old that she would not tolerate any topic of conversation of more recent date than the marriage of Queen Victoria'![39] Concerning her children, Katharine admits that much as she 'loved them very dearly', at this time they 'were not old enough, or young enough, to engross my whole mind'.[40] Besides, they would have been out of her sight for most of the day, 12-year-old Gerard at school at Blackheath, and Norah and Carmen, aged 9 and 7, instructed at home by their German governess. It was of course the case that Victorian children of a certain class were to a large degree brought up by servants and governesses, although the frequent references to family holidays by the seaside indicate that Katharine was by no means a remote maternal presence. Yet, unlike so many Victorian wives and mothers in her position, she had a life independent of her family, absorbed by her lover and stimulated by her political involvement. Gladstone, she says, always treated her with such respect, as if she was 'at least a compelling force in the great game of politics'.[41] She was also beginning a new family. The fact that she became pregnant again so soon would have helped her to recover from the death of baby Claude, and indeed from the distressful months of her previous pregnancy with Parnell imprisoned in Kilmainham Gaol. Within a matter of weeks, Katharine's life had undergone an extraordinary revolution.

We know little of O'Shea's movements in the period immediately after the Kilmainham embarrassment in the Commons, yet a note dated 23 June 1882 suggests that he had not seen a great deal of Parnell since the events of mid-May, or at least not to speak to, either in the Commons or at Eltham. Their last recorded contact is a dinner at Eltham on 24 May, when O'Shea got Parnell to promise in a speech to the Commons that he would 'repudiate Dillon and all his works' (meaning his obstructive tactics).[42] That Parnell's attitude in the House had come close to reneging on the terms of the Kilmainham treaty was naturally a cause of embarrassment to O'Shea. His letter of 23 June, addressed to 'My dear Parnell', reminds the Irish leader that a good deal of debating time had passed since, at Parnell's request, he had told Gladstone that obstruction to the Crimes Bill would cease.[43] On the same day, he also wrote peevishly to Chamberlain complaining that Parnell was, as he put it, 'in a "moony", drifting state of mind, nowadays, with which it is difficult to keep one's temper'.[44] There was of course an intriguing mixture of personal and political reasons for Parnell's evasiveness.

Chamberlain replied graciously to O'Shea's apologies for Parnell's behaviour, writing that if Parnell would not cease to obstruct the debates on the Crimes Bill, 'there is no power to make him'. He was only sorry that the possibility of future negotiations with Parnell through himself and O'Shea looked increasingly unlikely, since Parnell himself had ruined any chance of the '*modus vivendi*' he had been seeking.[45] Neither had an inkling that a *modus vivendi* between the Irish leader and Downing Street was already in place, nor that, while Parnell appeared to be obstructing the bill in public, in private he was, through Katharine, impressing upon Gladstone his desire to cooperate with the Government.[46] As Gladstone recalled to R. Barry O'Brien, 'She said that a great change had come over Parnell with reference to myself personally and with reference to the Liberal party, and that he desired friendly relations with us.'[47]

In August 1882, by which time Katharine would have had no doubt that she was again pregnant, her husband and lover were both in Dublin, where Parnell was studiously avoiding O'Shea. O'Shea checked into the Shelbourne Hotel as usual and on Saturday 26 August took it upon himself to deliver in person to the Lord-Lieutenant, Lord Spencer, his memorial for the reprieve of Francis Hymer, a small 'gentleman farmer', and 'very distant connection' of O'Shea, who had been sentenced to hang for shooting a man.[48] He found Spencer non-communicative. Hymer was subsequently hanged. The day before, O'Shea had visited the new Chief Secretary, George Otto Trevelyan, and was struck 'to see his three boys playing cricket in the grounds of his lodge with constabulary sentinels at each corner'. His haunting the lodges in Phoenix Park and his attempts to ingratiate himself with Spencer and Trevelyan all pointed to O'Shea's ambition to become the new Under-Secretary for Ireland. 'The lodges are charming places', he observed to Katharine, 'but I have not been in the Under-Secretary's'.[49] He even tried to get a photograph of the latter.

Otherwise, O'Shea complained that his work in Ireland was 'dreadful' and the weather 'beastly'. His despair deepened when he was thrown from a carriage, and broke his left arm and sprained his right, injuries now compounded by a return of gout. To cap it all, despite having a received a pleasing number of telegrams and personal enquiries, 'Mr Parnell, although in next street, never sent. P for pig!'.[50] Significantly, O'Shea continued to address Katharine as 'Dick', his pet name for her, and to sign himself 'Your Boysie', evidence enough, perhaps, to suggest that he may not have understood how fundamentally altered their relationship was since Parnell's release from Kilmainham. The next weekend, better able to write, he listed to Katharine the leading Liberals who had sent their commiserations: 'Nice note from Fawcett. Also from Harcourt. Nothing from Chamberlain. John Morley has been with me to-day for a couple of hours. I hope to see Trevelyan tomorrow.' But there was still not a peep from Parnell, who, he had heard, had left Dublin for England: 'I merely say he never took the trouble to send a message or write a line.'[51]

It would seem likely that Parnell had returned to Eltham to coach Katharine through her second interview with the Prime Minister, although it is possible that Katharine went to see Gladstone armed with no more specific information than that supplied in a letter she received from Parnell on 20 August. Writing to her from Morrison's, Parnell said that he hoped to have all his work done in a couple of days so that he would be able to spend a week at Avondale before returning 'to Wifie'.[52] In the briefest terms he explained to her that Dillon and Davitt had quarrelled with him because he refused to allow any further expenditure by the Ladies' Land League for the relief of evicted families, and because he had arranged to be responsible for such future payments himself.

Thus, while O'Shea was confined to his Dublin hotel, his wife had her second and third momentous interviews with Gladstone, now at 10 Downing Street. We know a good deal more of these meetings, a fortnight apart, on 29 August and 14 September, than we do about the first. Yet, very strangely, no letters survive in which either meeting is requested or a date set, even though Sir Edward Hamilton notes that the interview of 29 August was brought about 'at her earnest solicitation'.[53] Crucially, Hamilton's record of the substance of their conversation is in accord with Parnell's letter referred to above, and with Katharine's account of the interview in her book.

Hamilton's record of Gladstone's second meeting reads as follows:

> Mrs O'Shea told Mr G. that Parnell had broken up the Ladies' Land League, had stopped their supplies, had laid hold of the Land League funds – that is, arrested them, amounting to £60,000 – and was determined to confine himself with bonds of legality . . . She also said that Davitt and Dillon were both 'in great dudgeon' (as Mr G. termed it) with Parnell by reason of his restricted action on land and national questions. She regards Davitt as the incarnation of vanity and Dillon as a *tête montée*.* She, of course, reflects Parnell's views, and in doing so admitted the improvement of the state of Ireland.[54]

Hamilton could make these notes because he was privy to the account of the 29 August meeting which Gladstone sent to Lord Spencer, but the Prime

* A hothead.

Minister had ensured that he and Katharine talked alone. Katharine has
described how, when she was shown into Gladstone's room, 'he would rise
from his desk to greet me and, solemnly handing me a chair, would walk
down the room to the door at the end, which was always open when I
entered, close it firmly and, pacing back to the door of my entry, push it'.[55]
It was then his custom to invite her to take his arm and to talk while they
walked up and down the office, Katharine careful to voice Parnell's points in
the third person ('It is considered that, etc.,') and Gladstone referring always
to the views of 'Your friend'. When she finally asked him, 'What is it you
shut up in that room, Mr Gladstone, when I come to see you?', he replied,
'Persons, or a person, you do not come to see, Mrs O'Shea. Only a secretary
or so, and occasionally, in these times of foolish panic, detectives . . . no one
can overhear a word we say when we pace up and down like this.'[56]

The accuracy of Katharine's description of her interviews at Downing
Street was later challenged by Herbert Gladstone. In his book, *After Thirty
Years* (1928), Herbert goes so far as to print a photograph of his father's
study, clearly showing the double doors, and provides the exact dimensions
of the room (23ft 3in by 19ft 3in). His great concern was to quash
Katharine's story of Gladstone's conducting his interviews with her while
walking up and down the room so as not to be overheard, and he details
the physical impracticalities of circumnavigating a room so crammed with
furniture. He goes on to make the rather pompous statement that his father
would never have 'walk[ed] up and down a room arm in arm with a lady
while discussing politics': 'As a matter of fact, Mr Gladstone never even
stood when engaged in interviews. Not one of us ever saw him walking up
and down a room in discussion.'[57]

Katharine was not a Cabinet colleague, and nor was she, in these
conventional terms, a 'lady', despite her impeccable social connections. She
was an unorthodox woman, and by Herbert Gladstone's experience, one
hard to define or quantify. Mrs O'Shea operated outside the conventional
community of upper-class ladies, MPs' wives, who were valued as political
hostesses and who presided over dinner parties or open-house events where
politicians could meet informally, or who raised party funds. Not only did
she not have a fashionable London address, but she did not mix in society.
In town she could be found – unchaperoned – at Thomas's Hotel, perhaps
the nearest equivalent to a male club, where she could receive male visitors
discreetly. And this sense of independence, at once physical, moral and
intellectual, is reflected in the familiar way she often writes to Gladstone –
*exactly* as if she had been on such terms as to pace the Prime Minister's
study on the Prime Minister's arm.

The question raised by Lyons is whether Katharine talked too loosely to
the Prime Minister, going beyond the essential points conveyed to her by

Parnell. He notes that Gladstone immediately passed on to Lord Spencer Katharine's sensational information that the weekly expenditure of the Ladies' Land League 'had been as high as £7–10,000 a week', which, Lyons feels, was 'almost certainly . . . a gross exaggeration'.[58] Possibly so, but the substance of her conversation with Gladstone was concentrated upon the efforts Parnell had made to honour the terms of the Kilmainham treaty. In June 1882, Parnell, together with Biggar and McCarthy, took control of the Land League monies in Paris by instructing the bank only to release funds with their joint signatures added to those of Egan and Davitt (Egan would eventually resign as treasurer in October after Katharine had secured Gladstone's promise that he could return to Ireland without fear of arrest 'under the old or new Act'). As she explained in great detail, 'There is a sum of £16,000 in America which will very shortly arrive, and which [Mr Parnell] is anxious to hand over to Mr Egan's successor who . . . will be Mr Parnell's own nominee.'[59]

Katharine's own account of this meeting describes how she told Gladstone about the 'inner workings of the Ladies' Land League, about which he was curious'. She represented to him 'the enormous sum' spent by the ladies and how Parnell, finding it difficult to get them to moderate their activities, had forced them to disband by cutting off their access to the League funds.[60] Years later Parnell would admit to William O'Brien that his sister Anna had 'never spoken a word to me since I stopped [their] account'.[61]

The break with Anna came at a particularly difficult time for Parnell, for on 20 July his sister Fanny, who had inspired the foundation of the Ladies' Land League, had died of a heart attack at Bordentown, New Jersey. Katharine saw the announcement in the morning papers, and knowing that Parnell spoke of Fanny as his 'favourite sister . . . I thought it better to wake him and tell him of it, lest he should read it while I was away with my aunt'. 'For a time he utterly broke down', and Katharine stayed with him throughout the day until he received a telegram, sent on to Eltham from London, 'saying that his sister's body was to be embalmed and brought to Ireland'.[62] Both Parnell and Anna were horrified at such an idea. Anna was deeply affected and may have tried to take her own life; *The Times* reported that 'Miss Anna Parnell is dangerously ill with brain fever. Mr Parnell has been telegraphed for.'[63] Parnell sent Katharine up to London to wire his mother, 'absolutely forbidding the embalmment of his sister's body, and saying that she was to be buried in America'.[64] In a matter of weeks he lost one sister and all relations with the other had been severed: both had been actively, but troublingly, involved in their brother's political work. Significantly, that rupture came just at the time that Parnell had come to rely upon Katharine's very different political support.

That support was again of crucial importance in October of 1882. So concerned was he to demonstrate to Gladstone his honouring of the understandings embodied by the Kilmainham treaty that Parnell went so far as to forward him a draft of his speech to the Nationalist Convention, to be held in Dublin on Monday 17 October. On 6 October, Katharine informed the Prime Minister that 'should any of it [not] be likely to meet your view', Parnell would 'leave such points alone'.[65] A further letter of 20 October conveys Parnell's anxiety to keep Gladstone closely informed about the resolutions made by the Convention, most importantly the formation of the National League, a new organisation in place of the Land League. In his opening speech to the Convention, Parnell established its principal aims: Home Rule, giving Ireland 'the right of making her own laws upon Irish soil'; and a solution to the Land question which ensured for tenant farmers the right to purchase their holdings.[66] He also called for local self-government, extensions to the franchise nationally and locally, as well as measures for economic development.

Parnell let Katharine know that he 'got through the first day of the Convention very successfully',[67] yet he was under great strain. A week before the Convention he was feverish and had an attack of dysenteric diarrhoea; the doctor told him, 'my stomach must have been getting out of order for some time'.[68] Healy had to work on the draft constitution of the National League by Parnell's bedside at Morrison's Hotel. Nonetheless, Parnell saw off the two major dissenters, Dillon and Davitt, who objected to the Kilmainham treaty's pledge of future cooperation with the Liberals. (This resulted in Dillon's temporary retirement from politics, while Davitt went on a fund-raising tour of America.) Parnell was elected Chairman of the National League, with Biggar as one of the treasurers and Healy as secretary.

Katharine's letter of 20 October is of particular interest because it intimates to Gladstone her private relationship with Parnell. She explained, with reference to Parnell, that it had taken her nearly two years 'to penetrate through the habitual reserve' of Mr Parnell and his 'suspicion of the Saxon . . . sufficiently to induce him to make his view known *at all* and thus shake himself free of the set by which he was surrounded'.[69] In order to demonstrate that Parnell's opinions were 'not in accord with theirs', she enclosed two telegrams he had wired her on 15 and 16 October from the Dublin Convention, which Gladstone was asked to destroy. He did not do so. Both telegrams assert Parnell's control over the threatened dissension of Dillon and Davitt. One says, acknowledging Katharine's advice: 'I will not permit myself to be drawn or pushed beyond the limit of prudence and legality.' The other comments, 'have completely foiled other side'. These telegrams also show great anxiety to hear from Katharine, who, unknown to Gladstone, was by now four months' pregnant. On Friday 13 October,

Parnell had written asking for more letters from her, saying, 'you have no idea how . . . frightened and nervous I feel when, as sometimes happens, a whole day goes by without any news'.[70] The telegrams of 15 and 16 October add to their political messages: 'wire this evening how you are am very anxious am quite well and going out again today you may write more fully'; and 'wire how you are'.[71] Gladstone must surely have asked himself why Parnell was so pressing in his desire to know how Mrs O'Shea was keeping. The two enquiries after her health are perhaps not particularly revealing, yet a more guarded correspondent than Katharine clearly felt she needed to be could simply have quoted selectively from the two telegrams. Her decision not to do so, her laying her lover's telegrams openly before Gladstone, certainly supports her contention that at the conclusion of her first interview with Gladstone, he 'allowed me to know that he knew'.[72]

Katharine's letter to Gladstone is of further significance since it disregarded the Prime Minister's advice given her at the beginning of the month that the best channel for Parnell's future communications with the Government would be through 'my friend Lord R[ichard] Grosvenor'.[73] Since September, pressure had mounted on Gladstone to put an end to his communications with Mrs O'Shea: Lord Spencer told Gladstone that he 'quite dread[ed] the fact of her communications leaking out'; Lord Granville was shocked to learn that the correspondence was still kept up, and agreed that Grosvenor was the appropriate channel; while Lord Hartington (Secretary of State for India) was opposed to *any* form of parley with the Irish leader 'other than across the floor of the House'.[74] Despite this strength of feeling among Cabinet Ministers, Gladstone held to his belief in the importance of contact with Katharine, who, he said, 'has been of some use in keeping Parnell on the lines of moderation'.[75] He did, though, agree to a compromise, hence the instruction on 10 October not to write to him directly, since if the fact became known it would lead to 'suspicion and misapprehension'.[76]

A fortnight after the Dublin Convention, Katharine forwarded Gladstone a memorandum in Parnell's hand relating to what he regarded as defects in the Arrears Act. While she apologised to the Prime Minister 'for disobeying your wishes', Katharine explained that Parnell, on his side, 'objects to making his views known to you . . . in any way that will give rise to rumours, which are . . . very detrimental to his position in Ireland'.[77] Clearly, Parnell mistrusted any other channel of communication. At the end of November, Katharine was asked again to stop writing to Gladstone and to remember 'the course she was requested to adopt',[78] but throughout the winter she continued to disregard Gladstone's injunction. Her letters continued to receive second-hand replies through Grosvenor, although there is no evidence of annoyance on the part of Gladstone or Grosvenor.

Katharine was treated as courteously as ever, and her interest in Irish politics taken seriously. When on Wednesday 8 November, apparently at the House of Commons,[79] she asked for Gladstone's response to an enclosure of Parnell's she had posted a few days' earlier, in which he had suggested the introduction of a short bill to amend two particular aspects. of the Arrears Act, she got an immediate reply from Grosvenor. He regretted that Gladstone was unable to answer her letter personally, because he was about to attend a cabinet meeting and directly afterwards was to make a speech in the House. While Grosvenor pointed out that there was no time to consider any new legislation this session, Katharine was assured that 'In his speech today Mr Gladstone will contend that the interests of Ireland require *good* arrangements for the conduct of business. I hope that you will be able to stop for it,' he added, 'as he hopes to speak between 4 & 5 o'clock'.[80]

It is clear from O'Shea's surviving correspondence that he became aware to a limited degree that his wife had begun to carry messages from Parnell to the Prime Minister, and also that he expected Katharine to make use of that contact on his own behalf. Indeed, Sir Edward Hamilton believed – or perhaps Gladstone led him to believe – that Katharine's *prime* motive for seeing the Prime Minister was to beg the Irish Under-Secretaryship for O'Shea, and he was nettled to realise that Gladstone was almost swayed: 'Mr G. thinks the Government is under *some* obligation to O'Shea. I can't admit this at all.'[81] It is the contention of J.L. Hammond that Gladstone was partly deceived as to the exact nature of the O'Sheas' marital relationship by Katharine's persistent attempts to win favour for her husband, which involved her sending the Prime Minister, 'from time to time', copies of O'Shea's letters which addressed her in affectionate terms.[82]

Despite O'Shea's bungling of the Kilmainham treaty in the Commons, Gladstone clearly held to his belief that the Government was indebted to him for delivering to them Parnell's offer of cooperation, and at the beginning of September asked members of the Cabinet what they thought of rewarding O'Shea with the Irish Under-Secretaryship.[83] Grosvenor sent in an unequivocal assessment of O'Shea's manoeuvring: 'I always expected that he intended his participation in the "Kilmainham Treaty" business to make the foundation of a claim for a berth under Govt. *Every* Irishman, without a single exception, always jobs.' As to whether O'Shea was qualified to take up such a position of trust, Grosvenor wrote, 'I confess that the little I know of him does not impress me at all favourably.'[84] It would seem that at Katharine's third interview with Gladstone she did take the opportunity to ask about her husband's chances, because the following day she forwarded Gladstone a letter and telegram she had just received from O'Shea ('which I shall feel grateful if you will kindly read, and destroy, at your leisure'[85]) in which O'Shea confirmed that if offered the post of Under-Secretary for Ireland he would of course accept. 'My dearest wife,' he wrote, 'Yes, I should like to be under-secretary very much and I think I might make a useful one. I quite see that it would not be a bed of roses at first, but a Liberal Government can scarcely nowadays keep all, or almost all, the Irish appointments manned by Englishmen.'[86] The fact that he also sent a telegram to Katharine the day after she had seen Gladstone suggests a certain desperation to influence the Prime Minister.[87]

Gladstone's response to this unorthodox communication has not survived, although it is clear that Katharine was informed that the replacement of the Under-Secretary was a matter for Lord Spencer. 'Yes, I am afraid that the Grand Old Humbug is gammoning us,' was O'Shea's response, knowing that, 'Of course, Lord Spencer would not stand out one moment against the G.O.M.'s real wish.'[88] Unknown to O'Shea, Spencer had already conveyed to Gladstone that he could hardly think of a man 'more unfitted' for the Under-Secretaryship.[89] A month later, O'Shea was agitated to discover that Lord Spencer had his own 'immense favourite' lined up for the post, the Inspector General of Constabulary, a man named Jenkinson, who 'knows nothing whatever of the country'.[90] O'Shea's rising desperation is evident from the renewed enquiry Katharine felt 'constrained' to make at the end of October. That she felt constrained may be indicative of more than her understandable embarrassment. Referring to her husband's 'great anxiety', she wrote, 'he begs me to tell you that he is sure he could be useful in such a position and I hope you believe how anxious he is to be so and will forgive my writing to you on the subject'.[91] To Gladstone's memo on the reverse of Katharine's letter, 'What have I told her before?', Grosvenor reminded the Prime Minister, 'That you would refer her application to [the] Viceroy'. And thus, after months of fond expectation, O'Shea was forced to accept the fact that his chances of gaining a Government appointment as a mark of gratitude for his involvement in the Kilmainham negotiations were nil.

Aside from O'Shea's personal ambition, one of the reasons he so coveted the position of Under-Secretary for Ireland was his increasingly troubled financial situation in the latter half of 1882. It was already shaky in the spring of that year, before he made his first overtures to the Government. At the end of March he consulted Katharine about disposing of certain shares, but had high hopes that he would be proposed as the managing director of his bank.[92] In an undated letter of Katharine's which may well refer to this period, she advises him to take measures to protect his Irish land, 'and anything that could be touched', from legal proceedings.[93] By 1 May, O'Shea admitted to Katharine that, 'the dates of payments are staring me in the face', and that he was 'getting quite hopeless'.[94] He began to borrow heavily from a friend who was 'flush of stuff', but in July was still waiting to hear from 'my people' (although it is unclear whether 'my people' refers to his mother, his land agent in Limerick or his bank).[95] 'Damnation on a volcano kind of life', he exclaimed.[96] At the end of September, Katharine asked him for a full breakdown of all monies owed by him: 'I have £100 coming due on October 17th, £300 on November 13th, and £300 on December 3rd at the National Bank . . . I don't see any way out of it at all, and believe the end is at hand.'[97] Years later, O'Shea admitted to Joseph Chamberlain that 'especially in 1882, I was in want of money, owing to political expenses and, if you will, extravagant personal outlay, and I certainly pressed my former wife to keep her aunt up to her promises'.[98]

That Katharine was under great pressure from her husband is unmistakable. She had been obliged to try to influence the Prime Minister in his favour and had failed. Now she was being called upon to save him from bankruptcy. It is an interesting situation, in which O'Shea had quite probably been applying the leverage of whatever he understood to be the situation of Katharine and Parnell, and in which, now, Katharine could exact from O'Shea a ratification of their informal marital separation. Certainly the latter is the claim made by Henry Harrison, who, in the course of his study of Katharine's private papers relating to the Probate Action over her aunt's will, came across a particular letter from Katharine to O'Shea which 'made a deep impression on me'. Unfortunately, Harrison made no copy of this document, but he claimed that it dated from 1882, and in view of O'Shea's mounting financial difficulties we can safely date a financial settlement to the latter part of the year: 'In it she undertook to provide him with £600 a year out of moneys which she would receive from her aunt – on condition that he continued to leave her quite free and did not attempt to interfere with her life.'[99] However, according to O'Shea, he was already in receipt of an average income of over £2,500 from Mrs Wood, irrespective of any separate gift from the old lady.[100] If Harrison is right about Katharine's 1882 undertaking, it must have referred to an annual provision which she was prepared to make over to O'Shea out of the income she received independently from her aunt. Again, according to O'Shea, this amounted to some £4,000 a year.

Further questions remain, such as exactly how Katharine justified to O'Shea her sudden desire for 'conjugal freedom',[101] as Harrison puts it. Did she perhaps tell her husband that after having lost baby Claude she didn't want to risk becoming pregnant again? Or did she confront him with the truth that she was already almost four months' pregnant with Parnell's child? It is significant that having reprinted a letter of O'Shea's, posted from the Shelbourne Hotel on 17 October 1882, Katharine makes no reference at all to her husband's correspondence until October 1884. When his letters begin to be mentioned once more, they give every appearance of unaltered friendly relations between husband and wife (O'Shea continues to use their nicknames), but the two-year gap in their correspondence must surely have to do with the fact that during this period Katharine gave birth to one daughter by Parnell and was about to be delivered of another. Their daughter Clare was born in March 1883, and Katie in November 1884.

That these two girls were 'unquestionably' Parnell's daughters will be more fully discussed later. There is, though, one further piece of evidence which strongly suggests that Katharine bought her conjugal freedom from O'Shea in 1882. This evidence (which O'Shea put before his divorce lawyers and which they wisely suppressed) is an indignant letter which Katharine wrote to her husband early in April 1887, in reply to 'one of the many gross insults you are fond of writing to me'. She wrote: 'Your assertion that I at any time "concealed the fact of my being in the family way" is simply a foul lie – like many other things you have written to me – as I told you.'[102] If Captain O'Shea had any grounds for believing that he was the father of Clare and Katie (he did claim later that he was[103]), his accusation that Katharine had in the past 'concealed' the fact of her pregnancies would make no sense at all.

It is difficult to believe that there was no correspondence between Katharine and O'Shea from October 1882 to October 1884. The fact that it is not mentioned in her book allowed Katharine conveniently to evade the fact that she bore Parnell these two children. There is no mention of Clare or Katie in Katharine's book, and Henry Harrison was astonished – and delighted – to learn of Parnell's daughters when he first visited the family after Parnell's death.[104] When one puts together O'Shea's very serious financial position in late 1882 with Harrison's claim that an arrangement was offered to O'Shea as a means to ward off impending bankruptcy and ensure his future financial stability, even comfort, it is perhaps tempting to reassess the (unsubstantiated) claim Katharine made to Harrison that an agreement relating to her conjugal freedom had been made as early as July 1881 (see Chapter 3). There may, of course, have been two separate understandings: the first in which O'Shea was to turn a blind eye to Katharine's relationship with Parnell because of what she knew of her husband's infidelities; the second in which her husband was required to accept his wife's lover's children as his own in return for an assured income. But it is interesting that Katharine never once volunteered information to Harrison regarding this latter agreement, while she did speak a great deal about the 1881 'arrangement' conducted by her sister Anna. It may be that Katharine needed to suppress the truth of a nakedly financial agreement with her husband – one in which she was prepared to exploit her husband's economic insolvency – and was altogether easier describing an amicable agreement in which the two parties were equally free in their extra-marital relationships.

# CHAPTER 7

## *The Lost Years*

Clare Gabrielle Antoinette Marcia Esperance O'Shea was born on Sunday 4 March 1883. The announcement of her birth duly appeared on the front page of *The Times* the following Friday: 'On the 4th inst., at Eltham, the wife of WILLIAM HENRY O'SHEA Esq., MP, of a daughter.'[1] Yet she was the child of Parnell. It is an exceedingly complex situation, its implications difficult to comprehend. It has been noted that in her book Katharine avoids all mention of her two youngest daughters and reprints few letters from this period, and the years 1883–4 might be regarded as 'lost years' in terms of our understanding of how the births of Clare and then Katie affected the relationships between O'Shea and his wife and O'Shea and Parnell, with whom he appeared to continue to be on good terms. They certainly collaborated on a number of political projects during these years, and while the surviving documentary evidence from this period throws up a number of contradictions about O'Shea's position, it also points strongly to the fact that he was able to accommodate himself to Katharine's pregnancies by keeping a main eye on his own political career.

His behaviour regarding the announcement of Clare's birth and her subsequent baptism is one case in point. The strongest evidence of O'Shea's tolerance of the situation is, however, anecdotal. T.P. O'Connor tells a curious story of how the announcement of Clare's birth was placed in the *Freeman's Journal*. His source was J.M. Tuohy, then editor of the *Freeman's*, who was, O'Connor believed, 'the last man . . . to interpret wrongly, and . . . incapable of inventing any event'.[2] Tuohy described to him a particular night when O'Shea and Parnell arrived at the paper's Essex Street offices off the Victoria Embankment to deliver a political statement. When they had done so, 'Parnell took a piece of paper out of his pocket, and showing it to O'Shea, asked him whether he should also supply this information to the *Freeman's Journal*. O'Shea nodded an assent, and Parnell handed the document to Tuohy.' As O'Connor observes, it was 'an astonishing document under the circumstances'.[3] Parnell had just handed Tuohy an announcement of the birth of a daughter to the wife of Captain O'Shea. The story may seem incredible, but it is a fact that on the very day the notice of Clare's birth appeared in the *Freeman's*, Thursday 8 March 1883, the paper also published a long letter to the editor from O'Shea. This would appear to be the political statement that had been delivered to Tuohy, thus validating his extraordinary story and certainly implying a more tortuous relationship between O'Shea and Parnell.

O'Shea's letter in the *Freeman's Journal* was written in defence of 'my friend', Parnell. The Irish leader had been attacked in the Commons by Forster, who declared that Parnell had long colluded with outrages in Ireland, including even the Phoenix Park murders. Parnell had fought back, but with such verbal ferocity that the British press was horrified. O'Shea's letter reminded readers of Parnell's repeated statements against the agitation in Ireland, and argued that Forster's insinuation that Parnell had any connection with the Invincibles was absurd: 'When the news of the murders in the Phoenix Park reached London he came to me, and if ever a public man was overcome by horror and grief for public crime it was he.'[4]

O'Shea's attitude to Katharine at this time was perhaps less conciliatory. Just nine days after the birth, O'Shea wrote from Albert Mansions, asking Katharine to forward Gladstone several pages of a letter he had written her (a volubly pro-Chamberlain, anti-Spencer communication).[5] While the letter itself is not important, the fact that O'Shea chose to make use of Katharine in this way, so soon after the birth, suggests not only that he was aware of her continuing contact with the Prime Minister on Parnell's behalf, but that he was asserting himself by reminding her of her duties towards her husband. After all, he could quite easily have sent a letter directly to Gladstone himself. The fact that he left the registration of Clare's birth to Katharine is perhaps the strongest evidence available to us that he knew Clare could not have been his child. Indeed, there may have been some awkwardness over this, for Katharine did not officially register her daughter's birth until 19 April.

Yet, O'Shea does appear to have organised Clare's baptism on 2 May at the Catholic Church of St Mary Magdalene in Upper North Street, Brighton. Some time in late April Katharine and the children had moved down to Brighton, presumably on the grounds of restoring Katharine's and safe-guarding the baby's health. It would no doubt have been on Katharine's mind that it was exactly a year since Claude Sophie had begun to sicken, although this pregnancy does not appear to have affected Katharine herself so badly. At the divorce hearing, O'Shea stated that after Katharine's confinement he had taken a house in Bedford Square, Brighton, and that his wife 'was there some time. I used to go backwards and forwards'.[6] Harriet Bull, the maid employed by a Mrs Dalton, owner of the house, recalled that the Captain came to see his wife 'sometimes, but not often', although she remembered distinctly that he came down to Brighton for Clare's baptism.[7] Not only was Clare baptised a Catholic, but her godmother was chosen by O'Shea. She was Lady Mary O'Donnell, the wife of his friend and distant relation, Sir George O'Donnell of County Mayo.[8] As we have seen, Katharine had been so distressed at her daughter Carmen's baptism that she refused to attend the ceremony, which she watched from the porch of the Brompton Oratory. Now her daughter by Parnell was being baptised in her husband's faith. Bearing in mind her feeling that the Catholic Church had taken her children away from her, this must have been doubly painful for Katharine. It was no doubt forced upon her in order to avoid social and political scandal, and may have led to a paradoxically turbulent response: her defiantly public life in Brighton with Parnell once O'Shea had returned to London.

When asked at the trial whether Parnell was ever a guest at 39 Bedford Square, O'Shea was evasive: 'I was never there when he was there. It was not within my knowledge that he was visiting my wife there.'[9] In fact, Katharine and Parnell seem to have flaunted their relationship. Harriet Bull noted that besides the visits of O'Shea, another gentleman, whose name she never found out, had his own key and 'would come to the house every day', always when the Captain was absent: 'The children would go out for a drive, and there would be no one left at home with this gentleman and Mrs O'Shea. They would remain in the drawing-room together for hours.' Mrs O'Shea would also go driving with the gentleman, and on one occasion they appeared back at Bedford Square at midnight. Harriet Bull had waited up for her, since the house was generally closed up at eleven o'clock. 'Was there anything in Mrs O'Shea's appearance that attracted your attention?', she was asked by Sir Edward Clarke. 'Yes; her appearance was anything but that of a respectable woman. Her hair was all flying.' Harriet Bull was sufficiently offended by Mrs O'Shea's behaviour to tell Mrs Dalton. There was worse to follow: one afternoon, she had gone up to Mrs O'Shea's bedroom to give her a message, and 'I heard the voice of the co-respondent in her bedroom'. She tried the door but found it locked: 'I should think they came out about three-quarters of an hour after I had knocked at the door.' Again, she mentioned the matter to Mrs Dalton.

There is the suggestion, too, that evidence of the affair was leaked to certain of Parnell's colleagues. At the end of June 1883, while Katharine remained at Brighton, Parnell was in Ireland to orchestrate Healy's election campaign at Monaghan, which the Government believed to be a safe Liberal seat. For biographers of Parnell, 1883 and 1884 are generally regarded as the 'lost years', politically, because of his relative inactivity.[10] His parliamentary inactivity was largely imposed upon him by the Government, which, exhausted by the Irish Question since they had taken office, was now focused upon the introduction of the third Reform Bill, which was passed in December 1884. The resultant widening of the suffrage increased the Irish electorate from 200,000 to 700,000, which strengthened Parnell's position enormously. The next General Election was expected in late 1885, and until that time Parnell was, in fact, actively involved in every by-election in Ireland, working to ensure the victory of a Nationalist candidate pledged to support his leadership and to vote in unison with the party: 'a vote for his candidate was a vote of confidence in him as leader.'[11]

At Monaghan, Healy won by a clear margin of 300 votes, and he has described Parnell's delight at crossing the Liberals, 'who had persecuted him and reviled him . . . We toured the county that evening, and from our brake he shouted to every group at a cross-roads, "Healy! Healy! Healy!"'[12] Yet the party's victory in the north was overshadowed for Healy by an episode which had similarities with that of the opened letter in Paris in 1881. It was the apparent discovery of a private message which had preceded Parnell's arrival in Monaghan. He had been due to speak there on a Sunday evening, 'Yet he neither appeared nor sent an apology,' noted Healy. 'Miserable at Parnell's breach of faith,' Healy and Sexton travelled back to Monaghan town later that night. At their hotel they were met by the solicitor, J.F. Small, holding out a telegram. Healy says that they assumed that it was an apology from Parnell. It was, instead, a telegram *to* Parnell, and read:

The Captain is away. Please come. Don't fail. – KATE.[13]

Healy says that he was at first angry with Small for opening the telegram, and then hoped to put it back in its envelope to disguise the fact that it had been opened, but Small had already torn up the envelope. While the existence of the opened telegram is not in doubt,[14] its represented contents are hardly credible.

Katharine and Parnell had effectively been living together as man and wife for thirteen months since Parnell's release from Kilmainham. Back in Dublin after the Monaghan victory, Parnell wrote to Katharine as 'your husband'.[15] He had left Katharine safely lodged in Brighton with her young family, and nursing her 4-month-old baby. It has been established that her actual husband rarely visited them. She would not, then, have seized upon his brief absence to demand that her lover leave his campaigning in Ireland to come to her. Moreover, Katharine has said that they telegraphed in code: she would never have sent him such a dangerously explicit message. In fact, she wrote to Parnell the whole time he was in Ireland. 'Please continue writing,' he begged her. 'Your letters always give me the greatest happiness to read.' He made arrangements to have these 'kept out of sight'.[16] Katharine and Parnell were by now old hands at the art of maintaining their secret correspondence. Of course, it may be that Healy re-phrased the telegraphic message in order to make its message explicit to readers of his memoirs. But what most undermines Healy's recollection of the telegram's contents is the fact that Parnell was fully aware that 'The Captain [was] away'. O'Shea was in his constituency, West Clare, where Parnell intended to visit him the following week, sometime after a banquet in Cork held in his honour on 4 July.[17]

One of the matters Parnell would have needed to discuss with O'Shea was a scheme on which they had begun to collaborate to relieve the condition of the very poorest tenants along the north-west coast of Mayo. On 19 June, Katharine had sent Gladstone a private memo in Parnell's hand with measures for dealing with this problem, and enclosing a proof copy of a pamphlet he had produced on the 'Congested Districts of the County of Mayo'.[18] Parnell was 'very anxious' about this problem and proposed that the Government subsidise the purchase and improvement of currently unoccupied areas of bog land by private companies, and by giving each family a grant of £50, to encourage the re-settlement of tenants from over-populated villages, who were at present tied to land 'so poor that it seems difficult to allot to it any substantial value'.[19] Backed by the Prime Minister's 'strong recommendation' that these measures 'should be given careful consideration',[20] the Tramways and Public Companies (Ireland) Act, as it became known, passed into law before the end of the session.

The Irish Land Purchase & Settlement Company was subsequently launched, Parnell personally investing in it the considerable sum of £2,000. Early the following summer, the *Nation* carried two articles on the progress of the company, reporting that Parnell and O'Shea had looked at an estate in Tuam, Galway. They eventually purchased land at Kilcoony, but, according to Lyons, 'the landlords raised their prices as soon as they saw them coming . . . and since hardly anyone agreed to take shares in the company they had to wind it up afterwards'.[21] Relations between the two men seem at this point to have been perfectly amicable. At the conclusion of the Galway trip, Parnell invited O'Shea to Avondale for a couple of days.

In the winter of 1883 Katharine returned to Brighton, but not to the house in Bedford Square where she had aroused the suspicions of the maid and landlady. She and Parnell had already settled on a house in Second Avenue and Katharine had signed an agreement to take it, one of the first tangible signs of her independence from her husband. Under the recently passed Married Women's Property Act of 1882, Katharine's right to dispose of her 'separate property', the money she earned as her aunt's companion, was made unambiguous and she was now able to sign contracts as if she were a single woman.[22] Yet in this instance O'Shea immediately countermanded her and, in Katharine's words, 'insisted on my taking a house facing the sea in Medina Terrace'.[23] Number 8 Medina Terrace was taken for four months, from November to February 1884, and O'Shea seems to have remained the nominal head of the household. According to Katharine, 'Willie undertook to stay here to be with the children while I went back to my aunt (coming myself to Brighton for one or two days in the week)': a novel situation! Yet Caroline Pethers, the servant at the house, recalled that 'two or three days after Captain and Mrs O'Shea had taken the house a gentleman appeared' who went under the name of 'Charles Stewart'.[24] Parnell's presence there was apparently at O'Shea's invitation. Indeed, O'Shea admitted during the divorce that Parnell 'visited there pretty frequently. At that time there was a good deal of political activity, and I was a good deal with him.'[25] Yet no evidence survives of this urgent 'political activity'.[26]

On 15 December 1883, Parnell was in Dublin, where he was presented with a national testimonial of £40,000 by the Lord Mayor and attended a banquet held in his honour at the Dublin Rotunda. The money was raised after Parnell had advertised the sale of Avondale, which was heavily mortgaged. At this point O'Shea was expressing to Chamberlain his admiration for Parnell, who intended to use a small amount of this tribute to pay off his mortgages and to hand over the rest 'for public purposes', a gesture that would only increase his popularity.[27] At some point after the Dublin ceremony, Parnell returned to England in order to meet Katharine secretly at Eltham on Christmas Eve. She had come back to visit her aunt while O'Shea stayed in Brighton with the children, and got the train back on Christmas morning. This was a rare opportunity for the pair of them to spend a night in the house without the children and without fear of discovery. Parnell was unable to leave her side for a moment. Accompanying her through the deep snow-laden park to Eltham Lodge, they had to step back into the shadow of some trees to make way for the village carol singers taking a shortcut across the park. Later, Katharine joined her lover pacing up and down the wide terrace: 'We walked up and down in the moonlight till the carols died away, and we heard the church clocks strike twelve. Then we stood together to listen to the Christmas bells sound clear and sharp from many villages on the frosty air.'[28]

It is a romantic scene, painted tenderly by Katharine, a strong contrast to the duplicitous behaviour she is alleged to have resorted to that winter whenever Parnell visited her at Brighton. A number of incidents aroused Caroline Pethers's suspicions. According to her testimony at the divorce trial, 'Mr Stewart', as she knew Parnell, 'always came to the house the beach way', and commonly 'wore a light cloth cap over his eyes'; he 'drove out at night with Mrs O'Shea, but never in the day-time'; and, most incriminating of all, he and Mrs O'Shea 'were nearly always locked in a room together'. Katharine instructed her daughters Norah and Carmen to say that 'their mama did not like to be disturbed when she had anyone with her', and when Mrs Pethers had to take up messages to Katharine when she was engaged with 'Mr Stewart', 'I would wait five or ten minutes, and Mrs O'Shea would come to the door and open it just a little way'. While the Captain was away, Mrs O'Shea's visitor would sleep in her husband's dressing-room on the third floor. Katharine herself would take up his hot water and give orders for his breakfast. On one occasion, Mrs Pethers and her husband witnessed Katharine joining him in his bedroom: 'Mrs O'Shea and Mr Parnell were in the drawing-room until midnight. Mr Parnell came out first and went upstairs. Mrs O'Shea followed him upstairs . . . They were still in the bedroom when we went to bed.'[29]

This was clear evidence of Katharine's adultery, but more sensational in the minds of the public and in newspaper accounts of the trial was Caroline Pethers's astonishing account of an incident when Katharine and Parnell were surprised one evening by the sudden arrival of O'Shea. Mrs Pethers had already tried to enter the drawing-room to light the gas, but found that Mrs O'Shea and her friend had locked themselves in. Katharine called out that 'it didn't matter about the gas'.[30] At that moment, Mr Pethers was heard below admitting Captain O'Shea at the front door. Ten minutes later, according to Mrs Pethers, 'Mr Parnell rang the front door bell and asked to see Captain O'Shea. (Laughter.).' Since he could not have got down the stairs without being observed, the witness concluded that he must have used one of the rope ladder fire-escapes which were attached to the balcony. Katharine declared to Henry Harrison that, 'Nothing could have possibly been more unlike Mr Parnell than what was alleged against him. He considered himself a husband, and was sternly jealous in asserting the rights of his position in such ambiguities.'[31] Yet according to Caroline Pethers, this deception did not take place once, but 'three or four times'.[32]

While Lyons is content simply to dismiss Mrs Pethers's evidence as an 'uncorroborated story by a single witness, based apparently on half-heard conversation and on inference rather than observation',[33] Harrison devotes eight pages to discrediting the episode. He notes the discrepancy between Sir Edward Clarke's representation of Parnell being careful to keep out of O'Shea's way and O'Shea's own account of Parnell's visiting the house 'frequently' to discuss pressing political business, and he points out the absurdity of Parnell's being apparently known at the house under his own name *and* that of 'Charles Stewart'.[34] Harrison is most persuasive in his analysis of the fire-escape incident itself. Not only did the balcony in question face the Esplanade ('what of the neighbours and passers-by?'), but descent from a balcony by rope ladder 'involves a certain gymnastic proficiency', and what, asks Harrison, did Parnell do with his 'impedimenta', his hat and coat 'and possibly a bag containing political papers'?[35] Finally, he leaves the reader to picture the sheer absurdity of 'a bearded Romeo hurriedly descending by a rope ladder . . . in the presence of a Junoesque Juliet standing by to remove the apparatus of flight': 'Not such are the ways of middle-aged lovers, however defiant of the conventions.'[36]

Yet, as Harrison notes, the story of the fire-escape 'dominated' the mind of Justice Butt.[37] In his summing-up to the jury, the judge made two pointed allusions to the episode, as evidence ('so strong and conclusive') both of the respondent's adultery, and of the falsity of the respondent's counter-charge of connivance and condonation: 'why, when the husband comes to the door . . . should Mr Parnell . . . have gone out by the balcony and descended by a fire escape . . .?'[38] Katharine told Harrison that she knew of no such fire-escape at the house, and called Caroline Pethers's story a 'malicious fantasy'.[39] A fantasy it may have been, but it was not of Mrs Pethers's invention. Gerard O'Shea later told T.P. O'Connor that when interviewed by his father's solicitor he had been asked to account for Parnell's behaviour that day at Medina Terrace. Thus Gerard was the witness who believed that Parnell had been in the house when his father called and that he had subsequently reappeared at the front door. Gerard may have been mistaken, though, since he was clearly not in the drawing-room with his mother and Parnell and did not actually see Parnell make his escape. Pressed for an account of how Parnell could have exited the house unobserved, 20-year-old Gerard replied, 'I'm d——d if I know, unless he nipped down the fire-escape'.[40] He meant it as a joke, so he told O'Connor, 'never thinking the solicitor would take it seriously'.

It was apparently at Brighton that Katharine's and Parnell's youngest daughter was conceived. Katie was born on 27 November 1884, and was thus conceived in late February. It was Katharine's recollection that O'Shea came down to Brighton sometime in February to say goodbye to her and the children, before his departure on a long business trip to Lisbon and Madrid. The date of O'Shea's departure is an important consideration in establishing the paternity of Katie, and since the house in Medina Terrace was only taken up to the end of February 1884, Katharine's memory would seem to be accurate.[41] At the divorce trial, however, both O'Shea and his counsel were careful to stress that he left England in *March*.[42] We may infer from this that O'Shea had condoned his wife's behaviour at the time and knew that he could not possibly have been Katie's father, but that in order to pursue his case for divorce he had to make it appear that she had been conceived before he left the country. Why would they have been so insistent on what would otherwise have been an unimportant detail?

O'Shea was away for several months, his business trip apparently prolonged by an attack of gout. He would later claim that on his return to England in 'July or August 1884, I heard vague rumours that Mr Parnell had been at Eltham'.[43] As with his threat to call out Parnell in 1881,

O'Shea's response was both indirect (he chose to write to Parnell rather than confront him personally), and, in view of the fact that the rumours which reached him were 'vague', somewhat dramatic. 'You have behaved very badly to me,' he wrote to Parnell on 4 August: 'While I often told you that you were welcome to stay at Eltham whenever I was there, I begged of you not to do so during my absence, since it would be sure at the least sooner or later to cause a scandal.'[44] He was so offended by Parnell's behaviour that he announced his intention of resigning from Parliament before the end of the session and taking his family abroad. O'Shea's choice of phrase is significant, however. He nowhere makes an explicit accusation; his concern is solely that Parnell's behaviour may 'cause a scandal'.

Of course, to the divorce court, O'Shea's letter would have appeared to accuse Parnell of behaving in such a way as to give rise to rumours of an adulterous affair, but it is far more likely that O'Shea was reacting to the unpleasant discovery that his wife had become pregnant while he was abroad. He may have been able to come to terms with his wife having one child by Parnell, but this new pregnancy would have been a shock. Katharine called at Albert Mansions on Tuesday 5 August, the day after O'Shea wrote his letter to Parnell, and had presumably seen her husband at some point before then on his return to England. As Lyons has noted, she was now more than five months' pregnant: 'to the eye of one who knew her well enough to penetrate even the reticences of late Victorian clothing, she was plainly carrying a child.'[45] What is more, it is significant that she alludes to her pregnancy in a letter she wrote O'Shea two days later. On Thursday 7 August, presumably in response to an angry telegram demanding to know why she had not called to continue their discussion of Tuesday, Katharine replied that since that discussion had been so unpleasant, 'I could not imagine that you would expect me'. That, however, was not her chief excuse for not coming up to town: 'I was scarcely feeling strong enough to travel again in the heat yesterday, and for the children's sake I should not like to die yet, as they would lose all chance of aunt's money.'[46] The threat that the O'Sheas would forfeit Mrs Wood's fortune if the scandal alleged by her husband were to be made public, and he were to remove the family from Eltham, is made fairly plain, as is the allusion to her advancing pregnancy and the dangers of travelling up to town too often in the height of summer.

On 7 August, O'Shea also received a reply from Parnell, who, unlike Katharine, responded rather coolly: 'I do not know of any scandal, or any ground for one, and can only suppose that you have misunderstood the drift of some statements that may have been made to you.'[47] As to the matter of O'Shea's threatened resignation, Parnell expressed no false regret. Indeed, he advised O'Shea that it would be best if he did so a few days before the end of the present session. With that O'Shea was apparently satisfied. According to Sir Edward Clarke, having received written denials from both his wife and Parnell (although neither letter of 7 August quite qualifies as a 'denial' of specific wrongdoing), 'this matter was closed', and Clarke moved on swiftly to read out an invitation O'Shea sent Parnell to spend the evening with the family at Wonersh Lodge just before Christmas, which appeared to prove that O'Shea was still head of the household at Eltham. Parnell's belated reply (of 24 December) also appeared to demonstrate Clarke's point that, in the months immediately after the contretemps of August, Parnell had refrained from visiting Eltham except at O'Shea's request. He thanked O'Shea for his invitation, which 'would have given me a great deal of pleasure had I known in time', and went on, 'I will look for you to-morrow at Eltham, unless I hear that you are unable to leave town, in which case I will call at Albert Mansions'.[48]

There is some evidence that more care was taken over Parnell's visits to Eltham in the latter part of 1884, but he does appear to have been there when Katie was born. Of the birth itself we know even less than of her sister Clare's. Sir Edward Clarke did not mention Katie in his presentation of the case, while O'Shea referred to her briefly as 'our youngest child, Frances'.[49] Katharine herself says only that she was unwell in the autumn of 1884, and that 'Captain O'Shea was coming to Eltham a good deal'.[50] A letter of Parnell's she reprints, dated Friday 28 October 1884, appears to back this up. Apparently in code, Parnell wrote to Katharine to ascertain O'Shea's movements.[51] (O'Shea had been holding meetings in West Clare and let Katharine know that he intended to travel on Thursday 23 October.) However, there is little further sign of O'Shea's presence at Eltham. In fact the next five letters from Parnell published in Katharine's book are addressed from Eltham. The letters are not specifically dated, but they do appear to have been sent at the time of Katie's birth.

Harrison believes that Katharine was also in the house and that Parnell wrote her these notes because 'he had to leave too early and to return too late for sickroom hours'.[52] Certainly, Wonersh Lodge was registered as Katie's place of birth. Yet it may be that Katharine recuperated after the birth away from home, perhaps at a London nursing home. Whatever the precise arrangements, Parnell was able to visit Katharine on evenings when there wasn't much activity in the House, and of course they found a method of communicating daily ('I felt very much relieved by your letter last night. However, it is evident you must take great care'; 'you really must take care of yourself and not get up too soon'[53]). While he still had his rooms at the Westminster Palace Hotel, Parnell seems frequently to have slept at Wonersh Lodge, where he was waited on by Katharine's maid, Phyllis Bryceson ('had an excellent breakfast which Phyllis brought me'; 'Phyllis is looking after me first rate'[54]).

Katharine chooses not to explain the context of these five undated letters from Eltham, yet together they suggest very strongly a long-established pattern of domesticity at Wonersh Lodge, when, even in Katharine's absence, it is the home to which Parnell came to be looked after by her servants – and a home where neither he nor Katharine appeared to have any real fear of O'Shea's intrusion. The following year, 1885, Katharine would pay for an extension to the house to afford Parnell a private study, the panelling and fittings furnished with sweet-chestnut from Avondale. He also sent over for his telescope, a magnificent affair, which he mounted in Katharine's back garden, having made a pedestal from 'a few sacks of Portland cement'.[55] He gave her two Irish setters, 'Ranger' and 'Grouse', and at New Year 1885, bought a new horse for Katharine in Ireland. He was named 'Dictator', and was a 'very quiet and a very fine one', he reported to Katharine on 14 January: 'strong and short legs, with plenty of bone, a splendid fore-quarter, and a good turn of speed.'[56] The horse was also 'very shy and unused to town', and Parnell advised Katharine to have two grooms to meet 'Dictator' and his own horse, 'President', when they arrived at Euston: 'They should be walked carefully through London.' Interestingly, he sent Katharine this last message in a formal letter addressed to 'Mrs O'Shea', stating that he 'should feel very much obliged if you would allow them to stand in your stables *for a few days*, until I can make other arrangements'.[57] This precaution was necessary, according to Katharine, 'in case the horses should be noticed arriving in Eltham and the fact reported to Captain O'Shea',[58] yet for another year and a half O'Shea apparently remained unaware of the fact either that his wife's lover's horses were permanently stabled at Wonersh Lodge or that Katharine employed a new groom, Richard Wise.

Since so little correspondence from this period survives, it would be irresponsible to jump to conclusions. However, the few letters published by Katharine do suggest certain patterns of behaviour. While O'Shea maintained close contact with Katharine, he did so by letter or by asking her to call on him at Albert Mansions. His occasional visits to Eltham are requested by letter and appear to be brief. O'Shea was away in Ireland a month before the birth and returned there pretty shortly afterwards (Katharine reprints a letter of his from the Shelbourne Hotel dated 15 December 1884). And while the birth of another daughter to Captain O'Shea was duly announced on the front page of *The Times*, Thursday 4 December 1884, once more it was left to Katharine to register the birth of her daughter, and again she delayed doing so (this time, for two and a half months).[59] On 10 January 1885, O'Shea came down to Eltham for Norah's birthday – interestingly, while Parnell was away in Ireland – yet, in another undated note to Katharine which appears to belong to the January correspondence, he asks that 'the young ladies' be sent to meet him at Pope Street (New Eltham) Station at 12.22, which seems to indicate that he intended to take them back to town for lunch without having to call at Wonersh Lodge. Then, on 19 January, in a 'very low state' on account of his gout (his doctor told him he thought 'my heart affected'), he asked Katharine to drive up to Albert Mansions with Norah and Carmen.[60]

One other letter, also apparently from January 1885, may shed some further light on the O'Sheas' curious relationship at this period. Writing at one o'clock in the morning after having been called out to see Chamberlain at midnight, O'Shea was in possession of 'a communication of the most urgent and important character' to pass on to Parnell: 'I have just written to Mr Parnell to say that I shall be here [i.e. at Albert Mansions] at 12 o'clock, and shall wait for him.' It was all too involved for him to explain in writing, but he hoped that Katharine, too, would be free to come up to Albert Mansions some time in the afternoon when he promised to 'tell you all about it'.[61] He signs off, 'Your B.' The letter tells us, first, that O'Shea continued to regard his wife as his political confidante (he clearly liked to share political gossip with her), but that it was his practice to communicate with her in writing or to see her in London, not at Eltham; and, secondly, that in notifying Katharine about the appointment he was trying to arrange with Parnell, he appears to be aware she is more likely to see Parnell than he is, and that in her role as Parnell's unofficial secretary she would be able to tell him of the pressing need for the meeting. It is as if he knows that Parnell is at Eltham, and that in writing to her he is writing to him.

If O'Shea was indeed the conniving husband Katharine would later accuse him of being, and not only knew that he was being cuckolded but was prepared to accept his wife's lover's children as his own, there remains the question of how he was able to maintain a close professional relationship with Parnell. Certainly, his personal ambition did not flag and it alone may have driven him through this unpleasant episode, since Chamberlain flattered him that their collaboration over the question of Irish local government was sure to lead to a government appointment. However, this was to be the last political collaboration between Parnell and O'Shea. O'Shea was prepared to use his special relationship with the Irish leader in order to get close to the centre of political power, just as he had done over the Kilmainham affair. But whereas in negotiating the Kilmainham treaty, he was in effect merely facilitating a process urgently desired by both Parnell and Gladstone, the issue of local government was not one on which the Irish and the Liberal leaders were in agreement, and he was to find his own role as intermediary fraught with difficulty.

Joseph Chamberlain had revived the idea of granting a form of local government to the Irish. It had previously been aired by Gladstone, but dropped due to Cabinet opposition. As in 1882, Chamberlain once more relied upon O'Shea to mediate with Parnell, and Katharine recalls that they 'discussed the Local Government Bill at all hours, as Mr Parnell wished to find out what the views of Mr Chamberlain were and the Tories – better ascertainable by Willie than others'.[62] Clearly, despite the flare-up in the summer, the men could still work together politically. Their discussions led to O'Shea forwarding Chamberlain a memorandum of the conditions under which Parnell would accept a renewal of coercion: either that its re-enactment was limited to just one year, or that the new Crimes Bill should contain within it provision for a substantial measure of local government.[63] The memorandum was posted on Thursday 27 November 1884, the same day that Katharine gave birth to Frances Katie Flavia O'Shea.

The phrase 'local government' was interpreted rather differently by Parnell and by Chamberlain. The former had in mind an elected central board whose role was to be purely administrative, while Chamberlain envisaged, apparently more ambitiously, a legislative board with powers to raise taxation and to deal with questions of land, education, transport and communications. In fact, Chamberlain, an opponent of Home Rule, regarded the whole issue of local government as a *substitute* for it, while Parnell saw the scheme as 'absolutely separate', and ultimately insignificant.[64] Parnell's direction to O'Shea on 5 January could not have been more explicit: 'In talking to our friend [i.e. Chamberlain] you must give him clearly to understand that we do *not* propose this local self-government plank as a substitute for the restitution of our Irish parliament.'[65]

While the idea of local government was at best a side-issue for Parnell, O'Shea staked all on its success, but he seems to have promised Chamberlain more than he could deliver, and to have misled him by holding from him Parnell's strongly expressed position in his letters of 5 and 13 January. In early March he invited himself to Eltham in order to confide in Katharine that Chamberlain had as much as told him that after the General Election the post of Chief Secretary would be his: 'This is an enormous thing, giving you and the Chicks a very great position.'[66] He believed it to be in his grasp, perhaps unwisely repeating to Parnell a remark of Chamberlain's on the incautious speed at which they were proceeding, 'somewhat as if he were already Prime Minister and I Chief Secretary'.[67]

Yet Parnell had no wish to see Chamberlain succeed Gladstone, who was the only man he regarded as capable of carrying through Home Rule, and at some point in early January, in a repetition of his treatment of O'Shea during the Kilmainham negotiations, Parnell went behind the messenger's back and communicated independently with the Government. He drafted a local government bill to his own specifications and asked Katharine to forward it to the Prime Minister.[68] That he did so implies his mistrust of

O'Shea. We know from a letter of Lord Richard Grosvenor's that the document was 'written by a type-writing machine',[69] which suggests that it was produced at Eltham by Katharine, who had become an able typist.

Thus, when Chamberlain called at Downing Street to report a meeting he had had with O'Shea on 15 January, Gladstone 'told him that he had received a similar scheme embodying Parnell's views through Mrs O'Shea'.[70] What Chamberlain and O'Shea made of this is not recorded. However, O'Shea's subsequent behaviour suggests that he was very anxious to convince Chamberlain that Katharine was as much his own messenger as Parnell's. On 19 January, he wrote to Katharine, enclosing for Parnell a very long and breezy account of his meetings with Chamberlain. He had written out a copy for Chamberlain's benefit which he now asked Katharine to forward ('Please post the enclosed by the 10 o'clock post to Chamberlain. Seal with wax'[71]). There seems to be no reason at all for his requesting Katharine to do so (why not post it himself?) except to convey to Chamberlain an appearance of marital unity, and to blur the significance of his wife's acting independently of him, and on behalf of Parnell.

Nevertheless, by mid-March things had advanced so far that the Cabinet discussed bringing in separate local government bills for England and Ireland, the latter, O'Shea told Katharine, 'on the basis of the proposals which I handed C[hamberlain] in January'.[72] Lord Spencer now urged upon the Cabinet the danger of facing the next election with having done nothing for Ireland except renew coercion, and he put forward a four-point programme of remedial action which was to include 'a bill to establish representative local government in the Irish counties'.[73] Nervousness about a 'central board', possibly dominated by 'the present Irish parliamentary party, the Healys, the O'Briens and T.P. O'Connors', led to his preference to 'build up local government from the bottom'.[74] Cardinal Manning now became important to the process, promising the support of the Irish bishops for a local government scheme to pre-empt the question of Home Rule. This was something Parnell wished to avoid at all costs.[75]

At this point O'Shea was distracted by very serious money troubles. In mid-March he was about to return to Madrid on business relating to a Cuban investment scheme in which he was involved, yet he was prepared to postpone the trip for a day or two at Chamberlain's request, 'so as to let him know "P.'s mind"' ('He hasn't much,' O'Shea, typically, quipped to Katharine). Once in Spain, he expressed some impatience at Mrs Wood's accusation of extravagance (for, of course, it was she who financed all these visits to Spain and Portugal). He was, he claimed, doing 'everything [a] mortal could do about the Cuban business', including difficult negotiations with the Spanish Prime Minister, and he was exhausted, anxious to return to Parliament after the Easter Recess: 'but I greatly fear Bank and great bother in London.'[76]

He came back to a Government in disarray. An understanding with Parnell seems to have been arrived at, but the Cabinet was divided. On 28 April, Chamberlain instructed O'Shea to send word to Parnell that he and Dilke were prepared to make the failure of what had become the County and Central Board Government Bill a resignation matter if 'Parnell would publicly pledge his full support to the scheme proposed by him in January, and would prevent obstruction on the part of his followers to a renewal of the Crimes Act for one year'.[77] Two days later, O'Shea saw Parnell at Albert Mansions at seven o'clock, and recorded in his diary: 'After much conversation accepted proposal.' He then reported this to Dilke at eleven, who said 'he thought the Cabinet would break up on it'.[78]

The following day, Friday, O'Shea sent Katharine further news of the Cabinet meeting held that morning at eleven o'clock: 'Gladstone is very strongly in favour of our solution, and to C.'s surprise Hartington did not reject the proposal offhand as was expected.'[79] In fact, he gave her such detailed information that one suspects that he intended it for Parnell. Yet O'Shea had more than political concerns. He had, he said, 'nothing to do to-morrow', and wondered if he could come down to Eltham for the day. He makes a point of mentioning that he has a breakfast appointment with Chamberlain on Sunday morning (it was his boast that Chamberlain 'generally sees me twice a day now'[80]), which may or may not have been intended to indicate to Katharine that he was not going to stay the night at Eltham. No doubt he wanted to see Katharine about money matters, which were pressing since 'the Cuban business must take time'.[81] He was 'holding out against the bank, but only by the skin of my teeth, and it cannot continue many hours'.[82] He was open with Katharine that the reason for his anxiety about the local government proposals was personal, and no doubt financial: 'if Chamberlain has power, which I think he will in the next Parliament, he will offer me the Chief Secretaryship, or the equivalent position if the name is abolished.'[83]

Yet Parnell, who had no wish to divide the Cabinet over the issue of local government, finally reneged on his assurances to O'Shea, and announced on the night of Thursday 7 May, 'with a sort of wave of chivalry, that I might convey to Chamberlain that he didn't hold them to the bargain; that they were free to compromise with their comrades if they chose'.[84] On Saturday a split Cabinet voted to reject Chamberlain's scheme, and on Friday 15 May, Gladstone announced to the House that the policy of coercion *would* be renewed (although he refused to specify its duration), and that the Government proposed *no* remedial legislation for Ireland this session. The resignations of Dilke, Chamberlain and Shaw Lefevre followed.[85] Tim Healy writes that 'Few realised that the fall of Gladstone's Government was impending. I doubt that the Conservatives knew it',[86] but the agreement with Parnell that a local government bill would be introduced before the Coercion Bill had not been kept, and in the first week of June, Parnell marshalled his MPs for the second reading of the Budget Bill. The Tory MP, Sir Michael Hicks Beach, was to move an amendment condemning an extra sixpence on the price of spirits. On the evening of 7 June Parnell telegraphed Healy, then in Dublin, ordering him to get the morning mail to London. Healy arrived to a quiet House at 6 p.m. on Monday evening, to be met by Parnell, angry that two of his MPs were still in Dublin and would miss the vote. At 1.45 on the morning of 9 June the results of the division were called: the Government, opposed by a united front of Tories and Nationalists, had lost by a margin of fourteen votes, and 'Roar after roar of joy went up from the Irish benches'.[87] Gladstone resigned that day and Salisbury formed a temporary government before the calling of the General Election at the end of the year.

# CHAPTER 8

## *The Price of Silence*

The disappointment of O'Shea's political ambitions would give rise to considerable difficulties for Katharine and Parnell. This was particularly so as, during the few months of Salisbury's first brief Conservative Government, from June to December 1885, Parnell's increasing mistrust of Chamberlain's scheme for Irish local government became outright rejection. O'Shea's frustration was exacerbated by his anxiety about which seat he would fight at the forthcoming General Election. There was no possibility that the Nationalist electorate of County Clare would stomach his renewed candidacy. Nor was there the slightest hope that the Irish Parliamentary Party would support his candidacy elsewhere. When Parnell discussed this possibility with colleagues, T.P. O'Connor 'shook a very emphatic "No"', while James O'Kelly advised him either to let O'Shea stand as a Liberal in the North, 'or else make some provision for him outside politics'.[1] From being centrally involved in the months of negotiations between Chamberlain and Parnell, with the prospect, in his view at least, of being rewarded with the Irish Under-Secretaryship, O'Shea first saw these negotiations come to nothing and then had to face the humiliating prospect of having no constituency to represent.

O'Shea told Katharine that Parnell had 'promised me to secure my re-election "without trouble"',[2] and he would for ever after blame Parnell for not supporting him in the constituency he had represented for the past five years. In fact, he had only himself to blame. If Home Rule were to be achieved, discipline was essential for Parnell's new party, but O'Shea had made something of a boast of his refusal to take the party pledge now required of all Nationalist candidates: 'I pledge myself that, in the event of my Election to Parliament, I will Sit, Act, and Vote with the Irish Parliamentary Party.'[3] As he would explain to Gladstone in October of that year, it was impossible for him to subscribe to such a pledge, since he would then forfeit 'giving your policy the humble support which I am always anxious to offer it'.[4] He believed himself above such things as pledges.

O'Shea's was a sudden fall from grace, and his increasingly venomous anger towards Parnell, whom he firmly believed to be in his debt, threatened to blow apart the secure domestic life Katharine and Parnell had established at Eltham over the past two years. In order to pacify her increasingly troublesome husband, Katharine had to ask for help from the Prime Minister, and Parnell had seriously to compromise himself.

The first indication that Parnell was intending to reject Chamberlain's scheme for an Irish local government 'central board' was an attack in Parnell's paper, *United Ireland* (26 June), on the proposed tour of Ireland by Chamberlain and Dilke to test public opinion toward the scheme. The tour was condemned as 'a mere electoral manoeuvre' designed 'to curry favour once more with the Irish people', and the two Radicals were censured for 'their cynical hypocrisy'.[5] Chamberlain was astounded and sent the article to O'Shea with a mass of exclamation marks. O'Shea immediately had words with Parnell, but could not get him to promise that the paper's editor, William O'Brien, would retract the article. He sent Chamberlain two separate commentaries on their interview, the second revealing that 'Mr Parnell sat under a tree for an hour and a half reflecting on all my observations'.[6] It is likely that this Sunday afternoon discussion took place in the garden at Wonersh Lodge, with O'Shea, significantly, the visitor.

O'Shea then spent a week in Madrid. On his return Chamberlain presented him with a long letter to show to Parnell in an attempt to get him to say once and for all, 'as a gentleman and a man of honour', whether he was still interested in the question of local government.[7] Two days later he heard back from O'Shea that Parnell's position had been completely altered by the fact that there had been a change of government. As O'Shea put it, 'he has had a better offer': the Conservatives had decided against a re-imposition of coercion in Ireland and had made promises regarding remedial legislation; moreover, the new Lord-Lieutenant, Lord Carnarvon, appeared to be open-minded regarding the question of Irish 'legislative independence'.[8] To Chamberlain, O'Shea was able to rationalise the situation, but to Katharine he admitted 'that one looks such a fool, getting Mr C. to write such a letter as that . . . to no purpose'. He claimed to have 'told the *scoundrel* what I think of him', and rued the day when he was *asked*, as he construed it, to go to Kilmainham.[9]

His confiding to Katharine his treatment at the hands of the '*scoundrel*' Parnell certainly complicates the notion of O'Shea's connivance; so, too, does the fact that he could find comedy in his embarrassment. 'I am worried, if not out of my wits, out of my hair,' he wrote. 'The little left came out this morning after a sleepless night, and I am balder than a coot is.'[10] Yet his bitterness over Parnell's betrayal of the scheme he and Chamberlain had been nursing since the previous November led him to make the following comment in a letter to Katharine the next day. He had talked over Parnell's conduct with, apparently, scores of MPs of all parties, and reported that 'one and all spoke in astonishment and disgust of

Parnell's conduct to me. None of them, of course, knew the absolute baseness of it'.[11] This is not further explained, but it is difficult to avoid understanding it to be an allusion to the irregularity of their relationship.

One of the reasons Parnell dropped O'Shea and Chamberlain was that he had received independent enquiries about his present views on local government from another, far more important source – Gladstone himself. Once more Katharine played an important role. At Gladstone's request, Lord Richard Grosvenor wrote to her on 14 July, to ask whether Parnell still stood by the terms of the 'tolerably complete scheme' she had forwarded him earlier in the year.

There is little documentary reference to the domestic life of Katharine and her children during the latter part of 1885, but at this point she was at the seaside with her children and did not reply to Grosvenor's note until a week later. She and Parnell holidayed on and off that summer. According to the testimony of Jane Chapman, a temporary parlour-maid hired by Katharine for the months of July and August 1885, while the family were at Eltham, Mr Parnell was there 'all the time', and when Mrs O'Shea was away at the seaside, he went with them.[12]

On the same day Grosvenor's letter was dated, Gladstone's son Herbert, MP for Leeds, had made an incautious speech in his constituency in support of a Dublin Parliament, and Katharine's reply to Grosvenor ran thus: 'I believe, that nothing less than a scheme based on the lines of Mr Herbert Gladstone's last speech at Leeds would be acceptable now, or considered calculated to settle the Irish question. This is however only my own idea, and I will write to you again in a few days if you care to hear.'[13]

Despite the audacity of this latest development Gladstone responded favourably, since it provided him with a programme on which to fight the next General Election. It was the opinion of his Private Secretary, Sir Edward Hamilton, that, 'we have had enough of half measures for Ireland [and] had better "go the whole hog"'.[14] Yet for some weeks it remained unclear exactly what kind of Irish Parliament Parnell believed would settle the Irish question. Katharine failed to reply to Grosvenor's pressing demands for a 'plain' answer,[15] and on 4 August, Gladstone ('never . . . more embarrassed as to what to do', according to Mrs Gladstone[16]) wrote to Katharine himself, impressing upon her his anxiety to know Parnell's mind, since he was about to go on a three-week yachting expedition around the Norwegian coast.

Katharine replied the next day and apologised for her silence. She explained that she had been away and had not had her letters forwarded, and that she had just returned from Folkestone to find letters from him and from Grosvenor. It was a credible enough excuse, but, despite having only just got home, she was able to write Gladstone a three-page letter detailing the new

1. Rivenhall Place, Essex, the childhood home of Katharine, whose father Sir John Page Wood was the Vicar of Cressing.

2. Portrait of Katharine dated 1873. O'Shea 'was always worrying me to dress in the latest fashion'.

3. Watercolour sketch of William Henry O'Shea (1840–1905), then a Captain in the 18th Hussars.

4. Wonersh Lodge, Eltham, the roomy villa provided for Katharine by her wealthy Aunt Wood. In 1885, Katharine paid for an extension to the back of the house to provide Parnell with a study. His two horses were stabled at Wonersh Lodge.

5. Eltham Lodge, south-east London, the home of Aunt Wood.

6. Charles Stewart Parnell
(1846–1891), *c.* 1880.

7. The Ladies' Gallery, House of Commons.

8. Four envelopes showing some of the pseudonyms adopted by Katharine and Parnell.

9. Parnell (centre) and Irish MPs protest at the news of Michael Davitt's re-arrest (3 February 1881). All were suspended and forcibly removed from the House.

10. Land League supporters demonstrate at a forced sale of cattle seized in lieu of rent, June 1881.

11. Miniature of Katharine that Parnell had with him at Kilmainham.

12. Charles Stewart Parnell *c*. 1885.

13. Parnell interviewed in his cell at Kilmainham Gaol.

14. The Liberal Prime Minister, William Ewart Gladstone (1809–98).

15. One of the few surviving photographs of Captain O'Shea.

16. Katharine's very first letter to Gladstone, dated 23 May 1882, asking for a private interview

17. From a letter from Katharine of 23 October 1885, petitioning Gladstone for a seat for O'Shea at the next election.

**O ROMEO, ROMEO!"**

18. Post-divorce cartoon depicting Parnell using the fire escape to evade detection.

19. Parnell addressing a hostile crowd at the Kilkenny by-election in December 1890.

20. Katharine and Parnell's second daughter, Clare (1883–1908).

21. Katie O'Shea (1884–1947), Katharine's youngest daughter.

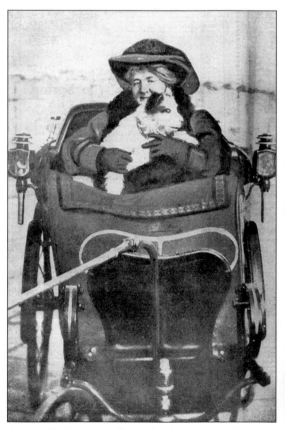

22. Clare's son and Parnell's only grandchild, Assheton Clare Bowyer-Lane Maunsell (1909–34).

23. Katharine Parnell on the front at Brighton in 1914.

position taken up by Parnell. Katharine's letter makes it clear that he was with her at Eltham: 'I have shown this letter to Mr Parnell who says it expresses exactly what he means.' Of the local government scheme she had submitted earlier in the year, Katharine would say only that it had been conceived 'in order to make it more easy for English statesmen to approach the question of [Home Rule]'. Parnell now believed that the country was ready 'to consider the question of granting to Ireland a constitution of a similar nature to that of one of the larger colonies'. If Gladstone was amenable to such a proposal, she offered to send him 'a draft of detailed propositions'.[17] This document had already been drawn up while she and Parnell were at the coast. We are given a glimpse of how intimately their domestic and political lives were intertwined as Katharine discloses that Parnell dictated 'A Proposed Constitution for Ireland' to her 'while I sat on the steps' outside Heatherbell Cottage, a house they had taken at Beachy Head.[18]

While Gladstone was careful to make clear to Katharine that he would not enter 'into any counter-bidding of any sort' against the Conservatives, he could not disguise his excitement at the proposal alluded to in Katharine's 'very interesting' letter: 'Too interesting, almost, to be addressed to a person of my age and weakened sight, since it substitutes for a limited prospect a field almost without bounds.'[19] According to Herbert Gladstone, who spoke to Sir Edward Hamilton on Friday 7 August, his father would fight the next election only 'if some specific work is put before him – some work with which the nation specifically entrusts him', and it was Herbert's understanding that 'The only work of such a kind which is likely to present itself is the Irish question'.[20] Parnell, though, allowed Gladstone to leave for Norway without further contact. August and September passed. On 6 October, Grosvenor informed Gladstone that there was 'no sign of any document from the lady',[21] and Gladstone seems to have resigned himself to the fact that Parnell must have 'throw[n] in his lot with the Tories'.[22] But Parnell had not gone so far as to do that.

On 23 October Gladstone and Grosvenor finally heard from Katharine (she sent out duplicate letters), although she was cautious about the matter of the draft constitution: 'I should have sent the Paper I mentioned', but was not 'sure if the offer would be desired'. Astonishingly, the main concern of this spontaneous and substantial communication (she covered nine sides of notepaper) was to beg Gladstone to intervene on her husband's behalf at the General Election. The substance of the deal she offered was simple: in return for the Government's assistance in getting O'Shea a Liberal seat, Parnell promised full collaboration on a Home Rule bill proposed by the Liberals. Implicit in this agreement is an understanding that Gladstone and Grosvenor knew full well why it was so important to Katharine and to Parnell that O'Shea was silenced.

Katharine did not send Gladstone Parnell's paper until he had given her assurances that he would act on behalf of her husband, even though this was leaving Gladstone very little time before the General Election in November to prepare his own mind and that of his party on the question of Irish Home Rule. Since the opposition from O'Shea's own constituency of County Clare was so '*very* great' (twice underlined), Katharine stated that she did not feel justified in asking Mr Parnell to support his standing again for Clare. The terms of the deal she proposed were extraordinarily favourable to the Liberals. In return for O'Shea's being accepted as the Liberal candidate for Mid Armagh ('I am sure he will be a very good supporter of the Liberal Party'), Gladstone was assured of the Irish vote in East Down, North Antrim, North Armagh, North Derry and Wolverhampton (where the Liberal MP Henry Fowler's seat looked vulnerable). 'But of course this cannot be carried unless you will intervene with the leaders of the Liberal Party in Ulster immediately'.[23]

Gladstone's personal intervention on behalf of Katharine's husband is of interest, quite aside from the fact that Parnell offered the Liberals such a generous deal in exchange for assisting O'Shea to a safe Liberal seat. Publicly, Gladstone persisted in his belief that the Liberal Party owed O'Shea a personal debt over the Kilmainham treaty, and, at Katharine's express wish, he put pressure on Grosvenor, writing to him on 27 October, 'I hope you will be cautious not to [reject?] in principle the O'Shea proposal though you may not be able to act upon it.'[24] It is surely no coincidence that Parnell's long-promised document on an Irish constitution reached Gladstone three days later (Katharine explaining that she had waited for Parnell to return from Ireland, 'to see if he wished to alter it in any way'[25]); nor that Katharine subsequently received a letter promising support for her husband's campaign in Mid Armagh. Gladstone dictated Grosvenor a letter assuring Katharine that 'Lord R.G. will I am sure do all he can to promote Captain O'Shea's views but his power at this advanced stage is limited & I wish the need could have been earlier known'.[26] In her book, Katharine would categorically deny that there was 'a loathsome treaty between Parnell, Willie and myself',[27] but the measures which she and Parnell were prepared to take to secure her husband a seat in Parliament do strongly suggest that they were desperate to avert scandalous exposure, and the conclusion that Gladstone and Grosvenor, his Chief Whip, were complicit in this is hard to avoid.

Henry Labouchère later confided to Tim Healy Gladstone's willingness to buy the silence of another cuckolded husband that same year. When Sir Charles Dilke was threatened with divorce Gladstone asked Labouchère to approach the aggrieved husband, Donald Crawford (also a Liberal MP), to 'make a settlement' to save Dilke's political career. Labouchère came back saying that it was impossible because Crawford demanded to be made a judge, too high a price, to which Gladstone replied, 'Why impossible? Can any good reason be brought forward against his being made an English judge?'[28] Similarly, O'Shea had to be silenced for the sake of political expediency, so that Gladstone could continue to work closely with Parnell, through Katharine as intermediary, to achieve Irish Home Rule, which he anticipated would be the crowning glory of the Liberal Party and his own last ministry.

While Parnell was campaigning in Dublin, Katharine was left to campaign on O'Shea's behalf. It is a measure of her influence, and also of Gladstone's recognition of the importance of her role as Parnell's intermediary, that she received the full cooperation of the Liberal leader. Remarkably, Grosvenor, who kept Gladstone closely informed of developments, found time to have several long interviews with her, despite its being less than a month before the General Election. Yet the hastily arranged campaign was beset by all manner of problems, and O'Shea himself felt that he 'was on a wildgoose chase'.[29] By the end of the month, Grosvenor learnt that their secret negotiations with the Ulster Liberals had been leaked to the press, and that O'Shea's chances in the North were hopeless ('I am very much afraid that they have made a fearful mess, as they always do with anything of the kind in Ireland'[30]). The most he could do would be to help him 'very silently' in another constituency.[31] The Liberal Party could be confident of one thing, however: 'It seems clear enough that Parnell is anxious to help O'Shea & us unconditionally as proposed.'[32]

This was not how O'Shea perceived the case. On 2 November, from the Shelbourne Hotel, O'Shea wrote separately to Parnell and Katharine. His letter to Parnell was curt, if not insolent. Ignoring the fact of Parnell's offer to the Liberals, it rankled with him that Parnell had insisted that he take the party pledge, which, to O'Shea's mind, had 'nothing to do with me'. Indeed, he found Parnell's whole attitude towards him at fault, and let him know that 'Several very important personages . . . are of the opinion, that, as a gentleman, you are under the clearest obligation to declare to your friends that you insist on my being returned to Parliament', or 'you will resign the leadership of your Party'.[33] As was his way, O'Shea had complained to a great many people about Parnell's failure to support him more strongly, such that there was 'much talk in Dublin about my affair. All agree that Parnell's conduct is loathsome.'[34]

O'Shea's 2 November letter to Katharine suggests that he would stop at nothing, even blackmail, to secure his re-election to Parliament. Distracted with self-pity ('I wonder the little girls have not written to me; no one cares a bit for me except my poor old mother'), and expressing small gratitude for Katharine's exertions ('Of course I knew nothing about your political movements and arrangements'), O'Shea let Katharine know that he was plotting his revenge against Parnell ('He won't be of high "importance" soon'):

All I know is that I am not going to die in a ditch. I have been treated in blackguard fashion and I mean to hit back a stunner. I have everything ready; no drugs could make me sleep last night, and I packed my shell with dynamite. It cannot hurt my friend [i.e. Chamberlain], and it will send a blackguard's reputation with his deluded countrymen into smithereens.[35]

What he intended we simply do not know, because Katharine immediately made an appointment to see Grosvenor, and at the end of this meeting the possibility of an *English* seat was held out to O'Shea, that of the Liverpool Exchange Division, which, according to T.P. O'Connor, 'had in its electorate a large number of English Liberals and even a larger number of Irish Nationalists'.[36] Here, too, the situation was complicated, and Katharine was now in daily communication with Grosvenor in order to ensure that everything was being done to help her husband, who was becoming increasingly agitated. On 7 November, Parnell called at Albert Mansions and, according to O'Shea, 'began to mumble' his regrets about Mid Armagh and hoped 'that an English seat might yet be found for me'. O'Shea took exception to what he saw as Parnell's rather too casual approach. The next day he posted Chamberlain a dramatic account of his meeting with Parnell. Whether it is an exaggeration of the truth or pure invention, O'Shea's extreme sense of grievance at the way he was being treated is clear:

I soon cut matters short by telling him that I did not want any more beating about the bush, that no man had ever behaved more shamefully to another than he had behaved to me, and that I wished to hold no further communication with him. He inquired whether I wished him to leave and I replied, most certainly. He then crossed the room and held out his hand. I informed him that I would not touch it on any account.

   I do not suppose he has feeling enough to have felt the blow long, but I never saw a man slink out of a room more like a cur kicked out of a butcher's shop.[37]

Parnell's response to this ugly scene was to draw up yet another generous deal to offer the Liberals in return for their support for O'Shea's candidacy in Liverpool ('giving Liberal candidates a fair chance of six divisions'[38]). However, on 13 November Katharine got word that another Liberal candidate, Stephens, had already been selected for Liverpool Exchange. By this time, she says, she was so determined that her husband should be returned for the seat that she authorised him to tell his Liberal friends that Parnell threatened to stand for election himself if O'Shea was not accepted: 'I can get that put in Liverpool papers tonight if you telegraph [Parnell].'[39] O'Shea, perhaps not quite trusting his chances in England after his embarrassment in Mid Armagh, telegraphed Katharine to say that he would not consider going up to Liverpool unless she could provide him with firm letters of recommendation from Grosvenor and Gladstone. Katharine 'did not wish to rouse the irritation of Mr Gladstone',[40] but, having no time to consult Parnell, she telegraphed Gladstone, who said he would consult with Grosvenor. Grosvenor had in fact already wired to Liverpool his support for O'Shea, but this was not enough. Gladstone's backing was essential. So she made another appointment to see Grosvenor, who took an amused view of Katharine's campaign of harassment: 'I am not at all sure that I approve of you in your political capacity,' he told her, 'you are so terribly strenuous and determined!'[41] However, he gave her assurances that Gladstone would act.

From Midlothian, where Gladstone was campaigning in his own constituency, he sent a telegram to Grosvenor in which he stated that, in view of O'Shea's role in the Kilmainham negotiations, and his being 'a genial supporter of Liberal policy', 'I shall have great pleasure in hearing that he's widely accepted, and is likely to be triumphantly returned by the election of the district'.[42] As Grosvenor had gently reminded Katharine, 'We have our own troubles, Mrs O'Shea, in this election'.[43] It is therefore all the more remarkable that Gladstone chose to intervene personally on behalf of O'Shea in Liverpool. It is only explicable in terms of Gladstone's awareness of how important Parnell was to him and to Irish politics, and of his vulnerability to O'Shea.

On Friday 20 November, O'Shea delivered his address to the electors of the Exchange Division, but local Liberals required a great deal of convincing, even with Gladstone's endorsement of his candidacy. That same day he wired Katharine in desperation, 'If Grosvenor would come all might be put right.'[44] Several times a day Katharine was left to field messages like this from her husband. On receiving this particular telegram, she went straight to London, 'and told Lord Richard that now he absolutely must go, as he had promised me he would'. Despite its placing him in a highly 'awkward position' (but no doubt persuaded by what he knew to be Gladstone's personal wishes in the matter), Grosvenor agreed to catch the night-train to Liverpool. He had, however, one condition: 'I want you to come with me,' he told Katharine.

I looked quietly at Lord Richard, and held to my self-control with all the force I possessed. Go with him to Liverpool to help by canvassing and by the influence of my personal charm, my husband by law to contest this seat, backed and aided in my efforts by the presence of my lover himself! Was Grosvenor mad? . . . Was this man a monk, a priest, an absolute child, to think these things could be?[45]

Unable to meet her eye, Grosvenor played with his blotting pad. 'Parnell is in Liverpool working quietly for Willie,' Katharine explained. 'He replied, still not looking at me: "I was not sure". I went on: "I cannot personally work for Willie in Liverpool".' With that, Grosvenor agreed to set off at once, but he cautioned her that his work on behalf of O'Shea must remain secret, and that in communicating with Katharine he would refer to her husband by the code-name 'Jack'. They then left in a cab together so that Katharine 'could explain exactly how matters stood in Liverpool'.[46] Grosvenor was always the courteous gentleman towards Katharine, but she sensed him to be 'a man of the world (no less than Gladstone)'.[47] Indeed, Gladstone was much later informed that when he arrived at Liverpool in the early hours of Saturday 21 November, 'he said in the hearing of several persons' that the reason Parnell had come to fight this particular seat in person was that 'he sleeps with O'Shea's wife'.[48]

In Saturday's papers it was announced that Parnell did indeed intend to stand as a Home Rule candidate for the Exchange Division. Then, as if the situation in Liverpool was not tense enough, at the very time that he was backing O'Shea's candidacy as a Liberal and countenancing Katharine's efforts to persuade Gladstone and Grosvenor to lend their support, Parnell suddenly renounced the Liberal alliance. Frustrated with Gladstone's failure to make a definite promise regarding Home Rule, and perhaps believing that a Conservative government was more likely to achieve it because of their strength in the House of Lords, Parnell issued a manifesto which called upon the Liverpool Irish to vote for the Tories if they could not vote for a Nationalist candidate. If his main aim was to see the Liberals defeated at this election, Parnell's defiant support for O'Shea looked all the more incomprehensible to those unaware of the private pressures he was under.

Parnell arrived in Liverpool on Sunday 22 November, intending to address a public meeting in the Concert Hall at three o'clock in the afternoon, but so many people turned out ('packed as close as herrings in a barrel'[49]) that he agreed to speak later that day from a wagon outside St George's Hall. A crowd of 10,000 stood in the streets to hear him. A canny tactician, Parnell never once mentioned the name of Captain O'Shea. Instead, he electrified his audience with a thorough denunciation of the Liberal enemy: 'The Liberals gave us chains, imprisonment, and death.'[50] Yet at noon the next day, when the nominations were read aloud outside the Town Hall, Parnell withdrew his candidacy and a bewildered Liverpool

Irish electorate were persuaded to transfer their votes to the official Liberal candidate, O'Shea. That evening in the League Hall, speaking first in support of T.P. O'Connor and John Redmond (the latter standing for the Kirkdale Division), Parnell began to praise O'Shea's former services to the party, his exemplary voting record, and so on. When his name was first mentioned, hisses were heard from the audience, but Parnell told them that O'Shea was worthy of their votes, 'as an Irishman and a Catholic'.[51]

On polling day, Wednesday 25 November, in wind and rain, Parnell drove about the three divisions in an open brougham, urging voters, 'We must return the three Irishmen'. O'Connor and Redmond were naturally disgusted at being 'bracketed with O'Shea'.[52] Indeed, O'Connor found the whole situation astounding: Parnell's 'presence was never more necessary in Ireland than at that moment', yet here he was 'concentrat[ing] all his efforts that day upon the one constituency of Exchange'.[53] Parnell was 'intensely excited' throughout the day, and behaved 'like a man possessed'. Large numbers of vehicles were borrowed, 'and if he were told of any voter who was doubtful or on his sick bed, in a second he was in a hansom and rushing down to the doubtful voter. He worked like a demon'.[54] Yet in the end the united endeavours of Parnell, Katharine, Grosvenor and Gladstone counted for nothing. In the final count O'Shea lost to the Conservative candidate by a mere fifty-five votes. Parnell won his main objective, however, which was to help return the Conservatives to government.

Parnell returned to Eltham where he found Katharine 'suffering from a nervous breakdown owing to the sudden relaxing of the intense strain and work that I had been through'. She was overcome with her 'bitter disappointment at Willie's defeat', and for several days 'Parnell nursed, soothed and comforted me as tenderly as a woman'.[55] Katharine was so anxious to see her husband remain in Parliament not solely because of her fear that he would make her affair with Parnell public. It was also because his political career and busy life in London 'gave him little time to come down to Eltham'. She explains that, 'When he did so the perpetual watchfulness and diplomacy I had to observe were extremely irksome to me. Years of neglect, varied by quarrels, had killed my love for him long before I met Parnell, and since the February of 1882 I could not bear to be near him.'[56] O'Shea's parliamentary career had to be saved.

On 4 December, Katharine renewed her campaign on his behalf, writing to Grosvenor to express her thanks for his patience and courtesy: 'I am *really* grateful for the trouble you have taken and especially for that cold journey to Liverpool.' Her voluble letter, which flits so lightly between matters political and personal, the former relating to Parnell, the latter to O'Shea, provides further evidence that Grosvenor understood exactly why her husband's return to Parliament was so important to her – 'for reasons I need not trouble you with in a letter'. Pointedly, Katharine went on to remind Grosvenor of Gladstone's promise to her back in November 1882 that he would remember her husband 'should a "suitable" appointment become vacant – This is nearly *1886!*'[57]

However, before anything could be done for O'Shea, Parnell needed Katharine to re-open negotiations with Gladstone. This was an audacious move coming straight after a General Election in which he had helped to defeat the Liberals, but just as Gladstone had pressed Katharine with enquiries about the local government scheme throughout the summer months, so she now harried him, trying to get him to commit the Liberal Party to Home Rule. Parnell's first ploy was to persuade Gladstone that the Irish were about to enter into negotiations with the Tories. On 10 December, Katharine asked him *'in confidence'* for his views on Parnell's 'Proposed Constitution', since she had 'private information that Mr P. is to see Lord C[arnarvon] in a day or two'.[58] In fact it was Justin McCarthy who had a private interview with the Conservative Lord-Lieutenant on 13 December, only to be warned that the prospects for Home Rule under the Tories were nil. The next day, Salisbury's Cabinet voted against it. Knowing nothing of this, Gladstone stated his belief that Parnell was quite right to negotiate with the Tories ('no such plan can properly proceed from any *British* source but one, viz. the Government of the day'[59]). However, he held out hope to Parnell by putting forward five questions as to the precise scope of his 'Proposed Constitution'.

On 15 December, the day after the Cabinet decision, Katharine sent Gladstone a letter which made a straightforward offer to the Liberals: on their promise to introduce a Home Rule bill Parnell would guarantee the Irish vote in English constituencies at the next election. She enclosed a further letter from Parnell which responded in detail to Gladstone's questions about the 'Proposed Constitution'. In fact, Parnell addressed this letter, which was supposedly written *to* Katharine, from North Park, Eltham. Whether he did this deliberately, or in a moment of forgetfulness, Katharine later used the letter as evidence that Gladstone was well informed of her intimate relations with Parnell. In her book, she not only prints a full transcription of this letter but also provides a facsimile of the first and last pages, which clearly show Parnell to be writing on Katharine's headed notepaper.[60] In it, Parnell put forward a strong case for Home Rule while also flattering the Liberal leader Gladstone that he regarded him as 'the only living statesman who has both the power and the will to carry a settlement it would be possible for me to accept and work with'. Time was pressing, however, and the Liberals and Nationalists needed to agree, before Parliament met, on 'the best way to turn out the present Government'.[61]

This was a remarkable proposal, yet Gladstone sat tight. While thanking Katharine for Parnell's 'able and comprehensive' enclosure, and assuring her that 'any letters now passing between us are highly confidential, I would say almost sacred', Gladstone repeated his advice that the 'proper persons' for Parnell to be doing business with were the present Government. Mindful of the advice given him just two days earlier by Grosvenor at Liberal Central Office ('Hardly a Liberal comes to see me here who does not say before leaving "Now mind *no* coquetting with Parnell"'[62]), Gladstone pointed out that if word got out of secret negotiations with the Nationalists, it would 'ruin a Liberal proposal',[63] because it would look as though Gladstone had bribed the Irish to break their alliance with the Tories. Among his own party, too, he smartly reminded Katharine, there was considerable 'irritation to soothe, as well as prejudice to overcome'.[64]

Katharine's reply was immediate and frank. The Nationalist–Tory 'Alliance' Gladstone referred to had had but one motive, which was to put in a government prepared to dispense with coercion.[65] The Conservatives had done so, she wrote, but Parnell had never expected that Lord Salisbury would agree to Irish Home Rule. The Nationalists held the balance of power, and the point now was whether Gladstone was prepared to see the Tories remaining in office, or whether he would signal to Parnell his endorsement of Home Rule, so that, in any vote of confidence, 'he may know how to direct his Party to act'.[66] This was fairly explicit, but not sufficiently so for Gladstone. With some impatience, he wrote to Katharine on Christmas Eve, repeating his specific objections to conducting secret negotiations with the Nationalists at the present time. Ignoring Parnell's demand that he make some public gesture of support for Irish Home Rule, Gladstone closed his letter with the demand that *Parnell* be the one to act. Describing himself as 'at present a man in chains', he concluded that nothing but a public statement to the effect that the Nationalist–Tory alliance was at an end 'could be of any avail'.[67]

As if her negotiations with Gladstone were not tense enough, Katharine also had domestic difficulties to deal with. Katharine and Parnell appear to have been together at Wonersh Lodge over Christmas, but on 22 December she had taken the children up to see O'Shea, whose mother had become quite feeble and infirm and was spending the winter in London (O'Shea's sister Mary, who had lived with their mother, had recently died). Mrs O'Shea stayed on at her son's apartments after Katharine had gone back to Eltham, and he clearly found his mother a handful. She would not leave until eight o'clock in the evening, 'in dreadful spirits' about her hotel, 'but does not know where she would like to go'.[68] He made it clear that he was anxious about her, and to preserve the appearance of a normal family life,

Katharine did agree to spend Christmas Day with O'Shea. She insisted, though, that she bring the children to Albert Mansions. There seems to have been no question that she would entertain O'Shea's mother at Eltham.[69] Presumably, this arrangement also enabled Katharine to leave her two youngest daughters (aged 1 and 2¾) at home. It was a highly disagreeable day for Katharine, quite aside from the strain of keeping up a façade of wifely solicitude for O'Shea. She was, she says, accustomed to her husband's mean ways of telling the children whenever he saw them 'that I am bringing them up very badly', an accusation she resented bitterly since O'Shea himself had never made 'any attempt at all to bring them up'. It was doubly galling to bear such criticisms from her mother-in-law, who, as Katharine later reminded O'Shea, 'thought it fair to attack me when acting hostess at your dinner table on Xmas Day'.[70]

Over the Christmas period, Katharine resumed her correspondence with Gladstone, telling him that she and Parnell had 'scarcely talked of anything else' but the Liberal leader's last letter. Writing on 29 December, as the time was 'now so short' before the opening of Parliament, she enclosed a further letter from Parnell, this time on official notepaper from the Irish Parliamentary Offices at Westminster.[71] How a new Liberal Government would deal with the question of coercion was an important issue. Parnell could hardly ask his party to turn out the present Government without firm assurances from the Liberals on Home Rule *and* coercion. Gladstone refused to make any such assurances, forcing Parnell to give ground.[72] On New Year's Day 1886, he confided to Gladstone that the Irish intended to move a series of amendments to the Queen's Speech which 'would be an assault along the whole line of English misgovernment in Ireland', and that he would urge all Nationalist members to sit on the opposition benches, alongside the Liberals.[73] If Gladstone responded to this communication, no letter survives, and further attempts to come to an understanding with the Liberals came to nothing.

The two leaders would not communicate again until the opening of Parliament, which took place on Thursday 21 January. Two days later, Katharine wrote to Gladstone to say that she was 'authorised by Mr Parnell to tell you that he and the Irish members will be willing, since your speech on Tuesday, to assist in ousting the Government', but only on condition that Gladstone would continue as leader. The fall of the new government was to be brought about by the Nationalists and Liberals voting against an innocuous amendment proposed by Liberal MP Jesse Collins: 'I know the Party will act up to it,' Gladstone was assured,[74] but he was only finally convinced of the termination of the Nationalist–Tory alliance when, on 26 January, Lord Salisbury betrayed it by indicating that his Government would re-introduce coercion. At one o'clock in the morning the

Conservative Government was defeated on Collins's amendment, and within days, Katharine was asking Gladstone how he proposed to have a 'full interchange of views' with Parnell about 'Irish Autonomy', advising him that it was Parnell's own wish that any messages should continue to be sent through Grosvenor or through herself.[75]

This last point was of no little importance. Gladstone had appeared recently to accept the overtures of the Liberal Henry Labouchère (editor of *Truth*, and, incidentally, a friend of O'Shea's) as a suitable intermediary with the Irish, but Parnell had not encouraged this, fearing that he might not be a discreet enough messenger. Katharine spent the second half of her long letter to Gladstone (a transcription of part of this letter is printed in her book) assuring him that 'as far as *I* am concerned I have not, and have never, had any desire to push myself forward as the means of communication. I have nothing to gain by it'. Significantly, she blamed herself, or so she told Gladstone, for originally suggesting to Parnell that he use her husband as an intermediary with the Government in April 1882, because she sensed 'the difficulty of my being made the means of communication of [Mr Parnell's] real views'. The difficulty she refers to could only have been the objection, on moral grounds and also on sound political grounds, that Mrs O'Shea was Parnell's mistress. Her letter makes it clear that, despite this 'difficulty', Parnell was 'not likely to express his real views to anyone except yourself and myself or if you think it advisable Lord R. Grosvenor'.[76]

Katharine had helped to bring about the fall of the Tory Government and the restoration of a Liberal Government committed to 'Irish Autonomy', yet she had still one matter to settle, that of restoring her husband's parliamentary career. Owing to the fact that T.P. O'Connor had been elected by two constituencies, Liverpool (Scotland Division) and Galway, the latter seat remained free, although if O'Shea intended to stand he would have to do so as a Nationalist after having just run a much publicised campaign in Liverpool as a Liberal! Prompted by Chamberlain, who asked whether there was any chance of his getting Parnell's backing ('It is really the least he can do for you after all you have done for him'[77]), O'Shea called on Parnell at the Commons and demanded that he give him his support for Galway. According to what Parnell told Katharine, he pointed out how difficult it would be to square O'Shea's nomination with the party, and 'Willie replied angrily that he was extremely popular in Ireland, and that he would be very sorry to be on terms of popularity with such a "rapscallion crew" as the party'. 'Well then', replied Parnell drily, 'you need not be sorry, for you are very unpopular with them'.[78] O'Shea 'fumed' while Parnell sat considering. Finally, when Parnell asked him if he would now take the pledge to vote with the party, O'Shea declared, 'No, he would sit where he liked, and vote as he pleased,' to which Parnell replied, 'Then the thing is not worth discussing further.'[79]

In order to force Parnell's hand, O'Shea threatened Katharine that he was about to depart for Ireland and 'meant to stand for Galway' whether Parnell would propose him or not, insisting that it was her 'duty' to see Parnell, and tell him that she would no longer be his 'cat's-paw' with Gladstone if he did not give his support.[80] O'Shea's demand that Parnell get him returned for Galway, and then his demand that Katharine force Parnell to do so, has been widely interpreted as 'the price of her husband's silence'.[81]

Katharine and Parnell talked the matter over at Eltham and finally resolved that she should go up to Albert Mansions to urge O'Shea to take the party pledge. Otherwise, his standing as a Nationalist candidate would be, to use Parnell's words, 'such a shock to my own men that they'll not be the same again . . . Tell him I cannot insult the others by proposing him without this'. Katharine found O'Shea house-bound with gout, indulging in self-pity, and obdurate – still harping on about Kilmainham and 'the man he let out of prison'.[82] When Parnell returned from the House that night, Katharine was waiting up and had a fire ready. He took her news calmly, saying that he had resolved to force O'Shea down the throats of the party in order to have done with him: 'We won't mind, Queenie, if it leads to worry and fuss . . . what shall be shall be.' He had that night informed T.P. O'Connor of his intention to propose O'Shea for Galway: 'You should have seen his face, my Queen; he looked as if I had dropped him into an ice-pit.'[83]

This was no exaggeration. O'Connor says that when Parnell made this announcement in Palace Yard, 'my blood ran cold'.[84] They argued it out, O'Connor taking little heed of Parnell's 'long list of the great services which O'Shea, in his private negotiations, had done for the Irish cause'. He at once telegraphed the news to Healy, then in Dublin, threatening to resign in protest and hoping to take Healy with him. He then fetched Biggar from his hotel bed and crossed over to Ireland by the night-mail, telling Healy to get onto Edmund Dwyer Gray, owner of the *Freeman's Journal*: 'An article tomorrow would kill the whole thing.'[85] At 11 p.m. on the night of Friday 5 February, Healy sat down to compose a letter of protest for the *Freeman's*, in which he lambasted O'Shea's hasty conversion to the Nationalist cause: 'For six years he sat in Parliament on the Government side of the House, and on nearly every critical occasion he either voted against the Irish Party, or else kept prudently away from embarrassing divisions.'[86] Parnell, meanwhile, telegraphed Gray to confirm his support for O'Shea, and in the early hours of the next morning Gray met Healy to say that he could not now publish his protest. Healy had hardly lain down to bed when O'Connor and Biggar arrived at his door with a copy of the *Freeman's* in which O'Shea's election address had been published, together with Parnell's endorsement. With just half an hour to go before the Galway train departed from Dublin, O'Connor changed his position, saying that, although the nomination of O'Shea was 'disgraceful', he could not go against Parnell now that his support for O'Shea had been made public. Biggar and Healy were still resolved to go to Galway, and Healy recalls O'Connor pleading with them from the doorstep of his house not to involve themselves.

Healy and Biggar arrived on Saturday 6 February, 'and found the town in uproar'.[87] A local Nationalist, Michael Lynch, had already been nominated, and the two set about addressing meetings in his support, at which Biggar 'did not shrink from scorching allusions to his opponent'.[88] These allusions, Healy implies, were to Parnell's affair with Mrs O'Shea, and 'set the town agog'. It is Healy's claim that he persuaded the *Freeman's* to suppress much of this, and it is the case that only Healy's speeches were recorded in the *Freeman's Journal*. Perhaps the question of whether either of them made *public* allusions to the scandal is less significant than the fact that, in private, gossip was rife about Parnell's true motives for giving O'Shea's candidature his personal endorsement.

At the Liverpool contest only the very vaguest public allusion had been made to Parnell's intervention,[89] yet in private talks with Galway Nationalists, both Healy and Biggar are alleged to have said, 'The candidate's wife is Parnell's mistress and there is nothing more to be said.'[90] A month later, Biggar wrote to Frank Hugh O'Donnell, saying that it was 'a case of blackmail, O'Shea having possession of incriminating letters and insisting on the seat to save exposure'.[91] The Bishop of Galway, Dr Carr, got word of the rumour shortly after O'Shea's arrival in Galway, and, in O'Shea's words, behaved towards him, in the circumstances, with understandable 'prudence . . . and reserve'.[92] Carr later told Healy that 'O'Shea had gone down on his knees before him and vowed there was no truth in any allegation which connected his wife's name with Parnell'.[93] When Parnell arrived in Galway to put down the Healy–Biggar opposition, the clergy expressed their support for O'Shea and urged Healy to cease his campaign.

O'Shea would later claim that Biggar and Healy 'reviled me at their meetings because I had been a supporter of a Government . . . guilty of wilful murder',[94] and, undoubtedly, the party's fierce opposition to O'Shea was political in origin. As T.P. O'Connor put it, 'It was the rotten politician and not the complacent husband against whom Galway, with all Ireland, stood up in revolt'; O'Shea sitting on the Government benches was 'really a traitor in the camp'.[95] The bitterness of the Liverpool Irish was so great that 600 Nationalists passed a resolution in support of the efforts of Healy and Biggar to 'remove once and for all a mischievous Whig intriguer from the field of

Irish politics'.[96] Whereas in Liverpool O'Shea had been castigated by the Liberals as Parnell's 'subservient tool', in Galway he was derided by Nationalists as 'a miserable Whig spaniel'![97] On Sunday 7 February, he wired Parnell, 'All hope gone unless you can come at once. Things have gone so far that the presence of anyone except yourself would not save the situation'.[98]

Unlike O'Shea's campaigns in Mid Armagh and Liverpool, where Katharine had had such an influential role behind the scenes, Parnell had to fight the Galway by-election without her help. He immediately telegraphed Biggar, begging him 'that now when the Irish Cause approached the winning-post he would not thwart the purpose of his old and faithful friend',[99] but to no effect. Biggar replied with the following curt telegram: 'The O'Sheas will be your ruin.' (According to Healy he had persuaded Biggar to soften his original message, 'Mrs O'Shea will be your ruin'.[100]) O'Connor, meanwhile, got prominent Nationalists to telegraph their disapproval to Healy, and on the morning of Tuesday 9 February, the *Freeman's Journal* carried an endorsement of Parnell's leadership signed by fifty of his MPs. Parnell himself arrived at Galway Station that day, flanked by O'Connor, Deasy (the party whip), Sexton, James O'Kelly and his secretary, Henry Campbell. Their reception was rough, with cries of 'To hell with Parnell and whiggery'.[101] O'Connor recalled that as Parnell steered him towards the Station Hotel, Captain O'Shea, white of face, could be seen in the distance, eager 'to approach and to welcome Parnell', but that 'Parnell got rid of him as soon as possible'.[102] Parnell continued to maintain a physical distance between himself and O'Shea during his time in Galway. They addressed meetings in different locations and Parnell did not once invite O'Shea to dine with him.

At the private meeting of the party immediately after Parnell's arrival, he appears to have given an assurance that O'Shea had agreed to take the pledge (which was certainly not the case), and Healy was persuaded to withdraw his opposition. Indeed, Healy appears to have been swayed the moment Parnell appeared. The reporter from the *Freeman's Journal* noted that he lingered behind the other MPs who followed Parnell into the Railway Hotel, and asked the crowd to conduct themselves 'in a peaceable and respectful manner': 'no groaning for Captain O'Shea,' he pleaded.[103] Only Biggar held out. Parnell next addressed a large gathering of Lynch's supporters at the Young Ireland Society Hall. Lynch was authorised to stand down, and Parnell persuaded the men of Galway that a vote for O'Shea was a vote of confidence in his leadership. 'I have', he said, 'a Parliament for Ireland in the hollow of my hand'.[104]

The following afternoon Parnell spoke at Castlegar, three miles away. He glossed over the controversy of the rival candidates as an unfortunate misunderstanding, saying that when he had endorsed O'Shea's candidature he had not realised that a local Nationalist had already come forward. He then pointed out the special merits of O'Shea. Whereas in Liverpool he had spoken of O'Shea's achievements as an intermediary with the Liberal Government, he reminded the electors of Galway that he had won the leadership contest back in 1880 by very few votes, one of them O'Shea's, and that it was therefore 'right for me to remember that service which O'Shea then rendered to the cause of Ireland as well as to myself personally'.[105] While not quite stating in plain language that O'Shea had agreed to take the pledge (he had, he said 'every confidence that he has fulfilled all the conditions which are required as preliminaries from members of the Irish Party'), Parnell did state categorically that O'Shea would sit with the Nationalists from now on. His closing words, however, skilfully took the minds of his audience beyond the personalities of the candidates. He told them to 'believe that the cause of Ireland is safe in my hands, and that in a very short time I will bring back to you an Irish Parliament to College Green (cheers), when you will be masters of your own destiny'.[106]

On the day of the election, Thursday 11 February, Parnell and O'Connor tirelessly worked the polling stations to ensure that the Nationalist vote went to O'Shea, and Parnell had the satisfaction of seeing his victory announced at 10.20 that night. From the magistrate's bench at the courthouse, first Parnell and then O'Shea made gracious speeches about Michael Lynch's willingness to stand down (the votes had fallen 912 to O'Shea and 54 to Lynch). But, as with the Liverpool election, the suddenness of Parnell's appearance and the abrupt re-direction of the campaign left much bitterness among Nationalist voters. When O'Shea began to express his 'great feelings of pride that I appear amongst you tonight to thank you for the very great honour which you have conferred on me today', a voice from the crowd shouted out, 'You may thank Parnell.'[107]

Two first-hand accounts survive of Parnell's relief, both at the result and at his having exerted his will over the party. O'Connor, who spent the evening with him, 'could not help noticing that Parnell was in a specially joyous mood . . . He was easy, talkative even, lolling comfortably in his arm-chair while he smoked a small cigar.'[108] Yet, just as the others were about to depart on the midnight train, William O'Brien recalls that he drew him into his room, 'and with something like a sob' talked of his gratitude to his party and his countrymen, saying: 'From this day forth this fellow can do no further mischief.'[109]

# CHAPTER 9

## *Scandal*

On 26 March 1886 Gladstone put a draft Home Rule bill before the Cabinet. Chamberlain and Trevelyan immediately resigned their posts (respectively, President of the Local Government Board and Secretary for Scotland). At the division on the second reading of the bill, the night of 7 June, Captain O'Shea, Member for Galway for barely four months, abstained from voting and also resigned – from Parliament. As Lyons has stated, 'This abrupt end to his career baffled contemporaries and is still difficult to explain.'[1]

What is clear is that O'Shea's attitude towards Parnell changed significantly in the immediate aftermath of the Galway by-election. At the divorce hearing O'Shea would state that during the campaign, 'I heard that statements were made referring to Mr Parnell and Mrs O'Shea,'[2] yet the only surviving evidence of communications between Katharine and her husband with reference to the scandal is a single letter from O'Shea, dated 23 April 1886. Its final paragraph was read aloud in court:

> With regard to Mr Parnell, I believed your assurances, but I have scores of times pointed out to you that, however innocent in themselves, the frequent visits of a man to a woman during the absence of her husband is an offence against the proprieties, and is sure sooner or later to be observed upon severely by society. I trust for Norah and Carmen's sake you have learnt your lesson.[3]

When O'Shea originally filed a divorce suit against Katharine, her adultery was alleged to date 'from April, 1886, up to the date of the petition',[4] and the extract above certainly suggests that by April 1886 he was losing his patience with Katharine's supposedly professional relationship with Parnell. However, the complete letter, which exists only as a lawyer's shorthand copy, reveals that the nature of the argument between O'Shea and Katharine was more complex than is suggested by this single paragraph. In the early part of the year it was not so much rumours of an affair that disturbed O'Shea, but the public slights upon his political integrity during first the Liverpool contest and then the Galway by-election.

Parnell's support for him at both these elections was, he had consistently argued throughout that autumn and winter, 'small return' for his having obtained Parnell's 'release from jail and save[d] his political career'.[5] Yet it appears from the shorthand letter that once the Galway election was over, worn down with anxiety and with O'Shea's ingratitude, Katharine let slip her guard and told her husband that in the spring of 1882 Parnell 'would have been released anyhow', with or without O'Shea's interference and his journey to Kilmainham. Her retort that Parnell was at the same time in talks with the Government through Justin McCarthy and that, if O'Shea had not pushed himself forward, Gladstone 'would have sent Mr McCarthy to Kilmainham', could not have been more hurtful to O'Shea. He held to his boast that 'when Mr Gladstone thanked me in his room . . . he believed that no-one but myself could have carried out the business', and claimed, too, that the Prime Minister had expressed a poor opinion of McCarthy.[6] Yet his political significance as the man who got the prisoners released, which O'Shea had so earnestly cultivated since that time, and alluded to so often in recent months, now looked decidedly diminished. It was not simply Katharine, Parnell and, of course, McCarthy who knew this, but Gladstone himself, and no doubt many members of the Cabinet.

For once, Frank Hugh O'Donnell comes close to the truth when he states that it was only after the Galway scandal that O'Shea learned that he had not been the sole intermediary in the Kilmainham treaty (although O'Shea seems to have told him that it was Katharine herself and not McCarthy who was Parnell's chosen negotiator). O'Donnell believed that his discovery of Gladstone's secret and confidential negotiations with Mrs O'Shea 'played a large part in the formation of Captain O'Shea's conviction of the guilt of his wife and Parnell'.[7] Of course, as we know, O'Shea had known of his wife's communications with Gladstone, on Parnell's behalf, almost from their very inception, and he himself had made use of her access to Downing Street. When O'Shea confided to O'Donnell, 'She never told me. Nor did Gladstone. Nor did Parnell,' and, O'Donnell said, 'applied strong language to Mr Gladstone for conducting such a transaction behind a husband's back', he was much more likely to be referring to his discovery that his visit to Kilmainham, from which he returned exultant with the treaty in his hand, was of less significance than he had thought.

O'Shea sent his admonitory letter to Katharine exactly one week after she had applied to Gladstone on his behalf, begging for 'the promise of some colonial appointment' (she stressed that her husband was 'willing to go *anywhere*'[8]). By 23 April O'Shea must have realised how hopeless were his chances. Since late 1882, Gladstone had held out the promise of a Government appointment ('which I told him at the time', Katharine hinted to Gladstone). She now informed him candidly that her husband was 'in *very great* pecuniary difficulties', and blamed this on the fact that he had been unable to collect rents in the current situation in Ireland and on 'other causes' – presumably the collapse of the Cuban investment scheme. Making another of her allusions to her life separate from O'Shea, she went on, 'My Aunt, with whom *I* have been living for many years . . . will she says assist my husband out of his present difficulties, for my sake, if she can see any hope of his getting any lucrative occupation – *but*, if not, she will not help him.'[9] A colonial appointment would certainly have resolved the domestic situation between the O'Sheas, that is, if Katharine and the children had been permitted to stay in England. Yet in her book, Katharine downplays her anxiety that her husband should be given such an appointment: 'I was willing to please him by asking for it, and it might have excited suspicion if I had not asked.'[10] This personal appeal, though, failed like all the rest.

This letter of 16 April is one of Katharine's few surviving communications with Downing Street during this period. On 18 March Gladstone had advised her 'that for the *moment*' he proposed to put the new Chief Secretary, John Morley, in touch with Parnell: 'I think we may look to Mr Morley alone & rely on all he says for accuracy as well as fidelity.'[11] A week later, Katharine wrote to assure him that Parnell was satisfied with this arrangement, and further that he was quite prepared to go anywhere for a private meeting with the Prime Minister: 'I hope you may be able to see him for I am sure it will do good if you do, and strengthen him.'[12] Yet the question of when and where they could meet privately was a difficult one.[13] Significantly, Gladstone did not respond to Katharine's suggestion that if he ever wished to see Parnell at her house 'what pleasure' it would be for her, promising, however, that in doing so he need not see her 'and certainly not anyone else!'[14]

The two leaders met on 5 April. 'We at once got to work. P. extraordinarily close, tenacious and sharp,' recorded Morley, who had arranged the meeting. When Gladstone took his leave at midnight, he muttered, 'very clever, very clever', as Morley held out the door for him.[15] The subject of their discussion was apparently 'all finance'. The Home Rule Bill refused the proposed Irish Parliament jurisdiction over customs and excise, and required it to contribute a fifteenth of the imperial budget; Parnell recommended a twentieth at the most.

On 7 April, two days after this meeting, Parnell called together the inner circle of the party to discuss the bill. As Healy describes it, 'We met on a raw, foggy night at the Westminster Palace Hotel with hearts aflame' and pulses 'quickened', yet as Parnell disclosed the details, they grew discouraged that Gladstone was so ungenerous about finance.[16] There were also two other significant quarrels with the Government's proposals: the Royal Irish Constabulary was not to come under the authority of the Irish

Parliament for some years yet; and the Irish Parliament was to consist of two Houses or 'orders', of which one would be elected and the other partly so, 'but also weighted in favour of property'.[17] It was also proposed that Members of the Irish Parliament would be excluded from the House of Commons. However, when the bill was introduced the following evening, with the backing of his party Parnell made a speech to the Commons in which he stated that, if satisfactorily amended, the Government of Ireland Bill would be 'cheerfully accepted by the Irish people and representatives as a solution of the long-standing dispute between the two countries'.[18]

No further communications appear to have been exchanged by Parnell and the Government until, on 8 May, at the end of the Easter recess, two days before the debate on the second reading was due to begin, Katharine received a telegram from Downing Street: 'Morley is most anxious to see Mr P. Is anything known at Eltham of his whereabouts? This is really urgent.'[19] A Government telegram was enclosed for her to send an immediate reply, and the fact that Katharine was able to do so suggests, of course, that Parnell was with her at the time. Morley was informed that Parnell would be at the Irish Parliamentary Offices at four o'clock that afternoon.[20] Among the matters they discussed was the question of whether Irish MPs would still sit in the House of Commons, for this remained a complex issue. According to Lyons, Parnell's concern was 'that a Dublin Parliament might be to some extent devalued if Irish MPs still came to Westminster'.[21]

The debate on the second reading began on 10 May, but already the Irish party had begun 'to anticipate defeat'.[22] In the event, on 31 May, Chamberlain called a meeting of fifty Liberal MPs as yet undecided whether to abstain or vote against the bill. He urged them to do the latter. When the result of the division was called, it was revealed that the Government of Ireland Bill had fallen by a margin of thirty votes. Eighty-five of the eighty-six Nationalist MPs voted for the bill; the one abstention was O'Shea's, which, as *The Times* commented, was 'no doubt a matter of interest to the Parnellite party'.[23]

Among Irish MPs, feelings ran high against O'Shea's unaccountable behaviour. Healy says that he caught sight of him 'grinn[ing] down on us from the Gallery gloatingly, in derision'.[24] O'Shea's resignation, perhaps the outcome of both personal grievances and political disappointments, was welcomed by such as William O'Brien, for whom his sudden departure 'cleansed the air of Irish politics'.[25] James O'Kelly reacted rather more strongly, writing to O'Shea that, in view of the party support he had been given at Galway, 'I regard your abstention from voting on the Home Rule Bill as a personal injury of so grave a nature as to entitle me to demand from you a personal reparation'.[26] O'Shea, however, made at once for Carlsbad on account of his health. O'Kelly did not receive a reply until

O'Shea's return to England two months later. He shrugged off the challenge and reminded O'Kelly, 'you are one of those who were released from prison owing to my intervention in 1882'.[27]

O'Shea's abrupt retirement from Parliament may be attributed in some measure to a number of allusions to Parnell's residence at Katharine's house which appeared in the press. It was this publicity that O'Shea himself would blame for ending his public life.[28] The first of these stories appeared in the *Pall Mall Gazette* while the debate on the second reading of the Home Rule Bill was in progress. On the night of Wednesday 21 May, Katharine's coachman Richard Wise met the 11.45 p.m. London train at New Eltham Station to drive Parnell back to Wonersh Lodge. Shortly after midnight they collided with a florist's van returning from Covent Garden market. The carriage suffered slight damage, but neither Parnell nor his driver was hurt. Rather surprisingly, an account of the incident was published in Saturday's *Pall Mall Gazette*, under the heading 'Mr Parnell's Suburban Retreat'. The paper volunteered information about Parnell's residence during parliamentary sessions, 'at Eltham, a suburban village in the south-east of London. From here he can often be seen taking riding exercise round by Chislehurst and Sidcup.'[29]

O'Shea was right to treat such gossip seriously. The campaigning editor of the *Pall Mall Gazette*, W.T. Stead, had a reputation for sensation. Only months before he had been imprisoned for his part in a stunt to demonstrate the ease with which under-age virgins could be procured in London for the purposes of prostitution. His sensational series of articles, published under the title 'The Maiden Tribute to Modern Babylon', had electrified the public when it appeared the previous year.[30] In the course of this exposé, Stead threatened to reveal the names of Members of both Houses whom he alleged were implicated in the trade in under-age prostitution.[31] As T.P. O'Connor puts it, 'on all sexual matters [Stead] was almost a monomaniac', and regarded it 'his sacred duty to track down any offence against sexual morality which was reported to him'.[32]

O'Shea says that he telegraphed Katharine immediately he saw the story in the paper, 'asking her what she had to say to it'.[33] Her response, as so often in crises of this kind, was remarkable. She first telegraphed and then wrote to him, quite unruffled, saying that she had 'not the slightest idea of what it means, unless, indeed, it is meant to get a rise out of you'. O'Shea received her letter on Sunday 25 May.

My Boysie, – . . . I saw the paper when I came from aunt's, but I was so wet I thought it best to change before I tellied to you. I do not see that it has anything to do with us, and I am inclined to agree with Charlie [Katharine's brother], from whom I heard this morning, who says, in respect to Healy, that 'it is better to put up with a great deal of abuse rather than retaliate, for it is ill-fighting with a chimney-sweep, for right or wrong, you'd only get soiled'. I should say the paragraph has been made up by Healy and Co. to annoy you, but I don't see why it should do so. However, it is not wonderful, after the notices I have received from some of the papers from Romeike [a press agency], and I should advise you to hold on to your seat, for I am sure you will annoy the sweeps most by doing so. I was sure there would be no end to their spite after your Galway success. We will call early tomorrow and talk it over.

Your K.[34]

There is a possibility that 'Charlie', here, refers to Parnell, and the use of 'We' at the end of the letter is puzzling. What is certain is that, on the Monday, Katharine called, alone, on O'Shea at Albert Mansions, to explain that she always communicated with Parnell through the Irish Parliamentary Offices, and that she knew nothing of his private address. Although she came alone, she brought with her a letter she claimed to have received from Parnell, coincidentally, that very morning:

> Irish Parliamentary Offices, Palace-chambers,
> 9, Bridge-street, S.W., May 26, 1886.
>
> My Dear Mrs O'Shea, – Your telegram in reference to the paragraph duly reached me. I had a couple of horses at a place in the neighbourhood of Bexleyheath, but as I am now unable to be much away from London, have turned them out to grass for the summer. I am very sorry that you should have had any annoyance about the matter, and hope to see you on Sunday. Kindly return me enclosures when you have had time to read them.
>
> Yours very truly,     CHAS. S. PARNELL

As Sir Edward Clarke stated in the divorce court, Parnell's letter to Katharine was a 'deliberately false letter, a letter invented for the purpose of setting Captain O'Shea's suspicions at rest': 'Mr Parnell was at Eltham on the night of the accident. He was there when the telegram came from Captain O'Shea.'[35] Further than that, both Katharine's and Parnell's letters make deliberate allusions to her role as Parnell's secretary and political confidante. She refers to the press agency Romeike's, while Parnell openly refers to an appointment at Eltham at the weekend, at which he wishes to discuss particular documents with her. This too was a deliberately false statement. There is no record of Katharine's involvement in any communications to Downing Street in the latter part of May 1886. She would next write to Gladstone from Eastbourne, in the middle of July.

One wonders how it was that O'Shea's suspicions were set at rest. Yet the *Pall Mall Gazette* story did not provoke him sufficiently to make him run down to Eltham to challenge Katharine or to inspect the stables attached to Wonersh Lodge. The fact that he could claim to have no knowledge that 'Dictator', 'President' and a third horse, 'Home Rule', had all been stabled at his wife's house for the past fifteen months provides further evidence of the fact that, since the birth of Katie in November 1884, he had been a rare visitor to Wonersh Lodge. He would admit to the divorce court that, 'At that time I knew nothing about the horses being at Eltham. I first heard about them in June of the following year [i.e. 1887], when my son told me about them.'[36] However, it is the case that Katharine and Parnell acted immediately to remove the horses from her stables. Richard Wise would testify that after the accident involving the carriage (that is, after it was reported in the *Pall Mall Gazette*), Katharine had them moved to adjoining stables at Messiter's Mews, known as 'the lower stables'. Wise's son-in-law, who remembered the accident, also recalled that Katharine and Parnell instructed him that 'all the things in the stable belonging to Mr Parnell [were] to be shifted to the next mews'.[37]

The *Pall Mall Gazette* did not stop there, however. On the following Saturday, under 'Occasional Notes', an unnamed correspondent identified Parnell's address as 'the house of Captain O'Shea', 'a little white-brick semi-detached suburban villa which rejoices in the name of Wonersh Lodge': 'Any of Mr Parnell's neighbours would be able to tell you that his home, for the present at any rate, is in the picturesque village of Eltham, in Kent, about eight miles from Charing-cross.' The reporter was particularly keen to probe the reason why 'Mr Parnell's personal appearance changes so often, according as he wears his beard long or short': 'I cannot understand where the secrecy comes in.'[38] However, despite the revelation that Parnell's 'home' at this time was Wonersh Lodge, O'Shea did not contest this with the paper, and made no effort to renew his questioning of Katharine. He admitted to the divorce court that he had considered taking 'criminal proceedings against the *Pall Mall Gazette* for such an atrocious libel', but (rather oddly), had suggested that Katharine, instead, instruct *her* solicitors to do so. Katharine, he says, 'appeared to think very well of the suggestion' at the time, but, presumably having talked over the matter with Parnell, she persuaded her husband 'that to take criminal proceedings would only be bringing the scandal into greater prominence'.[39]

Sometime towards the end of May, O'Shea had superintended his family's move to the Queen's Hotel, Eastbourne. He stated that he stayed there with Katharine for 'a couple of days', and that he continued to write to her there: 'I believed her to be residing the whole time at the Queen's Hotel.'[40] Yet once he had returned to London, Parnell came down to visit

Katharine and made other arrangements. Together they called on a Mr Samuel Lupton, the landlord of 2 St John's Road (Lupton recalled his 'impression they were staying at the Queen's Hotel'[41]), and after looking over the house agreed initially to take it for eight weeks, although this extended to nineteen. Lupton would state that it was the lady who signed the agreement and paid the rent. Lyons suggests that following the scandalous allusions in the *Pall Mall Gazette*, Katharine and Parnell were forced 'to be as discreet as they could and avoid newspaper gossip like the plague'.[42] Their private lodgings in St John's Road did allow them to cohabit much more discreetly than at the Queen's Hotel, but neither Katharine nor Parnell appears to have felt under much constraint.

While they lived at St John's Road, Mr Lupton 'heard a rumour that the gentleman was Mr Parnell',[43] and a cab driver frequently engaged to pick up Parnell from the station claimed to know him 'after a time as Mr Parnell'.[44] They were hardly secretive. Besides the children, Katharine brought two of her maids from Eltham, the page Thomas Kennett (known as 'Jimmie'), and her two grooms, Richard Wise and Thomas Partridge, to take care of 'President' and 'Dictator', who were now stabled at nearby Silverdale mews. Jimmie would testify that 'Mr Parnell often slept at the house. He would sleep there for a week and then go away and come back again.' This seems to have been while the second reading of the Home Rule Bill was being debated in the Commons: 'he used to go away in the afternoon and return very late at night – so late as 4 o'clock in the morning. Mrs O'Shea sometimes went away with him.'[45] (Katharine, of course, had to keep up regular visits to her aunt.) Parnell got into a routine of exercising 'President' in the mornings, and later going for a swim. Katharine said that the weakness of her heart prevented her joining him, but she recorded one May evening when Parnell persuaded her to wade out with him, fully clothed, 'till the waves came to my shoulder and threw me off my feet'.

> He held me tightly, laughing aloud as the ripple of waves and wind caught my hair and loosed it about my shoulders; and, as I grew cold and white, my wonderful lover carried me, with all the weight of my soaked clothing, back to the shore, kissing the wet hair that the wind twisted about his face and whispering the love that almost frightened me to death.[46]

In the dusk she was apparently able to get back to their lodgings without being observed 'in my wet things, half-walking and half-carried by Parnell'.[47] It was an episode that appealed to the romantic in both Parnell and Katharine, yet the consequences, should they have been discovered, are unthinkable.

They would often drive out in the surrounding countryside, just the two of them, 'Dictator' pulling Katharine's phaeton. On one occasion Parnell was spotted at Pevensey and an excited crowd stopped them, 'insisting on shaking hands with him, and throwing covertly interested glances at his companion'.[48] Knowing that the incident would lead to reports in the newspapers, they wrote a paragraph of their own which they sent to the Press Association, stating that '"Mr Parnell had been staying at Hastings with his sister, and on visiting Pevensey with her had", etc., etc.'. It was an act of considerable daring, but both Katharine and Parnell found it irksome that they could not be left in peace to live as man and wife, especially since O'Shea was safely in Carlsbad until early August: 'it was hard we could not have a few days' quiet amusement without having it boomed through the country.'[49]

This summer on the coast was, wrote Katharine, 'a peaceful little interlude in [Parnell's] strenuous political life, and we were very happy'.[50] One of their favourite diversions was to go house-hunting about the neighbourhood – at Beachy Head and nearby Birling Gap, a 'favourite haunt' of theirs, 'a site for the ideal house of our dreams . . . where we could be absolutely alone',[51] and as far along the coast as Bognor and Selsey. There is some confusion about the actual houses they did rent around this time. They had given up their lease on Heatherbell Cottage at Beachy Head; in early June they rented 2 St John's Road, Eastbourne, but at the same time took Moira House, in Staveley Road, for one year, again at Eastbourne. The number of addresses suggests that Katharine and Parnell were anxious to make a home for themselves free from interference, whether from O'Shea or from the press. As with Heatherbell Cottage, for which they had chosen Minton hall tiles, Katharine put a great deal of effort into making Moira House as much a home as possible. She had the whole house papered, installed 5ft trelliswork around the garden, and she paid the rent.

At the divorce hearing, Sir Edward Clarke, in stating that there was never any 'permanent occupation' of Moira House, but that Parnell was 'undoubtedly there with Mrs O'Shea',[52] implies that this second house was taken solely for them to meet in secret. Certainly, Katharine seems to have been extremely cautious in making her initial enquiries about the house. Ernest Vinal, an Eastbourne estate agent, was later able to produce the first letter he had received on behalf of Mrs O'Shea. It was dated 31 July 1886, and apparently from a Mr H. Campbell, but 'in the handwriting of Mrs O'Shea'.[53] Another letter bearing the signature of 'H. Campbell' offered to pay £150 for the house and a further £50 for the use of the stables. This unfortunate episode led later to Henry Campbell, Parnell's party secretary, being accused by the *Cork Herald* of hiring houses for Parnell for 'immoral purposes'. Six months after the divorce trial he sued the paper and Parnell provided Campbell's barrister with a letter explaining that 'Mrs O'Shea wrote the letters herself, and signed them with Mr Campbell's name, Mr Campbell having given him (Mr Parnell) permission to use his name'.[54] In order to divert attention from the fact that he had taken Moira House in order to cohabit with Katharine, Parnell, careful with the truth, claimed that 'I asked Mrs O'Shea to conduct the negotiation because I was shortly going to Ireland, and for the same reasons that I have frequently charged her with the conduct of vastly more important matters and negotiations'.[55]

This was a holiday for Katharine and Parnell, but while they were at Eastbourne they were also both working on parliamentary business relating to the Home Rule Bill and to the approaching General Election. Parnell had Henry Campbell bring his correspondence down to Eastbourne for Katharine to attend to. She actually wrote twice to Gladstone from Eastbourne in the middle of July, but was careful to give her address as the Queen's Hotel (which was still forwarding her mail), where she claimed to be staying 'for a few days, with my Babies'. Since Morley was then out of London and was not due back before the next meeting of the Cabinet, Katharine posted two separate enclosures in Parnell's hand and assured the Prime Minister, 'If I can convey any message or letter I shall be very happy to do so.'[56] She recollects sitting by the window, sorting Parnell's letters, only to see her page Jimmie Kennett brought back to the house by two policemen. It appeared that Parnell had thoughtlessly handed Jimmie, a boy of 14, a £50 note, telling him to get change at the grocer's. The grocer was suspicious and called in the police. Parnell, posing as 'Mr Stewart', explained to the police that all was in order. What is remarkable about this episode is Parnell's nonchalant attitude. While Katharine was 'horrified' to see Jimmie return to the house in the company of two policemen, Parnell joked that the boy must have been caught throwing stones: '*More paragraphs, sweetheart! You shouldn't have boys about.*'[57]

Yet newspaper allusions to the scandal of Parnell's 'suburban retreat' were to continue, and even followed O'Shea to Germany. He was on an excursion with a group of other hotel guests, when an American lady said suddenly,

'Here's your name in the press, Mr O'Shea.' She read about a paragraph or two, then suddenly stammered, being as red as a peony, and exclaimed, 'Oh, I am so sorry, I can't go on' . . . I knew what it was well enough; swore I didn't, etc. There it all was about Mr P.'s 'Aspasia'* at Eltham, Mr P.'s suburban retreat during the absence of the husband, and the rest of it.[58]

---

* Gifted Athenian courtesan, mistress of Pericles until his death in 429 BC. Thus, any charming, accomplished woman of easy morals.

This was a humiliating experience for O'Shea, yet he could write about it almost incidentally in a chatty letter, and it certainly did not prompt him to return more quickly to England.

While he was away, another General Election, fought on Home Rule, split the Liberal Party (a total of seventy-two Liberal Unionists, including Chamberlain, seceded) and led to a Conservative, or 'Unionist', majority of 117. Significantly, Parnell left for Ireland to address a meeting of the party at about the time O'Shea was expected back in England. It was clear that O'Shea had taken legal advice: he was now in constant communication with Katharine in order to resolve their domestic arrangements. The following letter, dated 20 August 1886, was read out in court:

> Dear Kate, – It will be advisable not to settle anything definite until my return. I hope today to conclude a provisional arrangement by which, should it be decided to carry into effect one of the proposals which you made the other day, I should be ready to take away the children on the 1st of October. Having most carefully weighed your second proposal, that we should live at Brighton or some place, and that you should go on frequent visits to Eltham, I find the objections to it quite insuperable. One of them is that it would allow the scandal to continue unabated in another form . . . Although I hope it is unnecessary, I repeat that I forbid you to hold any communication, directly or indirectly, with Mr Parnell.

Further to this, Katharine was required 'to make out an exact list of your debts, so that I may consider how the financial position may be met'.[59]

Rather than post this letter to Katharine, O'Shea entrusted it to Gerard, Norah and Carmen, who were visiting him, to give to their mother. Katharine considered the terms of this letter for five days before responding very angrily: 'Dear Willie, You have written me many mean & impertinent letters, but the last, which even you were ashamed to give me yourself . . . is one of the most mean and insolent you have ever written.' Knowing full well that her husband was unable to support himself financially, let alone his family, she was contemptuous. His threat to remove the family from Eltham on 1 October drew a blunt reminder: 'my Aunt says she will not give one penny to me either for the support of myself or the children . . . Of course in that case you will provide all monies for the children, and myself.'[60]

Katharine's letter of 25 August 1886 does appear to have been put before her husband's barristers for use in the divorce trial (an incomplete longhand and a complete shorthand copy of it survive), yet the letter was not produced in court. Nor have its contents been fully acknowledged by commentators on the case. Lyons quotes a passage from the incomplete longhand copy referred to above, yet the shorthand version is far more extensive, and significantly demonstrates that Katharine had herself taken legal advice and knew exactly what her legal position was as a wife whose spouse had 'wilfully lived away from [her] for more than two years'.[61] Under the terms of the 1857 Matrimonial Causes Act a wife who had been deserted 'without cause for two years' could apply before a local magistrate for a judicial separation, which would give her the same rights over her earnings as an unmarried woman.[62] Under the recently passed Matrimonial Causes Act of 1884, a wife could be awarded a judicial separation if her husband refused to live with her. Then, if he was found guilty of adultery after the separation, 'she could petition for divorce on the ground of his adultery coupled with desertion, even though the desertion might not be of two years' duration'.[63]

Regarding O'Shea's threat to assume custody of the children, Katharine told him that he was being 'childish': 'You cannot "take away" (as you call it) the children without their mother . . . no judge would give you the care of the children apart from me. Therefore you are bound by law to keep me.'[64] On this question she was bluffing, and recklessly so, since her husband would surely have taken an interest in the debates on the new Custody of Infants Act, which passed into law on 25 June 1886. Despite the reforms embodied in this new piece of legislation it 'remained patriarchal at its core' and the father's authority over legitimate offspring 'absolute'.[65]

Dismissing her husband's threats, Katharine offered her own comprehensive arrangement to be drawn up by her solicitor:

> that if my aunt proposes to keep up and pay the rent for your rooms at No.1 Albert Mansions until her death you will agree to live there. I will undertake to bring up the children and educate them and get aunt to pay all expenses for them and me and also allow you £800 a year board from me if you do not worry and annoy me by living under the same roof which really means quarrelling with me whenever you see me and telling the children all day that I am bringing them up badly.

If he agreed to her terms, she would permit him to see the children 'whenever you like and have them to see you'.[66]

Understandably, O'Shea's barristers suppressed this communication, which gave extensive proof of Katharine's assertion that he had treated her 'like a milch cow . . . ever since we were married', but it was a serious oversight of theirs to put before the court a further letter of O'Shea's, dated 13 September, in which he demanded that Katharine 'prepare a room for me, so as to live in the house [i.e. Wonersh Lodge]', since his permanent residence at Eltham would afford 'the only chance of mitigating the effect of the scandal on the children'.[67] Throughout the trial, O'Shea insisted that he was in 'constant communication' with his family: he would go down to Eltham on Sundays, 'and often besides, and Mrs O'Shea and my daughters constantly came up to Albert-mansions'. Among the 700 letters produced, there were, he said, 'a number of telegrams from Mrs O'Shea about her coming up to visit me and dine with me, and all the rest of it'.[68]

However, since Katharine's barrister was instructed to take no part in the proceedings, there was no counsel to cross-examine O'Shea with regard to his letter's implication that there was not, in 1886, a bed made up for him at Wonersh Lodge as a matter of course. It was evident, however, that the jury were not satisfied with his account of his relations with his wife and children. Justice Butt recalled O'Shea to the stand to take further questions from individual members of the jury in order to help them 'decide on the question of the petitioner's neglect of his wife'. One juror asked whether, since O'Shea was 'responsible for the maintenance of your family, did you look after the children and see that they were properly educated?', to which O'Shea replied, 'Certainly'. This was a lie. The truth lay in the suppressed letter of 25 August and Katharine's review of her continuing domestic responsibilities with her aunt's financial support, and O'Shea's failings; she reminded him that he had never 'made any attempt at all to bring them up'.[69] The same juror also asked O'Shea to account for 'his constant absence from home when Albert Mansions is only an hour distant from Wonersh Lodge'. Significantly, O'Shea could only claim that he was 'constantly' there 'up to 1880, when I got into Parliament'.

What do you mean by constantly? Do you mean you returned to your family every night? – I do not. I said I was constantly there up to the time I entered Parliament. No one has made the slightest pretence that there was a want of attention on my part. In fact, my diaries show clearly that I was a kind husband and a kind father. The diaries are put in and would be enough to satisfy anybody.[70]

O'Shea closed his letter of 13 September by informing Katharine that he would give her a week (while he was away on business in Paris) to make all 'necessary arrangements' for his room at Wonersh Lodge: 'I think it better and more quiet to write than to attempt the personal discussion which, as a matter of fact, is painful.'[71] In the meantime, in a series of letters, he encourages Katharine to seek the advice of her brother, Sir Evelyn Wood, and Horatio Pym, her aunt's solicitor. Repeatedly he urges her not to communicate with Parnell and relates this to the situation of the children, but significantly not the two young girls. He has in mind, he says, the effect of the scandal upon Gerard, Norah and Carmen, but in recommending that she talk to the solicitor he seems to have had in mind that Pym would warn Katharine that she was in danger of losing her children.

On O'Shea's return from Paris, he was met by Katharine's blistering riposte to his demand that she prepare a room for him. It has a very modern ring to it: 'I have not the slightest intention of allowing you to make the rest of my life utterly miserable by nagging at me from morning until night at Eltham . . . I only desire to be left in peace with my children, and that peace I deserve and will have when at home.'[72]

It now came to O'Shea's notice that Parnell had also been seen visiting Eastbourne that summer and that he intended to return there. On Thursday 30 September the *Sussex Daily News* had announced that Parnell intended to take a house on the Cliff, Grand Parade, Eastbourne, for the winter.[73] The next day the paper revealed that Parnell's companion at Eastbourne was to be his mother, over from America. Parnell had discovered that his brother Henry was also living at Eastbourne, which may have been what complicated the living arrangements of Parnell and Katharine that summer. His mother would now be near Henry and his young family.[74] The place was not only familiar to Parnell but also, presumably, beneficial to his health. Yet it is equally possible that, in view of the recent press interest in his movements, Mrs Parnell's presence at Eastbourne would have distracted attention from Katharine and Parnell. O'Shea was to testify to the divorce court that the *Sussex Daily News* also referred to Parnell's residing at Eastbourne 'with Mrs O'Shea, with Captain O'Shea's knowledge', yet in her letters to her husband, produced in court, Katharine clearly states that her name 'had not even been mentioned'.[75] She smartly dismissed her husband's enquiry as 'another method, under cover of an obscure newspaper paragraph, of renewing the demand [i.e. that she would have nothing to do with Parnell] which I have repeatedly and definitely refused to do', and she made another sharp threat about money. Katharine's postscript is much more revealing: 'The things you mention seem so petty after the real difficulty of existence, for they have no existence, and I cannot understand how a busy man can give so much time to them.'[76]

O'Shea evidently demanded a fuller explanation of the Eastbourne story, however, for Katharine was compelled to write again on Saturday 9 October: 'I know nothing about Mr P.'s movements in reference to Eastbourne, and I do not see why I should be expected to. I only know that his brother and family had a house there.' While she admitted that, from what the paper alleged, Parnell's stay at Eastbourne that summer did indeed coincide with the dates of O'Shea's trip to Carlsbad, she could assure her husband that Parnell was in Ireland at the beginning of August 'as he sent some grouse here'.[77] In this she was telling the truth: Parnell was in Dublin on 4 August, for the first meeting of the party after the General Election, and he appears not to have returned to England until 17 August, when he came straight from Avondale and turned up at McCarthy's house (where he had an appointment to see John Morley) in full hunting-dress. Once again, Katharine closed her letter to her husband with an unsubtle warning about money. Accusing him of dragging her name into a newspaper, she threatens legal action if it happens again, and then adds, 'I am writing in haste as I have to go to aunt about money matters.'[78] Her explanation appears to have worked, or perhaps it was her threat. O'Shea agreed to remain at Albert Mansions 'this winter', and acknowledged her refusal to be bound by his prohibition of further communication with Parnell. 'I have no means of enforcing it', he admitted, 'and I must seek some other'.[79]

On Parnell's return to the Commons he introduced a Tenants' Relief Bill which proposed to give the Land Court the authority to stay evictions if the tenants were 'ready to pay half the amount and arrears'.[80] He anticipated great suffering in Ireland that winter and warned the House of 'a renewal of turmoil'.[81] Although Parnell could count on the support of Gladstonian Liberals, 'the defeat of the bill was, in a conservative House of Commons, inevitable'. The bill lost by ninety-five votes at its second reading, yet 'it served its purpose', according to Conor Cruise O'Brien, 'as, on the part of the Irish leaders, a declaration of emergency'.[82] Within days of the close of the parliamentary session (24 September), the *Irish Times* published a letter from Parnell to the president of the Irish National League of America urging support for an anti-eviction fund in order to counter 'a trouble and peril which has seldom been equalled even in the troubled history of Ireland'.[83] His predictions of further suffering and turmoil were borne out, yet this appeal for funds was to be the extent of Parnell's involvement in the alleviation of distress in Ireland. A month later, on 23 October, *United Ireland* published an anonymous article entitled 'A Plan of Campaign', written by one of the National League secretaries, Timothy Harrington, which advised tenants to hold meetings on each estate and 'to consult together and decide by resolution on the amount of abatement they will demand'.[84] If that abatement was rejected by the landlord, tenants were asked to put the money they had saved towards a fund for the evicted. John Dillon and William O'Brien, editor of *United Ireland*, were the two leaders of this campaign, which developed into another land 'war' between 1887 and 1889[85] and for which both men were later, in 1891, imprisoned in Galway Gaol.

There are differing accounts as to Parnell's position on the 'Plan of Campaign', and whether he countenanced this return to the semi-revolutionary land agitation of the early 1880s, or even whether he had been informed of it. It is a fact that Parnell was seriously ill that autumn (it has been suggested that he was suffering from Bright's Disease, a chronic disease of the kidneys[86]), and his poor state of health was no doubt exacerbated by political and personal troubles. Yet the seriousness of his undisclosed illness was doubted by some at the time. The *Pall Mall Gazette* issued a rather spiteful paragraph in which the idea of Parnell's being 'so ill as to know nothing about the Plan of Campaign' was dismissed as 'nonsense': 'he could not deceive a Kerry cow.'[87] Two years later, in a public speech, Parnell would state that he 'knew nothing about the movement until weeks after it had started', but that, 'If I had been in a position to advise, I candidly submit to you that I should have advised against it.' He said that he was 'dangerously ill' at the time, 'so ill that I could not put pen to paper, or even read the newspaper . . . I was so feeble that for several months – absolutely up to the meeting of Parliament – I was positively unable to take part in any public matter'.[88]

That he was ill is indisputable. Katharine states that during the summer he had been depressed, 'and towards the autumn I became much worried about his lassitude and general feeling of illness. I tried different diets without success'.[89] On 6 November, she took him in a closed carriage to consult the famous surgeon, Sir Henry Thompson, whose record of this consultation differs from Katharine's. Thompson described to R. Barry O'Brien the 'reserved' manner of his patient, 'Mr Charles Stewart', who was plainly 'very anxious and nervous about himself'. When Thompson proceeded to give him dietary advice, Mr Stewart told him 'that there was a lady in the next room, and that he would be glad if I would give the directions to her . . . I don't really remember how Parnell described her'. Katharine then entered, seemed 'very anxious', and 'listened carefully'.[90] Several more consultations followed this, and eventually Sir Henry discovered the identity of his patient. His account of meeting Katharine O'Shea could not be more discreet. Katharine's recollection was that it was she who first spoke to Thompson, while Parnell sat behind a closed door in the waiting-room. The doctor was at dinner when they arrived and was extremely annoyed to have to attend a patient whom he did not know, but calmed down, let her describe Mr Stewart's symptoms, and 'helped Parnell into his room, where, after receiving a smile of assurance from Parnell, and having seen the relief in his face', Katharine says, 'I left them together'.[91] Thompson's advice to Katharine was to ensure that Parnell kept his feet warm, because his poor circulation affected his digestion. Thereafter, he travelled everywhere with a little black bag with a change of socks and shoes.

A month later, Parnell's health certainly alarmed William O'Brien. In early December, he met O'Brien and Morley separately about the 'Plan of Campaign'. He had to persuade Morley that the Liberal alliance was still his priority and that he had the authority to call an end to the 'Plan of Campaign'. To do this he had to handle O'Brien very carefully, yet at the end of their meeting O'Brien agreed to calm down the agitation, which would be restricted to ten or so estates.[92]

During the second week of December, O'Brien was summoned to see Parnell and went looking for him at Wonersh Lodge. He has left a rather confused account of this and does not disclose who gave him Parnell's address at Eltham: 'The name gave me an unpleasant start, resolutely though I had shut out any belief in the tittle-tattle which Parnell's enemies of the more verminous sort had associated with it.'[93] Parnell seems to have been taken by surprise. Katharine claimed that the visit was 'entirely uninvited',[94] and that she had to improvise a story about Parnell being in a nursing-home. O'Brien returned to the Westminster Palace Hotel only to find a telegram from Parnell asking him to meet him the next morning.

O'Brien was deeply shocked by Parnell's changed appearance, his 'ghastly' face, with its 'dead clay' complexion and unkempt hair and beard, remarking that 'the effect could scarcely have been more startling if it was his ghost I had met wandering in the eternal shades'. Parnell's other-worldly appearance was in part attributed by O'Brien to his choice of meeting-place – behind the Greenwich Observatory at 10.15 in the morning, 'in a clammy December mist that froze one to the bone'. The two men were able to talk freely in the park, but Parnell must also have chosen Greenwich for its proximity to Eltham. This may have been sensible in view of his feeble health ('I have been ill – very ill', he admitted to O'Brien[95]), but risky, too.

Of her first encounter with O'Brien, Katharine states merely that 'Parnell was not really well enough to see him', but says that O'Brien was admitted when he called at Eltham a second time, a visit of which O'Brien, discreetly, left no account, but, on both occasions, he must have been aware of O'Shea's absence.[96] Parnell was able to leave his room 'for the first time to go down to the sitting-room to see him. They had a long talk over the Plan of Campaign and other matters, and the interview left Parnell so exhausted that he was very ill again for some days afterwards.'[97]

According to Katharine, towards the end of 1886 her relations with her husband 'became violently strained'.[98] O'Shea continued to write her letters containing 'such disgusting and ungrateful expressions' about her. 'It is really too sickening, after all I have done,' she complained to him.[99] O'Shea countered with his sense of the difficulty of discussing their situation in person: 'Dear Kate, – I shrink from the possible eventualities of discussion with you, especially as today before our daughters.'[100]

The situation was not helped by more press revelations. On Saturday 18 December, O'Shea took Gerard to a benefit for the prize-fighter Jem Mace, middle-weight champion of the 1860s, at the Cannon Street Hotel: 'While there, or on the way there, Captain O'Shea saw a paragraph in a newspaper which suggested that Mr Parnell was at Eltham', yet 'from a natural anxiety not to speak against his mother', 16-year-old Gerard told his father that it was not true.[101] The story printed in the *Pall Mall Gazette* amounted to one apparently innocuous sentence: 'Mr Parnell is at present paying a visit to Captain O'Shea at Eltham,'[102] yet O'Shea acted immediately to quash it. He wired the Sunday *Observer* to 'contradict the statement in the *Pall Mall Gazette* of last evening', and wrote more fully to W.T. Stead, offering to call at his offices on Monday.[103] 'The fact is', he wrote to Stead, 'that I have had no communication whatsoever with Mr Parnell since May. You have been deceived probably by some Parnellite . . . dogs of his.'[104] Yet he was too late to prevent the publication of the leading article in the *Pall Mall Gazette* that same day, 'THE MYSTERY OF MODERN POLITICS, A CHARACTER SKETCH OF MR PARNELL', which stated that Parnell's ability to keep secret his private address for so many years 'in the heart of the greatest gossiping-shop in all England, is a phenomenon without precedent'. He was said to be 'the only member of the House of Commons who had no postal address . . . no one knew where to find him': 'He has dwelt and dwells apart.'[105]

At his interview with Stead, O'Shea claimed that, whatever their political differences, 'he had never had any reason whatever to suspect Mr Parnell of any improper intimacy with his wife'.[106] Stead admits that he was somewhat incredulous of this, since, as he remarked to O'Shea, the rumours 'had been very persistent'. O'Shea, though, was adamant that there was 'not a word of truth in the story': 'he was perfectly satisfied that the relation between Mr Parnell and his wife was quite correct, and one to which he could take no objection whatever.'[107] Stead says that he was relieved to hear so, yet on Wednesday of that week his paper, in its highly sceptical account of Parnell's recent illness, made yet another pointed reference to 'Eleusinian mysteries* at Eltham'.[108]

On Tuesday 28 December Parnell was reported to be staying with his mother at the Euston Hotel before departing for Dublin. O'Shea was out of the country. He had told Stead that he wanted to see him urgently, because he was leaving London on Tuesday 21 December. From O'Shea's surviving papers we know that he was staying at the Grand Hotel, Paris, on 29 December, and it therefore seems likely that he went to Paris to spend Christmas with his mother. There was to be no repeat of the strained family Christmas of the previous year.

---

\* The Eleusinian mysteries were religious rites originally performed at Eleusis in honour of Demeter or Ceres, the goddess of corn. Since little is known about the character of the rites, the phrase has come to mean something deeply mysterious.

# CHAPTER 10

## *Breaking Point*

A life together became increasingly difficult for Katharine and Parnell. As soon as he returned to England for the opening of Parliament in January 1887, Parnell began to look for a rented property with stables attached which would enable him to keep a discreet distance from Eltham. No doubt he wanted to avoid further explanations to O'Shea (who remained in Paris until April that year), as well as further scandalous hints in the press about his residence at Eltham. This involved a life of secret addresses and various aliases.

He first looked for a house in Brockley, about four miles from Wonersh Lodge on the way to central London. The estate agent, a Mr George Porter, was not at home, and when Parnell called he left a message to say that he would return the next day. He gave his name as 'Mr Fox'. The next day, Mr Porter showed him around a number of properties and Parnell settled on St John's Lodge, 112 Tresillian Road. He now stated that his name was 'Clement Preston', but when the agent said he thought it was Fox, Parnell had a quick reply: 'No, Fox is the name of the person with whom I was staying.'[1] This was awkward. So, too, was Parnell's manner of dealing with the conventional request for references: he refused, 'saying that a man with horses ought not to be called upon for references, and that he had never given references before'. Mr Porter had to be satisfied with that, and Parnell 'agreed to pay £50 down'. Parnell next interviewed a Mr Honey for the post of coachman, and sent Mrs Honey, who was to keep house for him, to meet 'his sister' – Katharine's name was never given – in the first-class waiting-room at Cannon Street Station. At the divorce trial, Susan Honey identified Parnell and Katharine from photographs, and testified that Mr Preston 'stayed there on and off', and that 'The lady used to come and meet him there . . . but she never slept in the house'. Mrs Honey's account is corroborated by Katharine's recollection that she 'never lived there, but used to drive over to see him when it was inexpedient that he should be at Eltham'.[2]

Parnell took the house in Tresillian Road for one year, but it appears to have been very much a temporary address. 'He never liked the house,' Katharine recalled. Even in Brockley Parnell was recognised, 'and hated the way people used to hang about to see him go in and out'.[3] In fact, this attempt to frustrate the attentions of the newpapers came to nothing. At the end of February the mystery of Parnell's continuing residence at Eltham was raised again by the Tory weekly, *St Stephen's Review*. On 26 February, the paper carried separate allusions both to Parnell's residence 'in the neighbourhood of Eltham' and to his considerable efforts to foil detection: 'It is a curious fact that Mr Parnell, when returning at night to his residence – or rather Captain O'Shea's residence – at Eltham, seldom or never goes twice in succession to the same station.'[4] The suggestion that Captain O'Shea was being cuckolded, much more strongly put than in the *Pall Mall Gazette*, could not be ignored. According to a now familiar pattern, in an exchange of carefully phrased letters, O'Shea never makes an explicit accusation of his wife's adultery, while Katharine never actually denies it. Both confine themselves to a discussion of the public scandal. Thus O'Shea writes to her, drawing Katharine's attention to the gossip, and she replies with an off-hand dismissal. 'No one thinks anything of *St Stephen's*,' Katharine told him, 'and that is so evidently the old rumour again'. Rather coolly, she advised him not to take legal action: 'I am quite sure that if any one finds they have been able to take a rise out of you by it, that they will go on for ever.'[5]

Katharine seems to have taken the *St Stephen's* gossip a good deal more seriously than her letter suggests, for, largely at her prompting, Parnell moved to another rented house, this time in central London, although 'He wearily said he did not want to live in London unless I would live there too.'[6] Katharine first approached the firm of Hedges and Brandreth with regard to the tenancy of 34 York Terrace, which runs along the south side of Regent's Park, and offered three possible references: one from the National Bank, but also, rather cheekily, one from 'Mr C. Preston, Tresillian Road, Brockley', and another from 'Mr C.S. Parnell'.[7] They chose the latter, and on receipt of Parnell's reference the house, which was fully furnished, was let to Katharine for two years, from March 1887 to March 1889. She was able to pay the rent in full. Esther Harvey, the parlour-maid hired by Katharine, 'knew Mrs O'Shea by the name of O'Shea', but her mistress 'did not at any time' tell her the identity of the gentleman who slept at the house.[8] She took him to be Mr O'Shea, but in court identified him from a photograph as Parnell. Katharine would sometimes visit and stay for dinner, and on occasion would bring with her one of the maids from Eltham, perhaps to help carry things for Parnell, his books and magazines on engineering and mining, subjects which 'he considered of pleasant relaxation'. In her book, Katharine admits that the move was necessitated in part by the fact that Parnell's residence at Eltham was now frequently noticed in the press, and that she 'had had unpleasant letters from Willie', with whom she was 'not now on speaking terms'.[9]

Of greater concern to Katharine than her relationship with O'Shea was the fact that Parnell's health had not had a chance to recover over the Christmas recess. She recalls that he was

> looking fagged and worn. His health, always an anxiety to me, seemed to fail, and the languor that grew upon him frightened me. I determined that he should be spared the long cold night-drive down to Eltham, and suggested his having a house near the House of Commons to which he could return and get immediate rest after a night sitting.[10]

This is apparently all he used the house for. Esther Harvey noted that while 'he slept there pretty frequently', he 'did not stop there regularly'.[11]

Every night that Parnell did stay at York Terrace he would telegraph Katharine 'good-night' at Eltham, and in fact he appears to have lasted out for just three weeks: 'You must not leave me here by myself' he had told Katharine, 'I don't want to be here without you!'[12] In one of her rather novelistic moments, Katharine describes herself, one night at the end of March, 'mechanically making up the fire in my sitting-room as I did when sitting up for Parnell after a late sitting of the House'.[13] Overwhelmed by loneliness, she sat on after the servants had all gone to bed. Hearing the clock from the village strike two, she threw open the window and listened, 'as I had always done, about this time, for the regular beat of the horse's hoofs' that would bring Parnell home to her: 'I could hear nothing, and my longing for his presence was so great that I called out under my breath, "I wish you would come. I do wish you would come."' Then at three o'clock she heard him.

> I held my breath to listen, my heart beating with an eager joy. I could hear the beat of the hoofs round the corner into the village as they came from the Common, then lost as they went up the High Street, and suddenly clearer with the jingle of the cab bells as they turned the top of the road and stopped. I knew now, and opened the door quickly as my love came up the little side-walk past the window, giving the familiar signal as he went up the two steps; and I was in his arms as he whispered, 'Oh, my love, you must not leave me alone again.'[14]

The taking-on of the York Terrace house for Parnell's use was an expensive outlay for Katharine, but for years she had been promised that she and her children would inherit a sizeable sum of money from her aunt, who, at the age of 95, had become terribly frail. As Katharine put it, by the spring of 1887, her life 'seemed to be like a flame flickering in the wind [which] might go out any day'.[15] On the evening of Tuesday 23 March 1887 Mrs Wood's solicitor, Horatio Pym, called at the Lodge, no doubt to consult with her about making a new will, for she drew up such a will on 7 April, leaving 'all my personal and real estate to my niece Katie O'Shea whom I appoint my executrix'.[16]

It was at this time that O'Shea's return from Paris provoked a row over the custody of Gerard, who was becoming increasingly a problem. Gerard, the O'Sheas' eldest child, was about to turn 17 in April 1887, and was beginning to spend a lot of time in his father's company. As O'Shea said to Chamberlain, the boy was 'devoted' to his father,[17] who gave the young man his entrée into London society. The Jem Mace benefit in December 1886 was typical of the kind of event to which O'Shea would take his son. Gerard would have found life at Albert Mansions – dining out at clubs and restaurants, visits to the theatre and to boxing matches – a world away from his mother's suburban villa and the company of his four younger sisters. Approaching manhood, his perception of his mother's relationship with Parnell, understandably, changed. He grew to resent Parnell's presence in his mother's house. Years later he admitted, 'Had I been a little older . . . I should certainly have shot him and I was very nearly doing so, as it was'. It was Gerard's belief that he was the means of causing Parnell 'to hide and slink about under cover of darkness and under many aliases like the cowardly wretch that he was – even in those days, when I was a lad of 15 or 16'.[18]

Katharine was now keen to keep Gerard with her at Eltham until the end of April. He was studying under a tutor, and, 'As Gerardie says he told you . . . he is very anxious to go on with him until then and he is working very well.' She put off seeing O'Shea ('I don't suppose our "talk" about Gerardie will matter for a day or two – will it?'), saying that they had all gone down with colds.[19] Four days later, O'Shea received a cheque from Mrs Wood for £300, which was endorsed by Katharine, although there is no indication as to whether or not this was a routine payment.[20]

If the money was intended to silence O'Shea, it did not work. He was obliged to take things further by the letter which Gerard sent him on Wednesday 13 April:

My dearest Father,

Although my news may not be pleasing to you, yet it must be told. On my return to London this evening I came in by the back way and as I came past the window of the new room that was built last year I heard the voice of that awful scoundrel Parnell talking to a dog – Grouse I suppose. So I asked my mother if it were and she says that he has come to dine and will be gone presently. Perhaps I ought to have gone in and kicked him out but I am anxious to avoid unpleasant scenes with my mother. And I also think that it is better for you to know about it before giving him a thrashing as you of course understand more about these things than I do.

However if you wish me to kick him you have only to say so and it shall be done on the first opportunity.[21]

This time it was not rumour or newspaper scandal which disturbed O'Shea's apparent acceptance of his wife's relationship with Parnell, but his son's sudden realisation of its impropriety. This forced him to issue his first threat that he would institute divorce proceedings. His extreme reluctance to do so hitherto, he claimed, was motivated solely by his fear that once Mrs Wood learned of Katharine's adultery, she, and therefore their children, would have been cut out of her will. 'I dare say a great many people have some notion of the state of affairs,' he explained to Chamberlain the following year, 'but I am most anxious for my children's sake that nothing about it should be actually published'. Neither O'Shea nor Katharine appears to have been reluctant to admit these testamentary constraints upon their lives. By his reckoning the children stood to inherit over £200,000. [22]

At the divorce hearing, O'Shea would testify that upon receiving his son's letter he immediately telegraphed Katharine, 'saying I should call the next day. I did go, and had a very painful interview with her.'[23] His claim was supported by an exchange of letters in which both he and Katharine referred to their 'conversation on Friday'. The implication is that he took immediate action. Perhaps he did go down to Eltham, as he said, yet a surviving letter of Katharine's suggests instead that O'Shea waited for Katharine to come to him – which somewhat diminishes the view of him as an angry husband, suddenly faced with the truth. In answer to her husband's telegram, she sent him the following note on the Thursday morning: 'I shall be in Town tomorrow Friday and will call at Albert Mansions but not before 12 o'clock as I have to see Mr Pym first.'[24] Over the weekend Katharine wrote again, asking her husband to state clearly in writing his 'definite wish . . . in reference to the subject of our conversation'. She also warned him that, 'if you put it in such an offensive manner as you did on Friday, it will be impossible for me to accede to it both for my children's sake and my own, – for you have no right to give such a reason for my not meeting any one'.[25]

Only the first half of Katharine's letter was read aloud in court. The letter goes on to explain that her consultation with Mr Pym was to check the validity of her aunt's new will, a copy of which she enclosed with her letter.

She may have been indicating to O'Shea how powerful her position was by intimating that if O'Shea divorced her he would forfeit his children's inheritance. If so, this point was not acknowledged. O'Shea, who was, incidentally, running through the money sent him with some style (his diary for that day records that he and Gerard ate out at luncheon and in the evening[26]), merely pointed out to Katharine that the will was faulty in one particular: in the unlikely case of her aunt surviving Katharine, 'the children will not have a penny of her money'. It was his view that 'the new Will ought to state that in case you predecease her, she leaves her real and personal estate to your children'.[27] In reply, Katharine pointedly advises him to 'wait until the codicil is done before you get into a correspondence with any of the Newspaper scoundrels'. Specifically, O'Shea is counselled against responding publicly to the allegations in *St Stephen's Review*: 'with the family on the look out it is very important that it should be allowed to die its own death.'[28]

The 'family', that is Katharine's siblings, appear to have been given warning of a will favouring their sister. There was certainly concern about Mrs Wood's control over her finances, a concern shared, apparently, by her solicitor, who on 24 April wrote asking Charles Page Wood, Katharine's eldest brother, to call on him at his London office. He told Charles that Mrs Wood was 'quite as well as usual', but, significantly, that 'she forgets everything as soon as spoken'. He then explained that he had supplied Mrs Wood with gold (i.e. ready money in gold sovereigns) in return for a cheque once a fortnight, but that recently

> Mrs O'Shea and Mary Ann [Allan, Mrs Wood's maid] have got it from the Post Office. I suppose it is Mrs O'Shea will not let me see the cheque book – and Mary Ann undertakes to get the Gold so that I never see the cheque book or the day book to see how her money is spent . . . I don't think your Aunt knows anything about the money.[29]

It may have been that Pym was over-suspicious. It was the case, as he would admit to Charles, that Mrs Wood's doctor counter-signed some of these cheques. The order made out to O'Shea on 12 April for £300 carries the doctor's signature as well as Katharine's. But Pym was clearly full of misgiving: 'your Aunt told me Mrs O'Shea wanted Dr Bader to see her sign some papers but she did not know what papers.'[30] Certainly Katharine had access to large sums of money. On 6 April, Mrs Wood received notice that the half-yearly dividend on her bonds had yielded £1,308.[31]

Charles had not been the most attentive of nephews. Pym noted that Mrs Wood 'ask'd me when you were coming. She could not understand how it was that she had not seen or heard from you for so long.'[32] Nevertheless, the older brother tried to wrest authority from his sister. The day after Mrs Wood wrote the will leaving everything to Katharine, Charles noted in his diary that his aunt had objected to his own heavy-handed interference: 'Dr Bader told me that Aunt was irate with "one of her relations" who had brought a lawyer to deprive her of her right to manage her own affairs.'[33] He also sought the advice of an old acquaintance of his aunt's, a Mr Wilkinson, but after seeing Mrs Wood, Wilkinson reported that while 'her memory & hearing were deficient', 'she was quite her own kind self'. What is more, he was sympathetic towards the old lady's 'wish to benefit her favourite niece', and begged Charles not to subject her to 'unfeeling & selfish brawls between relatives'.[34] Charles called again at the Lodge on 18 April. This was the day Katharine had promised to call on O'Shea in London, but she telegraphed Albert Mansions three times that morning to explain that she could not leave her aunt 'while he is here'.[35] Her concern was that Charlie or any of the family would take 'further steps'.[36] On 27 April her brother Evelyn now called on their aunt, apparently without forewarning Katharine, but his brief diary entry for that day ('To Eltham. Aunt on Charlie') suggests that Mrs Wood was still furious with Charles's efforts to interfere with her money matters.[37] Charles returned on 8 May to find Mrs Wood being nursed by Katharine ('Katie looked black as thunder, evidently hated my coming'), but, perhaps having forgotten their recent dispute, the old lady was delighted to see him, made him stay for luncheon, 'and cheered up so much that she offered to drive me to [Blackheath] station altho' she had not left the house for 10 days . . . [and] begged me to come again to see her'.[38] Yet these nephews' visits did not lead to any changes in the will.

At this point, the strain was heightened by a public accusation that Parnell was complicit in, or at the least sympathetic to, acts of terrorism. On the morning of Monday 18 April, the same day that Charles Page Wood visited Eltham with his solicitor, cuttings from *The Times* were found pasted to the gate of Wonersh Lodge. The paper had reprinted a number of letters written in an unknown hand but purporting to carry Parnell's signature. A facsimile was published of the most significant of these which was dated 15 May 1882, nine days after the Phoenix Park murders. It ran as follows:

Dear Sir, I am not surprised at your friend's anger but he and you should know that to denounce the murders was the only course open to us. To do that promptly was plainly our best policy. But you can tell him and all others concerned that though I regret the accident of Lord F. Cavendish's death I cannot refuse to admit that Burke got no more than his deserts.[39]

Katharine says that she tried to keep the paper from Parnell while he breakfasted, but that he insisted on reading it then, since, he said, 'he *must* finish a bit of assaying he had left over-night, before going to London, and would not have time for papers afterwards, so I told him of the letters, and propped the *Times* against the teapot as usual'.[40] In silence, he read on, 'meditatively buttering and eating his toast the while'. Then, having 'carefully clipped the end off his cigar', he 'tossed the paper at me, saying: "Wouldn't you hide your head with shame if [I] were so stupid as that?"'. He spent the rest of the afternoon at his assaying before leaving for the Commons. As she held out his coat for him, Katharine urged him to take legal action against *The Times*, but he replied that he had 'never taken any notice of any newspapers, nor of anyone. Why should I now?'[41]

In fact, *The Times* had intended to launch its campaign against Parnell at the time of the Queen's Speech in January, but had been warned against printing the letters by the Attorney-General, Sir Henry James, who had doubts about their authenticity. At the beginning of March, the paper satisfied itself with the publication of a series of three libellous articles, entitled 'Parnellism and Crime' (7, 10 and 14 March), which charged Parnell and his party with having been, and being still, 'in notorious and continuous relations with avowed murderers', and accused the Liberals of having allied themselves 'with the paid agents of an organisation whose ultimate aim is plunder and whose ultimate sanction is murder'.[42] Both Parnell and Gladstone ignored these articles. The publication of the forged letters Parnell could not ignore.

The letters published by *The Times* had a highly dubious provenance. They emanated from Richard Pigott (a 'seedy Irish journalist', Lyons calls him[43]), a newspaper proprietor and pornographer. It was from Pigott that Parnell had purchased the paper that he would rename *United Ireland*. Pigott therefore had correspondence to do with this transaction in Parnell's hand, and in that of Patrick Egan, then treasurer of the Land League. In 1886, finding himself in financial difficulties, Pigott offered to sell to the young *Times* journalist and Unionist, Edward Caulfield Houston, incriminating letters linking Parnell to terrorism. *The Times* had hesitated to publish the letters, taking heed of Sir Henry James's warnings, yet, extraordinarily, the paper's proprietors did not fully grasp James's chief objection, that the source was Pigott, since the name was apparently unknown to them.[44] Tim Healy took one look at the forged letter and pointed the finger at Pigott. So strong was his conviction that he persuaded Henry Labouchère to make the allegation in the latter's paper, *Truth*.[45] Parnell took the earliest opportunity to denounce the publication of the facsimile letter to an expectant House at one o'clock on the morning of 19 April: it was 'an audacious and unblushing fabrication'. The handwriting was, he said, 'entirely different' from his own 'cramped hand'. 'It is in fact a labour and a toil to me to write anything at all,' he admitted.[46] Certainly, the enclosures in his hand which in the past Katharine had forwarded to Gladstone justify this description. A crabbed and untidy hand might better describe it; his notepaper is littered with ink blots.

Little more happened at this stage. The Conservative Government rejected Gladstone's call for a Select Committee to investigate the forgeries, and John Morley strenuously advised Parnell against taking a libel action, since there was no knowing what an English jury might decide. Presumably there was also no knowing what else might be brought to light about Parnell's secretive living arrangements. Moreover, Parnell was still very ill, and while he was on a brief visit to Avondale a rumour of his death 'thrilled' the Commons.[47] When he appeared in the House on 18 May Justin McCarthy described his appearance as that of an apparition: 'no ghost from the grave ever looked more startling among living men . . . the ghastly face, the wasted form, the glassy eyes gleaming.' Running into John Morley a moment later, 'We both could only say in one breath, "Good God! Have you seen P.?"'[48] In July he was fit enough to preside over a meeting of the party, the first he had attended for a long time, 'But fancy,' McCarthy wrote to Mrs Campbell Praed, 'on such a burning day as this, he wore a thick outside coat and soft felt hat – and he shivered so often!'[49] On 21 July, Parnell was honoured at a banquet at the National Liberal Club, but for the rest of the year he was rarely to be seen in public, and was nursed back to health by Katharine.

Meanwhile, following Gerard's letter to his father about Parnell's continued visits to Wonersh Lodge, Katharine's relations with her husband continued to deteriorate. An extract from O'Shea's diary for Monday 18 April 1887 survives. It does not record his response to the publication that day of the facsimile letter in *The Times*, but dwells on his relationships with his wife and son: 'She wants Gerard back – replied letter & telegram offering her to give her time to see Pym first.'[50] His son had been with him that weekend, and on the Monday evening they attended a benefit for Gerard's boxing instructor, 'Bat' Mullins, where they saw Lord Queensberry. Her son's long visits to his father appear to have caused Katharine great anxiety, and the next day she telegraphed again, 'Please send Gerard home immediately . . . he can go up again if you wish after all settled.'[51] From O'Shea's diary entry for 19 April it seems that the wrangling over their son had reached a compromise: he went as usual to his tutor at Greenwich, returned home briefly to see his mother ('departed on friendly terms'[52]), and then went up to town to stay with his father, who took him to the Globe Theatre in the Strand. O'Shea also records that earlier that day he called on his wife's solicitor, and deposited with Pym his correspondence with Katharine dating from the previous summer, 'chiefly Augt & Sept'.[53] These were the letters in which he had repeatedly advised her to seek Pym's advice in order to diminish the effect of the scandal upon the children, but also, perhaps, so that she would be warned of her legal position. Unable himself to enforce his wife's compliance, O'Shea was hoping that Katharine's solicitor would advise it.

Not only did this not work, but Katharine, in a letter written by Pym on her behalf, began to challenge her husband on such matters as his connivance in her relationship with Parnell: 'The particular friend you alluded to . . . only became a friend of the family upon your introduction and by your wish.' She refused to behave 'with a discourtesy which the past friendship and kind favours shown to you by that friend do not deserve', and the communication ended with the customary covert threat: her aunt was suffering 'very serious annoyance and anxiety' about Gerard's absence from home.[54]

Stung by Katharine's suggestion that he was under obligation to Parnell, O'Shea wrote back 'The fact is the absolute reverse',[55] and in his second letter to Pym that day he demanded the immediate return of his papers. He then goes on to say what he had hoped from Pym's interference on his behalf: 'What I asked you to advise Mrs O'Shea about was this, and only this. That reports being wide and strong as to her relations with Mr Parnell it would for her children's sake be expedient that she should declare her renunciation of communication with him.'[56] The word 'expedient' is an interesting choice. He does not admit or deny the truth of these reports. He merely states that since the story has got abroad, Katharine should issue a public statement for the sake of her children.

Pym duly returned O'Shea's papers to him on Monday 25 April, but repeated Katharine's threat regarding Gerard's whereabouts, lest 'his position with Mrs Wood may be very seriously compromised'.[57] O'Shea was left with little alternative but to write to Parnell himself, which he did at the end of the week:

> It has come to my knowledge that in the face of the scandal which has been largely disseminated by your own associates and which I have no reason to believe you have ever made any effort to curb you continue to communicate with & to meet with Mrs O'Shea. I now personally call on you to discontinue all communication direct or indirect with her.[58]

No documentary evidence survives to suggest how Parnell and Katharine responded to this demand. The papers which provide such a detailed insight into Katharine's affairs throughout the spring of 1887 are those which were submitted by O'Shea as evidence in the probate suit which followed Aunt

Wood's death in 1889. These cease abruptly with the copies of two perfunctory telegrams she sent her husband on the morning of 2 June, letting him know that Norah and Carmen would meet him for luncheon at the Café Royal, and that she would call for them at Albert Mansions at about four o'clock.[59] Yet this glimmer of improved relations between Katharine and O'Shea was extinguished by his apparent discovery, less than a fortnight later, that the 1886 allegations made by the *Pall Mall Gazette* were true. Parnell had been staying at Wonersh Lodge.

O'Shea appears to have post-dated this discovery. We know that Gerard had written to his father about Parnell being at Eltham on 13 April, and yet O'Shea later told Chamberlain that it was on 13 June that he had learned about this and had then gone straight to his solicitors, Freshfield and Williams.[60] He seems to have been covering up the fact that it took him two months to take any action. Of course there may well have been two separate incidents at Eltham involving Gerard. He would much later claim that, on one occasion, 'on arriving home unexpectedly I found the blackguard there and broke a bottle of wine on his head – I wish I had killed him'.[61] It does appear that it was not until June that Gerard admitted to his father specifically that Parnell's horses were stabled at Wonersh Lodge, or so O'Shea testified at the divorce trial.[62] At any rate, his solicitor being away at the time, O'Shea sent Gerard back to Eltham with a threat that, unless Katharine gave him a written pledge of better behaviour, he would institute divorce proceedings against her and would make sure that she never saw her son again.[63]

If Katharine refused to give her husband a formal promise that she would cease to communicate with Parnell, she now agreed to make such a statement to her son, drawn up in exactly the terms that had been demanded by O'Shea back in April. Addressing Gerard as if she were responding to his, rather than his father's, personal objection to Parnell, Katharine wrote on 27 June: 'I am most anxious that everything should be made as pleasant as possible for you, and that nobody should come here who is in any way obnoxious to you, and, therefore, I readily agree that there shall be no further communication, direct or indirect, with [Mr Parnell]. Ever, my darling Gerard, Your loving Mother.'[64] The next day, she wrote a second time to Gerard in answer to her husband's further stipulations, confirming that she had given her groom notice and had given up the lower stables ('Dictator' was to be turned out into her aunt's park). However, she concluded this letter with a defiant message for O'Shea: 'I must tell you again that I am not afraid of any proceedings, and if Mr P. Williams's clerk comes, or any one else, on my premises, without my leave I shall take means to have them removed.'[65] She was clearly aware that O'Shea was keeping her under observation.[66] Then, apparently (and rather too easily) satisfied that his wife 'had kept her promise and had broken off communication with Mr Parnell', O'Shea departed for Carlsbad.[67] Significantly, he took Gerard with him.

O'Shea would testify that his suspicions were not aroused again until the end of 1887, when *The Times* tracked down Parnell's 'concealed residence' at Brockley, which he was again using regularly. More damaging still was the revelation that he had taken the house in Tresillian Road under the alias of 'Mr C. Preston'. The fact that 'the leader of a powerful Parliamentary party . . . should feel it advisable to go into hiding under an assumed name seems to require explanation,' exclaimed *The Times*.[68] While the clear inference to be drawn from the article was that Parnell feared for his life because of his dealings with Irish-American conspirators, the proximity of Brockley to Eltham can hardly have been lost on O'Shea. Yet still he did nothing.

At Avondale in early January 1888, Parnell himself now made out a new will, which, according to Henry Harrison, left his family home in Ireland 'and all that he had' to Katharine, Clare and Katie. Harrison had it in his hands only once, and while recalling that the will ran to two sheets of foolscap paper he could remember little of the detail, save that 'its immense significance – quite unforgettable – lay in its acknowledgment of the two little girls as his children'.[69] Why Parnell should have decided at this time to write out his will is a matter of interest, since what Katharine stood to gain from her aunt's will was not then in doubt, although it may be that he thought to do so because his health had been such a concern the previous year. On 7 March 1888, Anna Maria Wood signed another will drawn up by Horatio Pym, and had it witnessed by her housemaid, Mary Ann Allan, and her cook, Sarah Elizabeth Russell. The necessity of a new will remains unclear, since the terms of Mrs Wood's previous will remained essentially the same: her niece Katharine was named as executrix and sole beneficiary, 'free . . . from her present or any future husband'.[70] It may be that Katharine had taken heed of O'Shea's advice about the weakness in her aunt's previous will in the event of Katharine's dying before her aunt. In order to protect the interests of the children, Mrs Wood now named Pym and Charles Bader as the trustees and guardians of any of Katharine's children who remained minors at the time of their mother's death.

When Charles and Evelyn decided to contest this latest will on the grounds of their aunt's diminished responsibility, their petition to the Courts of Lunacy necessitated Katharine having her aunt's mental capacity assessed by a doctor. She chose Gladstone's own physician, Sir Andrew Clark, an eminent authority who may have been recommended by Gladstone himself.[71] Clark came down to Eltham on Saturday 7 April, and after spending about an hour and a half with Mrs Wood told Katharine that 'it was a cruel thing for anyone to say my Aunt was insane. He thought her [a] most charming cultivated woman.'[72] Clark's delay in writing up his report added to Katharine's anxiety. Having sent Clark three telegrams, she now wrote to Gladstone begging him to intervene: 'I know a word from you will induce Sir Andrew to attend to the matter at once.' Her aunt, she wrote, was suffering 'so cruelly from the suspense', and had 'not slept for more than ten minutes at a time'.[73] This may in fact more closely represent her own desperation, which was so great that she asked Parnell to write to the Prime Minister – the only time he had ever done so on a personal matter, but 'immediate action is of pressing importance'.[74]

Gladstone obliged, and Clark's statement was filed on 20 April. His assessment of Mrs Wood's mental faculties was conclusive: aside from 'an occasional forgetfulness' and 'a slight tendency to repetition' natural in a person of her great age, he found her mind alert and agile in responding to his questions. She was 'attentive . . . coherent and logical . . . full of old stories', and 'able to quote largely from the French poets'.[75] The legal case was eventually withdrawn, very likely on the strength of the medical report.[76] Katharine's family would wait until their aunt was dead before they mounted another legal challenge to her will.

On the matter of the forged letters published in *The Times*, Parnell had so far refrained from taking legal action. Frank Hugh O'Donnell did sue, on the grounds that his own reputation had been damaged by the accusations made more widely against the leaders of the Land League. His case finally collapsed at the beginning of July 1888, but in the course of its proceedings, Sir Richard Webster, counsel for *The Times*, repeated the paper's allegation that in 1882 Parnell had sanctioned acts of terrorism and murder. Parnell denounced the forged letters in the Commons a second time on the night of 6 July. With reference to one particular letter, supposedly written from Kilmainham and addressed to Patrick Egan, which had called for 'prompt action . . . to make it hot for old Forster & Co.,' Parnell declared, 'I never wrote it; I never signed it; I never directed it to be written; I never authorised it to be written and I never saw it'.[77] Although Gladstone was careful not to offer advice officially, a note was passed to Parnell in the Commons which read, 'you had better do nothing further'.[78] There was always the concern that Parnell's domestic situation might also be exposed: 'every fact in a man's life might be gone into.'[79]

Parnell did, however, press for a Special Committee to deal with the matter, and the Conservative Government, realising that such an inquiry could go far beyond the question of the authenticity of the letters, and be used to investigate the whole workings of the Land League, was quick to introduce a Special Commission Bill. Parnell was impotent to influence the scope of the commission, and when he criticised the bill, during the debate on the second reading, he had to endure the taunts of Chamberlain to the effect that Parnell's unwillingness to challenge *The Times* was a sign of his guilt. Animosity between Chamberlain and Parnell surfaced in a *Times* correspondence in which O'Shea participated, attacking Parnell as a weak leader.[80] Yet, while this very personal contest fizzled out, *The Times* now showed a sudden interest in O'Shea as a possible witness *against* Parnell.

The Special Commission, which was to call sixty-three Nationalist MPs and sixty-seven 'other persons' to give evidence, began sitting on 17 September 1888. (It would not conclude until 22 November 1889.) There was barely a month before the commission was to begin, and Parnell had many consultations with his solicitor, George Lewis. He appears to have confided in Lewis the delicate situation of his relations with Katharine, the estranged wife of one of *The Times*'s star witnesses.

On one occasion, Lewis requested that Katharine meet him at Wood's Hotel, close to his offices at Ely Place. In the hotel coffee-room they 'had a long business talk about the case', in the course of which they discussed some letters that Katharine had entrusted to him at an earlier interview, possibly to establish proof of handwriting. All the while, however, Katharine was conscious of people passing 'very close to us', who 'stared curiously at me before going out'.[81] She finally asked Lewis outright why he had asked to meet her in such a public place, but got an evasive reply. She was hurt and 'somewhat ruffled' by Lewis's failure to give her an explanation there and then, but at their next private interview at his offices he was able to explain to Katharine that someone had been impersonating her, 'with the hope of better entangling Parnell, and of preventing him from publicly protesting his honour for fear of dragging me into the case'.[82] It is clear, here, that Lewis knew of the affair, and of the risk that the Special Commission would expose it. What is of interest is the fact that O'Shea was just as anxious as Parnell to prevent such exposure, not simply of the affair, but of the fact of his complicity in it, as his evidence to the Special Commission shows.

O'Shea was called on 31 October. As he confessed to Chamberlain the next day, he 'went into the witness-box . . . under a very heavy load of anxiety owing to matters in themselves apart from Charges and Allegations'.[83] This anxiety was no doubt caused by his fear of exposure, and by his having to confront Parnell, with whom he had not communicated since April 1887, when he forbade him to see Katharine. Parnell was in court, sitting with Healy and O'Connor, and throughout O'Shea's testimony 'looked eagerly yet gravely towards him the whole time'.[84] There are differing accounts of O'Shea's state of mind that day. O'Connor recalled that he was 'in appearance what he had always been, only a little more so. He was very carefully dressed . . . and gave his evidence with an appearance of almost frank bonhomie.'[85] However, Alfred Robbins of the *Birmingham Post* was shocked to find him 'very much changed, in both figure and face, in the direction of what was then known as "the shabby genteel"', and noted that when he was called to the stand he was highly nervous, 'manifestly trying to repress his excitement, but his hands trembled a good deal'.[86] Sir Richard Webster took Captain O'Shea through the Kilmainham negotiations up to the time of his request for police protection on the day after the Phoenix Park murders. When asked to pronounce an opinion as to the authenticity of the Parnell letters published in *The Times*, he gave a studied reply: with a smile, he 'disclaimed any pretence to being anything like an expert on handwriting', but, casting his eyes over the document handed to him, gave the opinion that, 'from his extensive knowledge of Parnell's writing and of his signature, he regarded the signature as genuine'.[87]

He was then briefly cross-examined by Sir Charles Russell. It was O'Shea's boast to Chamberlain that, 'Once it came to fighting Russell . . . I had him down round after round',[88] but according to Alfred Robbins, Russell 'walked round' the witness just as delicately as the Attorney-General, and 'showed himself as reluctant as Webster to tempt him to speak freely, for neither trusted him, and each suspected he might say too much'.[89] Parnell had been against any cross-examination beyond that conducted by Russell, and had in fact opposed Russell's original request for Healy, a practising barrister, to represent the suspects.[90] There seems little doubt that Parnell was anxious that Healy might be tempted to take his revenge for Galway and lead O'Shea into making compromising revelations. When Healy asked for O'Shea to be recalled in order to question him further, Parnell's reaction was to clutch at Healy's jacket and demand to know what exactly he intended to ask. Healy replied, 'Nothing sensational.'[91]

The implication of Healy's account is that Parnell was concerned to prevent discussion in court of the nature of his relationship with O'Shea. This is not borne out by Parnell's own intervention in Russell's cross-examination of O'Shea. In the course of his testimony, O'Shea revealed that at some time during the debate on the second reading of the Home Rule Bill, he had learnt certain things about the Irish leader which caused him to break off their friendship. Russell, under instruction from Parnell, now pressed O'Shea to explain more precisely what these certain things were. Parnell was taking a terrible risk, but his challenge to O'Shea, and O'Shea's response, show that he was confident that, while Katharine's aunt lived, O'Shea would do or say nothing to bring the scandal to light. Robbins observed that O'Shea became 'more and more nervous. He unfolded his arms; leant an elbow on the ledge and his head on his hand; frequently wiped his face; hurriedly stroked his chin; and almost turned his back on the cross-examiner'.[92] His guarded reply was simply to restate the fact that 'certain things came to my knowledge at that time which absolutely destroyed the good opinion I had hitherto held of Mr Parnell'.[93] Russell did not pursue the matter any further. That evening Healy wrote to his brother, '[O'Shea] has not hurt us, but I don't think Parnell's character will be improved by the close relations he has held with the Eltham household'.[94] The immediate crisis was over, however. The evidence of the 'time-bomb' as Lyons calls O'Shea, which potentially could have been so damaging to Parnell, had in fact contributed little of substance to *The Times*'s case. O'Shea then departed for Spain, ostensibly to follow up his business interests in Madrid. He returned home briefly in early December to give support to Gerard, who was about to take his army entrance examination, but went back to Madrid before Christmas.

The investigation into *The Times*'s letters did not begin until 14 February, and Parnell was now in daily attendance. Pigott was finally called on the afternoon of 20 February. Patrick Egan had previously sent over from America evidence of Pigott's handwriting, in which his misspelling of the word hesitancy as 'hesitency' was consistent with the forged letters. On the second day of his examination, the letters were exposed as forgeries, and Pigott as the forger. By the time the commission adjourned for the weekend, he was out of his wits. On the Saturday he offered a full confession to Labouchère, which on the Monday was revoked by his solicitor, and then, on Tuesday 26 February, having absconded to Paris, he sent another confession to London, explaining in detail how he had executed the forgeries by tracing out words or phrases from letters of Parnell and Egan in his possession. He arrived in Madrid on Thursday 28 February and checked into the Hotel Embajadores under the assumed name of Roland Ponsonby. In Madrid, he shot himself in the head.

Pigott's choice of hiding-place had been absolutely sound, since Britain had no extradition treaty with Spain, yet the fact that O'Shea was also there is a remarkable coincidence.[95] O'Shea even caught sight of Pigott in the Calle de Sevilla in the company of an interpreter from his hotel, yet apparently made no attempt to approach him. He described this curious non-encounter to Chamberlain more than a week after Pigott's suicide. His delay in doing so is certainly uncharacteristic – O'Shea was never one to hold back political gossip – and his manner, too, of identifying Pigott also seems overly cautious. On the evening of Pigott's arrival, O'Shea had observed an Englishman order a beer and an English newspaper at the Café Inglés, and quickly identified him from having seen 'portraits of Pigott and . . . descriptions of his appearance, in newspapers'. The next day, he added, 'hearing of the suicide a few minutes after it occurred . . . I had no doubt of the identity'.[96] It is certainly true that Parnell suspected O'Shea's involvement in the procurement of the forgeries, and from O'Shea's correspondence with Chamberlain it is clear that he knew of Parnell's suspicions. Yet no evidence has ever been discovered implicating O'Shea or Chamberlain in *The Times*'s case against Parnell.

When news of Pigott's suicide reached England, Parnell was given a rapturous reception in the Commons. Katharine herself was too ill to attend the House on the night of 1 March. Justin McCarthy's friend Mrs Campbell Praed had been in her seat in the Ladies' Gallery since three o'clock in the afternoon and recorded how, when Parnell rose to speak some time after 11 p.m., 'the whole Opposition – including Mr Gladstone, Sir William Harcourt, and . . . many Tory members – stood up bare-headed and cheered the Irish leader for several minutes': 'I, too, felt to the quick the surge of excitement which swept the House at sight of that tall form in loosely-built clothes and the pale brown-bearded, statuesque face, as the man who was called "The Uncrowned King" waited until the storm of cheers had died down.'[97] When he returned to Eltham in the early hours of the morning, Katharine asked him, 'if he had not felt very proud and happy then, but he only smiled, and answered, "They would all be at my throat in a week if they could!"'[98] Yet, for a while, at least, Parnell was the toast of the Liberal Party: on 8 March the 'Eighty Club' held a dinner for him at which he was received 'with loud and prolonged cheers, the audience springing to their feet and waving their napkins over their heads'.[99] He responded with a speech in which he denounced the current Tory 'bastard plan' of governing Ireland through 'a semi-constitutional, a semi-coercive method'. The only proper way of governing Ireland was the Liberal plan 'of allowing her to govern herself in all those matters which cannot interfere with the greatness and well-being of the Empire of which she forms a part'.[100] On 19 March he dined with the Gladstones at the house of Liberal MP Sydney Buxton, and three days later spoke at a mass meeting in St James's Hall, presided over by John Morley; on 28 May Sir Charles Russell hosted another reception for him at which Parnell was made a life member of the National Liberal Club. 'It was', wrote Katharine, 'a time of adulation for him from first to last'.[101]

Yet though *The Times*'s letters were proved to be forgeries, it was still necessary for the commission to complete its investigation into the work of the Land League and for Parnell to clear his name of the charges made against him. Katharine says that the commission never caused him any real worry, 'except that it took up so much of our all too little leisure time, which was so precious to us'.[102] He finally took the stand on 30 April, his examination lasting nine days, and looked resplendent in a new frock coat, Lewis having objected to his 'shabby Irish homespuns'.[103] While his evidence regarding his links with named extremists displayed 'a forgetfulness amounting almost to amnesia',[104] Parnell was more than a match for Sir Richard Webster, and when the commission report was finally published in February 1890, Parnell and his party were exonerated of complicity in acts of terrorism, although the Land League was found guilty of encouraging tenants to withhold payment of rents and of accepting funds from the American Patrick Ford ('a known advocate of crime and the use of dynamite').[105] Parnell eventually won damages of £5,000 from *The Times*.

Domestically, too, there was relief for Katharine and Parnell. Eleven days after the examination of Parnell had been completed, Katharine's aunt died at the age of 97. Mrs Wood suffered an attack of bronchitis in April from which she never recovered. Katharine sat and read to her during the day, but 'a little smile and pressure of the hand I held was the only response she made'. Every night, Katharine devotedly returned to the Lodge, to ask, under Mary Ann's window, if her aunt was settled for the night: 'On these May nights', after having testified before the Special Commission by day, Parnell would drive back to Eltham and 'walk across the park with me and wait on a seat for me till I had obtained the latest bulletin'.[106] Katharine was with Mrs Wood the morning she died, 'looking as small and frail as a child'. Yet while there was sadness at her passing, Katharine admits that there was also inexpressible relief that she and Parnell were no longer 'tied to one place', a sensation she had 'sometimes felt so keenly hard'.[107] Katharine's desire to leave Wonersh Lodge was overwhelming. Until the house was in a state to let, she and the children moved into 'Woodcroft', a rented country house off the Mottingham Road, little more than a mile away, before settling into the house they still retained in Brighton, at 10 Walsingham Terrace. As soon as they left Eltham, 'the pretty garden was devastated by relic hunters, who pulled the place to pieces in obtaining mementoes of "the house where Parnell had lived"'.[108] The sudden move from Wonersh Lodge, her home of fifteen years, symbolised not simply a release from Katharine's former responsibilities as her aunt's companion, and the economic dependence which that entailed, but also broke one further link with her husband. O'Shea seems to have known nothing about his wife's domestic arrangements in Brighton. Norah and Carmen do not appear to have told him that Parnell was living at Walsingham Terrace, and if, as seems likely, Gerard was by then in the army, he may also have known nothing about it. Whether or not O'Shea was wilfully blind to the identity of the Brighton household, one other certainly was. That summer, T.P. O'Connor caught sight of Parnell out promenading with Katharine and, presumably, 6-year-old Clare on the pier at Brighton: 'There was a lady with him – I suppose it was Mrs O'Shea – and a child . . . I slid away, lest I should cause him any pain or embarrassment.'[109] Like William O'Brien, he kept his knowledge to himself.[110]

Their new life at Brighton was, by Katharine's account, happy and relaxed. The house was situated at a discreet distance from Brighton itself, but, beyond that, they made no great effort to hide the fact that they were living together. They could often be seen walking or riding on the Downs, and indeed, the public did find them out and 'used to walk or drive out to see "Parnell's house", but this was not particularly annoying'.[111] There is a new spirit of confidence, too, in their decision to expand the household by renting the adjoining house, 9 Walsingham Terrace, and to take on a large domestic retinue: besides the faithful Phyllis, and a nurse for Clare and Katie, Katharine now employed four other maids. Although O'Shea apparently remained in ignorance of these arrangements, Gladstone and Morley were informed of Parnell's new residence, and wrote to Katharine there in order to arrange a meeting with Parnell to discuss the terms of a second Home Rule bill. She says that it was her idea to suggest that Gladstone invite Parnell for a private conference at his home, Hawarden Castle. After receiving three pressing invitations,[112] Parnell finally went to Hawarden on 19 December on his way to Liverpool, where he was due to give a speech. It has been said that Parnell was at the zenith of his power when *The Times*'s letters were proved forgeries, but surely it came later in the year when, both politically and domestically, his position looked unassailable. His fall could not have been more dramatic.

# CHAPTER 11

## Divorce

The petition for divorce was finally filed on Christmas Eve 1889. The first notice of it was published in the *Evening News* on Saturday 28 December:

> The grounds alleged are the adultery of Mrs O'Shea during the period from April, 1886, up to the date of the petition, at the undermentioned places: – Eltham; 34 York-terrace, Regent's Park; Brighton; and Aldrington, Sussex. No damages are claimed.[1]

The paper had been reluctant to print the story until it was confirmed by O'Shea in an interview on the Saturday morning. He and Gerard were still at their breakfast when the *Evening News*'s reporter arrived at 124 Victoria Street and was shown up 'into a cosy sitting-room'. Reluctant to speak openly in front of 19-year-old Gerard, the reporter asked whether it would be possible to see O'Shea privately, only to be told, 'You may speak before my son.'[2] Still the reporter hesitated, and so Gerard was asked to leave the room. O'Shea then invited the man to sit down and coolly offered him a cigarette, but had little to add to the newspaper announcement beyond his rather offhand manner.

The first people to learn that Captain O'Shea was close to instituting divorce proceedings were Katharine's own family. In the first week of October 1889 he had been invited to the Barrett Lennards' home, Belhus Park, to discuss the situation with Katharine's two brothers, Charles and Evelyn, and her sisters Anna and Emma, Lady Barrett Lennard. O'Shea would state in his affidavit, which was read out in court on Tuesday 21 January 1890, that in taking proceedings against his wife he had 'the entire support and sympathy to the fullest extent' of her brothers and sisters.[3] Indeed, as he confided to Chamberlain a week or so after the meeting, Katharine's siblings had talked unrestrainedly of their hostility towards her in front of house-guests and friends from the neighbouring gentry. It was a typically strange situation for O'Shea to find himself in. He was seeking support from people who were at the same time intent on claiming a share of the fortune which would be his children's inheritance.

His letter to Chamberlain was primarily to tell him of the forthcoming legal challenge mounted by Katharine's brothers and sisters to contest the terms of their aunt's will, a case in which O'Shea's solicitors had already advised him to intervene on behalf of his children. He now felt it necessary to forewarn Chamberlain that he was considering whether some further 'strong action should not be taken by me', and wanted to explain to him certain 'personal matters':

> You are aware that I have had much domestic trial, complicated by considerations concerning the interests of my children, and my desire to avoid the injury certain to be inflicted on them by full publicity of a scandal gross in itself, but all the more re-echoing on account of the persons involved.[4]

O'Shea enclosed a paper which, he felt, would enable Chamberlain 'to judge of the perfidy of which I have been the victim'. In this document, in which he had copied out the May 1886 *Pall Mall Gazette* article, 'Mr Parnell's Suburban Retreat', together with separate denials of its content by Katharine and by Parnell, O'Shea admitted that since 13 April 1887, when Gerard had told him about Parnell's continued presence at Eltham, he had known that the newspaper's allegations had been accurate. It is as if O'Shea was building up a case to put before his lawyers and offering the evidence first to Chamberlain to test his reaction. Chamberlain's reply could not have been more carefully phrased: 'I have never listened to scandalous reports affecting my friends', he assured O'Shea, 'and in your case I have heard nothing, and knew nothing, beyond what you have told me.' His closing advice, however, carries an implication that O'Shea knew about his wife's affair before April 1887, and might have taken action earlier. Expressing the fear that in the days of the *Pall Mall Gazette* and such newspapers, 'these things cannot be hushed up', he advised: 'I am not sure that the boldest course is not always the wisest.'[5]

Before taking what he described as 'strong action', O'Shea sought dispensation from the Catholic Church which would allow him to divorce his wife on the grounds of her proven adultery. His diary entry for Saturday 19 October records a meeting with Cardinal Manning, head of the Catholic Church in Britain: 'Explained that while anxious to conform with the regulations of the Church, I saw no way outside applying for a divorce.'[6] When the Cardinal asked him what proof he had of his wife's adultery, O'Shea produced a paper similar to the enclosure he had prepared for Chamberlain, including the extracts from the *Pall Mall Gazette*. While Manning expressed considerable sympathy, it was his hope that O'Shea would be satisfied with a simple separation deed, and he ended the interview by asking for more time to consider how best to advise him. He kept him waiting until the end of November, by which time the Special Commission had concluded its sittings. A frustrated O'Shea told Manning that he was anxious to receive instruction and could wait no longer. It was 'imperative', he wrote, 'that my course of procedure should be determined. Personally I have everything to gain by the completest publicity.'[7] Manning wrote back straight away on 27 November, 'throwing cold water on Willie's desire for a separation', according to Katharine.[8] It is clear from the tone of O'Shea's immediate reply that Manning had not only wilfully undervalued the significance of his proof, but had gone so far as to accuse him of connivance and to suggest that this was for financial reasons: 'There has been no delay on my part,' protested O'Shea, in a fury about the Cardinal's 'informant' and his 'cowardly insult' about money.[9]

O'Shea had good cause to be angry. Katharine states that she first learnt of this correspondence with Cardinal Manning when she was handed the letters by Gerard for inclusion in her biography of Parnell: 'I do not know more about them.'[10] Yet, there is evidence that a month before O'Shea filed his petition for divorce, Katharine and Parnell had prior notice, both of the action and the scope of O'Shea's documentary proof of the adultery. While O'Shea was hanging on for an answer for the best part of six weeks, Manning made his own enquiries into the O'Sheas' domestic arrangements. Astonishingly, he went for advice to Parnell's own solicitor, George Lewis, and to Sir Charles Russell, who had conducted Parnell's defence throughout the Special Commission. Not only did Manning consult Parnell's legal representatives, but, according to Sir Edward Clarke, he put before them copies of various incriminating letters which O'Shea had given to him in confidence.[11] O'Shea was furious to think that Manning could have acted in such a way. Indeed, his own solicitors Freshfield & Williams suspected that Manning was deliberately 'trying to gain time and screen Parnell'.[12] Such manoeuvres would have been entirely in character for the politicking cardinal, but it is also highly probable that Manning contacted Parnell's solicitor in an attempt to prevent the divorce from taking place and to thwart O'Shea's application for a dispensation from the Catholic Church, which would have been unwelcome in Rome.[13]

O'Shea would later tell Chamberlain that he had finally decided to take proceedings against Katharine after going down to Brighton with Gerard, who was staying with him in London for the Christmas holidays: 'He called unexpectedly at one of his mother's houses there (she has two) and found a lot of Mr Parnell's things, some of which he chucked out of the window. There was a dreadful scene, and on our return to London we went to the lawyers and settled that an action should be immediately instituted.'[14] In the divorce court, O'Shea testified that it was on

20 December that he learned that Parnell and his wife were living at the same Brighton address.

Sir Edward Clarke, O'Shea's counsel, gives a different version of these events, in which O'Shea had proof that Parnell was living at Walsingham Terrace as early as October or November 1889: 'He had gone into a room and had there found Mr Parnell's dressing utensils and some of his clothes. He spoke to a friend about the discovery, and was advised to lay it before Cardinal Manning.'[15] Clarke's recollection is supported by a statement made by W.T. Stead a month after the divorce trial, to the effect that immediately after Gerard's discovery on 20 December, O'Shea had 'called a family conference', at which 'Every one of my wife's family concurred in advising me that nothing could be done but to begin proceedings at once'.[16] Yet, as we know, the Wood family conference took place in early October. A switch of dates would have enabled O'Shea to come up with a desperately needed 'dreadful scene' which would prove that Katharine had gone back on her 1887 promise never to receive Parnell at her house, and upon which he could represent himself to have taken decisive action.[17]

The day after notice of the divorce suit appeared in the *Evening News*, Parnell gave the *Freeman's Journal* his immediate response to the specific charges laid out by O'Shea. He asserted that from late 1880 to 1886 O'Shea had been aware that, in his absence, Parnell had frequently visited his wife at Eltham, and that since 1886 he had known that Parnell 'constantly resided there'.[18] This may have been no more than the truth, but it was an extremely rash statement to have published. O'Shea had formally charged Katharine with adultery dating from April 1886 to December 1889; Parnell now admitted to an affair lasting not a mere three years, but nine. On Monday 30 December, presumably on advice from his solicitor, Parnell issued a completely different statement to the *Freeman's*. Not only did he refute the 'extraordinary' charges made but, with reference to the forged letters, accused O'Shea of bringing on the suit 'entirely in the interest of *The Times*'.[19] Meanwhile, the *Evening News* dismissed Parnell's denial of adultery and his counter-accusation against O'Shea, calling it 'a far-fetched theory, as the relations of Mr Parnell and Mrs O'Shea have been the subject of gossip in Dublin for years past'.[20]

Katharine later told Harrison that she received the initial notice of the divorce proceedings calmly: 'I was sure that I should be able to deal with it. It was only another move in Captain O'Shea's game; necessitated by the changed [financial] situation – I read it so at the time. With all that money coming to me I was certain that, if I was willing to make sacrifices, I could arrange everything.'[21] The sole beneficiary of her aunt's fortune, Katharine could afford to bargain with O'Shea. While her husband had no legal claim to her inheritance because the money lay outside their marriage settlement, Katharine calculated that she could offer him a proportion of it in order to win a divorce on her own terms, and apparently offered O'Shea as much as £20,000.[22] And so, while George Lewis prepared to defend the divorce suit, Katharine went her own way and, largely through her sister Anna, and then, apparently, through Gerard, made repeated attempts to bribe O'Shea into dropping his suit against her: 'for many months there were off and on discussions . . . and there were quarrels and breakings-off and resumptions.'[23] As O'Shea told Chamberlain, 'My solicitors withal are constantly plied with suggestions for compromise, "No difficulty as to terms!"'[24]

Katharine may initially have been calm, but as the case developed her actions became much less controlled and much less predictably to her own advantage. Certainly, once the writs had been served, Katharine did her very best to hold up proceedings. On 19 March, O'Shea reported to Chamberlain the first of her dodges, that she had 'feigned illness for 10 days, so as to evade service of an amended citation'.[25] She then parted with her solicitors. According to O'Shea they 'threw up her case',[26] but O'Shea, too, was twice obliged to change his solicitors and his witnesses were accordingly required to make fresh statements. A vast number of statements were taken down: O'Shea reported in excess of 200 by mid-March, while on Katharine's side Sir Charles Russell claimed to have 900 documents in their possession, with more to come.[27] Aside from dealing with the necessary administrative hitches owing to the changes of legal personnel, O'Shea's lawyers were also called upon to respond to various statements issued by Katharine's counsel.

The chief of these was Katharine's counter-charge that her husband had not only condoned her affair with Parnell but had encouraged her. As evidence of the way in which he had used Katharine throughout their marriage, she submitted confidential letters she had received from O'Shea asking for financial assistance from Mrs Wood over and above the annual provision he had been guaranteed.[28] Months after Katharine and Parnell had both entered a simple denial of the alleged adultery, and having, as O'Shea put it, 'exhausted all the forms of obstruction',[29] Katharine, on 3 June and 25 July, at last submitted details of her defence and counter-charges. These counter-charges involved the admission of adultery:

The respondent alleged that the petitioner had been guilty of connivance in the adultery, of conduct which had been conducive to the adultery; that he had wilfully separated himself from the respondent; that he had himself been guilty of adultery; that he had unreasonably delayed instituting the suit; and that he had been guilty of cruelty towards the respondent.[30]

Up to this point, Katharine had still not submitted her affidavit of documents, and she received a sharp reprimand from Justice Butt on the morning of 9 August: 'He said there had been a most unreasonable delay & that the Respondent did not appear to have a proper idea of her legal obligations to comply with the orders of the Court.'[31] She was issued with a peremptory order requiring her to submit her affidavit within fourteen days. According to O'Shea, his counsel threatened her that if she continued to hold up proceedings they would apply to Justice Butt to have her imprisoned for contempt of court.[32]

Yet such treatment seems only to have caused Katharine to go on the offensive. Less than a fortnight before the start of the trial she made further counter-charges against O'Shea. Going beyond the initial statement made by Parnell in the *Freeman's Journal* of 29 December 1889, Katharine stated specifically that her husband had connived at the alleged adultery 'from the autumn of 1880 to the spring of 1886, by inducing, directing, and requiring the respondent to form the acquaintance of the co-respondent and to see him alone in the interest and for the advantage of the petitioner'.[33] While this made a nonsense of her denial of the affair, which remained on record, in accusing O'Shea of collusion in and connivance at the affair, Katharine was determined that he should not be seen as the innocent victim of a ruthless and systematic deception. Yet there is no doubt that it was an unsound decision with regard to her overall legal objective, which was to win a divorce from her husband on her own terms by pleading his adultery and desertion. If the collusion were proven, O'Shea would have been denied a divorce and Katharine and Parnell would not have been able to legalise their relationship.[34] If O'Shea's divorce suit were to fail, Katharine's adultery with Parnell would have become public knowledge to no end, with Parnell's career and the Nationalist cause badly damaged, and Katharine still tied to her estranged husband who would continue to be the legal guardian of her children, both his own and Parnell's.

Why, then, did she insist obsessively upon the formal accusation of O'Shea's collusion? Because it was the bitter truth: that her husband had for years treated her as his 'milch-cow', as she put it, and had, for his own political advantage, induced his wife 'to invite the co-respondent to her house in the absence of the petitioner'. Those who were privy to the case prior to O'Shea's filing of the petition told him that the evidence pointed to collusion: Cardinal Manning accused him of inexplicable delay, while Chamberlain warned his friend 'that any further hesitation would have given rise to an accusation of complacency under an injury which no honourable man can patiently endure'.[35] According to Katharine's solicitor, even O'Shea's own counsel regarded it as a clear case of collusion on the part of the husband. Katharine's solicitor told Harrison that, 'when instructions were first sent to Counsel on behalf of Captain O'Shea, he returned the papers saying that the facts relied upon as evidence showed knowledge of such long standing that they presented a clear case of condonation by the husband; and accordingly fresh instructions were furnished to him'.[36] This story is confirmed by Sir Edward Clarke, who recalls that on 4 February 1890, his junior counsel Lewis Coward 'came over to my room at the Law Courts to tell me that he had a very important divorce case in hand which gave him much anxiety, and . . . he did not wish to take any further step in it without having a consultation with the leader who would have to conduct it in court'.[37] Clearly Coward was apprehensive that O'Shea's case would fail.

While the charge of collusion was not, ultimately, in Katharine's own best interest, in entering another specific counter-charge she showed herself to be, at least legally, well-informed. On 25 July, her counsel submitted a motion which alleged that Captain O'Shea had committed adultery with Katharine's sister Anna on the night of 13 July 1881 (the night O'Shea stormed out of Wonersh Lodge after finding Parnell's portmanteau there). Why Katharine made this accusation involving her sister caused consternation at the time and has puzzled historians and biographers since.[38] At the close of O'Shea's examination on the first day of the trial he was questioned by Sir Edward Clarke and denied the charge of adultery with Mrs Steele. The suggestion was then made by Anna's solicitor, McCall, that Katharine had named her sister, with whom she had always been on intimate terms, because of ill-feeling over the impending probate suit. In fact the court had to be adjourned early on the Saturday because Anna herself was not in attendance.[39] She was the last witness to be called on Monday 17 November and made a simple denial of adultery 'on or about the 13th or 14th of July, 1881', or 'at any time'.[40]

O'Shea told Chamberlain that when he first heard of the charge he was stunned, since 'during the intervening nine years she has not hinted such a thing either to myself or to any member of her family'.[41] This is not to say that his wife's privately-held suspicions may not have been correct. There was, though, universal condemnation of Katharine's action in the press, *The Times* calling it a 'shocking charge' and finding it lamentable 'that such accusations should be put on record'.[42] Mr Justice Butt told the jury that the fact that the charge had been entered without any supporting evidence was 'simply shocking to my mind': 'You will remember also that she is the woman's own sister.'[43] Sir Edward Clarke later called the charge 'utterly base and wanton', adding, 'Who can have advised this step, or why Mr Parnell permitted it, was and is a mystery.'[44] Only one commentator, it seems, understood that the charge 'was probably connected with Mrs O'Shea's hopes of divorcing O'Shea, against whom she would have had to prove cruelty as well as adultery'.[45] Under the terms of the Matrimonial Causes Act of 1857, a husband could petition for divorce on the grounds of his wife's simple adultery, whereas a wife had to prove adultery together with incest or bigamy, or one of the new 'qualifying aggravations of adultery', which were 'desertion, cruelty, rape, buggery or bestiality'.[46] A husband's adultery with his wife's sister was, in law, 'incestuous adultery'.[47]

The fact that Katharine named her own sister demonstrates how fiercely determined she was to bring charges against O'Shea, although, in his interviews with Katharine a year later, Harrison got little out of her on the subject beyond the intriguing comment (referred to in Chapter 3) that 'Anna and he had constantly been hunting in couples for many years'. While Harrison did not ask her outright for an explanation, he got the impression that 'the accusation itself had been a blunder and that the topic was unwelcome'.[48]

There was, though, reference to her husband's infidelity with countless other women. Katharine gave Henry Harrison the impression that as many as 'seventeen ladies had been in attendance, subpoenaed, expenses paid, and ready to appear in Court'.[49] When Harrison was later given access to the evidence prepared by Katharine's counsel, evidence which of course was never produced in court, he found plenty of material which would have proved that O'Shea was 'not a fit and proper person to have charge of young girls'.[50] Yet, in her book, no doubt to spare Gerard, Katharine denies specific knowledge of her husband's extra-marital affairs. Rather, she states that it was the fact of O'Shea's 'practical desertion' of her that she hoped would result in divorce on her own terms: 'I knew absolutely nothing of his private life, and cared less.'[51] Of course, any such infidelities would have carried little or no weight with the court, unless the evidence was designed to substantiate the claim that she had been wilfully and cruelly deserted. It is clear from her letter to O'Shea of 25 August 1886, referred to earlier (in Chapter 10), that Katharine had knowledge of matrimonial law and knew exactly what her legal position was as a deserted wife.

Yet Katharine's legal acumen has been consistently denied by commentators on the case. The accusation levelled at Katharine is that the legal mess of contradictory pleas and counter-charges was her fault alone. Harrison, for example, concluded that 'during the twelve months prior to the divorce trial, Mrs Parnell's affairs were mis-managed and that she herself was responsible for their mismanagement'.[52] Marlow accepts uncritically O'Shea's complaints made to Chamberlain about his wife's imperious manner, her ignoring court orders and refusing to submit her evidence, while Lyons regrets that 'the headstrong Katharine' would not take the advice of their solicitor, George Lewis, with whom she quarrelled, or Sir Frank Lockwood, whom she dealt with 'in her own amateurish fashion'.[53] It is also T.P. O'Connor's assumption that Katharine was to blame for taking Lewis off the case,[54] yet all the evidence points to Parnell as responsible for dismissing Lewis as his solicitor and refusing to cooperate with Lockwood. Harrison only perpetuated this perception of Katharine as 'a client who was reputed to be *difficile* if not impossible'.[55]

None of these reactions to Katharine's involvement in the divorce proceedings show any understanding of her position as a woman under the law as it currently governed divorce. She wanted a divorce on her own terms, one which took account of O'Shea's failings as a husband and a father and as an adulterer, but this was not possible under the law as it stood, since her own adultery was so evident and, indeed, admitted. We can see in the inconsistencies in her actions the frustration of a woman who wanted to be treated justly by the law.

It is true that from the very first, Katharine did adopt an independent position which brought her into conflict with her legal representatives, aggravating them and giving grounds for Parnell's colleagues to condemn her. It is certainly true that she was of independent character, and had the inherited self-confidence of her class, with the added pluck and determination of the women of her family. She was also prepared to acknowledge publicly her adultery with Parnell, and never, in her interviews with her counsel, or later with young Henry Harrison, was there anything in her of the shame of a fallen woman: Katharine was always 'explicit, frank, and definite',[56] never flinching from Harrison's probing questions.

Katharine herself tells us little of her dealings with Sir George Lewis and Sir Frank Lockwood during the eleven months from the original filing of the petition in December 1889 to the divorce trial of November 1890. She notes only that she and Parnell were served separately with copies of the petition in November, and that Lewis then called on her at Walsingham Terrace to take down her evidence. She also states that Parnell went with her up to London to consult with her own counsel, Lockwood, on several occasions, but that 'Parnell declined to instruct any solicitor from the first to last'. 'What's the use?', he asked her, 'We want the divorce'.[57]

Tim Healy, not by any means a wholly reliable witness when it came to matters regarding Katharine, would later claim that Lockwood told him it was 'the woman's pressure' that made Parnell refuse to attend the hearing and make any defence: 'Mrs O'Shea wished for a divorce to marry her paramour.'[58] Lockwood knew that he could produce overwhelming evidence of O'Shea's collusion in his wife's adultery, which would throw out the case. Of course, as has been noted, such an outcome would do nothing to resolve Katharine's legal position. It was also the case, again according to Lockwood, that 'Parnell felt that the defence of collusion would not have helped with his countrymen'.[59] Understandably, the barrister was exasperated with his clients, and is reported on one occasion to have had a violent altercation with Parnell, whom he threatened to pitch out of the window.[60] Yet there are different versions here, too. Parnell told O'Brien that he and Lockwood had 'almost come to blows' because the latter *refused* to permit Parnell into the witness-box, while Katharine herself admits to a dispute with Lockwood when, on the eve of the trial, Lockwood begged her 'to get Parnell to let him fight it'.[61] She did her best to persuade him, 'but to no purpose'. According to her, it was Parnell who, independently, and in absolute contradiction of her own wishes, determined to let O'Shea have his divorce uncontested: 'Parnell would not fight the case, and I could not fight it without him.'[62]

The perception that Katharine was the main force behind the case is perfectly understandable in view of Parnell's refusal to involve himself in any way. It was Chamberlain who first warned O'Shea that if Katharine and Parnell failed to reach a settlement with him, Parnell might not defend the case.[63] It may be that Parnell looked to the precedent set by Sir Charles Dilke, who was named co-respondent in the Crawfords' divorce case of 1886 (and was also represented by Sir Charles Russell). While Virginia Crawford confessed to the adultery (it was her claim that Dilke seduced her – then a girl of 18 – six weeks after her wedding), no other legal evidence was brought against Dilke, and, since he refused to testify, Mrs Crawford's adultery was proven while his part in her seduction was not. Crawford won his divorce, but was ordered by the judge to pay Dilke's costs. As the *Morning Advertiser* observed, this was a situation 'almost impossible for an ordinary layman to understand', while in the *Pall Mall Gazette*, Stead was indignant that despite his involvement in so prominent a divorce, Dilke was 'welcomed back to public life with favour'.[64]

Parnell's sole intervention in the O'Shea divorce suit was unrelated to his own defence. As soon as the petition was filed he consulted the divorce lawyer Frederick Inderwick for advice about the custody of his two daughters, Clare and Katie. According to what Inderwick told Sir Edward Clarke (whose colleague he would be, oddly enough, in presenting O'Shea's case in the divorce court), Parnell had asked him 'whether there was any European country in which Mrs O'Shea, in spite of the orders of an English court of law, would be able to retain the custody of these children'.[65]

The law governing custody had been reformed, but remained problematic. Until 1872, a wife who had been declared guilty of adultery in a court of law forfeited all rights of custody and even access to her children, and while the New Infant Custody Act of that year did for the first time recognise the custody rights of such women, these were very limited: the law held that a wife, that is *any* wife, was allowed to petition the court for custody only under exceptional circumstances, and the court had full discretionary powers to decide each individual case.[66] Of course, if it could have been established that Katharine's two daughters by Parnell were illegitimate, full responsibility for their maintenance would have been handed over to their mother. However, since the suit was not contested, O'Shea was able to maintain that Clare and Katie were his own children. Clarke, after what Inderwick had told him, had no doubt about their paternity,[67] but if he had been forced in court to admit as much, O'Shea's case that he had been cruelly deceived for nine years would have been destroyed.

It is also unthinkable that Katharine would have considered for one moment making a public admission of her two youngest daughters' illegitimacy. In her book, published in 1914 (when her daughter Katie and grandson Assheton were still alive), she discreetly avoided all reference to them, relating only the brief life of their first child, Claude Sophie. It was a sensitive issue, and remained so. St John Ervine, who received evidence of Clare's paternity from her widower, Dr Bertram Maunsell, in 1937, assured him that if his 1925 biography of Parnell were ever reprinted, he could 'rely on my discretion'.[68] Henry Harrison was so careful of the girls' reputation that he delayed publication of his book until, as he thought, both Clare and Katie were no longer living. To do otherwise would be 'acutely embarrassing': 'In short, while Mrs Parnell and certain of her children were alive there was, as it seemed to me, an obvious propriety in leaving with them the responsibility for maintaining silence or for revealing the truth.'[69]

Harrison makes a virtue of Parnell's non-involvement in the sordid haggling that went on between Katharine and her husband for many months before the trial, and of his refusal to 'infringe' Katharine's independence. As he saw it, Parnell 'would not intermix himself with any bargain or negotiation with Captain O'Shea', and 'endured in disdainful silence' the 'hell-broth of the Divorce Court'. Harrison recalls Katharine as saying, 'He would do nothing – assist in nothing – consent to nothing – that would prevent the divorce taking place.'[70]

Yet, it is possible to interpret otherwise behaviour which Harrison perceives as Parnell's manly forbearance. It would perhaps be nearer the truth to say that Parnell was prostrated by the announcement of O'Shea's petition for divorce, in both his political and his private life, and felt powerless to act. While he dreamed of such unrealities as absconding to a European hideaway with Katharine and his little girls, she faced facts and, through her lawyers, issued statement after statement designed to pressure O'Shea into allowing her to divorce him, at any price he named, and to threaten him with the failure of the suit if he did not cooperate. If the case was thrown out because of O'Shea's proven connivance and collusion, he would endure public humiliation and would gain nothing at all from

Katharine's inheritance, which, as previously noted, lay outside her marriage settlement. As it turned out, O'Shea had other wholly unprincipled ways to get hold of a share of the money, but for the present, as Katharine made plain to Harrison, 'there had to be a divorce': 'Parnell insisted that there must be a divorce so that he could marry me.'[71]

To his party Parnell revealed nothing of these developments, and his silence led Justin McCarthy to observe that, 'It is beginning to be believed I don't know how or why that [Parnell] will be able to come out of the whole affair triumphantly.'[72] Throughout January he saw nothing of Parnell, who made his first appearance at the Commons in February, and, according to Morley, 'betrayed no trace in his demeanour . . . of embarrassment'.[73] That same month he failed to appear at Biggar's funeral or requiem service, and when Parnell finally made contact with McCarthy over Easter, his letter was restricted to the party's finances. McCarthy remained in doubt about whether the case would ever come on. People were beginning to say 'that O'Shea has thought better of it',[74] and McCarthy, who had once been perhaps the closest to Parnell of all the inner circle, was actually prepared to believe that his leader's long relationship with Mrs O'Shea had never gone beyond the bounds of propriety: 'he is a strange man quite capable of imposing on himself a powerful restraining law and not allowing a temptation to draw him too far.'[75] He was not alone in this view. The social reformer Josephine Butler, a committed Home Ruler, claimed that she had 'guessed a good while ago that [Parnell] had some unhappy attachment, some skeleton in the cupboard, but I fancied he had firmness enough to have kept on the side of right in *action*'.[76] Even Frank Hugh O'Donnell believed the relationship to have been 'absolutely correct', a mere 'brother-and-sister intimacy'.[77]

William O'Brien and Michael Davitt were the only members of the party to confront Parnell about the case. O'Brien's kindly phrased enquiry won him the following statement from Parnell, sent on Tuesday 14 January 1890, the day after the initial hearing at the Royal Courts of Justice (he would have replied sooner, he said, but that he was 'overwhelmed with law & other business'). 'If this case is ever fully gone into,' Parnell wrote to O'Brien, 'a matter which is exceedingly doubtful, you may rest assured that it will be shown that the dishonour & the discredit has not been upon my side.'[78] This was hardly an explanation of how matters stood, and yet his brief letter, if not going so far as to admit adultery, does imply, at least, a confidence that the allegations he had made in the *Freeman's Journal* about O'Shea's connivance and collusion would result in a swift divorce on his own terms. Davitt interpreted Parnell's assurances very differently. He had a long conversation with Parnell shortly after the divorce was filed: 'he said to me that there was no truth in it. He was most emphatic, *most* emphatic.

I never saw him in better spirits.' Parnell claimed to have evidence in support of his allegation that O'Shea was in league with *The Times*, and declared that he would come out of it 'without a stain on my name and reputation'. When Stead saw him shortly after, Davitt beamed, 'Charlie is all right'. Stead asked him whether he was quite sure that he had understood Parnell correctly, but Davitt was adamant that he had denied the act of adultery.[79]

The leaders of the Liberal Party were in no doubt as to Parnell's adultery. As Sir Edward Clarke has observed, 'That the result of the trial should come as a complete surprise' to them 'is difficult to explain. Mr John Morley had been for years the friend and adviser of the Irish leader.'[80] According to his private secretary, Gladstone did become apprehensive at Parnell's 'not having asserted himself much lately', which might mean that the Irish leader expected matters to go 'so disagreeably for him in the impending divorce case that he may have to withdraw from public life and that he had better commence to prepare for this'.[81] Yet as late as August 1890, Lord Rosebery intended to include Parnell in his planned informal 'Round Table' conference in Gladstone's constituency of Midlothian, where the leaders of the Liberal party would have an opportunity to meet with Gladstone. Rosebery only dropped the idea of asking Parnell when it became likely that the divorce case would be heard that autumn.[82]

The failure of both Parnell and the Liberals to anticipate the shocking revelations of the divorce case is illustrated in Parnell's conversation with John Morley on Monday 10 November, and Morley's reaction. They had a great deal of political business to get through, but Morley had gently hinted to Gladstone a week before the appointment, 'Is there anything else on which you wish me to speak to him?' Morley added that he had got private word 'that O'Shea was formally asked recently whether, if no defence was made, he would still insist on casting mud at Parnell. He replied, No, but he must be guided by his counsel. His counsel is Clarke, and I fear Clarke will be likely to do his best to get as many nasty things out as possible. I fear there are plenty of them.'[83]

A day later, Gladstone confided in the new Chief Whip Arnold Morley, 'I fear a thundercloud is about to burst over Parnell's head'.[84] Yet when Parnell kept the appointment with him at the Hotel Metropole, Brighton, John Morley found the Irish leader 'more than usually cordial and gracious'. Parnell's only sign of nervousness was his habit of averting his face whenever the waiter approached their table. Otherwise, Morley felt that he had never looked better: 'there was so much more ease between us, and I have never known him so really genial.'[85] This geniality persisted even when Morley approached the question of whether the findings of the divorce court would necessitate Parnell's disappearance from the House or at least his temporary retirement from the leadership of the party: 'He smiled all over his face, playing with his fork. "My disappearance! Oh no. No chance of it . . . The other side don't know what a broken-kneed horse they are riding".'[86] That was about as far as Morley felt he could go into the question, and he reported back to Gladstone that he had advised Parnell that if this was the case, he should return to his work in the Commons immediately. 'That', Parnell replied, 'is just what you may depend upon my doing. I assure you there will be nothing to prevent it.'[87]

Parnell's behaviour throughout this period is difficult to fathom – his apparent refusal to become involved in the legal proceedings, his choosing not to confide in anyone in his party, his unembarrassed demeanour when he did attend Parliament, his untroubled assurances to O'Brien and Davitt on the one hand and Morley on the other. As Gladstone exclaimed to Morley after reading the report of the first day's proceedings in Saturday's *Evening News*, 'What could he mean by his language to you?'[88] Parnell's position seems to have been that his private life was of no concern to anyone but himself, yet in this he was being naïve. His strange detachment from the proceedings of the case continued to the last, according to Katharine's detailed account.

On Thursday 14 November, Lockwood made one final attempt to delay the divorce hearing. A week earlier, Katharine's sister Anna had formally applied to the court to intervene in the case in order to publicly defend herself against the charge of adultery. According to what O'Shea was told, Anna was persuaded to do so by her brothers, presumably in order to strengthen the family's case against Katharine in their forthcoming probate suit.[89] Lockwood now argued that extra time was needed for his client to prepare an appeal against the intervener, but, as Sir Edward Clarke pointed out, 'The suit was ready for trial so long ago as the 12th of May last', and since then they had been subjected to all kinds of obstruction and delay on Katharine's part.[90] Justice Butt was in agreement, and the trial was set for the morning of Saturday 15 November.

Lockwood must also have wished for further time to persuade Parnell to testify. On the eve of the trial, Friday 14 November, Katharine and Parnell had their final consultation at Lockwood's chambers, Parnell refusing for the last time to be represented at the hearing. He would not even confirm whether he intended to accompany Katharine to the court, for *she* was determined to attend. Lockwood was told to expect a telegram by eight o'clock the next morning, saying whether or not they would attend. The London to Brighton train was packed and they could only find seats in a saloon carriage. Katharine was overcome by the strain of the last few weeks, culminating in her failure to get hold of £20,000 with which to buy off O'Shea, and in the knowledge that her own children had been subpoenaed to testify against her. She was suffering from an attack of neuralgia and had a splitting headache, and the journey home in such circumstances was a misery to her, but Parnell reassured her with 'a cheerful little smile now and then, and directly we got home he insisted upon my going to bed'.[91] 'Always the most gentle and tender of nurses,' he made her sip some wine and eat a little. Once he had had his own dinner he came and sat by her bed and smoked a cigar. She made one last attempt to get Parnell to agree to go with her to the court 'and make some fight in the case', but he was unshakeable. Later, she woke in the night and rehearsed what they were going to tell Lockwood in the morning, 'going over the pros and cons till my brain felt on fire', only to be told by her lover that he had written the telegram while she slept. Katharine now broke down and wept, 'for him and for his work'. Years later she could still recall what Parnell said to her. Calmly and gently, he told her to

> put away all fear and regret for my public life. I have given, and will give, Ireland what it is in me to give. That I have vowed to her, but my private life shall never belong to any country, but to one woman . . . you have stood to me for comfort and strength and my very life. I have never been able to feel in the least sorry for having come into your life. It had to be.[92]

Katharine awoke late on the morning of Saturday 15 November to find Parnell sitting by the bed with a tray of tea and toast. 'I've done you this time,' he told her with a smile, 'I sent the telegram long ago, and they must be enjoying themselves in Court by now!'[93]

# CHAPTER 12

## *Katharine Parnell*

The divorce trial was reported widely. Its evidence was sensational, and quickly led to newspaper cartoons and even to the sale of toy figures of Parnell slipping down the fire-escape and titillating music-hall humour.[1] Within a fortnight, a number called 'The Fire-Escape' was being performed at the London Pavilion:

> A sudden knock! – a thrill of fear –
> Here comes my husband, Charlie dear!
>
> .    .    .    .    .
>
> The fire-escape, the fire-escape,
> It was indeed a merry jape,
> When Charlie Parnell's naughty shape
> Went scooting down the fire-escape![2]

A matter of days after the divorce trial, W.T. Stead issued a penny pamphlet, 'The Discrowned King of Ireland', in which he painted a vivid picture of Ireland, on the verge of Home Rule, 'thrust back into the outer darkness by the sinister figure of Mrs O'Shea', while their leader 'dallied in the lap of Delilah'.[3] He was not finished with Katharine. In the December edition of the *Review of Reviews*, he likened her to a female werewolf who, having seduced her victim, left him to a fate worse than death, 'in the living grave of universal contempt'. She was condemned first as 'a woman of great ambition' who 'aspired to play a considerable part – first in English and then in Irish politics', and secondly as a woman sufficiently well known, apparently, for her 'certain freedom of manner'.[4] The Unionist *Vanity Fair* gave Katharine the title 'O'Shea who must be obeyed', after the heroine of Rider Haggard's 1887 popular novel, *She*.[5] Condemnation of Parnell's mistress was not universal. Ironically, it was the Tory *St Stephen's Review* which expressed the 'regret that a woman so attractive and popular as was Mrs O'Shea should have fallen a victim' to a cad like Parnell: 'a man of that calibre', so the paper argued, 'can do pretty nearly what he likes with a woman'.[6]

O'Shea also received his share of press attention. Many journalists came close to the libellous in their articles.[7] While *Truth* was forced to accept the jury's decision to acquit the cuckolded husband of the charge of connivance, its editor, Henry Labouchère, asked how it was that O'Shea never went down to Eltham to discover the truth for himself: 'He was perpetually writing to his wife, protesting against her allowing Mr Parnell to visit her,' yet all the while 'Mr Parnell was habitually residing in the house in which she and her children were living, and his stud of horses was being kept in her stables'.[8] A similar point was made by the satirical paper, the *Porcupine*, which noted that while Parnell was fighting to help O'Shea to a seat in Parliament, his horses were 'munching their corn in the stalls at Mrs O'Shea's residence'.[9] Captain O'Shea, said Labouchère, should have 'looked more carefully after his family, and less carefully after his political advancement'.[10]

Hardest of all on O'Shea was Stead. In his pamphlet he observed that if 'O'Shea, notwithstanding the finding of the court . . . was in reality a willing and complacent party to the dishonour of his wife . . . the weightiest part of the accusation against Mr Parnell would fall to the ground'.[11] Then in his December editorial he published a detailed account of his December 1886 interview with O'Shea, during which he had firmly denied any impropriety between his wife and Parnell. When O'Shea had called on him again after the divorce trial, 'I at once told him that he had deceived me'.[12]

The important question was: how would the political world respond to Parnell's proven adultery? Support seemed solid. It was John Morley's belief that 'the Irish will stomach it',[13] and this, initially at least, seemed to be the case. At a meeting of the Irish National League on Tuesday 18 November a pledge of loyalty to Parnell was carried, and on the Thursday a meeting in Dublin's Leinster Hall passed a resolution proposed by Justin McCarthy that 'no side issue shall be permitted to obstruct the progress of the great cause of Home Rule for Ireland'.[14] The following week, Parnell was re-elected party chairman for the forthcoming parliamentary session.

In England, the Liberal press was unanimous in its advice to the public that Parnell's private life was his own concern: it was, said one paper, 'arrant hypocrisy for London society to pretend to be scandalised at Mr Parnell's offence'.[15] Yet the question of what should be the official Liberal line proved so sensitive an issue that Gladstone was reluctant to express his opinion, even in private. The closest he came to doing so was to suggest his approval of an article in the *Daily Telegraph*, which, while advising Parnell to retire temporarily from public life, regarded the revelations of the divorce court as an 'irrelevant accident, wholly unconnected with the struggle in which we are engaged'.[16] Evidence of Gladstone's difficulty is to be found in the draft notes he prepared for John Morley's use at the annual

Liberal Federation meeting in Sheffield, due to start on Thursday 20 November. Three times, Gladstone urges his party to keep their great political cause 'clear from all entanglement with public questions which are secondary, or . . . irrelevant'; three times these statements are deleted. The final speech is little more than a brief rallying cry to Liberals not to 'slacken for a moment [their] devotion' to the 'sacredness of our great cause'.[17] This was not what his party wanted to hear.

Back in London after the conference, Sir William Harcourt told Gladstone's private secretary that his audience had been 'dying to hear some announcement from him . . . which would accord with their outraged feelings'.[18] In particular, Gladstone's refusal to appear to be speaking as Parnell's moral judge served only to exacerbate the strength of feeling among Nonconformists. Church leaders, such as the Baptist minister Dr Clifford and the Wesleyan Revd Hugh Price Hughes, were uncompromising in their condemnation of Parnell: 'What is morally wrong can never be politically right.'[19] Hughes was well known to be an extremist on matters of sexual morality, but such views demanded to be considered. As Stead wrote to Gladstone on Thursday 20 November, 'I know my Nonconformists well, and no power on earth will induce them to follow that man to the poll, or you either,' if the Liberal leader were to remain 'arm in arm' with Parnell.[20]

Faced with the reluctance of both the Irish party and the Liberals to condemn Parnell and demand his resignation, 'the moral indignation of the British public exploded'.[21] Throughout the week immediately after the divorce hearing, Gladstone was bombarded with letters from the public.[22] 'I'm sick of Parnell & the sympathetic cant of his Irish colleagues,' wrote a Methodist solicitor from Bradford: 'A set of traitors to our home life & murderers of the sanctity of marriage are not the most desirable men to govern a nation.'[23] 'Whose homes wd be safe if we condone such wretched conduct?', asked another.[24] It was precisely the very ordinariness and distinctly middle-class setting of the affair between Katharine and Parnell, the suburban villa and the houses rented at seaside resorts, which 'outrag[ed] the moral instincts of the great mass of people'.[25] The middle class and the newly enfranchised working class were prompted by the case to examine their own moral standards and to speak their minds in the letters pages of the newspapers. The *Star*, in particular, gave up columns every day to this spontaneous public debate.

Gladstone decided that he had to act. He called a conference of his inner circle on Monday 24 November, at which he responded angrily to Sir William Harcourt's uncompromising moral position: '"What," he cried, "because a man is what is called a leader of a party, does that constitute him a judge and accuser of faith and morals? I will not accept it."'[26]

Nevertheless, it was agreed that he would write to Parnell to make it clear that if he did not resign it would serve to keep the Liberals out of power and make Gladstone's leadership of his own party untenable.

In later years, Katharine recalled her bitterness at what she felt to be Gladstone's hypocritical response to the divorce. 'Why does it matter more now . . .?', she asked Parnell in 1890, 'they have all known for years'.[27] As she put it, disdainfully, Gladstone 'had taken full advantage of the facility this intimacy afforded him in keeping in touch with the Irish leader . . . But that was a private knowledge. Now it was a public knowledge, and an English statesman must always appear on the side of the angels.'[28] She had a right to be scornful. Stead, at least, had acknowledged that this middle-aged love affair was 'a very venial offence compared with the unspeakable moral turpitude of Sir Charles Dilke'.[29] But the Liberals had a number of adulterers among them, besides Dilke. As one clergyman pointed out to Gladstone, it would be unfortunate if the Irish were to 'retort with the case of Lord Hartington' (who, like Morley, was widely known to live with his mistress).[30] Parnell had a politician's resignation about this kind of hypocrisy, but also shared with Katharine 'a contempt unspeakable' for the shifts they were put to.[31]

John Morley passed on Gladstone's letter to Justin McCarthy, but neither he nor Parnell informed the party of its contents, and the re-election of Parnell as party chairman was passed as a formality. When Gladstone learned that his letter had not been acted upon, he ordered its immediate publication. The Irish, now feeling that they had been misled by Parnell, re-convened and re-opened the question of the leadership. When he returned home to Katharine, he took her in his arms and said to her, 'I think we shall have to fight, Queenie. Can you bear it? I'm afraid it is going to be tough work.'[32] Parnell's response was to compose a lengthy manifesto, 'To the People of Ireland', in which he revealed the nature of his confidential discussions with Gladstone about a second Home Rule bill at Hawarden Castle in December 1889. After disparaging the terms offered (quite inaccurately and unfairly, according to Gladstone), he then renounced the Liberal alliance which, he claimed, had 'sapped and destroyed' the integrity and independence of the Irish party.[33] Katharine watched him as he sat at his desk, 'absolutely absorbed in what he was writing':

I loved him so much, and I did so long to take him away from all the ingratitude and trouble – to some sunny land where we could forget the world and be forgotten. But I knew that he would not forget; that he would come at my bidding, but that his desertion of Ireland would lie at his heart . . . I knew him too well to dare to take him away from the cause he had made his life-work; that even if it killed him I must let him fight – fight to the end.[34]

Parnell seems to have understood what she was thinking, and putting his hand on hers, told her gently that it was for her to say whether he should give in, but, he added, 'I want you to promise me that you will never make me less than the man you have known.'[35] She promised. It was to mean that they spent much of their life apart in the short time left to them after the divorce.

On the morning of Saturday 29 November, Parnell's manifesto appeared in the press. Its effect was to split the party along two lines: Parnellites, urging unity and independence from the Liberals, and the anti-Parnellites, who were prepared to put the cause of Home Rule (whose only realistic chance was through an alliance with the Liberals) before loyalty to their leader. As Katharine puts it, 'War was now declared.'[36] After a prolonged and acrimonious debate in Committee Room 15 at the House of Commons, forty-five MPs seceded, and on Saturday 6 December elected Justin McCarthy as their leader. These included Dillon, Healy, O'Connor and William O'Brien. Parnell was left with just twenty-seven followers.

The first battleground was Kilkenny in the south of Ireland, where the parliamentary seat was vacant. Parnell's decision to fight on meant contesting with men who had been his closest allies and supporters, now 'anti-Parnellites', three successive by-elections at Kilkenny, North Sligo and Carlow. Because he insisted on returning to Katharine each weekend,[37] this involved a series of journeys back and forth across the Irish Sea, particularly exhausting for a man of failing health. On 9 December he left for Dublin where he addressed a vast public meeting at the Rotunda. 'The house rose at him,' said one eye-witness, 'everywhere around there was a sea of passionate faces, loving, admiring, almost worshipping that silent, pale man. The cheering broke out again and again; there was no quelling it . . .The people were fairly mad with excitement. I don't think anyone outside Ireland can understand what a charm Mr Parnell has for the Irish heart.'[38] When he had finished his speech Parnell was told that a group of anti-Parnellites had seized the offices of his newspaper, *United Ireland*. Early the next morning he arrived at the offices with Dr Kenny and apparently attacked the door himself with a crowbar. An almighty struggle took place, at the end of which a hatless Parnell ('his hair was tumbled, his face . . . and clothes were powdered with dust and plaster') leant out of an upstairs window to announce victory to the crowd below, who 'burst into a roar'.[39]

While Dublin was true to Parnell, Kilkenny was a humiliation. From the start of the campaign he was clearly unwell. To R. Barry O'Brien 'he looked like a dying man', but he showed 'wonderful vigour for a man in failing health' in what became a rough campaign.[40] At Castlecomer, lime was thrown at his face. Parnell was unhurt – he had kept his eyes closed – but he was unable to get a telegram to Katharine to reassure her. By the time his message arrived, 'I was nearly out of my mind. The newspapers had made the very most of the affair, and I thought my husband was blinded.'[41] It was at Kilkenny that Healy's virulent attacks on Katharine were first launched: she was accused of being 'a bad woman who hates Ireland, who cares nothing for Ireland, who has been spending the money of the Irish people and ruined Parnell', while, conversely, it was alleged that her only attraction for Parnell was her 'two hundred thousand pounds'.[42] The Kilkenny campaign also saw the marshalling of the priesthood against Parnell. The local Bishop of Ossory registered his approval that the priests were 'off canvassing in all directions' and would march their men to the polling place.[43] It was R. Barry O'Brien's view that it was 'the priests alone' who dominated the election at Kilkenny.[44] The electoral defeat on 22 December, by 2,527 votes to 1,326, was crushing.

In the New Year attempts were made to arrive at a compromise whereby Parnell could remain as President and joint Treasurer of the party so long as he agreed to retire temporarily, although he was of course to be involved in any Home Rule talks when they began. At a series of meetings in France, known as the Boulogne negotiations, Parnell made clear his determination to see William O'Brien succeed him rather than McCarthy, and promised to retire at once if Gladstone could be brought to commit to paper his intentions for Home Rule. Neither point could be agreed. When the Liberals did produce a memorandum on Home Rule, Parnell was dissatisfied with its terms. Throughout the negotiations he was at his most intractable. On 11 February Parnell finally made a public announcement that the negotiations had ended in failure, putting the blame firmly on the Liberal Party. It was now that the myth of Katharine's hardening influence upon Parnell came into being. According to Dillon, 'Hers was a disastrous influence . . . it was she who prevented him from accepting any compromise about the Chairmanship of the party.' He was also said to have made the spurious claim that 'every evening Parnell crossed the Channel back to spend the night at Eltham and return in the morning more obstinate than ever'.[45]

The decree absolute came through on 26 May. From then on, according to one local paper, 'the names of Mr Parnell and Mrs O'Shea have never been absent from the minds of managers of Press agencies, newspaper Editors, and politicians'.[46] They had intended to be married in their parish church, but after making enquiries of his bishop the local vicar was warned against conducting the marriage of a divorcée. They decided to marry in a registry office and to solemnise their marriage in London at a future date. On 23 June, a local reporter trailed Parnell to Steyning, where he went to get a special licence which allowed for a marriage to take place within three months, but the following day Katharine was observed to drive into

Brighton, where she called at a florist, 'and returned laden with choice flowers'. The *Sussex Daily News* readied itself for 'the anticipated sequel to the momentous divorce case of recent years'.[47]

Katharine and Parnell left home in the phaeton at 6.30 a.m. on Thursday 25 June. Their intention was to avoid newspaper men, but one local reporter had stationed himself at the end of Walsingham Terrace in time to see them leave, Parnell in a morning suit and overcoat, and Katharine wearing 'a dress of black silk brocade and a lace mantle', with pink roses trimming her black hat.[48] According to Katharine, Parnell arranged the whole thing: she was woken at dawn, 'Get up, get up, it is time to be married!', and then there began 'a humming and excitement . . . through the house as the maids flew about to get us and breakfast ready'. Phyllis Bryceson, Katharine's maid, who was to be one of the witnesses, was 'hustled off' by Parnell, who replaced the maid's posy at Katharine's breast with his own, made of white roses to match his own buttonhole. Katharine took the reins and drove into Steyning just before Phyllis and Elizabeth Leggett, the children's nurse, arrived on the 8.47 train. They were shown in to a front room on the ground floor, prettily decked out by the registrar's wife, and while they awaited the arrival of their witnesses, Parnell adjusted his buttonhole in the mirror and blew a kiss to Katharine, remarking, 'It isn't every woman who makes so good a marriage as you are making, Queenie, is it? And to such a handsome fellow, too!'[49]

Although they had lived together in Brighton as man and wife for the past two years, only Katharine gave her address as 9 Walsingham Terrace. For the sake of propriety Parnell gave his as the Euston Hotel, London. He was described as a bachelor, while Katharine's condition was formally registered as 'The divorced wife of William Henry O'Shea'. Besides their discretion in listing separate addresses, there is one further point of interest concerning their marriage certificate: Katharine took six years off her age. On the date they married, Parnell was two days short of his forty-fifth birthday, yet Katharine, a year and a half older, had been 46 in January. She can hardly have pretended to Parnell that she was six years younger than himself. It would have meant that she was only 16 when she married O'Shea. It may be that she did not want the press to know her age. By law, the certificate of marriage had to be made available to anyone who requested to see it, and in fact full details of the certificate were published in Saturday's *Sussex Daily News*. According to the paper's poetically minded reporter, who returned to the house that evening, there were 'sounds of festivity' coming from 9 Walsingham Terrace, 'and the rays from the highly-lit rooms on all floors made holes in the fog'.[50]

The following day, Parnell unexpectedly admitted a reporter from the Central News Association, to whom he spoke of the forthcoming Carlow by-election, for which he was about to depart for Ireland: 'He had not the slightest doubt of victory.' He would have liked to take his wife with him, but Katharine was, he said, 'a bad sailor'. They hoped to solemnise their marriage on his return from Ireland, Parnell adding wryly that 'he would endeavour to let no one know exactly when and where it would take place'. Of the effect his marriage might have on the political situation in Ireland he could say nothing. 'I and my wife', he said, 'are perfectly happy. As for myself, I can truly say that I am now enjoying greater happiness than I have ever experienced in the whole of my previous life.'[51] Indeed, what is remarkable about the whole episode is Parnell's capacity to abstract himself from all his political and other difficulties and, clearly, *be* so happy.

The marriage was greeted with favourable comment from a number of English papers. The *Daily Chronicle* expressed sympathy and admiration for Katharine for having 'borne with heroic self-restraint the punishment of brutal obloquy and cruel abuse which the leaders of the new Irish Party have for the last year heaped upon her', and the *Manchester Examiner* noted, 'There is no longer a "Kitty O'Shea" for Secessionist whitlings to sneer at and taunt.' For the majority of the British press the marriage had gone far to atone for Parnell's 'regrettable offences against the marriage law', and, in legalising his relationship with Katharine, he had 'done much to reinstate himself as a leader in Parliament'.[52]

In Ireland, the reverse was true: 'Parnell's marriage served only to aggravate his moral offence.'[53] Indeed, the moral reaction of the Irish to Parnell's marriage to Katharine was far greater than the relatively muted response to the revelations of the divorce court, which at the time were believed to stem from a malicious campaign on behalf of *The Times* to defame Parnell in revenge for his triumph at the Special Commission. Justin McCarthy was not alone in hoping that the divorce court revelations 'might be found to have been deceptive'.[54] But the marriage now proved that the sordid story was true. On the day they married, the Irish Catholic bishops declared to the Irish people, that 'Mr Parnell by his public misconduct, has utterly disqualified himself to be their leader'.[55] Katharine was described as the 'degraded partner of [Parnell's] guilty pleasure' in one paper and as the 'registered lady of Steyning' in another.[56] Taking its cue from the pronouncement of the Irish bishops, the *Freeman's Journal* declared that 'The marriage is no marriage according to the teaching of the Catholic Church.'[57]

There had already been a violent contest in April over the vacant seat of North Sligo, although the margin of defeat had been much less than at Kilkenny. The Carlow election of July 1891 would be the most vicious yet in terms of its expression of anti-Parnellite venom towards Katharine, and its result would be the worst of Parnell's three post-divorce election defeats.

At Carlow, Healy would be Parnell's undoing. Personal attacks on 'Kitty' or 'Mrs O'Shea' (as he still insisted upon calling her) had begun at Kilkenny, but now they formed the staple of Healy's speeches. When, at one public meeting, he was asked, finally, 'Why can't you leave her alone?', he retorted, 'Why could not Mr Parnell let her alone (*cheers and laughter*)'.[58] Accompanying such speeches was a constant barrage of noise kept up by the banging of kettles (the Parnellite candidate was the unfortunately named Andrew Kettle), and the hallooing of hunting-horns (in allusion to one of Parnell's more notorious pseudonyms, 'Mr Fox'). Effigies were seen, one of 'Kitty O'Shea' hung from a tree with a kettle in her hand, while in another town a banner showed Katharine and the kettle, with the inscription, 'Kitty I'm scalded'.[59] For Katharine, aware that 'Kitty O'Shea' was 'sung and screamed' throughout Ireland 'with all the filth that foul minds' could devise, 'it was a little thing to bear for the man who loved me as never woman has been loved before'.[60]

At home the situation was no less stressful. Both Katharine and O'Shea were in very serious financial difficulties. Not only were both waiting for the probate suit to be heard and Mrs Wood's fortune to be released, but both parties had two sets of lawyers' fees to settle. O'Shea now found himself 'in a corner, and a nasty one, for the moment', and was driven to asking Chamberlain for a loan.[61] His solicitors eventually served Parnell with a judge's order to pay O'Shea's costs. This happened on the evening of 22 April, just as he was about to board the Brighton train at Victoria Station: 'It had all been done very quietly,' said Katharine. 'No one saw what was done.'[62] The order amounted only to £778 ('insufficient to cover Counsels' fees!', O'Shea exclaimed to Chamberlain[63]), but Katharine and Parnell were in no position to pay it. In August it was still unpaid, and from Avondale, Parnell wrote to Katharine to instruct Pym to negotiate terms with O'Shea's solicitors: 'I think you might fix the end of the year as the time you and I would guarantee the payment of the costs.'[64]

Parnell was put to further rather desperate measures to meet their legal costs. While in Ireland, he was trying to set up a new newspaper, the *Irish Daily Independent*, for which he had negotiated a loan of £1,000 from the Hibernian Bank, and, judging by the bulletins he sent Katharine, it looks as though he intended to divert some of this money to Brighton. He was also in the process of raising a mortgage on Avondale, but more immediately he set aside £1,000 to send to Katharine from a separate bank loan secured by his land agent, William Kerr, for a business venture of theirs.[65] The strain of such makeshift and imprudent solutions to their problems must have been considerable.

On his return from Dublin, Katharine tried to make Parnell rest on a sofa by day. 'Tired, grey shadows were growing deeper upon his beautiful face,' but he wouldn't hear of calling on Sir Henry Thompson in London, 'saying that he could not waste a moment of his little time at home'. It was indeed a little time that Parnell had spent with Katharine since their marriage, and little enough since the divorce, yet he made it very clear to her that his political work must take precedence. 'I am in your hands', he had told her, 'and you shall do with me what you will, but . . . I would rather die than give in now'. As she 'gazed down into the deep, smouldering eyes, where the little flames always leapt out to mine', she knew that she could not ask this of him.[66]

Before the end of the month, against the advice of Dr Kenny, he was in Ireland again, this time to address an open air meeting at Creggs, a village on the border of Galway and Roscommon, where his hosts were the MP Pierce Mahony and his wife. Parnell's frequent telegrams to Katharine referred again and again to the constant rheumatic pain he was suffering from: he had to keep his arm in a sling the whole time he was in Ireland. On the way to Creggs, he also spoke at Broadstone and Athlone. Those who saw him were shocked at his appearance, his face 'livid and haggard'.[67] At Creggs, it was raining as he made his speech, but he refused an umbrella, and returning to Dublin, 'He was very ill and suffered much pain.'[68] After a short time in Dublin he made the crossing back to England, once more rejecting Dr Kenny's advice, to which he replied, 'No, I want to get home; I must go home!'[69]

He arrived back in Brighton on Friday 2 October in a weakened state. After dinner he dozed with the dogs at his feet and Katharine sitting with her head resting against his knees. 'This is really a beautiful rest,' he murmured, but he needed a walking-stick and Katharine's assistance to get up the stairs that night. His sleep was troubled over the weekend, and on the Monday he was much worse. He wanted to get out of bed but did not even have the strength to stand up. Yet he would not hear of calling out Sir Henry Thompson, chiefly because of the expense. Katharine put him back to bed, and it comforted him to have her lie on the bed next to him and hold his hand. In this fashion he was able to drift off to sleep now and then, but he spent yet another sleepless night and woke on Tuesday with a horribly flushed face. Dr Jowers, a local doctor whom Katharine insisted upon consulting, made his afternoon visit and advised sedatives, but Parnell refused them.

Late that evening Jowers got a sudden call to come out again. Parnell was unconscious. Katharine had lain down with him as he liked her to, and he asked, 'Kiss me, sweet Wifie, and I will try to sleep a little', but the lips that touched hers were burning. Katharine recalls raising herself up to look at him, 'and as I slipped my hand from under his head he gave a little sigh and became unconscious . . . my husband died without regaining consciousness, before his last kiss was cold on my lips'. She sat with the body all night long, 'watching and waiting for the look and the word he would never give me again. All that night I whispered to him to speak to me.'[70] A local reporter noted: 'It was a wild night; the wind howled round the great house, and gusts of rain beat on the windows of the sickroom,' and went on to add: 'There was a certain fittingness that the cause of so much turbulence, the hero of so many fierce battles, should take his farewell of earth while the elements were at their noisiest.'[71] Katharine herself wrote that 'the rain and the wind swept about the house as though the whole world shared my desolation'.[72] These were to be the last few hours she would have alone with the remains of her husband.

Because of the suddenness of Parnell's collapse, Dr Jowers conducted a post-mortem at noon the next day. The cause of death was given as rheumatic fever, hyperpyrexia (that is, an excessive temperature) and heart failure. Katharine insisted upon going in person to register the death, on Friday 9 October. She also issued a statement that her husband had died from natural causes, and had not committed suicide, as some papers had speculated.

Now, according to the local paper, Katharine 'completely broke down',[73] while the private house that she had shared with Parnell and their daughters for so short a time was given up to the receiving of visitors, Parnell's supporters, and reporters. James O'Kelly was the first to arrive at Brighton late on Wednesday night; Pierce Mahony and his wife, Parnell's hosts at Creggs, arrived the next day with Parnell's sister, Emily Dickinson; and then followed John Redmond, Harrington and others, who all put up at the Grand Hotel.

A young disciple of Parnell's, Henry Harrison, Nationalist MP for Tipperary, was in London on the Wednesday evening when he read the news of Parnell's death on the newspaper placards: 'It occurred to me that everything pointed to Parnell's widow occupying a position of complete isolation [and that] I must do all that in me lay to lighten her burden at the moment.'[74] He set off for Brighton, checked into a hotel at Hove, then called unannounced at Walsingham Terrace and offered his services. He would assume the task of leading visitors up to the death chamber. The body was apparently 'much swollen, and presented a pitiful sight', 'the jaw was bound up, the hands clenched', and there were still traces of the blood that had seeped from his eyes and mouth.[75]

It must have been 19-year-old Norah O'Shea who considered and accepted Harrison's offer to help. He would later write with admiration of the manner in which she 'uncomplainingly and efficiently assumed and discharged [every] onerous duty about the household'.[76] Besides nursing her mother, Norah had to supervise her two little step-sisters, who were at first told nothing of their father's death. The *Sussex Daily News* observed that Clare and Katie were kept at 9 Walsingham Terrace, out of the way of doctors, visitors and the undertaker's men next door. On the morning of Thursday 8 October the pair ('charming little flaxen-haired girls') could be seen running out with their hoops, in the company of their nurse, 'scarcely conscious of the misery of their surroundings'.[77]

Katharine had one more trial to overcome. She had sacrificed her husband to Ireland, and now had to give up his remains. She may have wished for a burial in Brighton, but she submitted to the arguments of her husband's colleagues that a public ceremony in Ireland was the rightful course. On Friday night, Parnell's body was lowered into an oak coffin of plain rectangular design (he had a morbid dislike of the conventional sloping shoulders of coffins), but the lid was left off until the next day to allow Katharine to place mementoes next to the body, among them a withered flower, the rose that he had taken up and kissed when they first met: 'when he died I placed it on his heart.'[78] The next day, the coffin was boarded onto a train at Brighton Station. Katharine was in no fit state to consider travelling with her husband's body to Ireland, but she entrusted Harrison with 'wreaths and particular flowers which Mrs Parnell wished to lie close, specially placed at the last, upon the surface of the coffin'.[79] The funeral procession passed through Dublin to Glasnevin Cemetery followed by 'a vast concourse of people', silent in their grief.[80] Harrison would never forget the day Parnell was buried: 'On that day, if ever, the heart of Ireland was revealed. Never have I witnessed such an immensity of public sorrow, no, nor such an intensity nor spontaneousness.'[81]

Harrison says that although he was at the house every day, he did not see Katharine for several weeks: 'She had suffered a shattering blow', and it was 'wonderful . . . that she rose at all after that blow'.[82] Thirty years later, Norah gave T.P. O'Connor 'a thrilling description of how [her mother] would get up in the middle of the night in a state of wild alarm, and call on them to go downstairs to the hall, where, as she thought, Parnell and O'Shea were fighting and attempting to kill each other'.[83] For a long time, Katharine remained haunted by the past and 'used to imagine that she heard the voice of Parnell, and carry on long conversations with him'.[84] According to Norah, up to the time of her mother's death, Katharine had 'the happy delusion that Parnell comes to her at night, when things are worst'.[85]

Her grief for Parnell's sudden death must indeed have been terrible. These were two people who could not bear to be without each other, and when they were apart would communicate daily by letter or telegram. After years in which their love had triumphed over the strains of a difficult and covert life, they had been made free to live together openly and happily. When Parnell died they had been married less than four months.

It is all the more remarkable, then, that not three weeks after his death, she had apparently determined to contribute to a biography of Parnell. It was to be written by Henry Harrison.[86] This was premature, and one wonders why Katharine agreed to a biography of her husband by a young man who was as yet a stranger to her, even though he had become, by his own account, a fairly permanent fixture at Walsingham Terrace. He worked in a little back room on the ground floor, and for many weeks, 'the bulk of the fetching and carrying of drafts and notes and written memoranda and of the to and fro discussions was conducted through Norah', who would take legal and financial papers up to her mother's bedroom for Katharine's signature or suggested amendments.[87] Harrison's chief companions were in fact Clare and Katie, 'with whom there were rompings and grave conversations and tellings of stories . . . and, for a time, walks twice daily, in fine weather'.[88] Clare he describes as having 'the delicate colouring, the typical brown eyes, the skin texture, the hair – all such marked resemblance as to stamp her indelibly and unmistakably as a child of Parnell'.[89]

For a while, Harrison made himself indispensable to Katharine's family. She was in great financial difficulty. She received nothing from Parnell's estate. According to Harrison, his will had needed to be re-executed after their marriage for it to remain valid. Harrison took measures to make 9 and 10 Walsingham Terrace impregnable to the many debt collectors and newspaper reporters: 'I ordered a liberal provision of sheet iron shutters and bars and bolts and arranged with the police for special supervision.'[90] He also applied to fellow MPs in order to stave off bankruptcy until the probate case came on, and got a cheque for £500 from the railway magnate Sir Edward Watkin.

It was Healy's assertion that Harrison went so far as to write on Katharine's behalf to supporters of Parnell, asking them to freeze the party funds, still held in Paris, in order that Katharine could lay claim to a portion of them.[91] Furious at what appeared to be an alliance between Katharine and what remained of the Parnellite movement, Healy uttered his worst slander yet, speaking publicly of Parnell's widow as 'a proved British prostitute'.[92] Now that Parnell himself was dead, such language served only to drive a wider gulf between the opposing factions within the party, and was indeed beginning to prove distasteful even to fervent anti-Parnellites. Henry Labouchère, at this time in Ireland, hoping to persuade the party to re-unite behind a second Liberal Home Rule bill, thought to ask Gladstone to intervene. Gladstone's reply, written in the form of a letter which could be shown to Healy, is scrupulous in not naming Katharine (nor does Gladstone make any reference to his personal knowledge of her), and in attributing no blame to Healy for his public references to 'the unhappy woman'. He makes the observation that 'the

Almighty has smitten the woman heavily. Nor will her social punishment be light,' and goes on to say that attacking her within weeks of her husband's death is 'hitting her when she is down. I cannot help hoping Mr Healy may now feel he has done enough in the matter.'[93] The carefully phrased message was effective, and Healy promised never again to slander Katharine publicly. The pity is that Katharine never knew of Gladstone's action. Politically expedient it may have been, but there is an indisputable air of decency about his defence of her.

Henry Harrison was also on hand to witness a scandalous attempt by O'Shea to blackmail Katharine. O'Shea, too, had suffered from the divorce and the treatment he had received from the press. Three months on, he confided in Joseph Chamberlain, 'I have not recovered health or spirits.' In particular he mentions that 'the absence of my eldest daughter, Norah, is a constant trial'.[94] When the Bishop of Galway repeated Healy's accusation that O'Shea had blackmailed Parnell into securing him the Galway seat in February 1886, he concluded that the Catholic hierarchy in Ireland, 'like the rest of the Gladstonians, hate me much more than Parnell'.[95] It must have seemed to O'Shea that the whole of public opinion was against him.

Any sympathy one feels for O'Shea is short-lived, however. Harrison recalls a day in February 1892 when Gerard or Carmen brought word that their aunt Anna intended to visit their mother. There had been no direct contact between them since the divorce trial, and Harrison assumed that the time had come for their differences 'to be wiped away in affectionate reconciliation'. However, after Anna had been shut away with Katharine for some time, Norah stepped outside the room to hand a letter to Harrison. It was a very brief message from O'Shea to Katharine telling her not to worry herself about his powers of custody over Clare and Katie: 'I do not propose to take them away from you' was the substance of the letter. It looked innocent enough to him until Norah hesitantly explained why it had been written: 'Father wants Mother to agree to something in the Courts to-morrow.'

Katharine and O'Shea were about to attend a formal hearing intended to renegotiate the terms of their marriage settlement in order to reimburse O'Shea for his legal responsibility in bringing up their children. Harrison now noticed that O'Shea had post-dated his letter to make it appear as though he had written it *after* the court hearing. The shocking implication could not be clearer: O'Shea was threatening to take Clare and Katie away from Katharine unless she made over a certain amount of money to him. There was no time to seek legal advice, and Katharine could do nothing but submit: 'Mother would sacrifice anything rather than let Father have Clare and Katie,' Norah told him.[96] Harrison was 'mortified to see Parnell's widow bullied out of her rights under my very eyes'.[97] It also struck him that this was by no means the first occasion on which O'Shea had used the threat of his legal custody of Parnell's daughters to procure funds from Katharine. Norah was fully aware of what was going on: 'There was nothing new to her in the episode save the falsification of the date of the letter.' 'It's terrible to have to believe such things of one's father,' she confided.[98]

The long-awaited probate suit over Aunt Wood's will was finally heard in March 1892. The dispute was a simple one: Charles and Evelyn Wood refused to acknowledge their late aunt's wills of 1887 or 1888, since at that time, they alleged, Mrs Wood was 'not of sound mind, memory, and understanding'. Besides that, they believed her to be under 'undue influence on the part of the plaintiff'.[99] The will they wished to have proven was a much earlier one, dated 15 April 1847, in which Anna Maria Wood presumably made equal provision for all her sister Emma's children.[100] Katharine, on her part, submitted the will of 7 March 1888 to be admitted to probate. This was the document which had been drawn up by Horatio Pym, and signed by Mrs Wood in the presence of himself and his clerk. Pym would testify that his client 'was then of sound mind'.[101] O'Shea's interest in the case was, ironically, to shore up Katharine's position. In support of Sir Andrew Clark's report on Mrs Wood's sanity, he got his solicitor to gather further testimonies that she was sane from Pym and his clerk, the author George Meredith, and the rector of Eltham, a Mr Roswell.

In fact, O'Shea's intervention only served to weaken the case for the 1888 will. As a result of Anna Steele's involvement in her sister's divorce case, her barrister had knowledge of the private papers submitted by the defendant, which of course included letters described by O'Shea as 'written in the most absolute confidence by a husband to a wife regarding the pecuniary assistance which the late Mrs Wood had promised me in my political career'.[102] Thus Anna and the rest of the Woods knew that the O'Sheas had drawn on large sums of money from their aunt. This would have afforded them justification in alleging that Katharine had influenced the elderly woman into making a new will entirely in her favour. Even though Katharine was able to produce not dissimilar begging letters sent to her aunt by Charles, who got 'a present of £2,000 on the plea of poverty',[103] and Evelyn, who was given all Mrs Wood's plate, first as a loan and then as a gift, O'Shea's correspondence was potentially so damaging that he and his solicitor spent a great deal of time working on 'an explanation which would be satisfactory to any jury'.[104]

As Henry Harrison notes, 'there existed in England no other individual of either sex that the general public would have preferred to see in the witness box, or under cross-examination, than Mrs Parnell',[105] and at 10.30 a.m. on Thursday 24 March, the courtroom was crowded. Yet there was to be no trial. Justice Jeune did not take up his seat until noon, by which time lawyers on both sides had agreed a compromise. The settlement was as follows: the last will and testament of Anna Maria Wood, which left her whole fortune of some £145,000 to her niece Katharine, was to be executed. (This became £130,000 after legal costs, a fact which incensed O'Shea.) However, half that sum was to be divided among the various defendants and interveners in the case (there turned out to be quite a number of them), and half was to be put into Katharine's marriage settlement with O'Shea. O'Shea had been intent on getting his hands on some of the money and was to share Katharine's life interest on her half of the remaining money, now reduced to £65,000.[106] Harrison was frustrated that her inheritance was so diminished, but the advice of Sir Charles Russell, representing Katharine, was that if the matter went to a jury 'she might lose everything'.[107]

Once Justice Jeune had accepted the settlement and dismissed the special jury, Russell asked for a private hearing in a few days' time in order to protect the interests of the children involved (in 1892, all four of Katharine's daughters, aged 9 to 19, were classed as minors). At a separate hearing, the five children were apportioned shares of their parents' life interest in the money on their deaths: Gerard was to get 40 per cent, and his two sisters 22.5 per cent, while Parnell's daughters were given a mere 7.5 per cent each, shares which must reflect an awareness of the children's different parentage.[108] Yet O'Shea retained the right to custody of Clare and Katie, and while he did so Katharine would remain vulnerable to further financial claims. As Harrison put the point to her solicitor, 'She mustn't be left in the position that O'Shea can squeeze more concessions out of her.'[109] Fortunately, the court, no doubt aware that they were Parnell's children, was prepared to transfer custody of the younger children to Katharine as part of the settlement. O'Shea, responding to 'many nasty hints . . . made as to my conduct therein', and careful not to admit that the girls were not his own, told Chamberlain that he had agreed to this out of a feeling of sympathy for Katharine. Her doctor had 'furnished two certificates to the effect that if I took them from their mother, he would not answer for the consequences to her. This was over and over again corroborated by my eldest daughter, Norah.' Interestingly, this letter betrays a distinction between 'my children', 'my eldest daughter', and '*the two* youngest children', '*these* children'.[110] But O'Shea had agreed that custody of Clare and Katie pass to Katharine. Never again would he be in a position to extort money from her. Never again would Katharine live with the fear of having them taken from her.

O'Shea would die of a heart attack at the age of 65 on 22 April 1905, the death certified by Carmen's husband, Dr Arthur Buck, and registered by his nurse, Adelaide Simpson. He was buried in the Catholic section of Hove Cemetery, and the funeral was a small affair, attended only by Gerard and Buck. A brief obituary appeared in *The Times*, but it was noted that the name of Captain O'Shea 'has disappeared for many years past from public knowledge'.[111]

There is no way of knowing whether Katharine's family became reconciled to her once the probate suit was resolved. The evidence is to the contrary. Evelyn dedicated his 1917 autobiography, *Winnowed Memories*, to Anna ('A sage counsellor in literature, an apt pupil in the hunting field'[112]), and in his account of his early life he makes no reference to his sister Katharine. Nor is there any mention of Katharine's presence at her brother's funeral in 1919. When her niece Minna, daughter of Charles Page Wood, married in Essex in 1893, local papers listed the generous wedding gifts given by Charles, Evelyn, Emma and Anna. Aunt Katharine was presumably not invited. Yet this is not to say that Katharine was entirely forgotten by the family. News of Katharine does find a place in the family scrapbooks compiled by Minna Bradhurst throughout her marriage. Minna was a keen reader of T.P. O'Connor's penny weekly, *M.A.P.* (*Mainly About People*), which now and then carried old pieces about the O'Sheas, but she also kept cuttings from London and Essex papers which carried up-to-date information about Katharine's whereabouts.

The account Katharine later wrote of her love affair concludes with Parnell's death and offers no suggestion of an afterlife for his widow. For Katharine's biographers, too, the remaining thirty years of her life would be a blank. Her life with Parnell abruptly ended, she passed her widowhood in quiet anonymity on an ever-decreasing income. One of Minna Bradhurst's cuttings from the *East Anglian Daily Times* reported that Katharine had leased Trematon Castle in Cornwall in 1899, where 'she now lives in utter seclusion, neither visiting nor visited, and . . . rarely steps outside her grounds'. Described as standing 'high and alone', and 'successfully isolated' from its surroundings, the castle is represented as a fitting expression of Katharine's desire to live alone with her memories.[113] Yet, she did not live in isolation. She had with her Norah, Clare and Katie. While Katharine could sometimes be observed attending alone the morning service at the Anglican St Stephens-by-Saltash, her daughters would have gone to the local Catholic church. From Trematon Castle they moved to South Down Cottage in Preston, a coastal village outside Weymouth in South Dorset, where they could afford to keep a cook and parlour-maid, a groom and an errand boy.

In 1891 T.P. O'Connor had declared, 'We have not heard [Katharine's] story, probably we never shall',[114] but some twenty two years later the story *was* heard, apparently in response to a remark made by William

O'Brien in the *Cork Free Press* on 6 September 1913. O'Brien, who had recently discovered a cache of old letters, published the one Parnell sent him on 14 January 1890, in which he had assured O'Brien that if the divorce case were fully investigated, 'it will be shown that the dishonour & the discredit has not been upon my side'. O'Brien interpreted this phrase to mean that throughout the affair Parnell had conducted himself blamelessly and had never attempted to deceive O'Shea, who both condoned and connived at his wife's adultery for his own political advantage. It was his assertion that if Parnell had been allowed to testify, there would have been no divorce. He was not original in this. What was new was his claim that Parnell would thus have been 'shown to be rather the victim than the destroyer of a happy home'.[115] This was just too much for Gerard O'Shea to bear, and on Wednesday 10 September *The Times* published his public refutation of O'Brien's 'scandalous insinuations', which were, he believed, 'a slander upon my late father and my mother'. Furthermore, Gerard quoted from a letter he had received from Katharine: 'I quite agree with you as to the insult to myself, your father's memory, and, above all, to my late husband . . . and I now propose, with your consent, to publish as soon as possible myself the letters of my late husband, which, as you know, I had left directions should be published after my death.'[116]

This project clearly became Katharine's book, *Charles Stewart Parnell: His Love Story and Political Life.* In her preface to its serialisation in the *Daily Sketch*, under the caption 'Why It Has Been Written', Katharine wrote that it was 'a very poignant pain to me to give to the world any account of the sacred happiness of eleven years of my life and of the agony of sorrow that once seemed too great to bear'. She excused the publication of Parnell's 'sacred' love letters, which 'no eyes other than our own should ever have seen', by saying that, while Gerard wished her to write a book that would restore his father's honour, she herself was determined to guard that of her lover and second husband.[117] The British press did not agree that she had done so, the *Daily Express* calling it a 'pitiful revelation, a dragging down of idols', in all 'a story that ought never to have been told'.[118] The *Saturday Review* conceded that it would 'probably be the most read and talked-of book of the year', yet asked what the world was to think of Katharine's 'discretion or taste in printing some of the love letters', while the *Spectator* believed that it could detect 'a certain lack of delicacy' in Katharine's account of her early character, years before she first met Parnell.[119] *The Times*, too, regarded Katharine's having bared the secrets of Parnell's heart a 'desecration' ('There are women whom nothing on earth could move to such an act'), and doubted whether William O'Brien's statements about the divorce case could in any way defend or justify her book.[120]

One specific reservation expressed by *The Times*'s reviewer was the fact
that Katharine had interspersed transcriptions of her lover's intimate
correspondence 'with scraps of poetry', and had employed 'all the arts of a
clever writer' to present her story.[121] There is an unease at Katharine's
editorial control over Parnell's letters, and unease, too, with the confidence
of her own voice. As Roy Foster notes, 'an original voice comes through'.[122]
While her book does belong to that peculiarly Victorian genre of the
devoted widow's biography of a famous man,[123] it is quite as much
Katharine's autobiography: the first thirteen chapters are taken up with her
girlhood and first marriage. Katharine's claim that this portion of the book
was 'suggested and urged upon me by my children'[124] is the conventional
apology which prefaces the writings of so many Victorian women
autobiographers.[125]

It is particularly the contention of Henry Harrison and more recent
commentators that Gerard O'Shea had an undue influence upon the
production of his mother's book.[126] In order to explain how it was that
Katharine's published account was 'in flagrant conflict' with the story she
had told him at Walsingham Terrace, Harrison could only deduce that
Katharine was, 'in her old age, her helplessness, her sorrow, her penury',
quite incapable of 'giving a comprehensive and critical supervision' of her
manuscript. Yet his description of Katharine as a 'stricken authoress' with
an 'enfeebled brain and wavering lips' belongs to the impression he gained
of Parnell's widow during the few months he worked at Walsingham
Terrace in 1891–2, and has little to do with the reality of Katharine as she
featured in an up-to-date photograph in the *Daily Sketch*, a plump and
comely old lady seated in a horse-drawn cab on the front at Brighton, in
fashionable broad-brimmed hat, holding a white furred terrier in her arms.

Essentially, Katharine told a complex story which differed from that told
in the divorce court, one in which it is difficult to fathom exactly what were
the relationships between Katharine, Parnell and O'Shea. It is a less
forthright story in some respects than the statements she had made to
Henry Harrison in the months immediately after Parnell's death. But could
she be expected, in 1914, to tell the world the true story of her relations
with both men during this period? She told the public all they needed to
know: that she had been a neglected, almost a deserted, wife; that her
relationship with Parnell was one of passionate love; and that, refusing to
be bound by moral convention, they regarded themselves as husband and
wife. While for the Irish 'the chief shock-value of the book lay in Parnell's
own letters, particularly those from Kilmainham Gaol',[127] it also revealed
how much of her domestic happiness with Parnell she had had to sacrifice
for Ireland. Harrison may have been convinced that Gerard interfered with
his mother's manuscript, but the portrait of his father is not a flattering

one. The many letters of O'Shea's that Katharine reprints reveal a distinctly lesser man than Parnell – pompous, self-pitying, grasping, self-important, malicious, petty and absurd. It is hard to see how the completed book in any way achieves Gerard's wish to defend his late father's reputation.

Presumably it was for commercial reasons that Katharine published her memoirs under her former married title, 'Katharine O'Shea', and the book certainly sold well. The two-volume British edition, which was circulated in both Canada and Australia, ran to three editions in the first two months, and aside from the income Katharine would have got from the *Daily Sketch*, an American publisher, George H. Doran & Co., also brought out a two-volume edition in 1914. The financial reasons for writing her memoirs cannot be discounted. Back in 1901, Katharine's then solicitor, Arthur Stopford Francis, began 'speculating wildly' with money from her trust fund. In all, he 'borrowed' £4,500, 'every penny of my small fortune'.[128] Katharine was indebted to the kindness of Sir George Lewis, who successfully took the case to court and got Francis suspended for six months, the missing money refunded, and all legal costs paid.[129] A similar thing then happened in 1913 when, according to Norah, 'Mother's Trustee absconded with as much as he could lay his hands on'. The little that could be retrieved was invested in the Grand Trunk Railway of Canada, but 'that stopped paying dividends just before the war'.[130]

One other motive for giving her story to the world was that Katharine believed herself, at the age of 69, 'so near him now'.[131] She had been diagnosed with heart disease and would suffer a number of attacks before she died, seven years later, in the spring of 1921. In her final years, Katharine and Norah moved about from one hotel to another along the Brighton coast. At the Royal Crescent Hotel at Kemp Town it was noted that she would often get up at two o'clock in the morning to walk down to the front.[132] In 1920 they took a modest villa in Walpole Road, also in Kemp Town, to be near Gerard and his wife (they may even have lodged with Gerard temporarily), but from there they moved to 39 East Ham Road in Littlehampton, and it was in this house that Katharine died. Her sister Anna had died not long before. At the age of 80, Anna slipped and fell at her house in Brighton in the early hours of 7 November 1920. She broke her right thigh bone and never recovered, dying of 'Exhaustion' on 12 December.[133] Within two months, Katharine was dead, too, of a heart attack on 5 February 1921, Gerard and Norah with her when she died. Four days earlier, Norah had written to Henry Harrison to tell him 'that your old friend is dying, slowly and painfully, of heart disease'. For some months past her mother had suffered attacks from which 'she struggles back with more difficulty and pain each time'. Yet in all this time, almost thirty years since her lover's death, Katharine 'never stopped mourning Parnell . . . Her periods of delusion have always been Parnell, Parnell, Parnell.'[134]

According to the *Weekly Dispatch*, Katharine died at the age of 70, rather than her actual age of 76. The press had only her certificate of marriage to Parnell to go on.[135] *The Times* reminded its readers that Katharine Parnell, to whom 'destiny allotted the terrible rôle of a Delilah', was 'the woman for whose sake Charles Stewart Parnell cast aside the unchallenged leadership of the Irish people'.[136] Katharine was buried at the parish church in Littlehampton at three o'clock on the afternoon of Tuesday 8 February. Only four family members attended: Gerard and his wife Christabel, Norah, and Clare's husband, Dr Bertram Maunsell. It was a muted end to a notorious life.

# Afterword

Throughout the period of the divorce, their mother's remarriage and Parnell's death, Gerard and Carmen remained in Brighton, living with their father. In 1896 Gerard married his cousin Christabel Barrett Lennard, and a year later, Carmen, aged 22, married Dr Arthur Herbert Buck, a young doctor at the Sussex County Hospital, with her father as one of the witnesses. Not a great deal is known of the later lives of either Gerard or Carmen. There is a story T.P. O'Connor relates that at some point in the period after Parnell's death, Katharine's mental state became so alarming that Carmen's husband, Dr Buck, advised that she be cared for at an asylum, where she is supposed to have stayed for two years.[1] Buck had some experience in the treatment of mental disorders, and while married to Carmen had patients to lodge with them.[2] Since Carmen married in 1897, however, this would have been some time after Katharine's bereavement.

Carmen's marriage was not to last. In 1914, at the age of 40, she too was divorced on the grounds of adultery, with a 55-year-old widower, Edward Lingard Lucas. By the time they married in 1915 he had inherited a baronetcy, but this marriage, too, was to end in separation soon after her mother's death in 1921. She did not attend Katharine's funeral, but sent flowers to the grave. She was living alone in a flat in Worthing, where she was discovered dead in her bed a few months later, on 23 December 1921. She died from chronic pleurisy and fatty degeneration of the heart.

As we have seen, Gerard reappears when he takes exception to William O'Brien's observations upon Parnell and the O'Shea divorce. He served in the First World War, and surfaces again in 1936 when he took legal measures to prevent the London staging of a play about his mother's affair with Parnell.[3] In a volte-face which might have been worthy of his father, he seems then to have gone to Hollywood to advise on a film of the play, *Parnell*, starring Clark Gable and Myrna Loy, and been well paid for doing so. Little more of him is known. Gerard died of heart failure at Slough Emergency Hospital in November 1943.

Of Katie O'Shea very little is known. In 1907, at the age of 22, she married Louis D'Oyly Horsford Moule, a Lieutenant in the East Lancashire

Regiment. There is something rather sad about the fact that both of Parnell's daughters chose to marry anonymously, in London, and not near their mother, but perhaps they did so to avoid the notice of local reporters in Brighton. Katie's temporary address in London is given as the Ladies' Army & Navy Club, Burlington Gardens, while Moule gives his as the Motor Club, Coventry Street. There is no evidence that Katharine or the family attended Katie's Westminster wedding, at which, in a moment of confusion, perhaps, Katie gave her late father's name as Henry William O'Shea instead of William Henry.

Shortly afterwards, Moule's regiment was posted to West Africa. According to what Clare's husband was told, Katie was a little unbalanced by her mother's notoriety, and when, some time after her marriage, she was asked to appear as a witness in a minor court case, and asked to confirm her name, 'she blurted out, "I'm Kitty O'Shea"'.[4] Yet both Clare and Katie, when they were young women, introduced themselves to the Parnellite John Redmond, who told Henry Harrison that 'they avowed and took pride in the fact that they were Parnell's children'.[5] In 1936, at the time when Gerard was attempting to prevent the staging of the play about his mother and Parnell, Katie, then Parnell's last surviving descendant, was discovered by the London papers and offered reminiscences of her father, in particular her memories of her parents' wedding and her father's death.[6] The Moules had only settled in England after Katharine's death and they had no children. A family tree shows Katie as having had one still-born child. She was the last of Katharine's children to die, a widow, in absolute poverty in 1947, paralysed after an accidental fall, having spent her last years in an asylum.[7]

One of the consequences of Norah's having brought up Clare was that Parnell's eldest daughter became a 'model Catholic'.[8] Clare took her first Holy Communion on Sunday 18 October 1903, when she was aged 20. Clare's Catholicism had been a compromise forced upon Katharine, yet she gave her daughter a Roman Missal in commemoration of this first communion. At around this time, Clare began contributing short articles to the *Catholic Fireside*, and had short stories accepted by a number of periodicals. Her first novel, *The Story of Audrey*, was serialised in the *Monthly Magazine of Fiction* in 1904. Under the pseudonym of 'Hatherley More', the name taken from her mother's uncle, Lord Hatherley, she also published an edition of Professor Charles Coupe's *Lectures on the Holy Eucharist* in 1906 (she received instruction from Father Coupe).

Clare met her future husband, Bertram Sydney Osmund Maunsell, a young Irish surgeon at Kettering General Hospital in Northampton, in October 1907. She was visiting friends, maybe members of the local Liberal Association, for she was apparently 'an enthusiastic worker on the social side of Liberal politics'.[9] Miss O'Shea struck Bertram as being 'a strong healthy girl, something above the average height with a beautiful figure, her face was that of one fond of out-of-door exercise', and her eyes 'flashed intelligence & more – she had eyes which do a soul betray'.[10] They were married three months later, on 8 February 1908, at the Catholic church attended by Clare, The Sorrowful Hearts of Jesus and Mary in the Fulham Road. Clare was then living at Selwood Terrace off the Fulham Road. Before the year was out, she was pregnant with her first child – Parnell's only grandchild.

Clare gave birth to a baby boy at 2.45 on the afternoon of Thursday 16 September 1909,[11] but after the birth she suffered a haemorrhage for which nothing could be done. As she lay dying, Clare begged Bertram to 'look after the little one'.[12] He was to be a 'pal' to their child (Norah's word), and was never to 'speak harshly to him or scold him'.[13] Clare died of heart failure at 4.45 p.m. on the afternoon of Friday 17 September. The funeral took place in Kettering on Tuesday 21 September. The 5-day-old Assheton Clare Bowyer-Lane Maunsell was christened before the reading of the requiem mass, which moved the large congregation to tears. Local people had lined the route to the church, and a large number gathered at the cemetery. Among the mourners were Norah and Gerard, but apparently not Katharine or Carmen. Both sent floral tributes, however: Carmen's reading simply, 'Mrs Arthur Buck, Brighton', while Katharine's bore the message, 'For my darling, from mother.'[14]

'Clare's death was a terrible blow to my father,' wrote Bertram's eldest son by his second marriage: 'His life was hell.'[15] He remarried in 1914, and had a further seven children, yet according to their son John (later Father John Maunsell), his second wife Mary 'never understood him'. Bertram would often speak privately to him 'of darling Clare' and named one of his daughters after her. 'Faithful Aunt Norah', as John remembers her, continued to visit Kettering after Bertram's re-marriage, and would often collect Assheton to take him on visits to see his grandmother, Katharine, who was 'never far from Brighton'.[16] According to Norah, Assheton's head was 'just the shape of his grandfather's, as was Clare's'.[17] Assheton trained at Sandhurst and joined the Lancashire Fusiliers in 1929. In service in India, he died from enteric (typhoid) fever on 29 July 1934, two months before his twenty-fifth birthday, and is buried in the military cemetery at Lahore. Assheton's death was 'the last straw' for Bertram: 'The last link with long lost happy days was snapped.'[18]

Norah died not long after her full sister Carmen. At the age of 48 she was left 'practically penniless' on her mother's death, and wrote to T.P. O'Connor asking his help in finding temporary work as a nursery governess. She began training as a nurse at Queen Charlotte's Hospital, the maternity hospital, then on the Marylebone Road, where she adopted her mother's maiden name of Wood, 'so as to avoid troublesome questions'.[19] She then contracted the skin disease Lupus Erythematosus, which causes the patient to suffer painful ulcerous lesions which eat into the skin and leave deep scars. In August 1922 she underwent a lengthy treatment for her condition which involved having her septic throat scraped. She wrote to Bertram that her face was much improved, but 'Hands awful'. Norah asked Bertram 'to be a real Pal' and tell her frankly whether she would ever be cured of the Lupus, since she could never get a straight answer from her doctors: 'I must *know* what to expect.'[20] She died eleven months later, on the evening of 16 July 1923, at a nursing home in the village of Datchet, outside Eton, near where her brother Gerard now lived at Farnham Common. Septic pneumonia had set in once she had caught another infection, owing 'to the state of her skin & generally debilitated condition'. As Gerard wrote to Bertram, 'you know, she had been in torture, for a year'.[21] Norah was buried in Littlehampton on Thursday 19 July in the plot she had bought which lay next to Katharine's. She left her brother a small sum to cover her funeral expenses, but, as Bertram's son put it, 'Gerard collared the money'.[22]

It was to Bertram that Norah had entrusted a box containing relics of her mother's relationship with Parnell. It was to be handed down to Assheton. Katharine had treasured the box for thirty years, and Bertram would do so for another twenty: treasured, 'but rarely brought out or discussed'. It was, though, Katharine's wish 'that one day these Parnell relics would find a lasting resting place *in Ireland*'.[23] They included the signet ring Katharine gave to Parnell when they became lovers, Katharine's wedding ring of intertwined bands of gold and silver, made by Parnell, locks of Katharine's, Parnell's and the girls' hair, a framed photograph of Clare as a baby (Parnell used to carry a miniature of this in his waistcoat pocket[24]), and portraits of Clare and Katie as young women. There were also a couple of Parnell's leather wallets, one of his walking sticks, the photograph taken by Katharine of Parnell sitting in the new room built at Wonersh Lodge, and the 1880 photograph of Katharine that he had with him at Kilmainham Gaol, as well as various papers, including the last letter he ever wrote – that to his doctor, written three days before his death.

After Bertram's death in 1941, Father Maunsell added to these relics various papers relating to Clare, including a complex family tree he had compiled. He added an extraordinary detail. After listing the births of Claude Sophic, Clare and Katie, Father Maunsell records a fourth child born to Katharine and Parnell, a son who died at birth, whom he describes specifically as a 'posthumous' child, that is, a child born after the death of his father, Parnell.[25] If Parnell's death did indeed cause Katharine to miscarry and perhaps give birth to a premature baby, it was a well-kept family secret which perhaps only Norah knew of, a secret she may have entrusted to her brother-in-law when she gave him the relics after her mother's death in 1921. Bertram was after all a doctor, and besides that a 'pal' to Norah, who had been a second mother to his wife, her half-sister Clare. One wonders whether young Henry Harrison was let into the secret. He does appear to hint that there was more to her prostration at the time of Parnell's death: 'She had suffered a shattering blow after a prolonged period of anxiety, excitement, nervous strain – a period filled with even more complicated preoccupations than the world yet [knows] of.'[26] While it is not impossible that Katharine could have conceived a child at the age of 46, there exists no official record of the death at this time of a baby boy by the name of Parnell. Yet it may have been that the child was born so premature as to be regarded as a miscarriage, and thus its birth was never registered, while to her Catholic daughter, Norah, and son-in-law, Bertram, the still-born baby rightfully took its place in the family records.

The relics were saved by Norah's good sense, but it was presumably her brother Gerard who took possession of his mother's papers and the manuscript of her book. The only letters of Katharine's to survive are those in the Gladstone Papers in the British Library, as well as lawyers' copies of odd letters exchanged between Katharine and O'Shea in the National Library of Ireland which date from the tense period 1886–7. The survival of the 1887 letters is in fact quite accidental: taken for scrap paper, the blank sides were used by a veteran of the First World War to compile his memoirs.[27] The great body of Katharine's correspondence with Parnell was no doubt destroyed by Gerard, whose animosity towards Parnell did not abate with the publication of his mother's book. When, in 1923, Bertram was approached by the writer St John Ervine, who was then beginning work on his biography of Parnell, he promised to get in touch with Gerard, then living in central London and working in the motor business, to ask whether he was willing to offer any information about his late step-father. The reply was categorical: Gerard had never heard of Ervine, 'nor am I the least interested in what he or anyone else may say about the late Mr C.S. Parnell, who was the most unmitigated and contemptible villain unhanged'.[28]

The last words of this book, however, go not to Gerard but to Father Maunsell. On 7 April 1956, he handed over most of the Parnell relics to Sir Shane Leslie, the Irish writer and historian, who would eventually give the collection to the Kilmainham Gaol Museum in Dublin, which is where they are now on public display. After Leslie's visit, Maunsell posted him a small parcel of lesser relics – some books and religious cards belonging to Clare, mementoes of her mother and Norah, including a Christmas card addressed to 'My Clare', from 'loving Mums'.[29] Again, he expressed his satisfaction that others would soon be able to treasure these mementoes, 'which at last are going home where they belong', adding that, in the light of man's 'frailty and weakness', 'I could never even think of daring to condemn what Parnell & Kitty did'.[30]

# Appendix: The Kilmainham Treaty

Letter from C.S. Parnell to Captain O'Shea, 28 [actually 29] April 1882, and which formed the content of the Kilmainham Treaty.

Kilmainham
April 28 [1882]

I was very sorry that you had left Albert Mansions before I reached London from Eltham, as I had wished to tell you that after our conversation I had made up my mind that it would be proper for me to put Mr McCarthy in possession of the views which I had previously communicated to you. I desire to impress upon you the absolute necessity of a settlement of the arrears question which will leave no recurring sore connected with it behind, and which will enable us to show the smaller tenantry that they have been treated with justice and some generosity.

The proposal you have described to me as suggested in some quarters, of making a loan, over however many years the payment might be spread, should be absolutely rejected, for reasons which I have already explained to you. If the arrears question be settled upon the lines indicated by us, I have every confidence – a confidence shared by my colleagues – that the exertions which we should be able to make strenuously and unremittingly would be effective in stopping outrages and intimidation of all kinds.

As regards permanent legislation of an ameliorative character, I may say that the views which you always shared with me as to the admission of leaseholders to the fair rent clauses of the Act are more confirmed than ever. So long as the flower of the Irish peasantry are kept outside the Act there cannot be any permanent settlement of the land question, which we all so much desire.

I should also strongly hope that some compromise might be arrived at this season with regard to the amendment of the tenure clauses. It is unnecessary for me to dwell upon the enormous advantages to be derived from the full extension of the purchase clauses, which now seem practically to have been adopted by all parties.

The accomplishment of the programme I have sketched would, in my judgement, be regarded by the country as a practical settlement of the land question, and would, I feel sure, enable us to co-operate cordially for the future with the Liberal Party in forwarding Liberal principles; so that the Government, at the end of the session, would, from the state of the country, feel themselves thoroughly justified in dispensing with further coercive measures.

Yours very truly,
C.S. Parnell

The complete text of the Kilmainham Treaty is reprinted in Katharine O'Shea, *Charles Stewart Parnell: His Love Story and Political Life*, London: Cassell & Co., 1914, I, pp. 253–4.

# Katharine's Family Tree

William Wood  m.  Catherine Cluse
1738–1809                d. 1798

Sir Matthew Wood, MP    8 other children    Benjamin Wood, MP
1st Baronet 1768–1843                        1787–1845
m. 1795                                       m. Anna Maria
Maria Page d. 1848                            Michell*
                                              1792–1889

Admiral Sampson
Michell
d. 1809

Admiral Sir          Anna Maria       Colonel Charles       Emma
Frederick            Michell*         Collier Michell       Carolina
Michell              1792–1889        1793–1851             Michell
d. 1873                                                     1802–1879

Western Wood
1804–63
m. 1829
Sarah Letitia
Morris

William Page          Catherine        Maria            m. 1820 Revd Sir John
Wood                  Wood             Elizabeth                Page Wood
1801–81               m. Charles       Wood                     2nd Baronet
Baron Hatherley       Stephens         m. Edwin                 1796–1866
m. 1830                                Maddy
Charlotte Moor

Katharine
Wood
1845–1921
(see below)

Anna                 (Henry)          Charles           Emma              Sir Francis         Clarissa         Maria ('Polly')    Frederick    John Page
Caroline             Evelyn           Page Wood         Wood              3rd Baronet         Wood             m. 1847            Wood         Wood
Wood                 Wood             b. 1836           m. 1853           1831–69             1830–47          Colonel Joseph     1823–31      1821–5
1840–1920            1838–1919        m. 1864           Sir Thomas        m. Louisa                            Chambers
m. 1858              m. 1867          Minna             Barrett           Mary                                 d. 1878
Colonel              Hon. (Mary)      White             Lennard           Hodgson
Charles              Paulina Anne
Steel                Southwell

3 other
children
died in
infancy

Francis Page Wood
b. 1862

Colonel Sir John Page Wood
b. 1860

Sir Matthew Wood
4th Baronet

Katharine Wood
1845–1921

m. (1) 1867
(divorced 1890)
Captain William Henry
O'Shea
1840–1905

m. (2 1891
Charles Stewart Parnell
1846–1891

Gerard Henry
William O'Shea
1870–1943
m. 1896
(Anna) Christabel
Barrett Lennard
1865–1945

(Mary) Norah
O'Shea
1873–1923

(Anna Maria del) Carmen
O'Shea
1874–1921
m. (1) 1897
(divorced 1914)
Dr Arthur Herbert Buck

m. (2) 1915
Sir Edward Lingard Lucas

3 children

Claude Sophie
O'Shea
February–April
1882

Clare Gabrielle
Antoinette
Marcia Esperance
O'Shea
1883–1909
m. 1908
Dr Bertram Sydney
Osmund
Maunsell
1875–1941

(Frances) Katie
Flavia Guadalupe
O'Shea
1884–1947
m. 1907
Captain Louis
D'Oyley
Morsford Moule

still-born son
born after the
death of Charles
Stewart
Parnell(?)

Assheton Clare Bowyer-Lane
Maunsell
1909–34

# Notes

## Abbreviations

BL    British Library Manuscripts Room
ERO   Essex Record Office
FRO   Flintshire Record Office
KGM  Kilmainham Gaol Museum
NLI   National Library of Ireland
UBL   University of Birmingham Library

## Introduction

1. T.M. Healy, *Letters and Leaders of my Day*, 2 vols, London, Thornton Butterworth, 1928, I, p. 158.
2. J.L. Hammond's 1938 biography of Gladstone appeared to draw a line under this, by contesting Katharine's account of the number of times she saw the Prime Minister and in asserting his belief that Gladstone had no knowledge of her affair with Parnell. See *Gladstone and the Irish Nation*, London, Frank Cass & Co. Ltd, 1964 [1938].
3. Jules Abels, *The Parnell Tragedy*, London, The Bodley Head, 1966, p. 145.
4. 'Her placing of events is notoriously inaccurate', 'Her recollections . . . are extremely unreliable' (F.S.L. Lyons, *Charles Stewart Parnell*, London, Collins, 1977, p. 151; p. 224).
5. *Ibid.*, p. 175. So, too, Parnell's colleague, and biographer, T.P. O'Connor: 'The letters are in the language of almost exaggerated affection which characterised all his communications with her' (*Memoirs of an Old Parliamentarian*, 2 vols, London, Ernest Benn Ltd, 1929, II, p. 247).
6. Henry Harrison, *Parnell Vindicated: The Lifting of the Veil*, London, Constable & Co. Ltd, 1931, p. 219; p. 232.
7. *Ibid.*, p. 127.
8. *Ibid.*, pp. 119–20.
9. Joyce Marlow describes Katharine's contact with Gladstone and the content of her letters in some detail, but she treats them as feminine confidences, not as calculated political negotiations (*The Uncrowned Queen of Ireland: The Life of 'Kitty' O'Shea*, London, Weidenfeld & Nicolson, 1975, p. 105). Mary Rose Callaghan's more recent biography confines Katharine's political role as Parnell's intermediary with the British Government to a single paragraph (*Kitty O'Shea: A Life of Katharine Parnell*, London, Pandora Press, 1989, p. 100).
10. R. Barry O'Brien's 1898 biography of Parnell prefers to eschew details of the divorce case affair, saying that 'Mrs Charles Stewart Parnell and her children are still alive. I

must consider her and them' (*The Life of Charles Stewart Parnell, 1846–1891*, 2 vols, London, Smith, Elder & Co., 1898, II, p. 236). Justin McCarthy, William O'Brien and Michael Davitt all make discreet references to the affair.

11. Gerard's hostility towards Parnell developed as he grew into manhood, and will be referred to in Ch. 10. When the divorce suit was filed, both he and his youngest sister Carmen chose to live with their father. Even though Norah was the one O'Shea child to stay with her mother, she later confided to Henry Harrison that 'my point of view and [mother's], and no doubt yours, is by no means similar, but in bringing up his two girls, Clare and Katie, for my mother's sake I have come to view a great man with inimical toleration' (Norah O'Shea to Henry Harrison, 1 February 1921, reprinted in *Parnell Vindicated*, p. 216).

12. Katharine Parnell, *Charles Stewart Parnell: His Love Story and Political Life*, 2 vols, London, Cassell & Co. Ltd, 1914, II, pp. 50–1.

13. *The Parnell Tragedy*, p. 145.

14. *Parnell Vindicated*, p. 218.

15. R.F. Foster, *Paddy and Mr Punch: Connections in Irish and English History*, London, Allen Lane, 1993, p. 137. Foster's is the first study to offer a sympathetic analysis of Katharine's book and its critical reception.

16. George Bernard Shaw's letter to the *Star*, Thursday 20 November 1890, p. 2. Shaw was writing in defence of Parnell's refusal to retire from the leadership of the Irish Parliamentary Party after the divorce trial. He regarded Katharine's relationship with Parnell 'a perfectly natural and right one', and argued: 'Until our marriage laws are remodelled to suit men and women . . . no verdict in a divorce case will force any man to retire from public life if it appears that he behave no worse than the law forced him to.'

## Chapter 1. Katharine O'Shea

1. Details of the first day's hearing of the divorce case are taken from *The Times*, Monday 17 November 1890, pp. 3–4 (the fullest and most accurate reporting of the case), the *Evening News and Post*, Saturday 15 November 1890, p. 3, and the *Star*, Saturday 15 November 1890, pp. 2–3.

2. *Evening News and Post*, Monday 17 November 1890, p. 4. The *Star* observed that Katharine always hired 'good-looking servant girls', Monday 17 November 1890, p. 2.

3. Quoted in *Evening News and Post*, Tuesday 18 November 1890, p. 4.

4. *The Times*, Monday 17 November 1890, p. 3.

5. *Ibid.*, Tuesday 18 November 1890, p. 14.

6. *Ibid.*, p. 13. O'Shea's statement in court that he was responsible for the maintenance of his family and the education of his children was another lie. When asked on this specific point by the first juror, O'Shea answered, 'Certainly'.

7. *Parnell Vindicated*, p. 122.

8. *Ibid.*, p. 123.

9. Lady Wood's father was an admiral, as was her elder brother Sir Frederick Michell, KCB. Her other brother, Charles Collier Michell, was a colonel in the Royal Engineers.

10. William Page Hatherley was knighted in 1851 and created Baron Hatherley of Hatherley in 1868.

11. Belhus Park is situated in South Ockenden, Essex, the grounds designed by Capability Brown. The house itself was destroyed in the 1960s.

12. *The Dictionary of National Biography*, ed. Leslie Stephen, 63 vols, London, Smith, Elder, 1855–1900, LXII, p. 371.

13. A copy of this letter is enclosed in UBL, Joseph Chamberlain Papers, JC8/8/1/166, W.H. O'Shea to Joseph Chamberlain, 30 March 1892.

14. Caroline was first offered the sum of £50,000 in return for her promise to renounce her claim to the title of queen and to continue to live abroad for the rest of her life. When she refused, George forced the Government, in July 1820, to introduce a divorce bill in order to dissolve his marriage, but such was the popular support for Caroline that the bill was withdrawn – it was feared that there might be a revolution over it (see Sir Evelyn Wood, *Winnowed Memories*, London, Cassell & Co., 1917, p. 53).

15. *Charles Stewart Parnell: His Love Story and Political Life*, I, p. 5.

16. *Ibid.*, I, p. 8.

17. BL, Gladstone Papers, Add. MS 44269, ff. 87–8, Katharine O'Shea to W.E. Gladstone, 17 June [1882].

18. It appears to have been Anna's decision to add an 'e' to the end of her married title.

19. *Charles Stewart Parnell: His Love Story and Political Life*, I, p. 10.

20. *Ibid.*, I, p. 18.

21. *Ibid.*, I, p. 4.

22. *Ibid.*, I, p. 13.

23. *Ibid.*, I, pp. 11–12.

24. *Ibid.*, I, p. 47; I, p. 46.

25. *Ibid.*, I, p. 47.

26. After the divorce case Katharine would regard him as 'one of my bitterest foes' (*ibid.*).

27. *Ibid.*, I, p. 23.

28. *Ibid.*, I, p. 24.

29. *Memoirs of an Old Parliamentarian*, I, p. 84. There is no evidence in support of Healy's malicious allegation that Henry O'Shea was a pawnbroker (*Letters and Leaders of my Day*, I, p. 154).

30. *Charles Stewart Parnell: His Love Story and Political Life*, I, p. 27.

31. *Ibid.*, I, p. 25.

32. *Ibid.*, I, p. 27.

33. J.L. Garvin, *The Life of Joseph Chamberlain*, 6 vols, London, Macmillan, 1932–69, I, p. 349.

34. *Memoirs of an Old Parliamentarian*, I, p. 47. The *Evening News & Post* called him 'the best dressed man' in the House of Commons, Tuesday, 18 November 1890, p. 2.

35. *Charles Stewart Parnell: His Love Story and Political Life*, I, p. 25.

36. UBL, Joseph Chamberlain Papers, JC8/8/1/166, W.H. O'Shea to Joseph Chamberlain, 30 March 1892.

37. *Charles Stewart Parnell: His Love Story and Political Life*, I, p. 23.

38. *Ibid.*, I, p. 26.

39. *Ibid.*, I, p. 31.

40. *Ibid.*, I, p. 22.

41. ERO, D/DL/C68, letters from John Clarke and Robert Keeley to Lady and Sir Thomas Barrett Lennard in a miscellaneous collection of Barrett Lennard correspondence. The

services of Clarke and the Keeleys were evidently thought highly of and they were well rewarded for their time and trouble.

42. *Charles Stewart Parnell: His Love Story and Political Life*, I, p. 34.
43. *Ibid.*, I, p. 35.
44. *Ibid.*, I, p. 38.
45. *Ibid.*, I, p. 44.
46. *Ibid.*, I, p. 51.
47. *Ibid.*
48. Years later, O'Shea confided to Joseph Chamberlain that Katharine's 'sole fortune . . . when I married her, was £120 per annum settled on herself' (UBL, Joseph Chamberlain Papers, JC8/8/1/160, 12 February 1891).
49. *Charles Stewart Parnell: His Love Story and Political Life*, I, p. 106.
50. Principal Registry of the Family Division, Probate Department, The will of The Right Honourable William Page Baron Hatherley, signed and witnessed on 1 July 1881. Lord Hatherley set aside £7,000 to be divided among the surviving children of his brother John Page Wood. This £7,000 was one fourth of the £28,000 left him by his father, Sir Matthew Wood. To Katharine's sister Emma he bequeathed a token £100 since she was 'otherwise amply provided for'; the remaining £6,900 was divided equally between Charles, Evelyn, Maria, Anna, Katharine, and their brother Frank's family.
51. *Charles Stewart Parnell: His Love Story and Political Life*, I, p. 53.
52. *Ibid.*, I, p. 73.
53. *Ibid.*
54. *Ibid.*, I, p. 76.
55. *Ibid.*, I, p. 88.
56. *Ibid.*, I, p. 87.
57. *Ibid.*, I, p. 88.
58. *Ibid.*, I, p. 118.
59. *Ibid.*, I, p. 98.
60. *Ibid.*, I, p. 103.
61. *Ibid.*, I, p. 98.
62. *Ibid.*
63. *Ibid.*, I, p. 99.
64. *Ibid.*
65. *Ibid.*, I, p. 101.
66. *Ibid.*, I, pp. 102–3.
67. *Ibid.*, I, pp. 106–7.
68. *Ibid.*, I, p. 110.
69. Lady Wood wrote an astonishing twelve novels after the death of her husband in 1866 until her death in 1879. Her 1870 novel *On Credit* may owe something to her son-in-law's chronic financial difficulties. Anna, who, like her mother, was published by Chapman & Hall, wrote in all seven novels as well as publishing a translation of Victor Hugo's *L'Homme Qui Rit*. Her first novel, *Gardenhurst*, published the same year as Katharine's marriage, was dedicated 'To my sister Katie (Mrs O'Shea)'. The *Daily News* said of *Gardenhurst* that it was 'one of the best novels we have met with for some time', while *The Times* commented that 'It is not often that we can commend a first novel . . . which seems to hold out such evident promise of "good fruit to come"' (press notices attached to Anna's 1872 novel, *Broken Toys*).

70. *Charles Stewart Parnell: His Love Story and Political Life*, I, p. 12. 'Evelyn was her idol', wrote Katharine, 'and never fell short of her expectations' (*ibid.*), while 'my mother and Emma were devoted to one another, and loved being together' (*ibid.*, I, p. 46).

71. *Parnell Vindicated*, p. 122.

72. *Charles Stewart Parnell: His Love Story and Political Life*, I, p. 110.

73. Eltham Lodge was built by Hugh May in 1663–4 as a suburban retreat for the banker Sir John Shaw. The original ornate plasterwork and wood carving survive. After Anna Maria Wood's death in 1889, the Lodge became the clubhouse for the Royal Blackheath Golf Club.

74. *Charles Stewart Parnell: His Love Story and Political Life*, I, p. 118.

75. *Ibid.*, I, p. 120.

76. *Ibid.*, I, p. 111.

77. *Ibid.*, I, p. 120.

78. *Ibid.* It is Healy's claim that Katharine 'was supposed to have been endowed by a banker named Christopher Weguelin, once MP for Youghal. When Sir Evelyn proposed the match to his subaltern, O'Shea at first pleaded that he was too poor to marry, but was assured that Miss Wood possessed £30,000' (*Letters and Leaders of my Day*, I, p. 154). He further claimed that at the divorce trial a letter was put before O'Shea's counsel in which Katharine had remonstrated against her husband's demands that she cease to communicate with Parnell, the gist of which was 'You did not object to Christopher'. Healy, it has to be said, is generally very ill-informed with regard to Katharine (he believed, for example, that Anna Maria Wood was Katharine's mother). As we know, O'Shea was never her brother Evelyn's subaltern, and Katharine did not possess a fortune at the time of her marriage; the letter Healy refers to need not be an admission of an affair with Weguelin. What we can be certain of is that Healy desperately wanted to believe in it. After the divorce trial, Healy was ill in Ireland and unable to attend the initial meeting of the party at which Parnell was re-elected chairman. A fellow MP sent him an account of Parnell's comments on the divorce which Healy seems to have wilfully misinterpreted. Of Parnell's discreet suggestion that O'Shea had colluded in his affair with Katharine, Healy took him to be saying 'that there was some other man in the case. This is of course Weguelin, so she must have been in relation with both. A precious piece of goods for [Parnell] to be tied to for the rest of his life' (*ibid.*, I, p. 333).

79. *Charles Stewart Parnell: His Love Story and Political Life*, I, p. 118.

80. Mrs Wood was fond of being read to and paid the novelist George Meredith £300 a year to come and read from the 'classics' every week (*ibid.*, I, pp. 114–17).

81. *Ibid.*, I, p. 123.

82. *Ibid.*

83. *Ibid.*, I, p. 125.

84. *Parnell Vindicated*, p. 127.

85. *Charles Stewart Parnell: His Love Story and Political Life*, I, p. 133.

86. *Ibid.*, I, p. 134.

87. See R.F. Foster, *Charles Stewart Parnell: The Man and His Family*, Hassocks, The Harvester Press, 1976, p. 108, for different family accounts of this episode.

88. Paul Bew, *C.S. Parnell*, Dublin, Gill and Macmillan Ltd, 1980, p. 9.

89. See *Charles Stewart Parnell: The Man and his Family*, pp. 149–65.

90. The Irish Parliament was abolished under the Act of Union of 1800. The British Prime Minister, Pitt the Younger, had intended to compensate the Irish by giving Catholics equal rights with Protestants, but George III refused to countenance Catholic Emancipation.

91. Fanny Parnell founded an American Ladies' Land League in October 1880 at the time Michael Davitt was in America. With his support, a sister organisation was launched in Ireland in January 1881 with Anna as its general secretary. Within its first year, the Ladies' Land League had formed 400 branches. While its priority was the alleviation of suffering of evicted families, and later the families of prisoners, through the distribution of food and the provision of prefabricated housing, the Ladies' Land League gained a reputation for radical politics.

92. *Charles Stewart Parnell: The Man and His Family*, p. 138.

93. 'I wish to say as publicly as I can that I do not believe, and never shall believe, that any murder was committed at Manchester' (quoted in *The Life of Charles Stewart Parnell, 1846–1891*, I, pp. 95–6).

94. *C.S. Parnell*, p. 21.

95. *The Life of Charles Stewart Parnell, 1846–1891*, I, p. 80; I, p. 174.

96. *Ibid.*

97. *Ibid.*, I, p. 163.

98. *Charles Stewart Parnell: His Love Story and Political Life*, I, p. 129.

99. Resolution of the Land League, quoted in *The Life of Charles Stewart Parnell, 1846–1891*, I, p. 195.

100. *C.S. Parnell*, p. 31. 'As the winter [of 1879] approached famine threatened the west, and committees were formed by the Duchess of Marlborough (the wife of the Lord-Lieutenant) and by the Lord Mayors to collect food and clothing for the starving peasantry' (*The Life of Charles Stewart Parnell, 1846–1891*, I, p. 197).

101. *C.S. Parnell*, p. 28.

102. 'Of the seven first chosen officers four were Fenians or ex-Fenians' (*The Life of Charles Stewart Parnell, 1846–1891*, I, p. 195).

103. As R. Barry O'Brien explains, Parnell's popularity was such that 'Three constituencies vied with each other for the honour of electing him – Meath [which he had served since 1875], Mayo, and Cork City' (*ibid.*, I, p. 214).

104. *Ibid.*, I, p. 225.

105. William O'Brien, *The Parnell of Real Life*, London, T. Fisher Unwin Ltd, 1925, p. 57.

106. According to Joyce Marlow, Parnell was relatively inexperienced, and, except for the American fiancée, he had never had a deep relationship with a woman: he was shy and reserved and had 'disciplined his inner feelings' (*The Uncrowned Queen of Ireland*, London, Weidenfeld & Nicolson, 1975, pp. 62–3).

107. He once told her that she was 'the only Englishwoman I can bear!' (*Charles Stewart Parnell: His Love Story and Political Life*, II, p. 139).

108. The term is R. Barry O'Brien's: 'A Revolutionist working with constitutional weapons', *The Life of Charles Stewart Parnell, 1846–1891*, I, p. 182.

109. *Charles Stewart Parnell: His Love Story and Political Life*, I, p. ix.

110. *Ibid.*, I, pp. 91–3.

111. *Ibid.*, I, p. ix.

## Chapter 2. Parnell

1.  *Charles Stewart Parnell: His Love Story and Political Life*, I, p. 135.
2.  Justin McCarthy, *Reminiscences*, London, Chatto & Windus, 1899, p. 108.
3.  *Charles Stewart Parnell: His Love Story and Political Life*, I, p. 136.
4.  *Charles Stewart Parnell*, p. 128.
5.  *Charles Stewart Parnell: His Love Story and Political Life*, I, p. 136. Parnell's original phrase, '*paces allons*', is not good French. Perhaps '*pas allants*' is meant ('lively steps'), which may be a term from dressage.
6.  On the death of Katharine's brother Frank in 1869 the baronetcy passed to his eldest son, Matthew Wood (1857–1908).
7.  *Charles Stewart Parnell: His Love Story and Political Life*, I, p. 137.
8.  *Ibid.*, I, p. 138.
9.  Jules Abels observes that his 'abortive affair with Miss Woods occurred three years before he entered politics' (*The Parnell Tragedy*, p. 144).
10. *The Life of Charles Stewart Parnell 1846–1891*, I, p. 233.
11. Conor Cruise O'Brien, *Parnell and his Party, 1880–1890*, Oxford, Clarendon Press, 1964 [1957], p. 51.
12. *Reminiscences*, p. 110.
13. *Charles Stewart Parnell: His Love Story and Political Life*, I, pp. 139–40.
14. *Ibid.*, I, p. 140.
15. *Letters and Leaders of my Day*, I, p. 98.
16. *The Life of Charles Stewart Parnell 1846–1891*, I, p. 264.
17. *Ibid.*, I, p. 265.
18. *Ibid.*, I, p. 140.
19. *Ibid.*, I, p. 141.
20. *The Parnell of Real Life*, p. 183.
21. Justin McCarthy, *Our Book of Memories*, London, Chatto & Windus, 1912, p. 255.
22.  *Ibid.*
23. *Charles Stewart Parnell: His Love Story and Political Life*, I, p. 141.
24. C.S. Parnell to Katharine O'Shea, 9 September 1880, reprinted in *ibid.*, I, p. 142.
25. *Ibid.*, 11 September 1880.
26. *The Life of Charles Stewart Parnell, 1846–1891*, I, p. 236.
27. Quoted in *ibid.*, I, p. 237.
28. *Parnell and his Party*, p. 53.
29. C.S. Parnell to Katharine O'Shea, 'Tuesday', n.d. [21 September 1880], reprinted in *Charles Stewart Parnell: His Love Story and Political Life*, I, p. 152.
30. *Ibid.*, 22 September 1880, I, p. 144.
31. *Ibid.*, 24 September 1880, I, p. 145.
32. *Ibid.*, 2 October 1880, I, p. 153; pp. 152–3.
33. *Parnell Vindicated*, p. 122.
34. *Charles Stewart Parnell: His Love Story and Political Life*, I, p. 146; I, p. 148.
35. *Ibid.*, I, p. 89.
36. *Ibid.*, I, pp. 90–1.
37. *Ibid.*, I, p. 91.
38. *Ibid.*, I, p. 89.
39. *Ibid.*, I, p. 92.

40. *Ibid.*, I, pp. 92–3.
41. *Parnell Vindicated*, p. 170.
42. *Charles Stewart Parnell: His Love Story and Political Life*, I, p. 188.
43. *The Times*, Tuesday 18 November 1890, p. 13.
44. *Charles Stewart Parnell: His Love Story and Political Life*, I, p. 149.
45. *Ibid.*, I, p. 150.
46. *Ibid.*, I, p. 162. According to Katharine, Parnell would often quote the following state-ment of Gladstone's when he addressed public meetings in Ireland that autumn and winter: 'in the circumstances of distress prevalent in Ireland a sentence of eviction is the equivalent of a sentence of death' (*ibid.*, I, p. 160).
47. *Ibid.*, I, p. 163.
48. *Ibid.*, I, p. 162.
49. *Charles Stewart Parnell*, pp. 128–9; p. 613.
50. *Memoirs of An Old Parliamentarian*, I, p. 234.
51. *The Parnell of Real Life*, p. 183.
52. Frank Hugh O'Donnell, *The History of the Irish Parliamentary Party*, 2 vols, London, Longmans & Co., 1910, II, p. 168.
53. *Reminiscences*, p. 91.
54. C.S. Parnell to Katharine O'Shea, 4 December 1880, reprinted in *Charles Stewart Parnell: His Love Story and Political Life*, I, p. 163.
55. Reprinted in *Charles Stewart Parnell*, p. 142.
56. *Our Book of Memories*, p. 5.
57. *Charles Stewart Parnell: His Love Story and Political Life*, II, p. 160.
58. Quoted in *The Parnell Tragedy*, p. 147.
59. *The History of the Irish Parliamentary Party*, II, p. 286.
60. *Parnell Vindicated*, pp. 121–2.
61. *Ibid.*, p. 120; *Charles Stewart Parnell: His Love Story and Political Life*, II, p. 247.
62. *Ibid.*, I, p. 123.
63. *The Times*, Monday 17 November 1890, p. 4.
64. C.S. Parnell to Katharine O'Shea, 17 October 1880, reprinted in *Charles Stewart Parnell: His Love Story and Political Life*, I, p. 153. The envelope bearing the direction 'Mrs O'Shea, Charing X Post Office, Strand, London' is reproduced in the *Daily Sketch*, Tuesday 5 May 1914, p. 10, and accompanies the serialisation of Katharine's book, *Charles Stewart Parnell: His Love Story and Political Life*, published that year.
65. O'Connor notes that this was something of an obsession with Parnell: 'One of the first things he looked at in a man was whether his hair was in good condition', and he would survey the House of Commons, observing 'What a number of bald-headed men there are' (*Charles Stewart Parnell: A Memory*, London, Ward, Lock, Bowden & Co., 1891, pp. 105–6).
66. C.S. Parnell to Katharine O'Shea, 22 October 1880, reprinted in *Charles Stewart Parnell: His Love Story and Political Life*, I, p. 154.
67. *Ibid.*, 4 November 1880, I, p. 156.
68. *Ibid.*, 11 November 1880, I, p. 158.
69. *The Life of Charles Stewart Parnell, 1846–1891*, I, p. 258.
70. *Ibid.*, I, p. 252.
71. *Ibid.*, I, pp. 240–1; I, p. 248.
72. *Charles Stewart Parnell*, p. 133.

73.  *Charles Stewart Parnell: His Love Story and Political Life*, I, p. 161.
74.  C.S. Parnell to Katharine O'Shea, 2 December 1880, reprinted in *ibid.*, I, p. 158.
75.  *Ibid.*, 4 December 1880, I, p. 163.
76.  *Ibid.*, 9 and 12 December 1880, I, p. 164.
77.  *Ibid.*, I, p. 168.
78.  C.S. Parnell to Katharine O'Shea, 'Xmas Eve', *ibid.*, I, p. 227.
79.  *Ibid.*, 28 December 1880, I, p. 170.
80.  *Ibid.*, 30 December 1880.
81.  *Ibid.*, I, p. 168.
82.  *Ibid.*, I, p. 171.

## Chapter 3. Discovery

1.  *Charles Stewart Parnell: His Love Story and Political Life*, I, p. xi.
2.  *Ibid.*, I, p. 171. The Nationalist Daniel O'Connell (1775–1847), MP for County Clare and then Dublin, founded the Catholic Association (1823) and led the campaign for Catholic Emancipation.
3.  Quoted in *The Life of Charles Stewart Parnell, 1846–1891*, I, p. 266.
4.  *Ibid.*, I, p. 286.
5.  *Ibid.*, I, p. 269.
6.  *Memoirs of an Old Parliamentarian*, I, p. 151.
7.  *Charles Stewart Parnell: His Love Story and Political Life*, I, p. 173.
8.  *The Life of Charles Stewart Parnell, 1846–1891*, I, p. 270.
9.  *Charles Stewart Parnell: His Love Story and Political Life*, I, p. 174.
10.  *Ibid.*, II, p. 123; I, p. 143.
11.  *Ibid.*, II, pp. 123–4.
12.  *Ibid.*, I, p. 187.
13.  *Parnell and his Party*, p. 59.
14.  Parnell's open letter to the Land League, written from Paris, quoted in *ibid.*, p. 62.
15.  *Letters and Leaders of my Day*, I, p. 107.
16.  *Ibid.*, I, p. 110.
17.  *Charles Stewart Parnell: His Love Story and Political Life*, I, p. 165.
18.  *Ibid.*, I, p. 166.
19.  *Ibid.*, I, p. 167.
20.  *Ibid.*
21.  *Letters and Leaders of my Day*, I, p. 110.
22.  In his published memoirs, Healy calls the woman 'Lizzie from Blankshire', and says that his information comes from a friend of Biggar's who went to enquire after her ('Her needs were provided for, and she was told where to apply should she require further help') (*Letters and Leaders of my Day*, I, p. 110). Frank Callanan's research shows that Healy was more forthcoming in an early draft of his book, in which he identifies 'Lizzie' as a barmaid working at the Wellington Hotel, Manchester, which was run by the Barkers, an English Catholic and his Irish wife, a hotel at which Parnell was known to have stayed after the 1880 General Election (*T.M. Healy*, Cork, Cork University Press, 1992, pp. 52–3). While there is no reason to reject the possibility of an affair between Parnell and this woman, Healy's second-hand narrative is unconvincing.

23. Michael Davitt, *The Fall of Feudalism in Ireland; or The Story of the Land League Revolution*, London & New York, Harper & Brothers Publishers, 1904, p. 306.

24. Katharine states, 'some years before [the divorce case] certain members of the Party opened one of my letters to Parnell' (*Charles Stewart Parnell: His Love Story and Political Life*, II, p. 165).

25. *Letters and Leaders of my Day*, I, p. 110; *Memoirs of An Old Parliamentarian*, I, p. 226.

26. *Letters and Leaders of my Day*, I, p. 109.

27. *Ibid.*, I, p. 110.

28. C.S. Parnell to Katharine O'Shea, 27 February 1881, reprinted in *Charles Stewart Parnell: His Love Story and Political Life*, I, p. 179.

29. *Ibid.*, 1 March 1881, I, pp. 179–80.

30. *Ibid.*, 27 February 1881, I, p. 179.

31. *Ibid.*

32. See *Parnell Vindicated*, pp. 305–6.

33. *The Life of Charles Stewart Parnell, 1846–1891*, I, pp. 289–90. Lord Cowper informed the Cabinet of troops being faced by stone-throwing mobs. There was, he said, 'the danger of a sudden overwhelming, by sheer weight of numbers, of small bodies of police or military'. 'In a word, the policy of the Government was everywhere met with denunciation and defiance, the Land League remaining supreme' (*ibid.*, I, p. 286–7).

34. *Charles Stewart Parnell*, p. 157; *The Life of Charles Stewart Parnell, 1846–1891*, I, pp. 292–3.

35. Quoted in *Charles Stewart Parnell*, p. 158.

36. *Letters and Leaders of my Day*, I, p. 124.

37. *Memoirs of An Old Parliamentarian*, I, p. 232.

38. *The Times*, Tuesday 18 November 1890, p. 13. Jane Lennister does not appear on the census record for Wonersh Lodge, taken in April 1881, presumably because she had already gone down to Brighton to prepare rooms for Katharine and the children. In her evidence at the divorce trial she states clearly that she was sent on ahead to Brighton, 'and Mrs O'Shea followed in a few days afterwards' (*ibid.*).

39. C.S. Parnell to Katharine O'Shea, 14 February 1882, reprinted in *Charles Stewart Parnell: His Love Story and Political Life*, I, p. 236.

40. *Ibid.*, I, pp. 182–3.

41. *Ibid.*

42. *Ibid.*, I, p. 175.

43. *Ibid.*, I, pp. 174–5.

44. BL, Gladstone Papers, Add. MS 56446, ff. 69–72, W.H. O'Shea to W.E. Gladstone, 13 September 1880.

45. *Ibid.*, Add. MS 44269, ff. 7–10, 'Confidential Memo.', 10 June 1881, enclosed in letter of the same date from W.H. O'Shea to W.E. Gladstone.

46. A second letter followed on 13 June 1881, *ibid.*, ff. 11–12.

47. *The Times*, Monday 17 November 1890, p. 3.

48. *Charles Stewart Parnell: His Love Story and Political Life*, I, p. 189.

49. *The Times*, Monday 17 November 1890, p. 3.

50. *Charles Stewart Parnell: His Love Story and Political Life*, I, p. 132.

51. *Ibid.*

52. O'Shea supplied a more dramatic account at the divorce trial. Having returned to Wonersh Lodge with Anna on 14 July to settle things with Katharine, he then went back to town with his sister-in-law, 'taking with him the portmanteau, which he flung out at Charing Cross', a statement that met with laughter in the divorce court, *The Times*, Monday 17 November 1890, p. 3.

53. *Charles Stewart Parnell: His Love Story and Political Life*, I, p. 190.

54. *Parnell Vindicated*, p. 124.

55. *The Times*, Monday 17 November 1890, p. 3.

56. *Parnell Vindicated*, p. 141.

57. *The Uncrowned Queen of Ireland*, p. 81.

58. See *Parnell Vindicated*, pp. 223–4; *The Parnell Tragedy*, p. 163; F.S.L. Lyons, *The Fall of Parnell 1890–91*, London, Routledge & Kegan Paul, 1960, p. 44.

59. *The Times*, Monday 17 November 1890, p. 3.

60. *Ibid.*

61. *Charles Stewart Parnell: His Love Story and Political Life*, I, p. 190.

62. *Parnell Vindicated*, p. 125.

63. *Ibid.*, p. 170.

64. C.S. Parnell to Katharine O'Shea, 20 July 1881, reprinted in *Charles Stewart Parnell: His Love Story and Political Life*, I, p. 190.

65. *Ibid.*, 22 July 1881, I, p. 191.

66. *Ibid.*, 25 July 1881.

67. *The Times*, Monday 17 November 1890, p. 3.

68. *The Life of Charles Stewart Parnell, 1846–1891*, I, p. 303.

69. *Charles Stewart Parnell*, p. 161.

70. Quoted in *ibid.*, p. 166.

71. *Ibid.*, p. 167; *The Life of Charles Stewart Parnell, 1846–1891*, I, p. 309; p. 308; p. 310.

72. *Letters and Leaders of my Day*, I, p. 136.

73. C.S. Parnell to Katharine O'Shea, 10 September 1881, reprinted in *Charles Stewart Parnell: His Love Story and Political Life*, I, p. 200.

74. *Ibid.*, 17 August 1881, I, p. 199.

75. *The Times*, Tuesday 18 November 1890, p. 13. The dinner at the Shelbourne was mentioned by Sir Edward Clarke on the first day of the trial, *ibid.*, Monday 17 November 1890, p. 3.

76. C.S. Parnell to Katharine O'Shea, 7 October 1881, reprinted in *Charles Stewart Parnell: His Love Story and Political Life*, I, p. 201.

77. *Ibid.*, 8 October 1881, I, p. 202.

78. *Ibid.*, 11 October 1881.

79. *The Life of Charles Stewart Parnell, 1846–1891*, I, p. 308.

80. Quoted in *ibid.*, I, pp. 316–17.

## Chapter 4. Kilmainham Gaol

1. *Charles Stewart Parnell: His Love Story and Political Life*, I, p. 204. One such code they used was phrases from the ballad 'The Dowie Dens of Yarrow'. Katharine recalls one occasion where Parnell had sent her a coded telegram from Ireland telling her the

results of a particular party meeting but not saying how he was. She wired back, 'O gentle wind that bloweth south', and he replied, 'He fareth well' (*ibid.*, II, pp. 259–60).

2.  *Ibid.*, I, p. 205.
3.  *Letters and Leaders of my Day*, I, p. 138.
4.  *Charles Stewart Parnell: His Love Story and Political Life*, I, p. 206.
5.  *Ibid.*, I, p. 207. By 'reactionary', Katharine appears to mean reactive to the Irish political situation. There is a usage of reactionary in which 'reaction' is a movement towards the reversal of an existing tendency or state of things, especially in politics. Katharine uses this term later when referring to 'the reactionary spirit [Parnell's arrest] had let loose in Ireland' (*ibid.*, I, p. 255).
6.  *Ibid.*, I, p. 207.
7.  C.S. Parnell to Katharine O'Shea, 21 October 1881, reprinted in *ibid.*, I, p. 212.
8.  *Ibid.*, 13 October 1881, I, p. 207.
9.  *Ibid.*, 14 October 1881, I, p. 210.
10. *Ibid.*, 13 October 1881, I, p. 207.
11. *The Life of Charles Stewart Parnell, 1846–1891*, I, p. 319. The manifesto was drawn up by William O'Brien but inspired by Patrick Egan, and Patrick Ford, of the American newspaper, the *Irish World*. It has been suggested that Parnell and his colleagues countenanced the manifesto since it marked a way of giving ground to American extremists on a measure which they knew would fail in practice: 'It fell absolutely flat' (*ibid.*, I, p. 320).
12. C.S. Parnell to Katharine O'Shea, 21 October 1881, reprinted in *Charles Stewart Parnell: His Love Story and Political Life*, I, 213.
13. *Ibid.*, 14 October 1881, I, p. 210. Indeed, by the 1890s the room in which Parnell had been confined, spacious and comfortable as he described it, was being used as a warder's office. See Tighe Hopkins, *Kilmainham Memories*, London, Ward, Lock & Co. Ltd, 1896, photograph facing p. 25. I am very grateful to Niamh O'Sullivan for sharing this information with me.
14. *The Life of Charles Stewart Parnell, 1846–1891*, I, p. 334.
15. C.S. Parnell to Katharine O'Shea, 17 October 1881, reprinted in *Charles Stewart Parnell: His Love Story and Political Life*, I, p. 211.
16. William O'Brien, *Recollections*, London, Macmillan & Co., 1905, p. 387; *The Fall of Feudalism in Ireland*, p. 348.
17. C.S. Parnell to Katharine O'Shea, 3 December 1881, reprinted in *Charles Stewart Parnell: His Love Story and Political Life*, I, p. 223.
18. *Ibid.*, 5 November 1881, I, p. 217.
19. *Ibid.*, I, pp. 217–18.
20. *Charles Stewart Parnell*, p. 187.
21. *Charles Stewart Parnell: His Love Story and Political Life*, I, p. 210.
22. C.S. Parnell to Katharine O'Shea, 13 October 1881, reprinted in *ibid.*, I, p. 207.
23. *Ibid.*, I, p. 210.
24. *Ibid.*, 22 December 1881, I, p. 227; *ibid.*, 21 November 1881, I, p. 220.
25. *Ibid.*, 21 November 1881, I, p. 221.
26. *Ibid.*, 7 January 1881, I, p. 230 (emphasis added).
27. *Ibid.*, 11 January 1882, I, p. 231.
28. *Ibid.*, 14 November 1881, I, p. 219.
29. *Ibid.*, 19 October 1881, I, p. 212.

30. *Ibid.*, 1 November 1881, I, p. 214. The 'cage' was presumably a designated area where common prisoners could receive visitors under close observation. As a political prisoner allowed the freedom of Kilmainham, Parnell naturally regarded the imposition of the cage as an indignity not to be borne.
31. *Ibid.*, 2 November 1881, I, p. 216.
32. *Ibid.*, 21 October 1881, I, p. 212.
33. *Ibid.*, 5 November 1881, I, p. 216.
34. *Ibid.*, 21 October 1881, I, p. 222.
35. *Ibid.*, 5 November 1881, I, p. 218.
36. *Ibid.*, 3 December 1881, I, p. 222.
37. *Ibid.*, 14 October 1881, I, p. 211.
38. *Ibid.*, 5 November 1881, I, p. 218.
39. *Ibid.*,14 October 1881, I, p. 211.
40. A photograph of an envelope addressed to 'Mrs Carpenter' and bearing this direction was reproduced by the *Daily Sketch* to accompany its serialisation of Katharine's book, Tuesday 5 May 1914, p. 11.
41. *Charles Stewart Parnell: His Love Story and Political Life*, I, p. 223.
42. C.S. Parnell to Katharine O'Shea, 29 November 1881, *ibid.*, I, p. 221.
43. *Ibid.*, 'Thursday' [1 December 1881], I, p. 222.
44. *Ibid.*, 7 December 1881, I, p. 224.
45. *Ibid.*, 9 December 1881.
46. *Ibid.*, 17 January 1882, I, p. 231; *ibid.*, 28 January 1882, I, p. 233.
47. *Ibid.*, 21 October 1882, I, p. 213.
48. *Ibid.*, 9 December 1881, I, p. 224.
49. *Ibid.*, 2 November 1881, I, p. 216.
50. *Ibid.*, 12 November 1881, I, p. 218. There was also money left in the 'Parnell Defence Fund'. £21,000 had been raised at the time of the State Trials in late 1880.
51. *Ibid.*, 29 November 1881, I, p. 221.
52. *Ibid.*, 7 January 1882, I, p. 230.
53. In the light of Katharine's later accusations of adultery between her sister Anna and O'Shea, it may have been that bitterness between Katharine and her family stems from just this time. Later ill-feeling over Aunt Wood's will may also have been rooted in favours shown to the youngest niece from much earlier on.
54. C.S. Parnell to Katharine O'Shea, 23 January 1882, reprinted in *Charles Stewart Parnell: His Love Story and Political Life*, I, p. 232.
55. *Ibid.*, 14 December 1881, I, p. 225.
56. *Letters and Leaders of my Day*, I, p. 157.
57. C.S. Parnell to Katharine O'Shea, 14 February 1882, reprinted in *Charles Stewart Parnell: His Love Story and Political Life*, I, pp. 235–6. In fact, Parnell had often confided in McCarthy that he hated making speeches, and McCarthy was convinced that Parnell thought himself 'a very bad speaker' (*Reminiscences*, pp. 97–8).
58. C.S. Parnell to Katharine O'Shea, 15 December 1881, reprinted in *Charles Stewart Parnell: His Love Story and Political Life*, I, p. 226. The facsimile of this letter referred to by Tim Healy is printed in *ibid.*, I, between pp. 226 and 227.
59. *Ibid.*, 16 December 1881, I, p. 226.
60. *Ibid.*, 'Xmas Eve' [1881], I, p. 227.
61. *Ibid.* This is the quarrel referred to at the end of Ch. 2.

62. *Ibid.*, 11 January 1882, I, p. 230.
63. *Charles Stewart Parnell*, p. 177.
64. *Recollections*, p. 409; p. 415.
65. *Charles Stewart Parnell: His Love Story and Political Life*, I, p. 244.
66. C.S. Parnell to Katharine O'Shea, 30 December 1881, reprinted in *ibid.*, I, p. 228 (emphasis added).
67. *Ibid.*, 3 January 1882, I, p. 229.
68. *Ibid.*, 7 January 1882.
69. *Ibid.*, 17 February 1882, I, p. 237; *ibid.*, 16 March 1882, I, p. 238.
70. *Ibid.*, 17 February 1882, I, p. 237.
71. *Ibid.*
72. *Ibid.*, 5 March 1882.
73. *Ibid.*, 16 March 1882, I, p. 238.
74. *Ibid.*, 7 April 1882, I, p. 243.
75. *Ibid.*, 16 March 1882, I, p. 238.
76. *Ibid.*, I, p. 239.
77. *Ibid.*, 23 March 1882, I, p. 240.
78. *Ibid.*, 27 March 1882.
79. *Ibid.*, 29 March 1882.
80. *Ibid.*
81. *Ibid.*, 23 March 1882.
82. *Ibid.*, 27 March 1882.
83. *Ibid.*, 29 March 1882, I, p. 241.
84. *Ibid.*
85. *Ibid.*, 30 March 1882, I, p. 241.
86. *Ibid.*, I, p. 244.
87. C.S. Parnell to Katharine O'Shea, 16 March 1882, *ibid.*, I, p. 238.
88. *Ibid.*, 30 March 1882, I, p. 242.
89. *Ibid.*
90. C.S. Parnell to Katharine O'Shea, 5 April 1882, *ibid.*, I, p. 243.
91. *Ibid.*, I, p. 244.

## Chapter 5. The Kilmainham Treaty

1. *The Times*, Tuesday 11 April 1882, p. 9.
2. BL, Gladstone Papers, Add. MS 44279, ff. 18–25, W.H. O'Shea to W.E. Gladstone, *Private*, 13 April 1882.
3. *Charles Stewart Parnell: His Love Story and Political Life*, I, p. 245.
4. C.S. Parnell to Katharine O'Shea, 13 April 1882, reprinted in *Charles Stewart Parnell: His Love Story and Political Life*, I, p. 245; *ibid.*, 15 April 1882, I, p. 246.
5. BL, Gladstone Papers, Add. MS 44269, ff. 18–25, W.H. O'Shea to W.E. Gladstone, *Private*, 13 April 1882.
6. *Ibid.*, f. 27, W.E. Gladstone to W.H. O'Shea, 15 April 1882.
7. *The Life of Charles Stewart Parnell, 1846–1891*, I, p. 329; p. 335.
8. As Harrison notes, 'on his two "parole" visits to London Parnell went straightaway to Eltham as his headquarters. On neither occasion was Captain O'Shea there to begin

with . . . on the second [occasion] he actually summoned him to Eltham by telegram. On neither occasion was there the slightest concealment from Captain O'Shea. It was, thus, Captain O'Shea who came to Eltham to see Parnell' (*Parnell Vindicated*, pp. 310–11). O'Shea testified before the Special Commission that Parnell 'remained several days [at Eltham] before he went to Kilmainham' ( *ibid.*, p. 321). However, at the divorce trial, he claimed that 'On [Parnell's] return from Paris he stayed at the Grosvenor Hotel and then went back to Kilmainham' (*The Times*, Monday 17 November 1890, p. 4).

9.  *The Times*, Tuesday 11 April 1882, p. 9.
10. BL, Dilke Papers, Add. MS 43936, 1882 Diary of Sir Charles Dilke, p. 87.
11. Dudley W.R. Bahlman, ed., *The Diary of Sir Edward Walter Hamilton 1880–1885*, 2 vols, Oxford, Clarendon Press, 1972, I, p. 253.
12. *Charles Stewart Parnell: His Love Story and Political Life*, I, p. 247.
13. *Ibid.*, I, pp. 256–7.
14. *The History of the Irish Parliamentary Party*, II, p. 122. Conor Cruise O'Brien is also convinced by W.S. Blunt's belief that as early as April 1882 both husband and wife were communicating with the Government on Parnell's behalf (*Parnell and his Party*, p. 75).
15. *Letters and Leaders of my Day*, I, p. 163.
16. *Charles Stewart Parnell: His Love Story and Political Life*, I, p. 247.
17. *The Life of Joseph Chamberlain*, I, p. 353.
18. BL, Dilke Papers, Add. MS 43936, 1882 Diary of Sir Charles Dilke, p. 88.
19. NLI, O'Shea Papers, MS 5752, f. 74, W.H. O'Shea to C.S. Parnell, 24 April 1882.
20. *Ibid.*, f. 70, 24 April 1882.
21. *The Fall of Feudalism in Ireland*, p. 353; p. 350.
22. O'Shea's statement to the Commons, *The Times*, Tuesday 16 May 1882, p. 8.
23. Reprinted in *The Life of Charles Stewart Parnell 1846–1891*, I, p. 341.
24. The text of the memorandum entrusted to McCarthy is reprinted in *ibid.*, I, pp. 341–2.
25. Reprinted in *ibid.*, I, p. 342 (emphasis added).
26. NLI, O'Shea Papers, MS 5752, f. 70, W.H. O'Shea to C.S. Parnell, 24 April 1882. O'Shea writes that 'my agent [i.e. Chamberlain] meets with great difficulty about the money [Davitt's release] but is very clever and painstaking. If he should succeed I shall have to come to Ireland, which will give me the opportunity of paying you a visit very soon.' In this communication, too, O'Shea requests a letter of recommendation for 'my agent', who has an appointment with 'a person on Wed. [i.e. the Cabinet] whose support is important to me must now'.
27. *Ibid.*, f. 74, W.H. O'Shea to C.S. Parnell, 24 April 1882.
28. *Ibid.*, f. 90, W.H. O'Shea to Joseph Chamberlain, 25 April 1882.
29. C.S. Parnell to Katharine O'Shea, 25 April 1882, reprinted in *Charles Stewart Parnell: His Love Story and Political Life*, I, p. 253.
30. *Ibid.*, I, p. 248.
31. *Ibid.*, I, p. 253.
32. Reprinted in J.L. Hammond, *Gladstone and the Irish Nation*, London, Frank Cass & Co. Ltd, 1964 [1938], p. 275.
33. See *Parnell Vindicated*, pp. 341–3.
34. C.S. Parnell to Katharine O'Shea, 30 April 1882, reprinted in *Charles Stewart Parnell: His Love Story and Political Life*, I, p. 255.

35. O'Shea's evidence before the Special Commission, reprinted in *Parnell Vindicated*, p. 342.

36. Reprinted in *Charles Stewart Parnell: His Love Story and Political Life*, I, pp. 253–4. The text of the Kilmainham treaty has been widely reproduced. The original, in Parnell's handwriting, is located with Forster's letters to Gladstone, BL, Gladstone Papers, Add. MS 44160, f. 168. The complete text is given in the Appendix.

37. Katharine states that McCarthy's enclosure was 'identical with the draft treaty, apart from a few verbal alterations', *Charles Stewart Parnell: His Love Story and Political Life*, I, pp. 252–3.

38. Quoted in *The Life of Charles Stewart Parnell 1846–1891*, I, p. 340.

39. Captain O'Shea's letter to *The Times*, August 1888, reprinted in *Parnell Vindicated*, p. 379.

40. *The Life of Charles Stewart Parnell, 1846–1891*, II, p. 133.

41. BL, Gladstone Papers, Add. MS 44160, f. 156, W.E. Forster to W.E. Gladstone, 'Mem. Of my conversation with Capt. O'Shea on Sunday morning April 30, on his return from seeing Parnell in Kilmainham'.

42. Reprinted in *Charles Stewart Parnell: His Love Story and Political Life*, I, p. 254.

43. BL, Gladstone Papers, Add. MS 44160, f. 160, W.E. Gladstone to W.E. Forster, 30 April 1882.

44. *The Fall of Feudalism in Ireland*, p. 351.

45. W.H. O'Shea to Joseph Chamberlain, 1 May 1882, reprinted in *Charles Stewart Parnell: His Love Story and Political Life*, II, p. 195.

46. *The Life of Charles Stewart Parnell 1846–1891*, I, p. 351.

47. BL, Gladstone Papers, Add. MS 44269, ff. 32–3, W.H. O'Shea to W.E. Gladstone, *Private*, 3 May 1882. Chamberlain's name was mentioned in *The Times* as a likely successor to Forster on 3 and 4 May (see *Gladstone and the Irish Nation*, p. 281).

48. BL, Gladstone Papers, Add. MS 44269, ff. 34–5, W.H. O'Shea to W.E. Gladstone, 4 [May 1882].

49. W.E. Gladstone to Earl Spencer, 6 May 1882, quoted in *Charles Stewart Parnell*, p. 206.

50. BL, Gladstone Papers, Add. MS 56446, f. 73, 'Friday' [5 May 1882]; *ibid.*, Add. MS 44766, ff. 71–2, W.E. Gladstone to Earl Spencer, 5 May 1882.

51. *The Fall of Feudalism in Ireland*, p. 356.

52. *Ibid.*, p. 357.

53. *Ibid.*, p. 362.

54. *Ibid.*, p. 357.

55. *The Times*, Tuesday 9 May 1882, p. 6.

56. *Ibid.*, p. 8.

57. *Charles Stewart Parnell: His Love Story and Political Life*, I, pp. 262–3.

58. *Ibid.*, I, p. 363.

59. *Ibid.* In Frank Hugh O'Donnell's memoirs, published a few years before Katharine's, he claims that 'having sent Parnell hot foot to the Westminster Palace Hotel', Katharine herself went to Downing Street, where she convinced the Prime Minister that Parnell was horrified by the murders, almost as much as Gladstone himself: 'from her lips, from her tearful appeals, from her own high courage and exhortations not to yield to the awful blow', Gladstone apparently gathered the resolve to honour the terms of the Kilmainham treaty (*The History of the Parliamentary Party*, II, p. 123). It

is an indulgent bit of scene-painting, and seems to derive from a misinterpretation of a phrase uttered by Gladstone to R. Barry O'Brien in 1897. When Gladstone says that 'I had a communication from Mrs O'Shea about this time', he is in fact referring to the first letter she wrote him on 23 May 1882 (*The Life of Charles Stewart Parnell, 1846–1891*, II, p. 361).

60. *Ibid.*, I, p. 357.
61. *Letters and Leaders of my Day*, I, p. 159.
62. *Ibid.*
63. BL, Gladstone Papers, Add. MS 44269, f. 42, W.H. O'Shea to W.E. Gladstone, 7 May 1882.
64. *The Life of Charles Stewart Parnell 1846–1891*, II, p. 361.
65. BL, Gladstone Papers, Add. MS 44269, ff. 38–9, W.H. O'Shea to W.E. Gladstone, 7 May 1882.
66. *Ibid.*, f. 40, 7 May 1882.
67. O'Shea's testimony before the Special Commission, reprinted in *Parnell Vindicated*, p. 325.
68. A.G. Gardiner, *The Life of Sir William Harcourt*, London, Constable & Co. Ltd, 1923, I, p. 438. The news that Parnell feared for his life and sought protection from the British Government was mentioned in the company of five Liberal MPs sharing a railway carriage on the way to Cavendish's funeral, and duly appeared in the *Standard*, on Friday 12 May.
69. *Charles Stewart Parnell: His Love Story and Political Life*, II, p. 59.
70. *Ibid.*, II, p. 56. In 1883 the Government tried again to get Parnell to accept police protection. Parnell asked Katharine to keep his appointment with Howard Vincent, head of the Detective Department at Scotland Yard (who expressed 'great surprise at seeing me'), but she was firm that 'Mr Parnell would, I was sure, not like that at all', and, moreover, she made Vincent admit that there had been no specific threats made against Parnell in order to justify such protection (*ibid.*, II, p. 58).
71. *Ibid.*, II, p. 55.
72. *Our Book of Memories*, pp. 97–8.
73. See *Parnell Vindicated*, Appendix B, Part II, pp. 314–27, and *The Parnell Tragedy*, p. 179. Harrison analyses the inconsistencies between McCarthy's recollection of leaving Chamberlain's house with Parnell on foot, and O'Shea's statement to the Special Commission, in which he claimed that Parnell made the request for police protection to him personally while driving away from Chamberlain's house in a cab (a claim strongly denied by Parnell who was in attendance while O'Shea gave his testimony before the Commission). From this, Harrison deduces that O'Shea was deliberately lying in order to conceal the fact that he had himself asked for police protection for Wonersh Lodge because he was well aware that Parnell was living there with Katharine.
74. *Letters and Leaders of my Day*, I, p. 155.
75. *Charles Stewart Parnell: His Love Story and Political Life*, I, p. 263.
76. *Ibid.*, I, pp. 263–4.
77. According to Katharine's recollections, 'Parnell at last roused himself and said: "Well, I will write to the G.O.M. and offer to resign, and abide by his decision"', (*ibid.*, I, p. 264). This statement is seized upon by Harrison, rather excitably, because of its 'demonstrable falsity' (*Parnell Vindicated*, p. 233). It is, of course, perfectly possible that Parnell threatened to resign more than once that day. He did so again the following Tuesday.

78. *Charles Stewart Parnell: His Love Story and Political Life*, I, p. 264.
79. *Ibid.*, I, pp. 264–5.
80. *The Times*, Tuesday 9 May 1882, p. 8.
81. *Letters and Leaders of my Day*, I, p. 160.
82. *Recollections*, p. 435.
83. 'Miss Anna Parnell on Irish Affairs', *The Times*, Tuesday 9 May 1882, p. 6.
84. In Dublin on 4 June 1882, Anna walked out in front of Lord Spencer's horse and held him up while she protested against 'the forced stopping of building huts for tenants evicted near Limerick' (*Charles Stewart Parnell: The Man and his Family*, p. 275).
85. *The Times*, Tuesday 9 May 1882, p. 6.
86. BL, Gladstone Papers, Add. MS 44269, ff. 48–9, W.H. O'Shea to W.E. Gladstone, 13 May 1882.
87. *Ibid.*, ff. 44–5, W.H. O'Shea to W.E. Gladstone, 10 May 1882.
88. *The Life of Charles Stewart Parnell 1846–1891*, I, p. 359.
89. BL, Gladstone Papers, Add. MS 44269, ff. 46–7, W.H. O'Shea to W.E. Gladstone, 12 May 1882. Healy had called it 'a Bill to give hanging powers to three Judges on any evidence that might be trumped up before them', and he singled out Justice May as 'a man for whom the people of Ireland spilt their blood in the county of Clare 20 years ago, and who would doubtless reward them by spilling their blood at the command of the Government. (Murmurs.)' (*The Times*, Friday 16 May 1882, p. 8). The extract from his speech given in the text is reprinted in *T.M. Healy*, p. 74.
90. BL, Add. MS 44269, ff. 48–9, W.H. O'Shea to W.E. Gladstone, 13 May 1882.
91. *Ibid.*, f. 53, W.H. O'Shea to C.S. Lewis, 15 May 1882.
92. *Ibid.*, ff. 284–91, Katharine O'Shea to W.E. Gladstone, 30 January 1886.
93. *The Times*, Tuesday 16 May 1882, p. 7.
94. *Letters and Leaders of my Day*, I, p. 161.
95. *Charles Stewart Parnell: His Love Story and Political Life*, I, p. 266.
96. *Letters and Leaders of my Day*, I, p. 162. As Conor Cruise O'Brien has observed, the treaty was 'essentially a business-like recognition' of the current situation. Having won a decent Land Act, 'it would have been merely mischievous for politicians to go on stirring up the land agitation' (*Parnell and his Party*, p. 78; p. 77). However, Parnell's promise of close collaboration with the Liberal enemy was felt to be a betrayal of the cause.
97. *The Times*, Tuesday 16 May 1882, p. 7.
98. *Ibid.*, p. 8.
99. *Letters and Leaders of my Day*, I, p. 162.
100. *Hansard*, 15 May 1882, quoted in *Parnell Vindicated*, p. 354.
101. *The Times*, Tuesday 16 May 1882, p. 8.
102. *Ibid.*
103. *Ibid.*
104. *Parnell Vindicated*, p. 351.

## Chapter 6. Gladstone

1. BL, Gladstone Papers, Add. MS 44269, ff. 75–8, Katharine O'Shea to W.E. Gladstone, 23 May 1882.

2. *Memoirs of an Old Parliamentarian*, I, p. 231.
3. *The Diary of Sir Edward Walter Hamilton 1880–1885*, I, p. 290.
4. FCRO, Glynne Gladstone MSS, GG2165, Sir George Leveson Gower to Sir George H. Murray, 4 August 1934 (Murray's copy which he forwarded to Henry Neville Gladstone on 12 August 1934).
5. *Ibid.*
6. *Gladstone and the Irish Nation*, p. 670.
7. FCRO, Glynne Gladstone MSS, GG2165, Sir George Leveson Gower to Henry Neville Gladstone, 27 August 1934.
8. *Ibid.*, Sir George H. Murray to Henry Neville Gladstone, 8 August 1934.
9. *The Times*, Thursday 3 February 1927, p. 5. Herbert stated that the rumours 'hardly existed in 1882. They grew', and that he 'never heard any definite statement of that kind'. He even claimed that O'Shea reassured him 'that it was important that [his wife] should see Mr Gladstone. He told me . . . that she was a great friend of Parnell's.'
10. FCRO, Glynne Gladstone MSS, GG2165, Sir George H. Murray to Henry Neville Gladstone. From 8 August to 14 September, a total of twenty-four letters passed between Henry Neville Gladstone, Sir George Murray, Sir George Leveson Gower and a Mr Bassett, archivist in the Department of Manuscripts at the British Library. While Leveson Gower's recollections are weak on several points (he says that Katharine's letters referred to the Kilmainham negotiations, and he says also that the Dilke case was 'recent', when in fact that took place in 1885–6), his story does ring true and, to his credit, he held out, warning that if any statement were issued denying Gladstone's awareness of the strong rumours in circulation in 1882, 'I should be compelled to contradict it' (*ibid.*, Sir George Leveson Gower to Henry Neville Gladstone, 27 August 1934).
11. BL, Dilke Papers, Add. MS 43936, 1882 Diary of Sir Charles Dilke, pp. 110–11.
12. BL, Gladstone Papers, Add. MS 44174, f. 127, Lord Granville to W.E. Gladstone, 24 May 1882.
13. *The Life of Charles Stewart Parnell 1846–1891*, II, pp. 361–2.
14. BL, Gladstone Papers, Additional Unbound, Add. MS 56446, f. 69, W.H. O'Shea to W.E. Gladstone, 13 September 1880.
15. *Ibid.*, Add. MS 44269, ff. 79–80, W.E. Gladstone to Katharine O'Shea, 23 May 1882.
16. *Ibid.*, ff. 81–2, Katharine O'Shea to W.E. Gladstone, 26 May [1882], although a note on the reverse suggests that it was sent on 25 May.
17. *Ibid.*, f. 83, Katharine O'Shea to [John] A[rthur] Godley [Principal Private Secretary to Gladstone], 26 May 1882.
18. *Charles Stewart Parnell*, p. 224.
19. *Charles Stewart Parnell: His Love Story and Political Life*, I, pp. 269–70.
20. See BL, Gladstone Papers, Add. MS 44269, f. 86, W.E. Gladstone to Katharine O'Shea, *Private*, 16 June 1882; *Charles Stewart Parnell: His Love Story and Political Life*, I, p. 270.
21. *Ibid.*, I, p. 275.
22. BL, Gladstone Papers, Add. MS 44269, f. 86, W.E. Gladstone to Katharine O'Shea, *Private*, 16 June 1882.
23. *Charles Stewart Parnell: His Love Story and Political Life*, I, p. 270. In the preface to her book, Katharine also speaks of her 'many interviews with Mr Gladstone [as] Parnell's messenger' (*ibid.*, I, p. xi).

24. J.L. Hammond provides an appendix giving details of Katharine's correspondence with Gladstone in his *Gladstone and the Irish Nation*. See for example F.S.L. Lyons's assertion that Katharine's relationship with Gladstone 'was not so intense as she subsequently claimed' (*Charles Stewart Parnell*, p. 224). However, even Herbert Gladstone was forced to admit that his father 'might subsequently have seen her once or twice [i.e. after the three documented interviews], but I cannot say' (*The Times*, Thursday 3 February 1927, p. 5).

25. BL, Gladstone Papers, Add. MS 44269, ff. 84–5, Katharine O'Shea to W.E. Gladstone, 16 June [1882].

26. Dudley W.R. Bahlman, ed., *The Diary of Sir Edward Walter Hamilton 1885–1906*, Hull, The University of Hull Press, 1993, p. 138.

27. *The Diary of Sir Edward Walter Hamilton 1880–1885*, I, p. 290.

28. W.E. Gladstone to Lord Spencer, 26 September 1882, quoted in *Gladstone and the Irish Nation*, p. 670.

29. *The Life of Charles Stewart Parnell 1846–1891*, II, p. 362. To O'Brien's question, 'Had you any written communications with Mrs O'Shea?', Gladstone answered, 'No, I wrote her no letters of importance. I wrote her letters acknowledging hers . . . *But all my communications with her were oral, and all my communications with Parnell were oral* [emphasis added]. I received only one letter from him, the letter after the Phoenix Park murders.'

30. On 2 March 1885 O'Shea airily telegraphed Katharine a message to pass on to Gladstone 'If you see [him] today', while on Friday 1 May he reminded her that he expected to see her at Albert Mansions at the weekend, 'that is if you had not been to see Mr G. today' (*Charles Stewart Parnell: His Love Story and Political Life*, II, p. 205; II, p. 209).

31. This letter of 25 August 1886 appears to have been submitted as evidence in the divorce trial, but was not produced. An incomplete lawyer's longhand copy and complete shorthand copy survive in the O'Shea Papers held in the National Library of Ireland, MS 3882. The significance of the letter will be discussed in Ch. 9.

32. Interview with Katharine Parnell to advertise the serialisation of her book in the *Daily Sketch*, Tuesday 5 May 1914, p. 8. This formed the preface to the book.

33. *Charles Stewart Parnell: His Love Story and Political Life*, I, p. 270.

34. *Charles Stewart Parnell*, p. 225; p. 291.

35. *Ibid.*, p. 229.

36. BL, Gladstone Papers, Add. MS 44269, ff. 93–6, Katharine O'Shea to W.E. Gladstone, *Private*, 26 June [1882].

37. *Charles Stewart Parnell*, p. 229.

38. BL, Gladstone Papers, Add. MS 44269, ff. 99–102, Katharine O'Shea to W.E. Gladstone, 10 July [1882]; *ibid.*, ff. 104–5, 11 July [1882].

39. *Charles Stewart Parnell: His Love Story and Political Life*, I, p. 91.

40. *Ibid.*

41. *Ibid.*, I, p. 275.

42. W.H. O'Shea to Joseph Chamberlain, 25 May 1882, reprinted in *The Life of Joseph Chamberlain*, I, p. 372.

43. NLI, papers relating to Captain O'Shea, MS. 5752, f. 144, W.H. O'Shea to C.S. Parnell, 23 June 1882.

44. *The Life of Joseph Chamberlain*, I, p. 372.

45. *Ibid.*, I, p. 373.

46. Parnell did so not only through Katharine. He also talked to Henry Labouchère, who, on the very day that O'Shea complained to Parnell about his obstructive tactics, wrote to Lord Richard Grosvenor to assure him that 'Kilmainham seems entirely to have changed him . . . You have therefore in dealing with Parnell, to deal with a man, who is very reasonable, and who is most desirous to join hands with the Liberals' (BL, Gladstone Papers, Add. MS 44315, f. 76, Henry Labouchère to Lord R. Grosvenor, n.d. Friday [likely to be 23 June 1882]).

47. *The Life of Charles Stewart Parnell 1846–1891*, II, p. 362.

48. *Charles Stewart Parnell: His Love Story and Political Life*, II, p. 196.

49. W.H. O'Shea to Katharine O'Shea, 26 August 1882, reprinted in *ibid.*, II, pp. 196–7.

50. *Ibid.*, 31 August 1882, II, p. 197.

51. Undated letter from W.H. O'Shea to Katharine O'Shea, reprinted in *ibid.* Henry Fawcett (1833–84) was appointed Postmaster-General in Gladstone's second administration, 1880. John Morley (1838–1923) was editor of the *Pall Mall Gazette* from 1880 to 1883, when he was elected Liberal MP for Newcastle-upon-Tyne; appointed Chief Secretary for Ireland in 1886.

52. C.S. Parnell to Katharine O'Shea, 20 August 1882, *ibid.*, II, p. 51.

53. *The Diary of Sir Edward Walter Hamilton 1880–1885*, I, p. 327.

54. *Ibid.*

55. *Charles Stewart Parnell: His Love Story and Political Life*, I, p. 274.

56. *Ibid.*

57. Herbert J. Gladstone, *After Thirty Years*, London, Macmillan & Co. Ltd, 1928, p. 301. A year before his book was published, Herbert was involved in a libel case brought by a Mr Peter Wright, whose book *Portraits and Criticisms* claimed that Gladstone had known of Parnell's relations with Mrs O'Shea from the very beginning. Herbert won the case, but he provoked laughter in the court when he admitted that he had examined the proportions of his father's study 'by the permission of the Office of Works', and concluded that 'all that could have happened was that Mr Gladstone and Mrs O'Shea walked arm-in-arm round the table' (*The Times*, Thursday 3 February 1927, p. 5).

58. *Charles Stewart Parnell*, p. 227.

59. BL, Gladstone Papers, Add. MS 44269, ff. 121–2, Katharine O'Shea to W.E. Gladstone, 22 September [1882].

60. *Charles Stewart Parnell: His Love Story and Political Life*, I, p. 273.

61. *Charles Stewart Parnell: The Man and His Family*, p. 282.

62. *Charles Stewart Parnell: His Love Story and Political Life*, II, p. 44.

63. Jane McL.Côtée, *Fanny & Anna Parnell: Ireland's Patriot Sisters*, Basingstoke, Macmillan, 1991, p. 225; see *Charles Stewart Parnell: The Man and His Family*, pp. 280–3, for Foster's account of Parnell's break with Anna.

64. *Charles Stewart Parnell: His Love Story and Political Life*, II, p. 45.

65. BL, Gladstone Papers, Add. MS 44269, ff. 124–5, Katharine O'Shea to W.E. Gladstone, *Private*, 6 October [1882].

66. *The Life of Charles Stewart Parnell 1846–1891*, I, p. 370; I, pp. 369–70.

67. C.S. Parnell to Katharine O'Shea, 17 October [1882], reprinted in *Charles Stewart Parnell: His Love Story and Political Life*, II, p. 53.

68. *Ibid.*, 10 October 1882, II, p. 52.

69. BL, Gladstone Papers, Add. MS 44269, ff. 137–8, Katharine O'Shea to W.E. Gladstone, *Private*, 20 October 1882.

70. C.S. Parnell to Katharine O'Shea, Friday evening, [13/] 14 October 1882, and Sunday, n.d. [it is possible that this second, undated, letter is in fact from 1883], reprinted in *Charles Stewart Parnell: His Love Story and Political Life*, II, p. 52; p. 53.

71. BL, Gladstone Papers, Add. MS 44269, ff. 139–40, C.S. Parnell to Katharine O'Shea, 15 October 1882; *ibid.*, f. 141, 16 October 1882.

72. *Charles Stewart Parnell: His Love Story and Political Life*, I, p. 270.

73. Quoted in BL, Gladstone Papers, Add. MS 44315, f. 95, Horace Seymour to Lord R. Grosvenor, 24 November 1882.

74. Quoted in *Gladstone and the Irish Nation*, pp. 308–11.

75. Gladstone's letter to Lord Spencer of 25 September is quoted in *ibid.*, p. 308.

76. BL, Gladstone Papers, Add. MS 44269, ff. 132–3, W.E. Gladstone to Katharine O'Shea, *Private*, 7 October 1882.

77. *Ibid.*, ff. 145–6, Katharine O'Shea to W.E. Gladstone, 2 November [1882].

78. On 24 November 1882 one of Gladstone's private secretaries, Horace Seymour, forwarded a memorandum from the Prime Minister to Lord Richard Grosvenor, asking him to remind Mrs O'Shea of the request made on 7 October that she direct any correspondence to Grosvenor himself (*ibid.*, Add. MS 44315, ff. 95–6).

79. *Ibid.*, ff. 151–2, n.d. Wednesday [8 November 1882]. Katharine writes on House of Commons Library notepaper.

80. *Ibid.*, Add. MS 44315, f. 94, Lord R. Grosvenor to Katharine O'Shea, *Private*, 8 November 1882.

81. *The Diary of Sir Edward Walter Hamilton 1880–1885*, I, p. 327.

82. *Gladstone and the Irish Nation*, p. 670. It is also the case that on occasion her personal representation of O'Shea and Parnell overlapped. For instance, on Tuesday 12 September, she wrote to Gladstone, no doubt prompted by her husband, to renew the appeal against Francis Hymer's death sentence, but also, on behalf of Parnell, to appeal against that of another of those sentenced for murder, a man named Walsh, 'who I am told is *known* not to have been guilty'. The letter goes on to describe Parnell's wider concern that the policy of Coercion had failed in Ireland, its administration serving only to increase distrust, unrest and hostility towards the Government: it made any understanding on the lines of the Kilmainham agreement unworkable (BL, Gladstone Papers, Add. MS 44269, ff. 108–13, *Private*, Katharine O'Shea to W.E. Gladstone, 12 September [1882]).

83. *Ibid.*, Add. MS 44766, f. 134, Memorandum as to Appointment for Captain O'Shea, 3 November 1882 (Granville and colonial secretary Lord Kimberley acknowledged their receipt of the memo that day, Harcourt and Spencer on 4 November).

84. *Ibid.*, Add. MS 44315, ff. 86–7, Lord R. Grosvenor to W.E. Gladstone, 3 September 1882.

85. *Ibid.*, Add. MS 44269, ff. 114–15, Katharine O'Shea to W.E. Gladstone, 15 September [1882].

86. *Ibid.*, f. 116, W.H. O'Shea to Katharine O'Shea, 13 September [1882].

87. O'Shea's telegram ran thus: 'I should be glad to accept believing that notwithstanding difficulties might be useful there' (*ibid.*, f. 118, 15 September 1882).

88. W.H. O'Shea to Katharine O'Shea, 29 September 1882, reprinted in *Charles Stewart Parnell: His Love Story and Political Life*, II, p. 198. (It is just possible that O'Shea

refers instead to Gladstone's referral of the Francis Hymer case to Lord Spencer, since Katharine had forwarded her husband's views both on this question and the Under-Secretaryship in mid-September 1882.)

89. Spencer's letter of 31 August is quoted in *Gladstone and the Irish Nation*, p. 307.
90. W.H. O'Shea to Katharine O'Shea, 17 October 1882, reprinted in *Charles Stewart Parnell: His Love Story and Political Life*, II, p. 199.
91. BL, Gladstone Papers, Add. MS 44269, f. 143, Katharine O'Shea to W.E. Gladstone, 30 October [1882].
92. See W.H. O'Shea to Katharine O'Shea, 31 March 1882, reprinted in *Charles Stewart Parnell: His Love Story and Political Life*, II, p. 194.
93. NLI, papers relating to Captain O'Shea, MS 5752, f. 23, Katharine O'Shea to W.H. O'Shea, n.d. 'Sunday'.
94. W.H. O'Shea to Katharine O'Shea, 1 May 1882, reprinted in *Charles Stewart Parnell: His Love Story and Political Life*, II, p. 195.
95. *Ibid.*, 29 September, II, p. 198; *ibid.*, 20 July 1882, II, p. 195.
96. *Ibid.*, 20 July 1882, II, p. 195.
97. *Ibid.*, 29 September 1882, II, p. 198.
98. UBL, Joseph Chamberlain Papers, JC8/8/1/166, W.H. O'Shea to Joseph Chamberlain, 30 March 1892.
99. *Parnell Vindicated*, pp. 191–2.
100. UBL, Joseph Chamberlain Papers, JC8/8/1/166, W.H. O'Shea to Joseph Chamberlain, 30 March 1892.
101. *Parnell Vindicated*, p. 192.
102. NLI, MS 35,982, W.H. O'Shea Papers, Katharine O'Shea to W.H. O'Shea, Good Friday, 9 [8] April 1887.
103. There is anecdotal evidence that O'Shea tried to persuade political colleagues that, despite living separately from his wife, marital relations were kept up and that he had fathered both Clare and Katie. Both T.P. O'Connor and Healy were told a story by Labouchère (although O'Connor hesitated to repeat a story emanating from such a source) that O'Shea had told him 'that Mrs O'Shea used to pay him occasional visits at Albert Mansions and – I need not be more precise, but suggest the humiliating and shameful compromises which married women who have a lover sometimes have to submit to' (*Memoirs of an Old Parliamentarian*, II, p. 229). Healy was more precise about the implications of this story: 'he told Labouchère that whenever Kitty came up to his flat in Victoria Street she insisted on renewing old relations, and he swears he will keep Clare on this account' (*Letters and Leaders of my Day*, I, p. 333). Of O'Shea, Labouchère, Healy and O'Connor, only O'Connor could be regarded as an entirely reliable witness, and he expressed reservations about his source.
104. *Parnell Vindicated*, pp. 102–3.


## Chapter 7. The Lost Years

1. *The Times*, Friday 9 March 1883, p. 1.
2. *Memoirs of an Old Parliamentarian*, I, p. 228.
3. *Ibid.*
4. *Freeman's Journal*, Thursday 13 March 1883, p. 3.

5. BL, Gladstone Papers, Add. MS 44269, f. 171, Katharine O'Shea to W.E. Gladstone, 13 March [1883]. Katharine did not receive a reply from Sir Richard Grosvenor until Friday 16 March, by which time it was too late to give her any answer of consequence.

6. *The Times*, Monday 17 November 1890, p. 4.

7. *Ibid.*

8. KGM, Parnell Papers, IE14 01, Certificate of Baptism for Clare Gabrielle Antoinette Marcia Esperance O'Shea. In 1881 O'Shea petitioned Gladstone on behalf of his 'friend and kinsman', the Baronet Sir George O'Donnell (spelt variously as O'Donnell or O'Donell), to use his old family title of Tyrconell (see BL, Gladstone Papers, Add. MS 44269, ff. 1–2, 5 April 1881; ff. 13–14, 5 August 1881). A letter from her sister-in-law Mary O'Shea, which Katharine reprints in her book, refers to Lady O'Donnell having seen Claude Sophie at Eltham before she died (*Charles Stewart Parnell: His Love Story and Political Life*, I, p. 248).

9. *The Times*, Monday 17 November 1890, p. 4. The testimony of Harriet Bull which follows is also taken from this page.

10. The term is Lyons's. See *Charles Stewart Parnell*, p. 238.

11. *Ibid.*, p. 252.

12. *Letters and Leaders of my Day*, I, pp. 191–2.

13. *Ibid.*, I, p. 190.

14. The telegram appears to have been held back by Small, only to resurface two years later (see p. 245, n. 90).

15. C.S. Parnell to Katharine O'Shea, n.d. [*c.* 3 July 1883], reprinted in *Charles Stewart Parnell: His Love Story and Political Life*, II, p. 65.

16. *Ibid.*, n.d. [*c.* second week of July 1883].

17. Parnell wrote to Katharine in the early hours of 4 July 1883 asking her to forward an enclosure for her husband since he had not got O'Shea's address in Ireland and wanted to arrange a meeting with him in West Clare (*ibid.*).

18. BL, Gladstone Papers, Add. MS 44269, ff. 186–212, Katharine O'Shea to W.E. Gladstone, 19 June [1883].

19. *Ibid.*, ff. 188–91, memo in Parnell's hand: 'Heads of a Bill for the Reclamation and Improvement of land in Ireland, and for the Resettlement of the population of certain districts.'

20. *Ibid.*, Add. MS 44315, f. 123, Sir R. Grosvenor to Katharine O'Shea, 21 July 1883 (Grosvenor's copy).

21. *Charles Stewart Parnell*, p. 264.

22. '(1) A married woman shall, in accordance with the provisions of this Act, be capable of acquiring, holding, and disposing by will or otherwise, of any real or personal property as her separate property, and in the same manner as if she were a feme sole [i.e. a single woman], without the intervention of any trustee. (2) A married woman shall be capable of entering into and rendering herself liable in respect of and to the extent of her separate property on any contract . . . in all respects as if she were a feme sole' (Married Women's Property Act, 1882 (45 & 46 Vict., c 75), 18 August 1882, reprinted in Lee Holcombe, *Wives and Property: Reform of the Married Women's Property Law in Nineteenth-Century England*, Toronto & Buffalo, University of Toronto Press, 1983, p. 247).

23. *Charles Stewart Parnell: His Love Story and Political Life*, II, p. 66.

24. *The Times*, Monday 17 November 1890, p. 4.

25. *Ibid.*

26. Katharine's own account at first seems to support her husband's. She claims that the two men discussed the Local Government Bill at Medina Terrace 'at all hours'. She is mistaken here. O'Shea did not communicate with Parnell about this particular bill, a project of Chamberlain's, until November 1884 (see *Charles Stewart Parnell: His Love Story and Political Life*, II, p. 66). O'Shea wrote to Chamberlain from 8 Medina Terrace on 8 December 1883. While he makes reference to a conversation he has had with Parnell, he does not say that Parnell has been staying with him (UBL, Joseph Chamberlain Papers, JC8/8/1/20).
27. *Ibid.*
28. *Charles Stewart Parnell: His Love Story and Political Life*, II, p. 67.
29. *The Times*, Monday 17 November 1890, p. 4.
30. *Ibid.*
31. *Parnell Vindicated*, p. 141.
32. *The Times*, Monday 17 November 1890, p. 4.
33. *Charles Stewart Parnell*, p. 241.
34. See *Parnell Vindicated*, pp. 296–7.
35. *Ibid.*, pp. 301–2.
36. *Ibid.*, p. 302; p. 299.
37. *Ibid.*, p. 300.
38. *The Times*, Tuesday 18 November 1890, p. 14.
39. *Parnell Vindicated*, p. 141.
40. *Memoirs of an Old Parliamentarian*, II, p. 277.
41. *Charles Stewart Parnell: His Love Story and Political Life*, II, p. 68.
42. See *The Times*, Monday 17 November 1890, p. 4. Sir Edward Clarke also states that 'In March 1884, Captain O'Shea had to leave England' (*ibid.*, p. 3).
43. *Ibid.*, p. 4.
44. W.H. O'Shea to C.S. Parnell, 4 August 1884, reprinted in *ibid.*, p. 3.
45. *Charles Stewart Parnell*, p. 242.
46. Katharine O'Shea to W.H. O'Shea, 7 August 1884, reprinted in *The Times*, Monday 17 November 1890, p. 3.
47. C.S. Parnell to W.H. O'Shea, 7 August 1884, reprinted in *ibid.*
48. *Ibid.*, 24 December 1884.
49. *The Times*, Monday 17 November 1890, p. 4. In the 1891 census return Katharine's youngest daughter is listed as Katie O'Shea.
50. *Charles Stewart Parnell: His Love Story and Political Life*, II, p. 70.
51. C.S. Parnell to Katharine O'Shea, Friday 28 October 1884, reprinted in *ibid.*, II, p. 69.
52. *Parnell Vindicated*, p. 236.
53. Two undated letters from C.S. Parnell to Katharine O'Shea, *Charles Stewart Parnell: His Love Story and Political Life*, II, p. 70; II p. 71.
54. *Ibid*, II, p. 70; II, p. 71.
55. *Ibid*, I, p. 192.
56. C.S. Parnell to Katharine O'Shea, 14 January 1885, *ibid.*, II, p. 75.
57. *Ibid.*, 3 February 1885.
58. *Ibid.* In fact, the station master at Pope Street (New Eltham) Station was subpoenaed as a witness at the divorce trial in order to establish the dates at which Parnell's horses arrived at Eltham (see NLI, MS 21,679, Acc. 3418, Subpoena and Correspondence re. W.A. Howlett and Parnell Divorce Case).

59. Katharine registered Katie's birth on 11 February 1885.

60. W.H. O'Shea to Katharine O'Shea, n.d. [appears to refer to the forming of the Salisbury government after 9 June 1885], reprinted in *Charles Stewart Parnell: His Love Story and Political Life*, II, p. 204.

61. *Ibid.*, n.d. 'Wednesday 1 a.m.' [possibly Wednesday 7 January 1885], II, p. 202.

62. *Ibid.*, II, p. 66.

63. Memorandum in O'Shea's hand, dated 27 November 1884, reprinted in *The Life of Joseph Chamberlain*, I, p. 578.

64. Joseph Chamberlain to John Morley, 21 January 1885, reprinted in *ibid.*, I, p. 587.

65. C.S. Parnell to W.H. O'Shea, 5 January 1885, reprinted in C.H.D. Howard, 'Documents Relating to the Irish "Central Board" Scheme, 1884–5', *Irish Historical Studies*, 8/31 (March 1953), p. 242.

66. W.H. O'Shea to Katharine O'Shea, n.d. [*c.* early March 1885], reprinted in *Charles Stewart Parnell: His Love Story and Political Life*, II, p. 206. As T.P. O'Connor has explained, the post 'carried a considerable salary', and would have 'given him considerable power and position – in short, it was just the kind of thing he would regard himself as especially fitted for and as especially fitted for him' (*Memoirs of an Old Parliamentarian*, II, p. 108).

67. W.H. O'Shea to C.S. Parnell, 18 January 1885, reprinted in *The Life of Joseph Chamberlain*, I, p. 585.

68. Parnell was in Ireland from 6 January, arriving back in Liverpool on 3 February. It is therefore likely that he composed this draft bill at Eltham before he left the country – at the same time that he wrote his first cautionary letter to O'Shea.

69. BL, Gladstone Papers, Add. MS 44316, f. 14, Sir R. Grosvenor to Katharine O'Shea, 14 July 1885 (Grosvenor's copy). Strangely, Katharine's letter and typed enclosure, or indeed any acknowledgement of their receipt, have not survived in the Gladstone Papers. In her book, Katharine refers to a 'non-committal acknowledgement of the receipt' she received from Sir Richard Grosvenor as late as 11 May 1884 (*Charles Stewart Parnell: His Love Story and Political Life*, II, p. 20).

70. C.H.D. Howard, 'Joseph Chamberlain, Parnell and the Irish "central board" scheme, 1884–5', *Irish Historical Studies*, 8/32 (September 1953), p. 337.

71. W.H. O'Shea to Katharine O'Shea, 19 January 1885, reprinted in *Charles Stewart Parnell: His Love Story and Political Life*, II, p. 204.

72. *Ibid.*, 17 March 1885, II, p. 206. This was O'Shea's memorandum, 'Local self-government in Ireland', which he drew up on 14 January 1885.

73. See 'Joseph Chamberlain, Parnell and the Irish "Central Board" Scheme, 1884–5', p. 340.

74. Earl Spencer to Joseph Chamberlain, 26 April 1885, reprinted in 'Documents Relating to the Irish "Central Board" Scheme, 1884–5', p. 258. For a detailed history of the local government negotiations, see the first chapter of Alan O'Day's study, *Parnell and the First Home Rule Episode 1884–87*, Dublin, Gill and Macmillan, 1986.

75. Dilke recorded Manning setting out his position thus: 'The bishops and clergy would be prepared to denounce, not only separation, but also an Irish Parliament' (cited in *Charles Stewart Parnell*, p. 272).

76. W.H. O'Shea to Katharine O'Shea, 10 April 1885, reprinted in *Charles Stewart Parnell: His Love Story and Political Life*, II, p. 208.

77. Joseph Chamberlain's diary, 28 April 1885, reprinted in *The Life of Joseph Chamberlain*, I, p. 600.

78. W.H. O'Shea's diary, 30 April 1885, reprinted in *ibid.*, I, p. 601.
79. W.H. O'Shea to Katharine O'Shea, 1 May 1885, reprinted in *Charles Stewart Parnell: His Love Story and Political Life*, II, p. 209.
80. *Ibid.*, 8 May 1885, II, p. 210.
81. *Ibid.*, 4 May 1885, II, p. 209.
82. *Ibid.*, 1 May 1885.
83. *Ibid.*, 4 May 1885.
84. *Ibid.*, 8 May 1885, II, p. 210.
85. In fact, Dilke, taking Chamberlain with him, resigned over Gladstone's announcement on 20 May that the Government would introduce an Irish land-purchase bill that Session, since they 'regarded this as a wrong order of priorities' (see *Charles Stewart Parnell*, p. 274). Shaw Lefevre, who 'had really been opposed to coercion all along', was strengthened by the action of his Cabinet colleagues and resigned the next day (see 'Joseph Chamberlain, Parnell and the Irish "Central Board" Scheme, 1884–5', p. 352).
86. *Letters and Leaders of my Day*, I, p. 209.
87. *Ibid.*, I, pp. 209–10. R. Barry O'Brien gives the margin as fourteen votes (*The Life of Charles Stewart Parnell 1846–1891*, II, p. 47), Healy twelve.

## Chapter 8. The Price of Silence

1. *Memoirs of an Old Parliamentarian*, II, p. 6; C.S. Parnell to Katharine O'Shea, 23 October 1885, reprinted in *Charles Stewart Parnell: His Love Story and Political Life*, II, p. 86.
2. W.H. O'Shea to Katharine O'Shea, 8 November 1885, *ibid.*, II, p. 92.
3. The full text of the pledge is reprinted in *Memoirs of an Old Parliamentarian*, II, p. 4.
4. BL, Gladstone Papers, Add. MS 44269, ff. 73–4, W.H. O'Shea to W.E. Gladstone, *Confidential*, 23 October 1885.
5. The *United Ireland* cutting sent O'Shea by Chamberlain is reprinted in *Charles Stewart Parnell: His Love Story and Political Life*, II, p. 212.
6. W.H. O'Shea to Joseph Chamberlain, 'Monday, 5 a.m.' [29 June 1885], reprinted in *The Life of Joseph Chamberlain*, II, p. 20.
7. Joseph Chamberlain to W.H. O'Shea, *Private*, 11 July 1885, *ibid.*, II, p. 22.
8. Chamberlain's 'Memorandum', *ibid.*, II, p. 25; W.H. O'Shea to Joseph Chamberlain, 13 July 1885, *ibid.*, II, p. 24.
9. W.H. O'Shea to Katharine O'Shea, 'Tuesday' [14 July 1885], reprinted in *Charles Stewart Parnell: His Love Story and Political Life*, II, p. 213.
10. *Ibid.*
11. *Ibid.*, 'Wednesday' [15 July 1885].
12. *The Times*, Tuesday 18 November 1890, p. 13.
13. BL, Gladstone Papers, Add. MS 44316, f. 18, Katharine O'Shea to Lord R. Grosvenor, 21 July [1885]. Curiously, Gladstone's secretary Sir Edward Hamilton notes in his diary that as early as Monday 20 July the Prime Minister was informed that 'Parnell has thrown over the Central Board scheme, and declines to accept such a scheme as even a partial solution of the Local Government question' (*The Diary of Sir Edward Walter Hamilton 1885–1906*, p. 1).

14. *Ibid.*
15. BL, Gladstone Papers, Add. MS 44316, f. 20, Lord R. Grosvenor to Katharine O'Shea, *Private*, 23 July 1885 (Grosvenor's copy). See also his letter to Katharine of 28 July, *ibid.*, f. 21.
16. *The Diary of Sir Edward Hamilton 1885–1906*, p. 1.
17. BL, Gladstone Papers, Add. MS 56446, ff. 78–83, *Private*, Katharine O'Shea to W.E. Gladstone, 5 August 1885.
18. *Charles Stewart Parnell: His Love Story and Political Life*, II, p. 112. Katharine provides a transcript of 'A Proposed Constitution for Ireland' in her biography of Parnell (*ibid.*, II, pp. 18–20), yet, confusingly, she appears to mistake it for Parnell's earlier local government scheme and states that she sent it in 'the early part of the year' (i.e. January 1884), *ibid.*, II, p. 18. The original paper, like Parnell's draft local government bill, appears not to have survived in the Gladstone Papers.
19. BL, Gladstone Papers, Add. MS 44269, f. 225, W.E. Gladstone to Katharine O'Shea, *Private*, 8 August 1885 (Gladstone's copy).
20. *The Diary of Sir Edward Hamilton 1885–1906*, p. 2.
21. BL, Gladstone Papers, Add. MS 44316, f. 42, Lord R. Grosvenor to W.E. Gladstone, 6 October 1885.
22. *The Diary of Sir Edward Walter Hamilton 1885–1906*, p. 6.
23. BL, Gladstone Papers, Add. MS 44269, ff. 226–9, Katharine O'Shea to W.E. Gladstone, *Private*, 23 October 1885. See also the virtually identical letter she sent to Grosvenor on the same date, Add. MS 44316, ff. 63–8.
24. *Ibid.*, Add. MS 44316, ff. 75–6, W.E. Gladstone to Lord R. Grosvenor, 27 October 1885.
25. *Ibid.*, Add. MS 44269, f. 232, *Private*, Katharine O'Shea to W.E. Gladstone, 30 October 1885.
26. *Ibid.*, f. 236, W.E. Gladstone to Lord R. Grosvenor, n.d. [*c.* 3 November 1885] (copy of letter drafted at Hawarden Castle, not in Gladstone's hand).
27. *Charles Stewart Parnell: His Love Story and Political Life*, II, p. 97.
28. *Letters and Leaders of my Day*, I, p. 215.
29. W.H. O'Shea to Katharine O'Shea, 25 October 1885, reprinted in *Charles Stewart Parnell: His Love Story and Political Life*, II, p. 89. Not only had the Secretary of the Ulster Liberal Association, Dr Wyllie, been for some time the accepted candidate, but the Ulster Liberals were so taken with Parnell's proposal regarding the Nationalist vote that they told O'Shea they 'wanted South Tyrone thrown in' – an added complication since William O'Brien was the Nationalist candidate there (BL, Gladstone Papers, Add. MS 44316, f. 70, W.H. O'Shea to Lord R. Grosvenor, *Private*, 25 October 1885).
30. *Ibid.*, ff. 77–8, Lord R. Grosvenor to W.E. Gladstone, 28 October 1885.
31. *Ibid.*, ff. 82–3, Samuel Walker to Lord R. Grosvenor, 31 October 1885.
32. *Ibid.*, f. 84, 1 November 1885.
33. NLI, MS 5752, Papers relating to Captain O'Shea, ff. 246, W.H. O'Shea to C.S. Parnell, 2 November 1885 (Captain O'Shea's copy).
34. W.H. O'Shea to Katharine O'Shea, 8 November 1885, reprinted in *Charles Stewart Parnell: His Love Story and Political Life*, II, p. 92.
35. *Ibid.*, 2 November 1885, II, p. 90.
36. *Memoirs of an Old Parliamentarian*, II, p. 7.
37. W.H. O'Shea to Joseph Chamberlain, 8 November 1885, reprinted in *The Life of Joseph Chamberlain*, II, p. 117.

38. *Charles Stewart Parnell: His Love Story and Political Life*, II, p. 96.
39. Katharine O'Shea to W.H. O'Shea, 14 November 1885, reprinted in *ibid.*, II, p. 93.
40. *Ibid.*, II, p. 94.
41. *Ibid.*, II, p. 95.
42. BL, Gladstone Papers, Add. MS 44316, f. 111, W.E. Gladstone to Lord R. Grosvenor, 18 November 1885.
43. *Charles Stewart Parnell: His Love Story and Political Life*, II, p. 95.
44. W.H. O'Shea to Katharine O'Shea, 20 November 1885, reprinted in *ibid.*, II, p. 97.
45. *Ibid.*
46. *Ibid.*, II, p. 99.
47. *Ibid.*, II, p. 98.
48. BL, Gladstone Papers, Add. MS 56448, ff. 52–5, Edward R. Russell (Editor of the *Liverpool Post*) to W.E. Gladstone, *Secret*, 22 November 1890.
49. *Liverpool Courier*, Monday 23 November 1885, p. 5.
50. *The Times*, Monday 23 November 1885, p. 11.
51. *Ibid.*, Tuesday 24 November 1885, p. 7.
52. *Liverpool Courier*, Thursday 26 November 1885, p. 5; *The Times*, Thursday 26 November 1885, p. 8; *Memoirs of an Old Parliamentarian*, II, p. 7.
53. *Ibid.*, II, p. 10.
54. *Ibid.*
55. *Charles Stewart Parnell: His Love Story and Political Life*, II, p. 103.
56. *Ibid.*, II, p. 85.
57. BL, Gladstone Papers, Add. MS 44316, f. 128, Katharine O'Shea to Lord R. Grosvenor, *Private*, 4 December 1885.
58. *Ibid.*, Add. MS 44269, ff. 237–40, Katharine O'Shea to W.E. Gladstone, *Private*, 10 December 1885.
59. *Ibid.*, ff. 241–2, W.E. Gladstone to Katharine O'Shea, *Private & Confidential*, 12 December 1885 (Gladstone's copy).
60. See *Charles Stewart Parnell: His Love Story and Political Life*, II, p. 27. The transcription of the complete letter is reprinted on p. 26, and continued on pp. 28–9.
61. *Ibid.*, II, pp. 28–9. The original letter is in BL, Gladstone Papers, Add. MS 44269, ff. 247–8.
62. BL, Gladstone Papers, Add. MS 56446, ff. 182–3, Lord R. Grosvenor to W.E. Gladstone, 14 December 1885.
63. *Ibid.*, Add. MS 44269, ff. 249–50, W.E. Gladstone to Katharine O'Shea, 16 December 1885 (Gladstone's copy).
64. *Ibid.*, ff. 256–7, W.E. Gladstone to Katharine O'Shea, *Private & Confidential*, 19 December 1885 (Gladstone's copy).
65. On 4 July, soon after forming their interim Government, the Conservatives had decided not to renew the expiring Coercion Act (see *Charles Stewart Parnell*, p. 283).
66. BL, Gladstone Papers, Add. MS 44269, ff. 260–5, *Private*, Katharine O'Shea to W.E. Gladstone, 23 December 1885.
67. *Ibid.*, ff. 268–9, enclosure in Gladstone's hand, sent with his letter to Katharine on 24 December 1885, *Private & Confidential*, ff. 266–7.
68. W.H. O'Shea to Katharine O'Shea, 22 December 1885, reprinted in *Charles Stewart Parnell: His Love Story and Political Life*, II, p. 214.

69. The only other reference to O'Shea's mother being in London is in Katharine's telegraph to O'Shea (then staying at the Shelbourne Hotel, Dublin) on 4 November, in which she informs him that she is about to take the children up to town to see their grandmother (*ibid.*, II, p. 91).

70. NLI, MS 3882, Katharine O'Shea to W.H. O'Shea, 25 August 1886 (transcription of shorthand copy, provided by Susan Henry).

71. BL, Gladstone Papers, Add. MS 44269, ff. 270–2, Katharine O'Shea to W.E. Gladstone, *Private*, 29 December 1885.

72. Katharine refers to a memorandum sent by Gladstone on 31 December in which he refused to pledge the Liberals to a non-return of Coercion in Ireland, but a copy of this communication has not survived in the Gladstone Papers (*Charles Stewart Parnell: His Love Story and Political Life*, II, p. 31).

73. C.S. Parnell to Katharine O'Shea, n.d. [*c.* first week of January 1886], reprinted in *ibid.*, II, p. 32 (again, a copy of the original enclosure and Katharine's covering letter have not survived in the Gladstone Papers).

74. BL, Gladstone Papers, Add. MS 44269, ff. 280–3, Katharine O'Shea to W.E. Gladstone, *Private*, 23 January 1886.

75. *Ibid.*, Add. MS 44269, ff. 284–91, *Private*, 30 January 1886 (Katharine reproduces a much-shortened version of this letter in *Charles Stewart Parnell: His Love Story and Political Life*, II, pp. 33–4).

76. *Ibid.*

77. Joseph Chamberlain to W.H. O'Shea, *Private*, 22 January 1886, *ibid.*, II, p. 234.

78. *Ibid.*, II, p. 104.

79. *Ibid.*, II, p. 105.

80. *Ibid.*, II, p. 106.

81. *Charles Stewart Parnell*, p. 324.

82. *Charles Stewart Parnell: His Love Story and Political Life*, II, p. 107.

83. *Ibid.*

84. *Memoirs of an Old Parliamentarian*, II, p. 94.

85. T.P. O'Connor to T.M. Healy, 5 February 1886, reprinted in *Letters and Leaders of my Day*, I, p. 239.

86. *Ibid.*, I, pp. 239–40.

87. *Ibid.*, I, p. 240.

88. *Ibid.*, I, p. 241.

89. 'He has always had some mysterious affinity to Captain O'Shea', observed the *Liverpool Courier*, Tuesday 24 November 1885, p. 4.

90. Memorandum by John Muldoon, formerly a reporter on *The Galway Vindicator*, n.d., cited in *Parnell and his Party*, p. 179. There was similar trouble at the Louth constituency, where Parnell opposed the candidacy of one of the Nationalist MPs, Philip Callan, who was reported to have asked Parnell what there was in O'Shea's 'political character or private history' that was 'superior to that of Phil Callan and his wife' (*Charles Stewart Parnell*, pp. 306–7). Callan is supposed to have seen a copy of the telegram opened at Monaghan in 1883.

91. Joseph Biggar to Frank Hugh O'Donnell, 3 March 1886, reprinted in *The History of the Irish Parliamentary Party*, p. 289.

92. W.H. O'Shea to His Grace the Primate of All Ireland, Armagh, 10 March 1891, reprinted in *Charles Stewart Parnell: His Love Story and Political Life*, II, p. 230.

93. *Letters and Leaders of my Day*, I, p. 241.

94. W.H. O'Shea to His Grace the Primate of All Ireland, Armagh, 10 March 1891, reprinted in *Charles Stewart Parnell: His Love Story and Political Life*, II, p. 230.

95. *Memoirs of an Old Parliamentarian*, II, p. 101.

96. Reprinted in *Letters and Leaders of my Day*, I, p. 244.

97. *Liverpool Courier*, Wednesday 25 November 1885, p. 5; *Freeman's Journal*, Monday 8 February 1886, p. 7. Healy asked the crowds assembled in Eyre Square, 'If the Government went wrong would you expect O'Shea to bark? (laughter).'

98. Reprinted in *Letters and Leaders of my Day*, I, p. 243.

99. *Ibid.*

100. *Ibid.*

101. *Freeman's Journal*, Wednesday 10 February 1886, cited in *Parnell and his Party*, p. 181.

102. *Memoirs of an Old Parliamentarian* II, p. 99.

103. *Freeman's Journal*, Wednesday 10 February 1886, p. 6.

104. *Charles Stewart Parnell*, p. 331.

105. Parnell claimed that he had won the leadership contest by a mere two votes, one of them O'Shea's, whereas in fact he had won by five votes.

106. *Freeman's Journal*, Thursday 11 February 1886, p. 5.

107. *Ibid.*, Friday 12 February 1886, p. 5.

108. *Memoirs of an Old Parliamentarian*, II, p. 106.

109. William O'Brien, *Evening Memories*, Dublin and London, Maunsel & Co., 1920, p. 105.

## Chapter 9. Scandal

1. *Charles Stewart Parnell*, p. 333.

2. *The Times*, Monday 17 November 1890, p. 4.

3. *Ibid.*

4. *Evening News and Post*, Saturday 28 December 1889, p. 3. Tim Healy is the only commentator to notice that the original 'writ assigned the dates of his wife's misconduct to occasions after the Galway election', which he interpreted as a deliberate measure on O'Shea's part to evade accusations that Galway was the price of his collusion in the affair (*Letters and Leaders of my Day*, I, p. 241).

5. NLI, MS 3882, W.H. O'Shea to Katharine O'Shea, 23 April 1886 (shorthand copy transcribed by Susan Henry).

6. *Ibid.*

7. *The History of the Irish Parliamentary Party*, p. 296.

8. BL, Gladstone Papers, Add. MS 56446, ff. 98–103, Katharine O'Shea to W.E. Gladstone, *Private*, 16 April [1886].

9. *Ibid.*

10. *Charles Stewart Parnell: His Love Story and Political Life*, II, p. 37. It was the case that, as Katharine explained to Gladstone, she delayed sending her husband's message, even though 'Captain O'Shea's unfortunate position admits of no delay', until eight days after the Home Rule Bill was introduced on 8 April 1886 (BL, Gladstone Papers, Add. MS 56446, ff. 98–103, Katharine O'Shea to W.E. Gladstone, *Private*, 16 April [1886]).

11. *Ibid.*, Add. MS 44269, f. 299, W.E. Gladstone to Katharine O'Shea, *Secret*, 18 March 1886.

12. *Ibid.*, Add. MS 56446, ff. 92–5, Katharine O'Shea to W.E. Gladstone, *Secret*, 25 March 1886.

13. Already there seems to have been a rather suspect attempt to bring about a meeting. A lady named Mrs Rae who, according to Katharine, 'haunted the ladies' gallery of the House of Commons, and whom I and Mr Parnell were not always successful in avoiding' (*Charles Stewart Parnell: His Love Story and Political Life*, II, p. 37), asked Parnell to come up to the gallery and told him that Gladstone wished to meet him at the house of a Mrs Tennant. Parnell took little notice of this, but Gladstone was thankful to Katharine for having warned him of the matter, BL, Gladstone Papers, MS 44269, W.E. Gladstone to Katharine O'Shea, *Secret*, 18 March 1886 (Gladstone's copy).

14. *Ibid.*, ff. 293–6, Katharine O'Shea to W.E. Gladstone, *Private*, 16 March 1886.

15. *The Life of William Ewart Gladstone*, III, p. 231.

16. *Letters and Leaders of my Day*, I, p. 251.

17. *Charles Stewart Parnell*, p. 344. See pp. 343–6 for a discussion of the terms of the first Home Rule Bill.

18. *Ibid.*, p. 345.

19. BL, Gladstone Papers, Add. MS 44269, ff. 300–1, Downing Street telegram to Katharine O'Shea, marked *Urgent*, 8 May 1886.

20. *Ibid.*, f. 302, Katharine O'Shea to Mr Primrose, 8 May 1886 (the telegram was sent at 2.37 p.m.).

21. *Charles Stewart Parnell*, p. 346.

22. *Ibid.*, p. 345.

23. *The Times*, Wednesday 9 June 1886, p. 7.

24. *Letters and Leaders of my Day*, I, p. 258.

25. *Evening Memories*, p. 105.

26. NLI, Papers relating to Captain O'Shea, MS 5752, f. 312, James O'Kelly to W.H. O'Shea, 8 June 1886.

27. *Ibid.*, f. 318, W.H. O'Shea to James O'Kelly, 12 August 1886.

28. On 10 October 1886, O'Shea had written to Katharine that 'one of the effects of [your name] having been [in the newspapers] has been to end my public life' (reprinted in *The Times*, Monday 17 November 1890, p. 3).

29. 'Mr Parnell's Suburban Retreat', *Pall Mall Gazette*, Saturday 24 May 1886, p. 8.

30. See Jane Jordan, *Josephine Butler*, London, John Murray, 2001, pp. 222–30.

31. *Pall Mall Gazette*, Thursday 9 July 1885, p. 3.

32. *Memoirs of an Old Parliamentarian*, II, pp. 201–2.

33. *The Times*, Monday 17 November 1890, p. 4.

34. *Ibid.*, p. 3. (Parnell's letter is also from this source.)

35. *Ibid.*

36. *Ibid.*, p. 4.

37. *Ibid.*, Tuesday 18 November 1890, p. 13.

38. *Pall Mall Gazette*, Saturday 21 May 1886, p. 5.

39. *The Times*, Monday 17 November 1890, p. 4.

40. *Ibid.*, p. 3.

41. *Ibid.*, Tuesday 18 November 1890, p. 13. Lupton believed that it was in May that Parnell first called on him to enquire about the property.

42. *Charles Stewart Parnell*, p. 342.
43. *The Times*, Tuesday 18 November 1890, p. 13.
44. *Ibid.*
45. *Ibid.* The cab driver Samuel Lupton was able to produce his account book in which he had recorded the dates he had been hired to take Parnell to the station, 10 and 16 June 1886, and those occasions on which he had taken Parnell and Mrs O'Shea, 25 June and 6, 13 and 25 July, *Evening News*, Monday 17 November 1890, p. 4.
46. *Charles Stewart Parnell: His Love Story and Political Life*, II, p. 108.
47. *Ibid.*, II, p. 109.
48. *Ibid.*, II, pp. 110–11.
49. *Ibid.*
50. *Ibid.*, II, p. 109.
51. *Ibid.*
52. *The Times*, Monday 17 November 1890, p. 3.
53. *Ibid.*, Tuesday 18 November 1890, p. 13.
54. *Spectator*, 27 June 1891, p. 879.
55. *Ibid.*
56. BL, Gladstone Papers, Add. MS 44269, ff. 305–7, Katharine O'Shea to W.E. Gladstone, 14 July 1886. Katharine sent a second enclosure from Parnell on 16 July.
57. *Charles Stewart Parnell: His Love Story and Political Life*, II, p. 119.
58. *The Times*, Tuesday 18 November 1886, p. 13.
59. W.H. O'Shea to Katharine O'Shea, 20 August 1886, reprinted in *The Times*, Monday 17 November 1890, p. 3,
60. NLI, MS 3882, Katharine O'Shea to W.H. O'Shea, 25 August 1886 (longhand copy).
61. *Ibid.* (transcription of shorthand copy, provided by Susan Henry).
62. Mary Lyndon Shanley, *Feminism, Marriage, and the Law in Victorian England, 1850–1895*, Princeton, Princeton University Press, 1989, p. 45. This was a radical reform of ecclesiastical law which had demanded that the absent spouse return home or face imprisonment. See also *Wives and Property*, p. 99.
63. *Ibid.*, p. 105.
64. NLI, MS 3882, Katharine O'Shea to W.H. O'Shea, 25 August 1886 (shorthand copy transcribed by Susan Henry).
65. *Feminism, Marriage, and the Law in Victorian England, 1850–1895*, p. 132.
66. *Ibid.*
67. W.H. O'Shea to Katharine O'Shea, 13 September 1886, reprinted in *The Times*, Monday 17 November 1890, p. 3.
68. *Ibid.*, Tuesday 18 November 1890, p. 13.
69. NLI, MS 3882, Katharine O'Shea to W.H. O'Shea, 25 August 1886 (shorthand copy transcribed by Susan Henry).
70. *The Times*, Tuesday 18 November 1890, p. 13.
71. *Ibid.*, Monday 17 November 1890, p. 3.
72. *Ibid.*
73. *Sussex Daily News*, Thursday 30 September 1886, p. 5.
74. Henry Parnell (1850–1915) married in 1882 and lived largely at various resorts on the south-east coast. Roy Foster calls him 'the most absentee of landlords', whose earlier land speculations had brought his brother into disrepute in 1875 and again in 1880 (see *Charles Stewart Parnell: The Man and His Family*, pp. 222–4).

75. *The Times*, Monday 17 November 1890, p. 3. Katharine's undated letter was written in response to her husband's communication of 4 October 1886. The paragraph to which O'Shea took objection has not been identified. On 30 September, 1 and 5 October, the *Sussex Daily News* carried three short announcements to the effect that Parnell planned to winter at Eastbourne with his mother.

76. *The Times*, Monday 17 November 1890, p. 3.

77. Katharine O'Shea to W.H. O'Shea, n.d. [9 October 1886], reprinted in *ibid*.

78. *Ibid*.

79. W.H. O'Shea to Katharine O'Shea, 10 October 1886, *ibid*.

80. *The Life of Charles Stewart Parnell 1846–1891*, II, p. 160.

81. *Ibid*., II, p. 169.

82. *Parnell and his Party*, p. 201.

83. Quoted in *ibid*.

84. Quoted in *ibid*., p. 202.

85. As R. Barry O'Brien describes it, 'Evictions were multiplied, peasants and police were brought into collision, and the old feeling of hatred and mistrust between rulers and ruled was kept painfully alive. Ireland was once more a prey to lawlessness upon one side and to arbitrary authority on the other' (*The Life of Charles Stewart Parnell, 1846–1891*, II, p. 173).

86. Lyons notes Alfred Robbins's diagnosis at the time (*Charles Stewart Parnell*, p. 378).

87. *Pall Mall Gazette*, Wednesday 22 December 1886, p. 4.

88. Parnell's speech to the Eighty Club (8 May 1888), reprinted in *Charles Stewart Parnell: His Love Story and Political Life*, II, p. 114.

89. *Ibid*., II, p. 115.

90. *The Life of Charles Stewart Parnell 1846–1891*, II, p. 161.

91. *Charles Stewart Parnell: His Love Story and Political Life*, II, p. 116.

92. See Sally Warwick-Haller, *William O'Brien and the Land War*, Dublin, Irish Academic Press, 1990, pp. 87–90.

93. *Evening Memories*, p. 177.

94. *Charles Stewart Parnell: His Love Story and Political Life*, II, p. 114.

95. John Morley, *The Life of William Ewart Gladstone*, 3 vols, London, Macmillan & Co., 1903, III, p. 280; *Evening Memories*, pp. 177–8.

96. *Ibid*. There is, apparently, no supporting evidence of Katharine's claim of O'Brien's second visit to her house (conversation with Dr Philip Bull, 3 July 2004, Chester University). It is, though, quite possible that Parnell trusted O'Brien to be discreet about his visit to Eltham. O'Brien was the only colleague to whom Parnell disclosed details of Katharine's marriage to O'Shea (see Ch. 11).

97. *Charles Stewart Parnell: His Love Story and Political Life*, II, p. 115.

98. *Ibid*., II, p. 218.

99. Katharine O'Shea to W.H. O'Shea, 'Sunday, December', n.d. [likely to be 12 December 1886], reprinted in *ibid*.

100. W.H. O'Shea to Katharine O'Shea, 12 December 1886, *ibid*.

101. *The Times*, Monday 17 November 1890, p. 3. James Mace (1831–1910) was the last surviving representative of the old prize ring.

102. *Pall Mall Gazette*, Saturday 18 December 1886, p. 9.

103. See the *Observer*, Sunday 19 December 1886, p. 5, and the *Pall Mall Gazette*, Monday 20 December 1886, p. 9.

104. W.H. O'Shea to W.T. Stead, 19 December 1886, reprinted in *Charles Stewart Parnell: His Love Story and Political Life*, II, p. 219.
105. *Pall Mall Gazette*, Monday 20 December 1886, p. 1.
106. W.T. Stead, 'The Discrowned King of Ireland, With Some Opinions of the Press on the O'Shea Divorce Case', London, *Review of Reviews*, 1890, p. 12.
107. Stead offered a more detailed account of their interview in *Review of Reviews*, December 1890, p. 599.
108. *Pall Mall Gazette*, Wednesday 22 December 1886, p. 4.

## Chapter 10. Breaking Point

1. *The Times*, Tuesday 18 November 1890, p. 13.
2. *Charles Stewart Parnell: His Love Story and Political Life*, II, p. 125.
3. *Ibid.*
4. *St Stephen's Review*, 26 February 1887, p. 7.
5. *The Times*, Monday 17 November 1890, p. 4.
6. *Charles Stewart Parnell: His Love Story and Political Life*, II, p. 125.
7. Mr William Henry Hedges stated at the divorce trial that he first received enquiries about the tenancy from Mrs O'Shea in February of that year, while Katharine herself states that she took the house in March because 'there had been various annoying happenings owing to new reports of his life at Eltham having been put about' (*Charles Stewart Parnell: His Love Story and Political Life*, II, p. 124). If Katharine enquired about the property before the publication of the two notices in *St Stephen's Review*, her seeking a new address for Parnell far away from south-east London was timely.
8. *The Times*, Tuesday 18 November 1890, p. 13.
9. *Charles Stewart Parnell: His Love Story and Political Life*, II, pp. 124–5.
10. *Ibid.*, II, p. 125.
11. *The Times*, Tuesday 18 November 1890, p. 13.
12. *Charles Stewart Parnell: His Love Story and Political Life*, II, p. 125.
13. *Ibid.*, II, p. 126.
14. *Ibid.*, II, p. 127.
15. *Ibid.*, II, p. 126.
16. NLI, MS 35,982, W.H. O'Shea Papers, will made by A.M. Wood on 7 April 1887 (copy), witnessed by two of her servants, Ezra Willsher, footman, and Rosa Aldridge, housemaid.
17. UBL, Joseph Chamberlain Papers, JC8/8/1/127, W.H. O'Shea to Joseph Chamberlain, 13 October 1889.
18. KGM, Parnell Papers, IE13 06, Gerard O'Shea to Dr Bertram Maunsell, 27 January 1923.
19. NLI, MS 35,982, W.H. O'Shea Papers, Katharine O'Shea to W.H. O'Shea (copy), 'Good Friday', 9 [actually 8] April 1887.
20. *Ibid.*, order for £300 for Mr W.H. O'Shea made out by Anna Maria Wood on 12 April 1887.
21. *Ibid.*, Gerard O'Shea to W.H. O'Shea, 13 April 1887. This letter was read out at the divorce trial (see *The Times*, Monday 17 November 1890, p. 4).
22. UBL, Joseph Chamberlain Papers, JC8/8/1/115, W.H. O'Shea to Joseph Chamberlain, 3 November 1888.

23. *The Times*, Monday 17 November 1890, p. 4.

24. NLI, MS 35,982, W.H. O'Shea Papers, Katharine O'Shea to W.H. O'Shea (copy), 14 April 1887.

25. *Ibid.*, 17 April 1887.

26. *Ibid.*, extract from Captain O'Shea's Diary (copy), Sunday 17 April 1887.

27. *Ibid.*, W.H. O'Shea to Katharine O'Shea (copy), 17 April 1887.

28. *Ibid.*, Katharine O'Shea to W.H. O'Shea (copy), n.d. Although Katharine's letter refers to the February issue of *St Stephen's Review*, there is strong evidence to suggest that she is writing to her husband on 17 April, since she refers both to her aunt's codicil and to her brother Charles's visit on the morrow and he is known to have called at the Lodge on 18 April.

29. *Ibid.*, unknown writer [likely to be Horatio N. Pym] to C.P. Wood (copy), 24 March 1887. The contents of this letter suggest strongly that Charles Wood's correspondent is Pym. We also know that Katharine telegraphed Pym on 22 April asking him to call on her aunt the next day.

30. *Ibid.*

31. *Ibid.*, Hitchens Harrison & Co. to Mrs A.M. Wood (copy), 6 April 1887. At this time her bonds were valued at £90,220.

32. *Ibid.*, unknown writer [likely to be Horatio N. Pym] to C.P. Wood (copy), 24 March 1887.

33. *Ibid.*, extract from Mr C.P. Wood's Diary (copy), 8 April 1887

34. *Ibid.*, H. Wilkinson to unknown recipient [likely to be C.P. Wood] (copy), n.d.

35. *Ibid.*, Katharine O'Shea to W.H. O'Shea (copy of telegram), sent 9.27 a.m., n.d. [18 April 1887]. To O'Shea's immediate reply, she telegraphed again at 11.15 to repeat her message: 'cannot go before he leaves' (*ibid.*).

36. *Ibid.*, Katharine O'Shea to W.H. O'Shea (copy), n.d. [likely to be 17 April 1887].

37. *Ibid.*, extract from Sir Henry Evelyn Wood's Diary (copy), Wednesday 27 April 1887.

38. *Ibid.*, extracts from Mr C.P. Wood's Diary (copy), Monday 9 May 1887.

39. *The Times*, Monday 18 April 1887, p. 8.

40. *Charles Stewart Parnell: His Love Story and Political Life*, II, p. 129.

41. *Ibid.*, II, p. 130.

42. *The Times*, 7 March 1887, p. 8. In her account of Parnell's reaction to the publication of the forged letter in *The Times* of Monday 18 April 1887, Katharine appears to conflate these two days. She says, mistakenly, that the forged letter appeared on 7 March 1887, and then states that on the day that the letter was published, Parnell 'got home before I did that evening', whereas it is on record that he made a speech to the House at one o'clock in the morning (see *Charles Stewart Parnell: His Love Story and Political Life*, II, pp. 129–31).

43. *Charles Stewart Parnell*, p. 368.

44. *Ibid.*, p. 371.

45. *Letters and Leaders of my Day*, I, p. 271.

46. *The Life of Charles Stewart Parnell 1846–1891*, II, pp. 199–200.

47. *Our Book of Memories*, p. 107.

48. *Ibid.*, p. 108.

49. *Ibid.*, p. 117.

50. NLI, MS 35,982, W.H. O'Shea Papers, extract from Captain O'Shea's Diary (copy), Monday 18 April 1887.

51. *Ibid.*, Katharine O'Shea to W.H. O'Shea (copy of telegram), n.d. [19 April 1887].

52. *Ibid.*, extract from Captain O'Shea's Diary (copy), Tuesday 19 April 1887.

53. *Ibid.*

54. *Ibid.*, H.N. Pym to W.H. O'Shea (copy), 22 April 1887. The full letter, including the closing reference to Gerard, was produced at the divorce trial (*The Times*, Monday 17 November 1890, p. 4).

55. *Ibid.*, W.H. O'Shea to H.N. Pym (copy), 22 April 1887.

56. *Ibid.*, second letter sent by W.H. O'Shea to H.N. Pym (copy), 22 April 1887.

57. *Ibid.*, H.N. Pym to W.H. O'Shea (copy), 25 April 1887.

58. *Ibid.*, W.H. O'Shea to C.S. Parnell (copy), 29 April 1887.

59. *Ibid.*, Katharine O'Shea to W.H. O'Shea (copies of 2 telegrams), 9 a.m. and 9.15 a.m., 2 June 1887.

60. The solicitor Peter Williams had been recommended to O'Shea by Katharine's own solicitor, Horatio Pym. Pym had assured O'Shea that if Williams would act for him they would avoid 'any future chance of friction' (*ibid.*, H.N. Pym to W.H. O'Shea, n.d. [22 April 1887] (O'Shea's copy)).

61. KGM, Parnell Papers, IE13 06, Gerard O'Shea to Dr Bertram Maunsell, 27 January 1923.

62. *The Times*, Monday 17 November 1890, p. 4. O'Shea testified that, at the time of the first *Pall Mall Gazette* story of May 26 1886, 'I knew nothing about the horses being at Eltham. I first heard about them in June of the following year, when my son told me about them.'

63. UBL, Joseph Chamberlain Papers, JC8/8/1/128, enclosure sent by O'Shea with his letter to Chamberlain of 13 October 1889.

64. *The Times*, Monday 17 November 1890, p. 4.

65. *Ibid.*

66. O'Shea later told W.T. Stead that, since his interview with Stead of 20 December 1886, 'I determined to put her under observation' (*Review of Reviews*, December 1890, p. 600).

67. *The Times*, Monday 17 November 1890, p. 4.

68. *Ibid.*, Saturday 26 November 1887, p. 9.

69. See C.S. Parnell to Katharine O'Shea, 4 January 1888, reprinted in *Charles Stewart Parnell: His Love Story and Political Life*, II, p. 133; *Parnell Vindicated*, p. 108.

70. Principal Registry of the Family Division, Probate Department, the last will and testament of Anna Maria Wood, 7 March 1888.

71. A surviving letter of Katharine's to Gladstone, dated 13 April 1888, suggests as much (BL, Gladstone Papers, Add. MS 44503, ff. 159–63). In 1892, Clark, Gladstone's physician for twenty-five years past, was required to give Sir Edward Hamilton confirmation of Gladstone being of sound mind after concerns were raised by Cabinet Ministers about his becoming 'confused and feeble'. See *Gladstone*, p. 585.

72. BL, Gladstone Papers, Add. MS 44503, ff. 159–63, Katharine O'Shea to W.E. Gladstone, 13 April 1888.

73. *Ibid.*

74. *Ibid.*, ff. 157–8, C.S. Parnell to W.E. Gladstone, *Private*, 13 April 1888.

75. UBL, Joseph Chamberlain Papers, JC8/8/1/161, 'In the Matter of Anna Maria Wood a supposed person of unsound mind', report submitted by Sir Andrew Clark, sworn on 17 April and filed on 20 April 1888, which O'Shea showed to Chamberlain in February 1891.

76. This took some time, however. Fearing that the proceedings were still to go ahead, Katharine wrote again to Gladstone on 1 May, this time to beg that he would urge Sir Charles Russell to take on the case: 'all the happiness that my Aunt has in life depends on the favourable issue of this case' (BL, Gladstone Papers, Add. MS 44269, ff. 310–12, Katharine O'Shea to W.E. Gladstone, 1 May 1888).

77. Quoted in *Charles Stewart Parnell*, p. 391.

78. *Our Book of Memories*, p. 158.

79. *Ibid.*, p. 102.

80. O'Shea also offered an extraordinary account of his visit to Kilmainham Gaol in April 1882: 'I stood over Mr Parnell as he signed his surrender'. The full transcript of O'Shea's letter to *The Times*, 2 August 1888, is published in *Parnell Vindicated*, pp. 378–80.

81. *Charles Stewart Parnell: His Love Story and Political Life*, II, p. 136.

82. *Ibid.*, II, p. 137.

83. UBL, Joseph Chamberlain Papers, JC8/8/1/114, W.H. O'Shea to Joseph Chamberlain, 1 November 1888.

84. Alfred Robbins, *Parnell, The Last Five Years: Told from Within*, London, Thornton Butterworth Ltd, 1926, p. 67.

85. *Memoirs of an Old Parliamentarian*, II, p. 146.

86. *Parnell, The Last Five Years*, p. 68.

87. *Memoirs of an Old Parliamentarian*, II, pp. 146–7.

88. *The Life of Joseph Chamberlain*, II, p. 394.

89. *Parnell, The Last Five Years*, p. 68.

90. See *Letters and Leaders of my Day*, I, pp. 287–94, for Healy's account of this.

91. T.M. Healy to Maurice Healy, 31 October 1888, reprinted in *Letters and Leaders of my Day*, I, p. 300.

92. *Parnell, The Last Five Years*, p. 68.

93. O'Shea's testimony is reprinted in *Parnell Vindicated*, p. 271.

94. T.M. Healy to Maurice Healy, 31 October 1888, reprinted in *Letters and Leaders of my Day*, I, p. 300.

95. J.L. Garvin is the only commentator to ask, 'Why Madrid? Did he know – as some of those he had imposed on knew – that O'Shea was there?' (*The Life of Joseph Chamberlain*, II, p. 395).

96. W.H. O'Shea to Joseph Chamberlain, 9 March 1889, reprinted in *The Life of Joseph Chamberlain*, II, p. 395.

97. *Our Book of Memories*, p. 177.

98. *Charles Stewart Parnell: His Love Story and Political Life*, II, p. 138.

99. *The Life of Charles Stewart Parnell 1846–1891*, II, p. 229.

100. *Ibid.*

101. *Charles Stewart Parnell: His Love Story and Political Life*, II, p. 139.

102. *Ibid.*, II, p. 132.

103. *Ibid.*, II, p. 135.

104. *Charles Stewart Parnell*, p. 430.

105. The conclusions drawn by the Special Commission are reprinted in *The Life of Charles Stewart Parnell 1846–1891*, II, pp. 369–72.

106. *Charles Stewart Parnell: His Love Story and Political Life*, II, p. 144; p. 145.

107. *Ibid.*, II, p. 146.

108. *Ibid.*

109. *Charles Stewart Parnell: A Memory*, pp. 137–8.

110. When Justin McCarthy heard that Parnell was at Brighton in November 1889, and 'looking much better', he seems to have believed that he visited the seaside for this health (*Our Book of Memories*, p. 202).

111. *Charles Stewart Parnell: His Love Story and Political Life*, II, p. 147.

112. Katharine refers to two letters in August 1889 and another on 16 October, yet neither of these letters appear to have survived (*ibid.*, II, p. 42).

## Chapter 11. Divorce

1. *Evening News & Post*, Saturday 28 December 1889, p. 3.

2. *Ibid.*

3. *The Times*, Wednesday 22 January 1890, p. 4.

4. UBL, Joseph Chamberlain Papers, JC8/8/1/127, W.H. O'Shea to Joseph Chamberlain, 13 October 1889.

5. *Ibid.*, JC8/8/1/129, Joseph Chamberlain to W.H. O'Shea, 14 October 1889.

6. Diary of W.H. O'Shea, 19 October 1889, reprinted in *Charles Stewart Parnell: His Love Story and Political Life*, II, p. 221.

7. W.H. O'Shea to Cardinal Manning, 26 November 1889, *ibid.*, II, p. 222.

8. *Ibid.*

9. *Ibid.*, W.H. O'Shea to Cardinal Manning, 27 November 1889, II, p. 223.

10. *Ibid.*, II, p. 227.

11. *The Story of my Life*, p. 284.

12. O'Shea refers to his 'bitter correspondence' with the Cardinal in UBL, Joseph Chamberlain Papers, JC8/8/1/130, W.H. O'Shea to J. Chamberlain, 30 December 1889.

13. Ironically, at this very time W.T. Stead was at the Vatican and quashed all suggestion of the scandal owing to the assurances given him by O'Shea at their interview in May 1886, 'The Discrowned King', p. 12. Manning himself enjoyed personal visits from Parnell at Westminster (see *Our Book of Memories*, p. 121), and does not appear to have shared O'Shea's view that the Irish leader was guilty of the 'grossest personal and political treachery' over the Local Government scheme of 1885 (W.H. O'Shea to Cardinal Manning, 13 December 1889, reprinted in *Charles Stewart Parnell: His Love Story and Political Life*, II, p. 225). He was, of course, obliged to call for Parnell's resignation after the divorce case, writing to Gladstone that 'No political expediency can out-weigh the moral sense', BL, Gladstone Papers, Add. MS 44250, f. 296, *Private*, Cardinal Manning to W.E. Gladstone.

14. *The Life of Joseph Chamberlain*, II, p. 400.

15. *The Story of my Life*, p. 283.

16. *Review of Reviews*, December 1890, p. 600.

17. Katharine, who provides full details of other such 'scenes' with her estranged husband, says nothing in her book about this one, and as Harrison points out, the alleged discovery of Parnell's 'dressing utensils' reads suspiciously like the earlier 'portmanteau' episode at Eltham in 1881, *Parnell Vindicated*, p. 143. In terms of its timing, the 'discovery' does seem to be extraordinarily fortuitous, coming immediately after Parnell's triumphant visit to Hawarden.

18. *Freeman's Journal*, Sunday 29 December 1889, p. 5.

19. *Ibid.*, Monday 30 December 1889, p. 5. O'Shea promptly sued the *Freeman's Journal* and won £100 in damages. His action against the proprietors of three newspapers took up the initial hearings of the divorce suit, from 13 January to 18 February. The *Star* was charged with having reprinted the libellous statements made in the *Freeman's Journal*, while the *New York Herald* had run a separate story in which it was suggested that after the Galway election of 1886 the scandal was talked about fairly openly in the Commons and that there were 'frequent allusions to *le mari complaisant*', UBL, Joseph Chamberlain Papers, JC8/8/1/130, W.H. O'Shea to Joseph Chamberlain, 30 December 1889. Justice Butt threw out the case against the *New York Herald*, arguing that the allusion to O'Shea's *complaisance* was based upon gossip and did not amount to a statement of fact.

20. *Evening News & Post*, Monday 30 December 1889, p. 5.

21. *Parnell Vindicated*, p. 128.

22. Katharine believed that if she had been able to raise £20,000 O'Shea could have been bought off (*ibid.*), a claim later verified by Sir Edward Clarke, who recalled that even up to 'the week before the trial we had consultations almost every day, and we heard all sort of rumours', *The Story of my Life*, p. 289. There continued to be press speculation that Parnell would arrange terms with O'Shea (see *St Stephen's Review*, 25 October and 8 November 1890). O'Shea himself told Chamberlain that the final offer made on the eve of the trial 'was equivalent to over £60,000', but he was no doubt exaggerating (quoted in *Charles Stewart Parnell*, p. 463).

23. *Parnell Vindicated*, p. 129.

24. UBL, Joseph Chamberlain Papers, JC8/8/1/144, W.H. O'Shea to Joseph Chamberlain, 3 August 1890.

25. *Ibid.*, JC8/8/1/138, 19 March 1890.

26. *Ibid.*, JC8/8/1/148, 7 September 1890.

27. *Ibid.*, JC8/8/1/138, 19 March 1890; *ibid.*, JC8/8/1/146, Wontners to W.H. O'Shea, 9 August 1890 (O'Shea's copy).

28. *Ibid.*, JC8/8/1/166, W.H. O'Shea to Joseph Chamberlain, 30 March 1892.

29. *Ibid.*, JC8/8/1/144, 3 August 1890.

30. *The Times*, Monday 17 November 1890, p. 3.

31. UBL, Joseph Chamberlain Papers, JC8/8/1/146, Wontners to W.H. O'Shea, 9 August 1890 (O'Shea's copy).

32. *Ibid.*, JC8/8/1/148, W.H. O'Shea to Joseph Chamberlain, 7 September 1890.

33. *Ibid.*, JC8/8/1/146, Wontners to W.H. O'Shea, 9 August 1890 (O'Shea's copy).

34. A similar situation governed the novelist George Eliot's relationship with her partner, George Henry Lewes. Since Lewes had condoned his wife's adultery with his friend Thornton Leigh Hunt, and also the children born of that union, he was 'forever precluded from appealing for divorce' (Gordon S. Haight, *George Eliot: A Biography*, Oxford, Clarendon Press, 1968, p. 132).

35. UBL, Joseph Chamberlain Papers, JC8/8/1/131, Joseph Chamberlain to W.H. O'Shea, 10 January 1890.

36. *Parnell Vindicated*, p. 142. Harrison's informant was Katharine's solicitor (Pym's successor), Mr Bourchier F. Hawksley.

37. *The Story of my Life*, p. 283.

38. Joyce Marlow suggests that Katharine was 'particularly furious with her sister over the part she had played in the Lunacy Petition and the probate action' (*The Uncrowned*

*Queen of Ireland*, p. 221); F.S.L. Lyons, equally perplexed, takes Harrison's line that if Katharine had assembled 'proof of some seventeen infidelities by Captain O'Shea . . . then the charge against her sister was indeed unnecessary' (*The Fall of Parnell, 1890–91*, p. 69). Frank Callanan dismisses the whole thing as an 'improbable allegation' (*T.M. Healy*, p. 249). See also *Parnell Vindicated*, p. 147.

39.  According to Clarke, Anna was down in Brighton on the Saturday, an extraordinary fact in view of the likelihood of Anna and Katharine travelling up to the divorce court on the same train, although Anna was maybe staying at the Brighton house of their other sister, Lady Barrett-Lennard, for moral support.

40.  *The Times*, Tuesday 18 November 1890, p. 13.

41.  UBL, Joseph Chamberlain Papers, JC8/8/1/144, W.H. O'Shea to Joseph Chamberlain, 3 August 1890. 'You can imagine the indignation of her brothers and sisters,' he wrote. 'Low as she has sunk with him before, I confess I was astounded when I heard of the depths to which Parnell has dragged her.'

42.  *The Times*, Tuesday 18 November 1890, p. 9. Joseph Cowen MP's paper, the *Newcastle Daily Chronicle*, declared that 'Mrs O'Shea wilfully violated all the decencies of family life by seeking to involve her sister in the charge' (quoted in 'The Discrowned King', p. 17), while *St Stephen's Review* called Katharine's 'positively monstrous' action 'utter madness' (22 November 1890, p. 5).

43.  *The Times*, Tuesday 18 November 1890, p. 14.

44.  *The Story of my Life*, p. 289.

45.  *Gladstone and the Irish Nation*, p. 615.

46.  Sybil Wolfram, 'Divorce in England 1700–1857', *Oxford Journal of Legal Studies*, 2/5 (1985), p. 157; Françoise Basch, *Relative Creatures: Victorian Women in Society and the Novel 1837–67*, London, Allen Lane, 1974, p. 24.

47.  'Divorce in England 1700–1857', p. 157. Indeed, there are only four recorded cases, prior to 1857, of divorce suits successfully brought by injured wives: in two of these cases, brought in 1801 and 1831, the husband's proven 'incestuous adultery' with his wife's sister was accepted by the court (*ibid.*, pp. 174–5).

48.  *Parnell Vindicated*, p. 141. T.P. O'Connor tells of an occasion where he caught sight of O'Shea walking with a lady down the Vauxhall Bridge Road. O'Connor spared his embarrassment by pretending that he had not seen him, and was surprised when O'Shea seemed eager to explain the matter to him later that evening at the Commons. O'Shea told him 'that the woman I had seen him with was a maid to a very important lady of the social world whom it was his duty to conciliate or consult. I could not help thinking even at the time that his manner suggested that of a man – as the Americans say – covering his tracks' (*Memoirs of an Old Parliamentarian*, I, p. 228).

49.  *Parnell Vindicated*, p. 140.

50.  *Ibid.*, p. 114.

51.  *Charles Stewart Parnell: His Love Story and Political Life*, II, p. 159.

52.  *Parnell Vindicated*, p. 138.

53.  See *The Uncrowned Queen of Ireland*, pp. 222–3; *Charles Stewart Parnell*, p. 462; p. 461.

54.  'Mrs Parnell: "Uncrowned King's Death"', *Daily Telegraph*, 9 February 1921, p. 9. O'Connor claims that 'Mrs O'Shea insisted on stating her views; her opinions are said to have been entirely erroneous; but Lewis had to sit and listen patiently, with Parnell standing by, silently, and if not approvingly, at least submissively'.

55. *Parnell Vindicated*, p. 107. Harrison's comment originates in an aside apparently made to Pym by George Lewis, who said of Katharine that she was 'a charming lady but an impossible one!'

56. *Ibid.*, p. 167.

57. *Charles Stewart Parnell: His Love Story and Political Life*, II, p. 157; p. 159.

58. *Letters and Leaders of my Day*, I, p. 318. The perception that it was Katharine who wanted the divorce, 'consumed by the desire to "regularise" her position', while 'Parnell probably had other views', was shared by T.P. O'Connor, 'Mrs Parnell: "Uncrowned King's Death"', *Daily Telegraph*, 9 February 1921, p. 9.

59. The substance of Lockwood's conversation with Tim Healy is recorded in *Letters and Leaders of my Day*, I, p. 318.

60. *Ibid.* It is as well, though, to remember that this anecdote is retold by Healy, whose venomous attitude towards Katharine is well recorded, and whose comments on Lockwood's story are quite unhinged: Healy, for example, makes the extraordinary assertion that 'Lockwood noted how she held her fan before her face to shield him from her offensive breath!' (*ibid*).

61. *Cork Free Press*, Saturday 6 September 1912, p. 7; *Charles Stewart Parnell: His Love Story and Political Life*, II, p. 158.

62. *Ibid.*

63. UBL, Joseph Chamberlain Papers, JC8/8/1/145, Joseph Chamberlain to W.H. O'Shea, 5 August 1890.

64. Quoted in *Pall Mall Gazette*, Saturday 13 February 1886, p.1.

65. *The Story of my Life*, p. 291.

66. The first Infant Custody Act of 1839 provided limited powers to a select class of women wealthy enough to petition their suit in Chancery. A woman separated from her husband was granted the power to petition in the equity courts for custody of those children under the age of 7, and for periodic access to those children aged 7 or older: 'However, no woman was to benefit from the act if she was guilty of adultery' (see Holcombe, *Wives and Property*, p. 54). The second Infant Custody Act of 1872 extended the mother's right to petition under civil law for custody and access to those children between the ages of 7 and 16. The only other legal alternative, barring the admission that Clare and Katie were the illegitimate daughters of Parnell, was for Katharine to secure their custody under a separation order from her husband (*ibid.*, p. 106). It is quite probable that she could have done so, but a legally binding separation from O'Shea would have left her unable to marry Parnell.

67. Sir Edward Clarke knew that Clare and Katie O'Shea 'were unquestionably' Parnell's daughters (*The Story of my Life*, p. 291).

68. KGM, Parnell Papers, St John Ervine to Dr Bertram S.O. Maunsell, 16 April 1937.

69. *Parnell Vindicated*, p. 5; p. 4. Harrison's book was published in 1931, long after the deaths of Katharine and her daughter Clare; Katie did not die until 1947.

70. *Ibid.*, p. 259; p. 172; p. 171; p. 129.

71. *Ibid.*, p. 129; p. 128.

72. *Our Book of Memories*, p. 212.

73. *The Life of William Ewart Gladstone*, III, p. 428.

74. *Our Book of Memories*, p. 238.

75. *Ibid.*, p. 214.

76. Josephine E. Butler to her son, Stanley Butler, 29 November 1890, Liverpool University Library, JB 1/1 1890/11/29 (I).
77. *The History of the Irish Parliamentary Party*, II, p. 149; II, p. 167. Even after the publication of the details of the divorce case, some doubted the truth of Parnell's adultery. An admirer of Gladstone begged him to support Parnell: 'If you only say this story is untrue everybody will believe you,' while Margaret Sandhurst, a personal friend of the former Prime Minister, wrote to say that she firmly believed in Parnell's innocence (BL, Gladstone Papers, Add. MS 56448, f. 17; ff. 143–5).
78. *Cork Free Press*, Saturday 6 September 1912, p. 7.
79. W.T. Stead recounts his conversation with Michael Davitt in *Review of Reviews*, December 1890, p. 600.
80. *The Story of my Life*, p. 290.
81. *The Diary of Sir Edward Walter Hamilton 1885–1906*, p. 112.
82. Noted in Hamilton's diary entries of 9 August and 16 September 1890, *ibid.*, p. 123; p. 124.
83. BL, Gladstone Papers, Add. MS 44256, ff. 61–2, *Secret*, John Morley to W.E. Gladstone, 3 November 1890.
84. *The Life of William Ewart Gladstone*, III, p. 429.
85. *Recollections*, p. 251; p. 254.
86. *Ibid.*, p. 254.
87. BL, Gladstone Papers, Add. MS 44256, ff. 63–6, *Secret*, John Morley to W.E. Gladstone, 13 November 1890.
88. *The Life of William Ewart Gladstone*, III, p. 430.
89. UBL, Joseph Chamberlain Papers, JC8/8/1/166, W.H. O'Shea to Joseph Chamberlain, 30 March 1892. Katharine's brothers may also have induced Anna to intervene in order that her barrister be given access to the O'Sheas' (extensive) private papers which were submitted to the divorce trial. Certainly, it was the case that McCall discovered evidence of Captain O'Shea's regularly acquiring large sums of money from Mrs Wood through the medium of Katharine, information which the Woods used against Katharine in the contest over their aunt's will (see Ch. 12).
90. *The Times*, Friday 14 November 1890, p. 14.
91. *Charles Stewart Parnell: His Love Story and Political Life*, II, p. 158.
92. *Ibid.*, II, p. 160.
93. *Ibid.*, II, p. 161.

## Chapter 12. Katharine Parnell

1. Healy wrote to his wife on 30 November 1890, 'Everywhere the Divorce case is being sung about in the music-halls. Passing through the Strand you hear the itinerant hawkers shout some toy or picture: "Mr Parnell and Mrs O'Shea"' (*Letters and Leaders of my Day*, I, p. 329).
2. Reprinted in *St Stephen's Review*, Saturday 29 November 1890, p. 12.
3. 'The Discrowned King', p. 6.
4. *Review of Reviews*, December 1890, p. 529, p. 598.
5. *Vanity Fair*, 22 November 1890, p. 438.

6. *St Stephen's Review*, 22 November 1890, p. 5.

7. As Alfred Robbins, Editor of the *Birmingham Post*, observed, 'public sympathy . . . was largely absent from O'Shea', and it was at first doubted whether the divorce scandal would necessitate Parnell's withdrawal from public life (*Parnell: The Last Five Years*, p. 151). The Liberal *Star* called O'Shea 'the most simple-minded of husbands', and suggested that the story told in the divorce court was incomplete: there remained 'untested evidence' (Tuesday 18 November 1890, p. 5).

8. *Truth*, 20 November 1890, p. 1044.

9. BL, Gladstone Papers, Add. MS 56448, ff. 52–5, *Secret*, Edward R. Russell to W.E. Gladstone, 22 November 1890. Russell forwarded Gladstone this newspaper cutting, adding that he had 'little doubt that there has been prolonged and mercenary connivance' on the part of O'Shea. O'Shea would continue to be the butt of slanderous innuendo in the press, such as an American story which claimed that Katharine had been the mistress of a Governor of the Bank of England, and that O'Shea married her for her 'infamous fortune which I was said in hundreds of American papers to have received in consideration!!!' (UBL, Joseph Chamberlain Papers, JC8/8/1/160, W.H. O'Shea to Joseph Chamberlain, 12 February 1891).

10. *Truth*, 20 November 1890, p. 1044.

11. 'The Discrowned King of Ireland', p. 9.

12. *Review of Reviews*, December 1890, p. 600; p. 601.

13. BL, Gladstone Papers, Add. MS 44256, ff. 72–3, *Private*, John Morley to W.E. Gladstone, 17 November 1890. When John Morley was in Ireland, two months before the divorce trial, he had asked John Dillon what he thought the Irish party would do if the charges against Parnell were upheld: 'His view was clear, that so far as Ireland was concerned, the proof of the charge would make no difference in P.'s authority, *provided* there was no disclosure of nauseous details.'

14. *The Life of Charles Stewart Parnell, 1846–91*, II, p. 243.

15. *Bristol Mercury* quoted in *Review of Reviews*, December 1890, p. 604. Stead berated the editors of the *Daily News*, the *Star*, the *Pall Mall Gazette*, *Truth* and the *Manchester Guardian* for their reluctance to pass judgement on Parnell.

16. W.E. Gladstone to John Morley, 18 November 1890, quoted in *The Life of William Ewart Gladstone*, III, p. 430.

17. BL, Gladstone Papers, Add. MS 44256, ff. 75–8, *Secret*, W.E. Gladstone to John Morley, 19 November 1890.

18. *The Diary of Sir Edward Walter Hamilton 1885–1906*, p. 129.

19. Quoted in *Charles Stewart Parnell*, p. 488.

20. BL, Gladstone Papers, Add. MS 56448, f. 30, W.T. Stead to W.E. Gladstone, 20 November 1890.

21. *Review of Reviews*, December 1890, p. 630.

22. As he noted to his Chief Whip Arnold Morley on 23 November 1890, he received 'bundle[s] of letters every morning on the Parnell business, and the bundles increase', quoted in *The Life of William Ewart Gladstone*, III, p. 433.

23. BL, Gladstone Papers, Add. MS 56448, ff. 43–4, J. Wright to W.E. Gladstone, 21 November 1890.

24. *Ibid.*, f. 51, Isaac Chapman to W.E. Gladstone, 22 November 1890.

25. An anonymous correspondent writing in the *Star*, Saturday 22 November 1890, p. 2.

26. *Recollections*, I, pp. 259–60.

27. *Charles Stewart Parnell: His Love Story and Political Life*, II, p. 162.
28. *Ibid.*, II, p. 164.
29. 'The Discrowned King of Ireland', p. 5.
30. BL, Gladstone Papers, Add. MS 56448, ff. 21–2, Revd M. McColl to W.E. Gladstone, 19 November 1890.
31. *Charles Stewart Parnell: His Love Story and Political Life*, I, p. ix.
32. *Ibid.*, II, pp. 161–2.
33. Parnell's manifesto, 'To the People of Ireland', was published on Saturday 29 November 1890. The full text is printed in *ibid.*, II, pp. 166–74.
34. *Ibid.*, II, pp. 162–3.
35. *Ibid.*, II, p. 163.
36. *Ibid.*
37. *Ibid.*, II, p. 181.
38. Katharine Tynan's account is reprinted in *ibid.*, II, pp. 177–8.
39. *Ibid.*, II, p. 180.
40. *The Life of Charles Stewart Parnell, 1846–1891*, II, p. 300.
41. *Charles Stewart Parnell: His Love Story and Political Life*, II, p. 182.
42. Quoted in Frank Callanan, *The Parnell Split 1890–91*, Cork, Cork University Press, 1992, p. 66.
43. *Charles Stewart Parnell*, p. 543. Priests were also acting at the polling booths as 'personation agents', to be present when illiterates declared their votes, *ibid.*, p. 544.
44. *The Life of Charles Stewart Parnell, 1846–1891*, II, p. 305.
45. Wilfred Scawen Blunt, *My Diaries, Being a Personal Narrative of Events, 1888–1914*, 2 vols, London, Martin Secker, 1920, II, pp. 397–8. Blunt records the essence of a conversation with John Dillon on 10 March 1912. If Parnell had returned to England every evening, it would have been to Brighton.
46. *Sussex Daily News*, Friday 26 June 1891, p. 5.
47. *Ibid.*
48. *Ibid.*
49. *Charles Stewart Parnell: His Love Story and Political Life*, II, p. 253.
50. *Sussex Daily News*, Friday 26 June 1891, p. 5.
51. *The Times*, Saturday 27 June 1891, p. 12.
52. Extracts from the national press, quoted in the *Sussex Daily News*, Saturday 27 June 1891, p. 5.
53. *The Parnell Split 1890–91*, p. 126.
54. *Charles Stewart Parnell*, p. 480.
55. *Ibid.*, p. 592.
56. *Weekly National Press* and *National Press* quoted in *The Parnell Split 1890–91*, p. 127; p. 133.
57. Quoted in *Memoirs of an Old Parliamentarian*, II, p. 299.
58. Quoted in *The Parnell Split 1890–91*, p. 129.
59. *Ibid.*, pp. 130–1. T.P. O'Connor also notes the cartoons of Katharine and Parnell, 'which went beyond all the bounds of good feeling. Her petticoat was constantly mentioned as either the flag under which Parnell sailed or the cloak behind which he took refuge' (*Memoirs of an Old Parliamentarian*, II, p. 291).
60. *Charles Stewart Parnell: His Love Story and Political Life*, II, p. 183.

61. UBL, Joseph Chamberlain Papers, JC8/8/1/162, W.H. O'Shea to Joseph Chamberlain, 23 February 1891. The divorce and probate suits combined had so far cost him over £5,000. He needed £800, and half of that before the end of the month. As he explained to Chamberlain, he had besides to provide a home 'for the children who are living with me', that is, Gerard and Carmen. According to the *Sussex Daily News*, this was 'a splendid mansion overlooking the Channel' (Friday 9 October 1891, p. 5).

62. *Charles Stewart Parnell: His Love Story and Political Life*, II, p. 192.

63. UBL, Joseph Chamberlain Papers, JC8/8/1/162, W.H. O'Shea to Joseph Chamberlain, 23 February 1891.

64. C.S. Parnell to Katharine Parnell, 15 August 1891, reprinted in *Charles Stewart Parnell: His Love Story and Political Life*, II, p. 261.

65. See Parnell's letters of August and September 1891, reprinted in *ibid.*, II, pp. 261–3.

66. *Ibid.*, II, p. 264.

67. Arthur Griffith quoted in *The Parnell Split 1890–91*, p. 179.

68. Mr Russell, a reporter, quoted in *The Life of Charles Stewart Parnell, 1846–1891*, II, p. 350.

69. *Charles Stewart Parnell: His Love Story and Political Life*, II, p. 265.

70. *Ibid.*, II, p. 275.

71. *Sussex Daily News*, Thursday 8 October 1891, p. 5.

72. *Charles Stewart Parnell: His Love Story and Political Life*, II, p. 275.

73. *Sussex Daily News*, Thursday 8 October 1891, p. 5.

74. *Parnell Vindicated*, p. 92.

75. *Ibid.*

76. *Ibid.*, p. 93; p. 105.

77. *Sussex Daily News*, Friday 9 October 1891, p. 5.

78. *Charles Stewart Parnell: His Love Story and Political Life*, I, p. 136.

79. *Parnell Vindicated*, p. 99.

80. *The Life of Charles Stewart Parnell, 1846–1891*, II, p. 352.

81. *Parnell Vindicated*, p. 100.

82. *Ibid.*, p. 103.

83. *Memoirs of an Old Parliamentarian*, II, p. 324.

84. *Ibid.*, II, p. 326.

85. Norah O'Shea to Henry Harrison, 1 February 1921, reprinted in *Parnell Vindicated*, p. 216.

86. *Ibid.*, p. 5. On 31 October 1891, Harrison issued an announcement in *The Times* to the effect that, 'on his widow's behalf and at her request', he himself would offer the world the first authorised biography of Parnell.

87. *Ibid.*, p. 105.

88. *Ibid.*, p. 193; p. 108.

89. *Ibid.*, p. 103.

90. *Ibid.*, p. 183.

91. *Letters and Leaders of my Day*, II, p. 370. Healy went to Paris in person 'to block Mrs O'Shea's claim to the funds there', and reprints a letter to his wife from Paris dated 29 November 1891.

92. Healy's speech is quoted in *The Parnell Split 1890–91*, p. 187.

93. Draft letter from W.E. Gladstone to Henry Labouchère, 24 November 1891, reprinted in *ibid.*, p. 189.

94. UBL, Joseph Chamberlain Papers, JC8/8/1/160, W.H. O'Shea to Joseph Chamberlain, 12 February 1891.

95. *Ibid*. Like W.T. Stead, Dr MacCormac, now Bishop of Galway, felt that he had been deceived personally by O'Shea's assurances and issued a statement to the press on 14 February 1891 to the effect that in 1886 Parnell was guilty of 'prostituting the Galway City constituency as a hush gift to O'Shea'. O'Shea protested against this libellous statement in his letter to His Grace the Archbishop of Tuam, 21 February 1891, reprinted in *Charles Stewart Parnell: His Love Story and Political Life*, II, p. 229. (The charge was made less offensively in Henry Labouchère's paper *Truth*, 18 December 1890, p. 1267.)

96. *Parnell Vindicated*, pp. 110–11.

97. *Ibid*., p. 112.

98. *Ibid*., p. 116.

99. *The Times*, Friday 25 March 1891, p. 8.

100. The original will of 1847 ran to eleven codicils, seven of which were accepted by the Wood family (*ibid*.).

101. *Ibid*.

102. UBL, Joseph Chamberlain Papers, JC8/8/1/166, W.H. O'Shea to Joseph Chamberlain, 30 March 1892.

103. *Ibid*. As O'Shea observed to Chamberlain, Evelyn's was a begging letter to beat all others. On his return from the Zulu Wars (1879–81), for which he was created a KCB, Evelyn sent Mrs Wood the following account of his wife's conversation with Queen Victoria: 'Paulina put on a very old and thread-bare water-proof when driving with her majesty, who, examining it with interest, said, "I suppose you wore that all through Zululand?" "Yes," said Paulina, – she might have added "and for several years previously".'

104. A copy of Mr W. Capel Slaughter's memorandum of negotiations which took place before the trial, which he wrote out for O'Shea on the morning of 24 March 1892, is enclosed in *ibid*.

105. *Parnell Vindicated*, p. 199.

106. *Ibid*., p. 204.

107. *Ibid*., p. 203.

108. *Ibid*., p. 204–5. Harrison is not sure that Gerard may have been given 35 per cent and his sisters 25 per cent each, 'but I am quite clear as to the much smaller shares of Clare and Katie. The discrimination against Mrs O'Shea's two children, of whom Parnell was the true father, was so conspicuous as to emphasise their special position very strongly.'

109. *Ibid*., p. 203.

110. UBL, Joseph Chamberlain Papers, JC8/8/1/166, W.H. O'Shea to Joseph Chamberlain, 30 March 1892.

111. *The Times*, Monday 24 April 1905, p. 4.

112. *Winnowed Memories* is dedicated to 'A.C.S.'.

113. 'Personal Gossip', *East Anglian Daily Times*, n.d. 1899, n.p., cutting pasted into family scrapbook compiled by Minna Bradhurst, ERO, T/B 224/1, p. 149.

114. *Charles Stewart Parnell: A Memory*, p. 133.

115. *Cork Free Press*, Saturday 6 September 1913, p. 7.

116. Gerard's letter to *The Times* is reprinted at the end of Katharine's preface to *Charles Stewart Parnell: His Love Story and Political Life*, I, pp. xii–xiii.

117. *Daily Sketch*, Tuesday 5 May 1914, p. 8. Katharine's apology formed the preface to *Charles Stewart Parnell: His Love Story and Political Life*.

118. *Daily Express*, 19 May 1914, n.p., cutting pasted into family scrapbook compiled by Minna Bradhurst, ERO, T/B 224/1/2, p. 188.

119. *Saturday Review*, 23 May 1914, p. 675; *Spectator*, 30 May 1914, p. 912. In fact, Katharine makes a point of saying that she is not giving the reader all Parnell's letters, but 'just a few of the little messages of my husband's love [which] in these last days I must keep for my own heart to live upon' (*Charles Stewart Parnell: His Love Story and Political Life*, II, p. 260).

120. *The Times*, Tuesday 19 May 1914, p. 6.

121. *Ibid.*

122. *Paddy and Mr Punch*, p. 125.

123. Harold Nicolson writes dismissively of the innumerable elegiac and commemorative 'widow' biographies produced during the Victorian period, remarking that 'they will survive only as literary curiosities, or at best as works of reference' (*The Development of English Biography*, London, Hogarth Press, 1927, p. 126).

124. *Charles Stewart Parnell: His Love Story and Political Life*, I, p. x.

125. Valerie Sanders refers to the example of Ellen Terry's 'Apologia' to her 1908 autobiography, *The Story of My Life*, *The Private Lives of Victorian Women: Autobiography in Nineteenth-Century England*, London, Harvester Wheatsheaf, 1989, p. 116. As Sanders observes, 'Clearly, everything about [the nineteenth-century] womanly ideal is the direct opposite of the qualities needed to initiate an act of self-writing, or indeed to see oneself as a separate being, detached and motivated, claiming an audience in one's own right' (*ibid.*, p. 8).

126. R.F. Foster also finds evidence of a 'double stream of composition', although he does state that Katharine 'was much more responsible for her book than chivalrous Parnellite champions like Henry Harrison allowed' (*Paddy and Mr Punch*, p. 135; p. 137).

127. *Ibid.*, p. 129.

128. *Charles Stewart Parnell: His Love Story and Political Life*, II, p. 135. The probate agreement had left Katharine with a life interest in £25,000, plus a capital sum of £6,000. It may have been this latter amount which Francis 'borrowed' from.

129. The *Daily Graphic* ran the story of 'Mrs Parnell's Trust Fund' on Thursday 4 April 1901, p. 215.

130. Norah O'Shea to Henry Harrison, 1 February 1921, reprinted in *Parnell Vindicated*, p. 216.

131. *Charles Stewart Parnell: His Love Story and Political Life*, I, p. viii.

132. '"Kitty O'Shea" Dead', *Weekly Dispatch*, 6 February 1921, n.p., cutting pasted in family scrapbook compiled by Minna Bradhurst, ERO, T/B 224/1/3, p. 174.

133. *Sussex Daily News*, Wednesday 15 December 1920, p. 2.

134. Norah O'Shea to Henry Harrison, 1 February 1921, reprinted in *Parnell Vindicated*, pp. 215–16.

135. *Weekly Dispatch*, 6 February 1921, n.p., cutting pasted in family scrapbook compiled by Minna Bradhurst, ERO, T/B 224/1/3, p. 174.

136. *The Times*, Monday 7 February 1921, p. 12.

## Afterword

1. *Memoirs of an Old Parliamentarian*, II, p. 326.
2. The 1901 census records that Dr Buck had a 57-year-old 'imbecile' and his attendant lodging at his house in Hove.
3. This was written by the American playwright, Elsie T. Schauffer.
4. KGM, Parnell Papers, IE13 12, Revd John V.F. Maunsell to Sir Shane Leslie, 8 February 1956.
5. *Parnell Vindicated*, p. 214.
6. The fact that Katie signs herself by the fanciful title of Guadalupe Katarina Flavia O'Shea on her marriage certificate has led Joyce Marlow to doubt her identity and speculate that the Mrs Moule who surfaced in the 1930s was in fact an imposter and more likely a Spanish love-child of O'Shea's (see *The Uncrowned Queen of Ireland*, pp. 302–4). This Katie's reminiscences of Parnell could easily have been lifted from Katharine's book, so Marlow argues. Yet it is a fact that Mrs Moule was able to supply her date of birth, 27 November 1884. In the 1901 census, Katie is listed as living with her mother and sisters in Preston, Devon, where she gives her name as 'Katie G.F. O'Shea'. Further evidence of Katie's identity is offered in a document which traces the pedigree of Katharine's nephew, the 4th Baronet, Sir Matthew Wood, which lists Katharine's youngest daughter as 'Guadalupe Katie Flavia O'Shea' (ERO, T/B 224/1, p. 20, family scrap book belonging to Minna Bradhurst, the daughter of Katharine's brother Charles Page Wood). It should be remembered that Katie's sister Clare also acquired another middle name. At her birth, she was registered under the name of Clare Gabrielle Antoinette Marcia O'Shea, yet her certificates of baptism and death also carry the name Esperance. She, too, acknowledges her full name in the 1901 census, where she is registered as 'Clare G.M.A.E. O'Shea'.
7. KGM, Parnell Papers, IE13 20. The family tree was compiled by Revd John V.F. Maunsell, a son from the second marriage of Dr Bertram Maunsell who had married Clare O'Shea in 1908.
8. *Ibid.*, IE14 16, Revd John V.F. Maunsell to Sir Shane Leslie, 13 December 1966.
9. *Ibid.*, IE14 01, Cutting from the *Kettering Guardian*, Friday 24 September 1909, pasted into Clare's *Office of the Blessed Virgin Mary*.
10. *Ibid.*, IE13 15, Recollections of Clare written by Dr Bertram S.O. Maunsell. The year before Clare met Bertram she had her handwriting analysed. The resultant character sketch was later copied out for Clare's son Assheton, and it is tempting to read something of her mother's character in the description of the daughter. She has intellectual faculties 'of a very high order', and characteristics such as 'a good deal of independence, cool & sober judgement. Yet an inclination to be hasty & passionate at rare intervals' (*ibid.*).
11. As the local Kettering paper put it, 'the case was within a little time known to be a bad one, which later became desperate'. The night before, Bertram had rushed Clare to a private London hospital at 20 Margaret Street, off Upper Regent Street. *Ibid.*, IE14 01, cutting from the *Kettering Guardian*, Friday 24 September 1909, pasted into Clare's *Office of the Blessed Virgin Mary*.
12. *Ibid.* Among the Parnell relics is an envelope in which Bertram has preserved a tiny piece of cotton wool, 'stained by a drop of Clare's blood – shed at the birth of Assheton' (*ibid.*).

13. *Ibid.*
14. *Ibid.*, IE14 01, cutting from the *Kettering Guardian*, Friday 24 September 1909.
15. *Ibid.*, IE13 12, Revd John V.F. Maunsell to Sir Shane Leslie, 8 February 1956.
16. *Ibid.*, IE14 16, 13 December 1966.
17. Norah O'Shea to Henry Harrison, 1 February 1921, reprinted in *Parnell Vindicated*, p. 216.
18. KGM, Parnell Papers, IE13 12, Revd John V.F. Maunsell to Sir Shane Leslie, 8 February 1956.
19. *Memoirs of an Old Parliamentarian*, II, p. 327.
20. KGM, Parnell Papers, IE13 26, Norah O'Shea to Dr Bertram S.O. Maunsell, 13 August 1922. Norah signs herself 'Norah (Wood) please'.
21. *Ibid.*, IE14 09, Gerard H.W. O'Shea to Dr Bertram S.O. Maunsell, 20 July 1923.
22. *Ibid.*, IE13 11, Revd John V.F. Maunsell to Sir Shane Leslie, 30 January 1956. 'It cost me about £90 to stop his bankruptcy & pay the bill,' Bertram recalled (Dr Maunsell's comments are written on Gerard's letter referred to above).
23. *Ibid.*, IE16 26, 11 March 1956.
24. Details supplied in *ibid.*, IE13 13, 31 March 1956.
25. *Ibid.*, IE13 20, family trees compiled by Revd John V.F. Maunsell. The project was begun in the early 1940s, after the death of Maunsell's father, Bertram, on 4 May 1941, and that of John's brother Tom who was killed in action in Tunisia in February 1943. The family trees were completed before Katie's death in 1947, which is entered with a heavier pen.
26. *Parnell Vindicated*, p. 103.
27. NLI, MS 35,982, W.H. O'Shea Papers. These papers were later bound and used by a C.G. Buckton to compile his memoirs, 'With the Heavy Artillery in France & Flanders', originally entitled, 'Experiences of the Great War'.
28. KGM, Parnell Papers, IE13 06, Gerard H.W. O'Shea to Dr Bertram S.O. Maunsell, 27 January 1923.
29. *Ibid.*, IE13 26. The card was found stuck behind a portrait of Katie, and Bertram has written on it a note of explanation for Assheton: 'This is from your Grandmother Mrs Parnell to your Mother.'
30. *Ibid.*, IE13 14, n.d.

# Bibliography

British Library, Dilke Papers, Add. MSS 43936

British Library, Gladstone Papers, Add. MSS 44160, 44250, 44256, 44269, 44314, 44315, 44316, 44503, 44506, 44766, 44787. Additional Unbound, Add. MSS 56445, 56446, 56447, 56448, 56449

Essex Record Office, T/B 224, T/Z 151/44, D/DL/C68

Flintshire Record Office, GG2165

Kilmainham Gaol Museum, Parnell Papers, IE13 and IE14

National Library of Ireland, MS 3882, MS 5752, MS 21,679, MS 21,936, MS 35,982

Principal Registry of the Family Division, Probate Department

University of Birmingham Library, Joseph Chamberlain Collection, JC8/8/1/176


Abels, Jules, *The Parnell Tragedy*, London, Bodley Head, 1966

Asquith, Lord, *Lord James of Hereford*, London, Ernest Benn Ltd, 1930

Bahlman, Dudley W.R., ed., *The Diary of Sir Edward Walter Hamilton 1880–1885*, 2 vols, Oxford, Clarendon Press, 1972

——. *The Diary of Sir Edward Walter Hamilton 1885–1906*, Hull, University of Hull Press, 1993

Basch, Françoise, *Relative Creatures: Victorian Women in Society and the Novel, 1837–67*, London, Allen Lance, 1974

Bew, Paul, *C.S. Parnell*, Dublin, Gill and Macmillan Ltd, 1980

Blunt, Wilfred Scawen, *The Land War in Ireland*, London, Stephen Swift and Co., 1912

——. *My Diaries, Being a Personal Narrative of Events, 1888–1914*, 2 vols, London, Martin Secker, 1920

Boyce, R. George and Alan O'Day, eds., *Parnell in Perspective*, London, Routledge, 1991

Callaghan, Mary Rose, *Kitty O'Shea: A Life of Katharine Parnell*, London, Pandora Press, 1989

Callanan, Frank, *The Parnell Split 1890–91*, Cork, Cork University Press, 1992

——. *T.M. Healy*, Cork, Cork University Press, 1996

Chamberlain, Joseph, *A Political Memoir 1880–1892*, ed. C.H.D. Howard, London, Batchworth Press, 1953

Clarke, Sir Edward, *The Story of My Life*, London, John Murray, 1918

Davitt, Michael, *The Fall of Feudalism in Ireland, or The Story of the Land League Revolution*, New York, Harper & Bros, 1904

Emden, Paul Herman, *Behind the Throne*, London, Hodder & Stoughton, 1934

Ervine, St John, *Parnell*, London, Ernest Benn Ltd, 1925

Foster, R.F., *Charles Stewart Parnell: The Man and his Family*, Hassocks, The Harvester Press, 1976

——. *Modern Ireland 1600–1972*, London, Penguin Books, 1989 [1988]

——. *Paddy and Mr Punch: Connections in Irish and English History*, London, Allen Lane, 1993

Gardiner, A.G., *Life of Sir William Harcourt*, London, Constable & Co. Ltd, 1923

Garvin, J.L., *The Life of Joseph Chamberlain*, 6 vols, London, Macmillan, 1932–69

Gladstone, Viscount (Herbert J.), *After Thirty Years*, London, Macmillan & Co. Ltd, 1928

Haight, Gordon S., *George Eliot: A Biography*, Oxford, The Clarendon Press, 1968

Hammond, J.L., *Gladstone and the Irish Nation*, London, Frank Cass & Co. Ltd, 1964 [1938]

Harrison, Henry, *Parnell Vindicated: The Lifting of the Veil*, London: Constable & Co. Ltd, 1931

——. *Parnell, Joseph Chamberlain and Mr Garvin*, London, Robert Hale, 1938

Healy, T.M., *Letters and Leaders of my Day*, 2 vols, London, Thornton Butterworth, 1928

Holcombe, Lee, *Wives and Property Reform of the Married Women's Property Law in Nineteenth-Century England*, Toronto & Buffalo, University of Toronto Press, 1983

Howard, C.H.D., ed., 'Documents Relating to the Irish "Central Board" Scheme, 1884–5', *Irish Historical Studies*, 8/32 (March 1953), 237–63

——. 'Joseph Chamberlain, Parnell and the Irish "Central Board" Scheme, 1884–5', *Irish Historical Studies*, 8/32 (September 1953), 324–61

Jeyes, S.H., *Life of Sir Howard Vincent*, London, George Allen & Co. Ltd, 1912

Jordan, Jane, *Josephine Butler*, London, John Murray, 2001

Kettle, Andrew J., *The Material for Victory*, ed. L.J. Kettle, Dublin, C.J. Fallon Ltd, 1958

Key, Robert, *The Laurel and the Ivy: The Story of Charles Stewart Parnell and Irish Nationalism*, London, Hamish Hamilton, 1993

King, Carla, *Michael Davitt*, Dundalk, Dundalgan Press Ltd, 1999

Kingsmill, Hugh, *After Puritanism 1850–1900*, London, Duckworth, 1929

Lucy, Henry W., *A Diary of Two Parliaments*, London, Cassell & Co., 1886

Lyons, F.S.L., *The Fall of Parnell 1890–91*, London, Routledge & Kegan Paul, 1960

——. *Charles Stewart Parnell*, London, Collins, 1977

McCarthy, Justin, *Reminiscences*, London, Chatto & Windus, 1899

——. *Our Book of Memories: Letters of Justin McCarthy to Mrs Campbell Praed*, London, Chatto & Windus, 1912

McL. Côtée, Jane, *Fanny & Anna Parnell: Ireland's Patriot Sisters*, Basingstoke, Macmillan, 1991

Marlow, Joyce, *The Uncrowned Queen of Ireland: The Life of 'Kitty' O'Shea*, London, Weidenfeld & Nicolson, 1975

Meredith, George, *Diana of the Crossways*, London, Virago, 1985 [1885]

Morley, John, *The Life of William Ewart Gladstone*, London, Macmillan & Co. Ltd, 1903

——. *Recollections*, London, Macmillan & Co. Ltd, 1917

Nicolson, Harold, *The Development of English Biography*, London, Hogarth Press, 1927

O'Brien, Conor Cruise, *Parnell and his Party*, Oxford, Clarendon Press, 1964 [1957]

O'Brien, R. Barry, *The Life of Charles Stewart Parnell*, 2 vols, London, Smith, Elder & Co., 1898

O'Brien, William, *Recollections*, London, Macmillan & Co., 1905

——. *Evening Memories*, Dublin & London, Maunsel & Co., 1920

——. *The Parnell of Real Life*, London, Fisher Unwin, 1925

O'Connor, T.P., *Charles Stewart Parnell: A Memory*, London, Ward, Lock, Bowden & Co., 1891

O'Connor, T.P., *Memoirs of an Old Parliamentarian*, 2 vols, London, Ernest Benn Ltd, 1929

O'Day, Alan, *Parnell and The First Home Rule Episode 1884–87*, Dublin, Gill and Macmillan, 1986

O'Donnell, Frank Hugh, *The History of the Irish Parliamentary Party*, London, Longmans & Co., 1910

O'Shea, Katharine, *Charles Stewart Parnell: His Love Story and Political Life*, 2 vols, London, Cassell & Co. Ltd, 1914

Robbins, Alfred, *Parnell, The Last Five Years: Told from Within*, London, Thornton Butterworth Ltd, 1926

Sanders, Valerie, *The Private Lives of Victorian Women: Autobiography in Nineteenth-Century England*, London, Harvester Wheatsheaf, 1989

Shanley, Mary Lyndon, *Feminism, Marriage, and the Law in Victorian England, 1850–1895*, Princeton, Princeton University Press, 1989

Stead, W.T., 'The Discrowned King of Ireland', London, The Offices of *Review of Reviews*, 1891

Stephens, W.R.W., ed., *A Memoir of the Right Hon. William Page Wood, Baron Hatherley*, 2 vols, London, Richard Bentley & Son, 1883

Warwick-Haller, Sally, *William O'Brien and the Irish Land War*, Dublin, Irish Academic Press Ltd, 1990

Williams, Charles, *The Life of Lieut. General Sir Henry Evelyn Wood*, London, Sampson, Low, Marston & Co., 1892

Wolfram, Sybil, 'Divorce in England 1700–1857', *Oxford Journal of Legal Studies*, 5/2 (1985), 155–86

Wood, Sir Evelyn, *Winnowed Memories*, London, Cassell & Co., 1917

# Index